Performing Afro-Cuba

Performing Afro-Cuba

Image, Voice, Spectacle in the Making of Race and History

KRISTINA WIRTZ

The University of Chicago Press
Chicago and London

Kristina Wirtz is associate professor of anthropology at Western Michigan University. She is the author of *Ritual, Discourse, and Community in Cuban Santería.*

Publication of this book has been aided by a grant from the Bevington Fund.
The University of Chicago Press, Chicago 60637
The University of Chicago Press, Ltd., London

Printed in the United States of America

23 22 21 20 19 18 17 16 15 14   1 2 3 4 5

ISBN-13: 978-0-226-11886-4 (cloth)
ISBN-13: 978-0-226-11905-2 (paper)
ISBN-13: 978-0-226-11919-9 (e-book)
DOI: 10.7208/chicago/9780226119199.001.0001

Library of Congress Cataloging-in-Publication Data

Wirtz, Kristina, author.
Performing Afro-Cuba : image, voice, spectacle in the making of race and history / Kristina Wirtz.
pages cm
Includes bibliographical references and index.
ISBN 978-0-226-11886-4 (cloth : alkaline paper)—ISBN 978-0-226-11905-2 (paperback : alkaline paper)—ISBN 978-0-226-11919-9 (e-book) 1. Blacks—Race identity—Cuba. 2. Blacks—Cuba—Social life and customs. 3. Blacks—Cuba—Social conditions. 4. Folklore—Cuba—History. I. Title.
F1789.N3W57 2014
305.896'07291—dc23
2013038110

♾ This paper meets the requirements of ANSI/NISO Z39.48–1992 (Permanence of Paper)

Contents

Agradecimientos

A word of thanks hardly repays the debt of gratitude I owe to ever-growing numbers of friends and colleagues whose generosity and insight have shaped the very possibility of this book. May their gifts and my thanks continue our cycle of friendship and exchange into the future: to those named herein and those who remain unnamed, I say: thank you, *gracias, modupwe.*

I begin by thanking my Cuban interlocutors, many of whom have become dear friends over the course of my engagement with Cuba, which now spans more than a decade. Some have watched me "grow up" from my days as a graduate student and neophyte in matters of Cuban culture; I hope that I have made them proud and that they see how important their patient introductions and explanations have been, even if my interpretations may sometimes surprise them. Foremost I must thank my mentor Licenciado Ernesto Armiñán Linares, and my *hermanas cubanas*, María Isabel Berbes Ribeaux and Teresita de Jesús Reyes Guerrero, who offered incomparable companionship and whose entire families offered me a place to call home. I also thank my *hermanos*, A. Abelardo Larduet Luaces and Marcos Antonio Salomon Guerra. Maritza Martínez Martínez and Mabel Castro taught me passion for the conga and carabalí, as did Benito Rodriguez and Imilce William of Olugo. Conversations over the years with Luisa María Ramírez Moreira, Olguita Portuondo Zúñiga, and more recently with Gladys Gonzalez and with Suitberto Goire, alas now with the ancestors, gave me much food for thought. Nurina Salas always tended to my spiritual well-being. This list barely scratches the surface, and so I must express my gratitude to all those in Cuba who have demonstrated such tremendous hospitality and openness.

I especially want to highlight the generosity of many groups in Santiago de Cuba who immeasurably enrich Cuban arts, letters, and life, and without whose welcome my ethnographic explorations would not have been possible: I thank the *Taller de Religiones Populares* of the Casa del Caribe and its director Orlando Vergés Martínez, the Ballet Folklórico Cutumba and its director Idalberto Bandera Guerrero, the Ballet Folklórico de Oriente and its director Milagros Ramirez Gonzalez, the Conga and Conga Infantil de los Hoyos, the Cabildo Carabalí Isuama, and the Cabildo Carabalí Olugo.

My fellow American travelers in Santiago have provided love, moral support, and intellectual rigor: Grete Viddal, Jalane Schmidt, Hanna Garth, and most especially my Western Michigan University colleague Sarah Hill, whose superb ethnographic eye and "*comadrazco*" on many trips to the field have immeasurably helped this project. Sarah also first drew my attention to the work of Goire and convinced me to attend to issues of materiality more generally.

I thank additional colleagues at Western Michigan University and especially in the Department of Anthropology, as well as department chairs Robert Ulin, Ann Miles, and LouAnn Wurst for the supportive academic environment, as well as Maria Pérez-Stable, librarian extraordinaire, for help in tracking down old references to *bozal*, and my colleague Pablo Pastrana Pérez in the Department of Spanish for help with the early Spanish context of *mamarrachos*.

Being a faculty fellow of the Ethnographic Video for Instruction and Analysis Digital Archive Project at Indiana University in summer 2009 provided precious time to delve into my earliest field video recordings, from which emerged key insights shaping this book. Western Michigan University provided the needed financial support for my research between 2006 and 2011 through College of Arts and Science Teaching and Research Awards, International Education Faculty Development Fund Awards, and especially a substantial Faculty Research and Creative Activities Award in 2009. These made possible my National Endowment for the Humanities Summer Stipend Award in 2012.

Many readers and listeners have engaged earlier versions of my work and encouraged me to clarify, deepen, sharpen, and widen my interpretations, conference paper by conference paper, chapter by chapter, and sometimes in toto. Their incisive critiques have challenged me to improve despite my own limitations, which no doubt remain evident. I especially thank Hilary Parsons Dick, Paul Christopher Johnson, Stephan Palmié, Matt Tomlinson, Bonnie Urciuoli, Allen Webb, anonymous reviewers, and participants in the Michicagoan linguistic anthropology faculty seminar (for valuable collective and individual feedback and encouragement), the Caribbean: Identities and Conflicts Cuba Conference at the University of Bergen, the University of Chicago Monday seminar, the Michigan State University Latin American Studies seminar, and the Western Michigan University Department of Spanish seminar.

I thank my editor, T. David Brent, assistant editor Priya Nelson, manuscript editor Yvonne Zipter, and the staff of the University of Chicago Press for their excellent and meticulous work in taking this book through the production process. My heartfelt thanks to TDB, especially, for his encouragement throughout the process.

My family has cheerfully accompanied me to Cuba or stayed behind when I went, tolerated endless hours of obsessive research and writing, and helped me toward insights only loving nonanthropologist spouses and small children can provide. Ed, Yasmin, and Naim have also ensured that everything I do keeps its context of love, compassion, and humanity. I hope Yasmin and Naim will understand that my drive to understand racialization and other inequalities is in the hope of a better world for them. I thank my family—Monika, Steven, Jaquelyn, Stan, and Mimi, and especially my mother Almut for always believing in me, while keeping me honest. I dedicate this book to my father, Jack Wirtz (1941–2007), who was there at its beginnings and would have read it with great interest, and whose voice I miss more than I can say.

Material from chapters 5 and 6 appears in different form in an article titled "Cuban Performances of Blackness as the Timeless Past Still among Us," *Journal of Linguistic Anthropology* 21, no. S1 (2011): E11–E34. A version of chapter 7 appears in "A 'Brutology' of Bozal: Tracing a Discourse Genealogy from Nineteenth-Century Blackface Theater to Twenty-First-Century Spirit Possession in Cuba," *Comparative Studies in Society and History* 55, no. 4 (2013): 1–34.

Illustrations

Figures

Maps

1

Semiotics of Race and History

Señores, hasta aquí llegamos, al compás de este vaivén
Saludando al territorio, y pa' la Isuama también

Gentle audience, we have arrived as far as here, in time with this journey
Greeting the territory, and the Isuama [society] as well

A memory: Two dancers sweep onto the floor before the audience as the song begins. They are elegantly dressed, Sergio in a grey suit with tails and Maura daintily holding up the skirt of her ruffled, floor-length white dress, and their postures are regal, even haughty (fig. 1.1). They are royalty, stepping high to the drums.

Que la reina del cabildo, ja, ja, ja, es la que se va coronada

That the queen of the cabildo, ha ha ha, is the one who bears the crown

So sings the lead singer, Manolo Rafael Cisnero Lescay, in his operatic baritone, backed by three other singers as the chorus, repeating his lines. A sly, crouching figure watches: a male dancer clad only in loose white britches gathered just below the knee, head wrapped in a red kerchief. Wielding his machete, he follows the pair with awe, then beckons to five companions, who join him in pantomiming their fascination with the elegant pair and their dance. The elegant couple exits and the men repeat their steps, intermingled with dances of carrying loads and cutting sugarcane: the labor of slaves. The song's lyrics now repeat a new refrain between lead and chorus:

Eso es verdad, eso es así, Olugo me trajo a Cuba a bailar carabalí

That's the truth, that's how it is, Olugo brought me to Cuba to dance carabalí

Suddenly, a striking figure appears, moving with fierce energy: Chirri is dressed in loose britches like the other "congos," his bare chest is crisscrossed with white strips of cloth and a long pendant, and his cheeks are hatched

FIGURE 1.1 Sergio Hechavarría Gallardo and Maura Isaac Álvarez perform a Carabalí dance as another dancer in the role of a "Congo" watches, in *Trilogía africana*, by Ballet Folklórico Cutumba, Santiago de Cuba, July 2006. Line drawing by Jessica Krcmarik of still image from author's video recording, used with permission.

with painted African "country mark" scars, bright white on his dark skin. As he dances around the others, intimidating them, he puffs at a cigar stub and rolls his widened eyes, his face frozen in a fixed stare (see fig. 1.2). He conjures the *brujo*, witch; he throws the others into paroxysms of possession trance on the floor. He works his dark magic, pulling snakes from a tall, carved wooden vessel that evokes both drum and witch's cauldron, then duels with a challenger, and after that stalks the very edge of the audience with two thin torches, burning each along the length of his arm. In a nifty theatrical trick, he blows streams of fire from his mouth then extinguishes the flaming wands in his mouth.

I have seen Santiago de Cuba's Ballet Folklórico Cutumba rehearse and perform this piece, *Trilogia africana*, several times over the years, but my memory always fixes on this one performance in 2006, in the colonial ambience of the Casa de Estudiantes, just off the old central Parque de Céspedes plaza in Santiago de Cuba, eastern Cuba.[1] The Casa de Estudiantes, which closed soon thereafter for renovation, is a classically Spanish colonial two-

FIGURE 1.2 Robert (Chirri) Nordé LaVallé dances the role of the *brujo*, "witch," in *Trilogía africana*, by Ballet Folklórico Cutumba, Santiago de Cuba, July 2006. Line drawing by Jessica Krcmarik of still image from author's video recording, used with permission.

story mansion, built as a square around an open-air central courtyard, with its expanse of tile floors, and graceful, arched columns, the folding chairs set out facing an area for performance and with the Cutumba musical ensemble—percussionists and singers—lining the opposite wall. All around was Caribbean yellow with white trim—decrepit, crumbling, and therefore much more evocative of times past. A large Cuban audience surrounded a group of visiting European dance aficionados perched on metal folding chairs, everyone responding with excitement, gasps, even shouts and squeals, as the performance progressed.

This is my memory, aided by my video recording of the event. The performance itself is a remembrance, a re-creation of some imagined past of Afro-Cuba set amid the colonial architecture. All of its elements of music, dance, choreographed narrative, instruments, costumes, makeup, and even the dancers' brown-hued skin convey a sense of what the traditions and legacies of African-descended Cubans are and, thus, of what Cuba's African heritage means today. In this book, I examine how performing particular stories about the past, on stages, in streets, and during rituals, shapes processes of racialization in the present. William Faulkner's aphorism echoes for me in Cutumba's performance: "The past is never dead. It is not even past" (from *Requiem for a Nun* [1951]). The past moves in and through the present, like a ghost, or a memory, or a sense of tradition, and it does so because living people selectively animate particular pasts, choosing what will be remembered as history, what kinds of things will serve as signs of that history, what will be forgotten, and what relationship those signs defined as "past" will have with the present moment. While some tellings of the past gain a hegemonic hold on particular locations of the present, histories are heterogeneously conceived, being active creations in and of each moment of the present. The prevalence of performances like the "African Trilogy" tells us that some remembrance of Cuba's colonial past as a slave society has significance for Cubans today. I take this observation as the opening for investigating: What significance? For whom? And why?

Consider the ongoing relevance of the transatlantic slave trade and slave societies in the Americas: What does this history, shared throughout the Western hemisphere and the wider Atlantic World, mean to us in this present moment of the early twenty-first century? The persistent racial hierarchies evident in African Diaspora societies throughout the Americas are proof enough of slavery's legacy. But in many American societies, not least among much of the U.S. population, the times of slavery feel very distant. In some societies—Mexico, Peru, Uruguay, Argentina—the past of African slavery has faded almost into oblivion. To others—many Cubans, Surinamese Saramaka, African Americans—the era of slavery feels quite recent still.[2] Why these differences? What stake do we have in situating slavery in the distant versus the near past, in citing or denying its contemporary relevance?

In a groundbreaking critique of "verificationist" approaches to studying historical consciousness in and of the African Diaspora, David Scott (1991, 278) argues for replacing concerns about authenticating the historical narratives of subaltern groups with questions about how such narratives construct "relations among pasts, presents, and futures" and with what consequences. Notable among responses to this call, Edmund Gordon and Mark Anderson (1999) and Paul Johnson (2007) have examined shifting "horizons" of historical consciousness among Garifuna and Nicaraguan Creole communities that destabilize anthropological assumptions that who "belongs" to the African Diaspora (or doesn't) is necessarily obvious. As Gordon and Anderson (1999) suggest, ethnographies of diaspora identification are needed. I would extend this call to understand the historical consciousness of subaltern groups not only in themselves but also in relation to other often powerful forms of historical and racial consciousness that may construct Blackness (alongside other racialized categories) and thus membership in the African Diaspora (or its impossibility) as self-evident categories.

Too often, the very concept of race, and particularly of Blackness, gets divorced from its history of conquest, slavery, and normalized inequality to be set on a timeless, eternal plane as an inescapable biological reality, written in phenotype and genealogy. Such naturalized notions of Blackness, in turn, are linked to longstanding imaginings of Africa as a continent unified into a homogenous, culturally and racially deterministic region like no other (Mudimbe 1994). At the broadest level, a contribution of this book is to demonstrate anew that concepts of race do have a history, that racial logics, including ideologies of racial embodiment, require continued cultural effort to be sustained, and that the historical imagination is inextricably entangled with the racial imagination. Blackness is neither a straightforward natural category nor a straightforward historical category. It is, rather, a complex series of cultural constructions whose various, overlapping histories encompass several continents and oceans over half a millenium.

Cuba is but one site where Blackness is a salient category, and it is the site I focus on in this book. Cubans recognize Blackness both as a matter of African descent that, because of miscegenation, may or may not quite always align with racialized phenotypic markers, and as a cultural inheritance from Africa and African descendants in Cuba. Tremendous complexities result from this dual realization of Blackness as genealogical *and* cultural heritage—complexities only hinted at by formulations such as Fidel Castro's (1975) claim that Cuba is not only Latin American but "a Latin-African nation" because "the blood of Africa runs abundantly in our veins." On the occasion of Castro's speech, claims of Blackness "in the blood" were a rhetorical strategy situating racial discrimination in Cuba's prerevolutionary past and antifascist, anti-imperialist "internationalist" struggle in its present and future. The ways in which Blackness is temporalized are evident in folkloric as well as political performances, where the latter in fact often implicitly point to the former.[3] I suggest that studying links between folklore performances of Blackness and Cuban national historical consciousness can tell us something more general about how racialization works everywhere.

One strand of my argument will be to trace out the performative effects of folklore performance, and here I must pause to explain my terminology. The distinction between performance and the performative that I follow in this book is not a new one, but I find the interface between the two to be productive. Quite a lot of the data I present concern performances, meaning events framed as virtuosic displays, in the sense developed by Dell Hymes and Richard Bauman, among others (Bauman 1993, 2011; Bauman and Briggs

1990; Hymes 1972). This is because so much of folklore performance in contemporary Cuba has focused on figurations of Blackness. But to speak of racialization processes, as I do, is to also invoke the performative, in the sense proposed by natural language philosopher John Austin and developed by more recent social theorists such as Judith Butler, and meaning the capacity of social actors to constitute their worlds. The most simple case is Austin's speech acts—paradigmatically, constructions such as "I promise," "I command"—but notice that the performative effects of such utterances depend, among other things, on social norms arising out of histories of use that presuppose what such constructions "do" in the world. Clearly, the performative function of language exceeds the limited case of verb constructions that explicitly state their intended effect (Silverstein 2001). In the work of Butler and others, the notion of the performative has been developed to explain how seemingly durable but sociohistorically specific constructs—gender, race, class—are given social force through their ongoing reiterations that create subjects as well as the (gendered, raced, classed, etc.) subject positions we occupy. The performative need not co-occur with specially framed performances, in the first sense above, since the performative permeates everyday interaction and larger-scale discursive processes alike. But I am particularly interested in the performative effects of folklore performances in mobilizing figurations of Blackness that do indeed have wide impact, or so I argue, on how Blackness matters in the Cuban historical imagination and as a contemporary subject position.

The particular story that unfolds in this book—of race and history, of folk religiosity and folklore performance, of pride and prejudice—began for me in mingled bedazzlement and puzzlement. From my first days in the eastern Cuban city of Santiago de Cuba in early 1998, my attention was drawn to folkloric and religious dances that enacted, I was told, traditions of enslaved Africans and their Afro-Cuban descendants. Performers and audiences, mostly self-identifying as Afro-Cuban in this most "Caribbean" of Cuban cities, expressed pride in these traditions. Not only professional performers of folklore but also amateur enthusiasts, musicians and dancers in carnival comparsas (Cuban carnival ensembles), and practitioners of Cuba's host of folk religions partook in reanimating African and slave figures from Cuba's past.

Sometimes, these performances brought me face to face with the kind of caricatured depictions of "primitive" and "wild" Africans, like the *brujo* (witch) and his corps of dancing slaves, that uneasily reminded me of North American traditions of blackface minstrelsy and Wild West shows featuring "primitive" Indians. To complicate matters, many of the performance tropes of folklore shows—bulging eyes, fixed stares, grimaces and inarticulate cries, fierce displays with machetes, speech keyed as "African"—were also evident in semiprivate religious ceremonies, when saints and spirits possessed people to mingle among the living and dispense advice. These riveting and unsettling performances demanded my attention, and in 2006 I began to study these stereotyped and instantly recognizable figures of Africans, slaves, maroons (escaped slaves), and Black witches. Such characterizations are staples of folkloric dance choreographies by amateur clubs and professional ensembles alike, in which they may interact with each other in dramatic tableaus that Cubans have long called "theaters of relations." They appear not only as physical types, marked by distinctive costumes, props, speech styles, choreographies, and behaviors—and significantly, darker skin color of the performers—but also as discursive figures and voices in songs from a wide array of religious, folkloric, and popular music genres. In raising the ghosts of Cuba's colonial slave society, these performances raise questions about how the past is imagined and what role these images of the past have in the present.

It will be apparent that the story goes back much further than my relatively recent ethnographic encounter with Cuba at the end of the 1990s. Racializing performances of Blackness have a history as long as the history of African presence in Cuba and indeed its colonizer, the Iberian Peninsula. In the age of Cervantes, Spanish writers were producing comic dialogues and sacred song lyrics representing a distinctive, parodied "African" voice, one that became the sound of *bozal*, or "wild," African-born slaves. This imagination of a new category of sub-Saharan Africans, in turn, drew on an older history of Christian-Moor-Jew-Gypsy relations in southwestern Europe, one whose traces remain evident.[4] And, in turn, the legacy of early age-of-exploration Iberian genres such as the *negrillo* is evident throughout colonial Latin America as well, from Sor Juana Inez de la Cruz's literary production in late seventeenth-century New Spain (now Mexico) to Cuba's mid-nineteenth-century teatro bufo and the twentieth-century blackface performances that followed. There is also a somewhat more obscure lineage of African critiques and counterparodies, less visible in the written historical record and more evident in performance traditions of religious cofraternities and societies of mutual aid and latter-day folklore societies and carnival ensembles. More apparent yet are twentieth- and twenty-first-century spaces of Afro-Cuban self-definition, pride, and autonomy, including these same folklore and carnival societies but also religious practices, grassroots carnival traditions, and other family- and neighborhood-centered interactional spaces.

To add to the complexity, the Cuban revolutionary state has, since taking power in 1959, prioritized the cultural forms identified with the lower classes—peasants and proletariat—that comprise what the Cuban Ministry of Culture characterizes as the "folk" and "popular" realms of culture. Such official attention, oscillating between surveillance, celebration, preservation, appropriation, and control, has been a mixed blessing. With it has come state support for what it designates to be "carriers of tradition," "aficionado" groups, and professional ensembles serving as "interpreters of tradition" for local, national, and international audiences (the terms in quotes are official categories). Cultural forms identified as African or Black have, in the course of these processes of folklorization, become almost synonymous with "the folkloric" in Cuba (Duany 1988), an identification that began even before the sea change of the 1959 revolution. These forms encompass kinds of ritual practice, sociality, music, and dance. Perhaps most prominent are popular religious practices, such as Santería and the Reglas de Palo. Diverse kinds of associations are keyed as Black, even though participation has long been racially inclusive: in western Cuba there are Abakuá men's secret societies and wide-open rumba jams; where I do research in eastern Cuba, traditional folklore societies organized by neighborhood are prominent, including the Carabalí cabildos and the "congas" or carnival comparsas. And emanating from these and other sites marked for their "Black" authenticity are many genres of "Afro-Cuban" folkloric music and dance, now well-cataloged in the repertoires of state-sponsored folklore ensembles. As such, these forms and the social groups they mark have become essential to the work of historical imagination by the state and by its citizens, at various scales and in numerous contexts. Indeed, one director of a professional folklore ensemble told me that she must constantly push back against the common public perception that Cuban folklore is reducible to, in her words, "blacks and drums."

This book is neither a historical study nor a work of historical anthropology, except insofar as the ethnographer's present quickly becomes the past, but rather an anthropological study of history making as a dynamic cultural process of situating subjectivity in space-time. As a linguistic anthropologist, I apply a semiotic perspective in which the scope exceeds "language" narrowly conceived to provide an analytic for relating broad-scale discourses to the moment-to-moment, unfolding interactions of life as we live it. Admittedly, I give much attention to events set apart as performances, to consider how contemporary performances explicitly or tacitly evoke earlier genres or present themselves as part of ongoing traditions, and how, in doing so, they contribute to a process of creating recognizable performance registers featuring distinctive figurations of Black characters and associated African or Afro-Cuban cultural forms. In examining such processes of intertextuality—or, in updated, discourse-focused terminology, interdiscursivity—and enregisterment, I propose a move away from overly linear, even teleological models of speech chains to explore more complex possibilities for the temporal ordering of performance events into recognizable genres. Indeed, this approach reveals surprises in how contemporary Cuban religious and folklore performances echo earlier traditions of blackface performance like the teatro bufo (comic theater) by borrowing their dramatic devices, character tropes, speech registers, and aesthetics.

I also examine the performance of history as a way of knowing the past, focusing on public, commemorative, and often deeply embodied presentations of history such as dramatic reenactments and spirit possessions, asking how these moments matter in the experiences of their participants. I examine their contribution to the creation of memory, understood as a direct connection to past experiences evident in personal and collectively shared narratives and thus a constitutive part of biographical personhood. Such narratives articulate with historical performances and with artifacts identified as tangible signs of and from the past. Because of the theoretical and practical difficulties of neatly distinguishing between the realms of history and memory, and because the same semiotic engagement with constructing the past is evident whether we are listening to someone's account of their own past experience or to someone's recounting of "oral history" about a distant time, I will mostly refer to that amalgam, *historical memory*, although pointing out moments of contact or divergence between what people distinguish as biographical memory versus history.

Memory and history are both performative, breathing life into temporal and spatial frameworks of subjective experience, frameworks that Bakhtin (1981) called chronotopes: *chrono-* meaning "time" and *-tope* meaning "space" and hence "time-spaces," directly echoing what in Bakhtin's day was the intellectually novel idea in physics of "space-time" relativity theory. Bakhtin described chronotope as a "fusion of indicators" of time and space—or perhaps, more accurately, of history and place. Although seeking to describe chronotope as a holistic domain of experience, he gave priority to time as "the dominant principle in the chronotope" because of its stronger effect on subjective experience (84, 86). But place, too, is intimately connected with historical imagination. Moving through it, sensing it, describing it helps structure subjectivity across interactions and practices of all sorts, including those structuring our experiences of embodiment—our bodies after all exist in space and time. I am especially interested in how chronotopic frames and the practices that create them help constitute embodied experiences out of the identifications we make of ourselves and other *as* particular kinds of people, fitting or not into various categories of identity, where identities are more than abstractions but also performative and chronotopic constructions we inhabit in and through social interaction. Rather than assuming a universal, empty, neutral space-time, I examine the cultural production of intertwined localities-histories-persons.

One consequence of using Bakhtinian chronotope as an analytical frame is that reflexive processes of *recognition* assume importance, since a text or performance's signs of time and place must be meaningfully taken up in order to create chronotopic subjectivities. This raises the question: How do differently positioned social actors recognize what is past and in doing so take a stand on how its being past is relevant? Moreover, interdiscursive processes of recognizing particular events as instances of types—genres of performance, for example—are linked to relational processes between people that, in a Hegelian view, are constitutive of selves (Butler 2004, 147–48).[5] And so we can ask: How do the spatiotemporal alignments that emerge from these processes of recognizing the past—the experiencing of patinas, nostalgias, traditions, innovations—affect processes of recognition among subjects in the present, including the kinds of interpellations of Black subject positions evident in Afro-Cuban performances?

We can only recognize the past and its representations insofar as we mark time more broadly: past-present-future, ongoing or completed, cyclical or hypothetical, event series, simultaneities, or flows, cause-and-effect or coincidence. But these are not the only possible delineations. Indeed, in Benjamin Whorf's formulations of what later became the linguistic relativity hypothesis bearing his and his mentor Edward Sapir's names (the Sapir-Whorf hypothesis), he proposed contrasting the grammatical treatment of basic categories such as time, space, and substance across very different languages, in order to look for correlations between obligatory grammatical categories and cultural predispositions that might reflect their influence. He saw such systemic, habitual aspects of linguistic classification systems, operating as they do largely below our conscious awareness, as the primary mode through which language could shape thought and action. His contributions to the notion of linguistic relativity posit that the mind habitually interprets reality in terms of the categorical distinctions required by its primary language(s), suggesting that obligatory but covert grammatical distinctions have perhaps the most powerful effect on thought precisely because we tend not to notice, and thus question, them (Lucy 1992, 1997; Whorf [1956] 1997). This notion that what does not rise to the level of conscious reflection constitutes the most powerful cultural logics has become a tenet of contemporary linguistic and cultural anthropological analysis.

In addition, any particular language in itself offers diverse resources for handling a given conceptual realm, such as temporality, in multiple, creative ways, even when a particular metaphor is prevalent, such as the spatialization of time as a segmentable, "masslike" thing, a substance in need of structure, in "Standard Average European" languages. John Lucy (1997, 2004) has pointed out that, in addition to the broad questions of language's influence on thought and of comparative linguistics and cross-cultural cognition, Whorf's work also suggests a "discursive relativity hypothesis" to investigate the influences of discourse practices within a language on the perceptions of those who engage in them, a possibility this study takes as a starting assumption. I am particularly concerned with exploring how the poetics of language use—and more broadly, of performance in all of its multimodal complexity—offer particular models of time, subjectivity, and history compelling enough that they are repeatedly taken up, gaining a certain cultural force through reiteration.

Wide-ranging, recent work on the poetic resources of language and language ideologies has identified an abundance of tropic and metric devices, parallelisms, metapragmatic cues, and other patterns that are salient even when not consciously identified by interactional participants. Reflexive attention to cultural forms exerts its own effects on their sensible experience and recognizability, and those effects must also be considered.[6] Greg Urban's (2001) definition of metaculture to describe cultural forms that draw attention to and thus aid in the entextualization and recirculation of other cultural forms sidesteps issues of cognition entirely, focusing instead on tangible evidence of cultural replication and dissemination as indices of social-interactional salience. Judith Butler's (1993) reformulation of Austinian performativity in light of Derrida and Foucault, coming at similar issues from a very different theoretical paradigm, takes a highly relativist stance in focusing on the way frequently reiterated, even obligatory discourses (e.g., of gender) constitute subjects and subjectivities. Reflexivity is both a necessary analytical perspective and a metacultural process in itself (see, e.g., Cameron 1995; Lucy 1993).

In this light, I am mindful that the deployment of scholarly categories in a study such as this exerts its own metacultural force on the ethnographic materials it presents.[7] Although unavoidable, a clearly laid out, explicit interpretive frame may serve as a partial mitigation. In the following sections, I ruminate over concepts such as time, place, performance, and recognition that serve to anchor my analysis throughout the book. Perhaps most in need of explanation is my use of racial terms like Blackness.

On Blackness

Labels can be a problem when it comes to analyzing racializing discourses without inadvertently replicating them or the cultural logics that naturalize them and often render them invisible as "common sense." One early reader of a chapter of this book commented that critical studies of race do not seem to have recourse to an umbrella term like "gender" or "queerness" that at least potentially can challenge normative logics by pointing to an "abject" position beyond biologically naturalized constructs such as race, sex, or sexuality (Susan Philips, personal communication, May 6, 2011). Consider the difficulties many social scientists encounter in the classroom when conveying the understanding that "race is a social construction," a formulation that many students comprehend as the ontologically distinct claim that "race does not exist." In that case, they ask, why talk about it? Aren't using the labels and discussing the stereotypes doing more harm than good? In short, how does one talk about race, and about one significant but still historically particular racial category, without repeating the oppressive logics applied to people of African descent to such devastating and lasting effect?

Consider the problem of navigating the proliferation of terms haunting an American scholarly book about race in Cuba: Black and White or black and white? Afro-Cuban, Black Cuban, or Cuban of color? What of descriptors of complexion, such as *prieto, parda, mulato, trigueña, blanco,* which don't quite translate as "dark," "brown," "mulatto," "wheatish," "white"? *Congo* or *criollo,* as the *muertos,* spirits of the dead, would have it? White in Cuban terms, White in U.S. terms, a white foreigner (or is that redundant in Cuban terms)? *Negro* in Cuban Spanish, which is nothing like Negro in American English. All of these terms for racial categories and skin colors are in overlapping use, within and across the society I describe and the society I call my own, whose very different racial politics shapes my ethnographic eye in ways beyond what I can hope to consciously control. As the Cuban aphorism has it, "él que no tiene de congo tiene de carabalí": if you're not part congo, you're part carabalí, where both of these colonial categories of African "nation" continue to resonate today in ways this book will explore. And then there are conventions of politeness, euphemisms, and acknowledgments that we are all mixed, all a little bit African, aren't we? Or maybe not, but *we* respect *their* culture, don't we, *compañera*?

Must I be consistent, should I be polite, should I take a stand, and if so, how do I justify my choices to you, my multifarious readers? What stance do I take toward the material of this book (what stance do I encourage *you* to take?), and how does it matter that I write as a White American anthropologist, comfortably middle class, raised in a liberal and multicultural Northeastern milieu with racial segregation just under the surface, child and great-grandchild of northern and eastern European immigrants but heir nonetheless to American White supremacy? A book about racial representations and performances of Blackness in Cuban society cannot help but add yet another interpretive layer in presenting ethnographic inscriptions of racial representations, in what becomes a hall of mirrors, of half-guessed intentions and unintended resonances. Taking, as I do, a view of discourse profoundly shaped by the work of M. M. Bakhtin and his interlocutors in semiotic approaches to linguistic anthropology, I agree that "there are no 'neutral' words and forms—words and forms that belong to 'no one'; language has been completely taken over, shot through with intentions and accents" (Bakhtin 1981, 293). So any pretense to false objectivity, to a stance outside of history, to having a privileged "view from nowhere" would ring false indeed. It could only reinforce a particularly entrenched form of racial privilege as the unmarked and neutral—White, elite—observer, who is of course anything but disinterested (di Leonardo 1998; Fabian 1983; Frankenberg 1997).[8]

I do not claim consistency in the labels I deploy, except to remain as true as memory, notes, and recordings permit to actual uses I witnessed in my ethnographic engagement in Cuba. These uses seldom included the labels preferred by American and Cuban scholars: Afro-Cuban, *afrocubano*, *afrodescendiente*, and other variants, of which the first two, in any case, are most often applied to cultural forms rather than people (but see Pérez Sarduy and Stubbs 1993, 2000). But precisely because of this scholarly usage and its creep from cultural forms like Santería to people phenotypically dark skinned, I have used "Afro-Cuba" in this book's title, where it highlights the creative metacultural work accomplished by labeling.

The term I heard Cubans most frequently apply to themselves or others to describe Blackness or African descent was *negro* or *negra*, which are best translated as "black." And so my umbrella term to describe people and cultural forms is Black, usually in somewhat roundabout formulations such as "people and cultural forms marked as Black" that emphasize Blackness as a socially meaningful quality *marked by* certain signs in a larger semiotic order, rather than *intrinsic to* anyone or anything. Indeed, in chapter 3 I will consider some of the ideologies and practices of embodiment that give race an apparent existence as an intrinsic physical quality, written in one's melanin, so to speak. To highlight the politics of claiming Blackness oneself or applying it to another, I follow an American tradition begun by Black Nationalists by capitalizing "Black" as a racial or cultural ascription. And in order to highlight how important Whiteness is precisely because it so often goes unremarked and assumed, I generally capitalize White as a racial ascription. Blackness, of course, like Whiteness, has its own discourse histories, with usages ranging from pejorative to positive formulations, and for this reason, I do not pretend my usage can somehow be neutral—hence, the capital *B*.

I define Blackness as configurations of signs that index African origins or ancestry, together with some combination of otherness, exoticness, cultural resistance, and social danger. Blackness, in Cuba, is construed as a descriptor of an intrinsic and genealogically warranted property of some bodies, persons, social groups, and cultural practices. As such, that seemingly unitary property of "Blackness" is semiotically complex, variously fractioned into phenotype, practice, tradition, or genealogy, depending on who or what is being ascribed. As I see it, Blackness has long constituted a racializing discourse in the Atlantic World (and beyond) in its emphasis on dangers posed by a categorical type of person. At particular historical moments and locations, Blackness also has been (and continues to be) an ethnicizing configuration in its emphasis on exoticness or other markers of cultural otherness. In adapting Bonnie Urciuoli's (1996) distinction between racializing and ethnicizing discourses, I do not want to overplay the contrast so much as point out that the interplay between discourses of (racialized) Blackness as social danger and (ethnicized) Blackness as exotic but perhaps ultimately superficial cultural difference allows some racist discourses to circulate "covertly" as it were, without much challenge, as is the case for "folkloric" Blackness in Cuba, where Blackness can also become a marker of pride and cultural resistance that minimizes historical legacies of racism (see Dick and Wirtz 2011).

Blackness is a configuration of signs that can mark physical bodies, social persons whether as individuals or groups, material artifacts, social locations, dispositions and practices, and cultural forms. The particular signs in that configuration vary in modality, by context, and over time, but it is in fact their co-occurrence that produces Blackness (just as "race" more generally has never been just about phenotypic markers, never just about place of origin). By referring to these signs as a configuration, I wish to highlight their interaction within a broader semiotic order that includes both synchronic comparisons (e.g., to other racial configurations such as Whiteness) and diachronic comparisons (e.g., interdiscursive connections to past, concurrent, and hypothetical configurations, such as those invoked by labels such as "Africa," "Negro," or "slave"). As Bonnie Urciuoli (2011) argues, such comparisons are taken up in processes of social marking that render some configurations racially normative and others marked as atypical, reinforcing the hierarchical ordering of racial categories. Hence, the normative subject of folklore in Cuba is cultural forms marked as African derived and associated with Black Cubans—a commonsense configuration whose semiotic workings, once unpacked and historicized, no longer seem natural.

In discussing the performative construction of Blackness in folklore performance, I use the notion of figures as semiotic objectifications that emerge and circulate in discourse and that only seem to represent a preexisting world of bodies and persons in action, whereas the relationship between what may appear to be enduring figures of discourse and preexisting bodies is, I would argue, a more complex, creative, and never-ending process of mutual semiotic constitution. The notion of figuration derives from critiques and expansions of Erving Goffman's (1981) taxonomy of participant roles, in which, for example, the role of speaker is itself composed of fractions such as author, animator, and principal that may or may not be held by the same participant. In a critique suggesting that there are endless possible participant role fractions and presenting some additional possibilities arising out of her analysis of interactional data, Judith Irvine (1996) proposes "figure" to describe persons, things, or social types that may or may not be present in an interaction but that are projected into participants' imaginations through the interaction. In this sense, I suggest that figures of Blackness circulate through visual, auditory, and embodied sign configurations, including the cues of costume, setting, and movement I will describe in chapter 2, the phenotypic and physical Blackness described in chapter 3, and the racialized "voices" described in chapter 4. Human bodies themselves are "figured" as racialized signs, with consequences for the subject positions of persons, not just when they play characters and project racialized figures in performances but as they move through their everyday lives as well—dynamics I explore in chapter 3.

To tease apart the everyday performative effects of moments of racialized folklore performance, we have to confront the degree to which, for North Americans and Cubans, at any rate, race appears to be a self-evidently intrinsic property of the body (and note the parallels with the sexing of the body; e.g., Butler 1993). It might seem so obvious as to scarcely bear repeating that a small set of visible phenotypic markers have come to index racial identifications, sometimes unmistakably and sometimes more ambiguously, based on a calculus of skin color and facial features—call this "somatic race." In most everyday talk about race, its a priori physical existence is presupposed, with only the meanings of physically evident race and its interactional relevance coming into question, whether implicitly or explicitly. Somatic racial ascriptions are obligatory and thus unavoidable; a person can appear racially ambiguous but can't exist outside of race. Not in a racial society (one is reminded of frequent anthropological accounts of working in clan-organized societies, where the Western anthropologist's protestations to "having no clan" are met with disbelief). Race, then functions as a presupposition, a set of signs so naturalized that somatic race appears to our senses as a "natural index," like Charles Sanders Peirce's grass bending in the wind. What meanings we assign to it and what attitudes we hold about it may vary tremendously, but at the level of an observable—a qualia—that we can see in bodies, sometimes hear in voices, and so forth, it seems to have an existence beyond the racializing logics of any particular moment or performance. A critical question, then, is to ask what semiotic ideologies drive this indexical anchoring of racialization in the body.

Throughout the book, I use Blackness as my key analytical term to highlight its dual character as unstable but perduring and familiar, such that Blackness is readily essentialized as an intrinsic and obligatory characteristic of some bodies, persons, locations, and cultural forms and thus comes to seem the natural order. But at the same time, the meanings of Blackness, as well as who and what Blackness is applied to (or claimed by), and in what cultural, genealogical, or somatic sense, clearly shift across time and space.

On Time

Temporal marking is a semiotic process evident in many aspects of meaningful social behavior reaching far beyond the verbal tense and aspect systems that so fascinated Whorf. Indeed, a foundational assumption of this book's approach is that the way we talk about—and more broadly speaking, semiotically engage with—time and history shapes our experiences as temporal beings and historically situated subjects. And all semiotic resources for marking time, from the most mundane or grammatically obligatory to the most novel and denotationally explicit, contribute to our temporal sensibilities.

Consider the familiar case of the historical present, in which our excitement about last night's ballgame or last century's struggles is heightened by using the present tense to relate events we understand to have already happened as if they are currently unfolding—an example is my use of the historical present tense in this chapter's opening account of a dance performance. The historical present has also been a conceit of ethnographers writing in the "ethnographic present" that freezes a community or society observed in a particular moment for all time (Fabian 1983). Ethnographic endeavors, much as they may seek to be of the moment, can at best be histories of the very recent past, since social life continues even as the ethnographer pauses to describe what has always already happened. The "ethnographic present" works to obscure this already-past character of ethnography. As Fabian's (1983) work highlights, using the historical present to describe another society as if it were unchanging can deny it coeval status with the describer, an irony given the immediacy conveyed by the "historical present." Another example of the semiotic potential of historical-present forms to give immediacy while preserving temporal (and social) distance occurs during Cuban spirit possession performances and similar evocations of historical figures in folklore performances, in which African deities and sorcerers and deceased slaves and maroons become immanent among the living.

As a semiotic process, temporal marking fundamentally involves deixis, the pragmatic function of anchoring texts in time, space, and social relations. Rather than speaking of text and context, where the latter is taken to exist a priori, we might more accurately speak of deixis as a process of cocreating text and context, of pointing out which are the salient stimuli to attend to in creating meaning (Gumperz 1992; Silverstein 1992). Tense and aspect markers are deictic—their reference changes depending on the context of their appearance and always in reference to a projected timeline, where time zero, t_0, usually is the moment of utterance. To examine narratives and performances keyed as historical, then, is to attend more broadly to temporal framing, or how unfolding events (or types of events—e.g., genres) are grouped, then related to the occurrence of other events (or types of events) in temporal sequences. Broadening out from verb tense and aspect to all kinds of ways of marking time, we find almost infinite semiotic possibilities, including discursive moves ranging from the poetics of internal textual coherence to the choice of registers, accents, and voices, to the poetics of interdiscursive references to other events. The semiotics of temporal framing also includes such material markers as costumes and props, song lyrics and instrumentations, even bodily gestures and movements like dance steps. Temporal frames often shift as well, even developing a timeline or trajectory of linked events. Through all of these metalevel shifts and comparisons, temporal frames emerge with a particular feel to each, whether of novelty or nostalgia, forward- or backward-looking, of the moment or bearing the patina of past times (Wilce 2009).

In order to elucidate the temporal frames acting in any case, we must attend to patterns of temporal marking in speech and more broadly in all kinds of semiosis, since actions and things can also index temporal frames. Where we see robust and durable temporal framings emerge, we might ask what processes and subjectivities produce them, with what effects on historical imaginings of those whose lives and practices are situated within them. We can imagine different ways of putting any particular temporal puzzle pieces together: a past event or epoch may be relevant in *contrast to* the present or because it is *continuous with* the present—ongoing, let us say. Or perhaps we recognize its episodic nature, as in the cycle of seasons and holidays. Maybe it is not now carnival season, but we remember carnivals past and know carnival will come again.

On Chronotope and Memory

Chronotope, or space-time, in Bakhtin's (1981) coinage, expresses how texts create temporal and spatial motifs within themselves that permit differing kinds of subjectivities to be conveyed. In his analysis of genres of literature from ancient epic poems to modern novels, Bakhtin tied it closely to characterizations of language itself (what he called "language consciousness") and, thus, to we might today call language ideologies. For example, in an essay comparing the epic to the novel, Bakhtin contrasts the epic's heroic "absolute past" of national tradition, which is sealed off from the present, to the modern novel's cotemporaneous, progressive temporal frame of potentialities, openness, and uncertainty (Bakhtin 1981, 84–258). While the epic reflects a completive, authoritative single voice and language, or monoglossia, the novel's play of voices and characters contrasts and "interanimates" multiple languages or registers of speech, a situation Bakhtin dubbed "heteroglossia" (Bakhtin 1981, 288–94). Thus, Bakhtin's notion of chronotope was about the semiotic construction of space-time subjectivities, which turns out to be inextricable from ideologies of language, including not only ideas about how language works but also notions about the social value of different voices and uses of languages.

The concept of chronotope, thus, was from its inception about more than space-time in written genres, and it has since been extended from literary analysis to performance and from the carefully crafted written word to the realm of spontaneous everyday speech—*parole*, as Saussure called it. When Bakhtin identified chronotopic motifs characteristic of particular literary genres, contrasting the effects of motifs such as "the road," "the threshold," "the idyll," "biographical time," and "adventure-time," he pointed out the kinds of narrative events, characters, and relationships made possible within each. The development of novels with biographical time and familiar, realistic interior spaces, for example, aided in the emergence of a new concern with characters' inner lives (Bakhtin 1981, 34–38). In the kinds of performances I examine, Blackness itself is given chronotopic flavor, corresponding to particular neighborhood locations and traditions and evoking a particular epoch of colonial slavery, marronage, and rebellious struggle. While these historical-locational resonances contribute to different kinds of social projects, they all have the effect of giving contemporary relevance to Black identities and cultural forms by projecting a particular historical imaginary.

This points to another characteristic of chronotope that Bakhtin examined: that chronotopes are relational constructs, in dialogue with one another in the world of authors, performers, and audiences. Different chronotopes "may be interwoven with, replace, or oppose one another, contradict one another or find themselves in ever more complex interrelationships" (Bakhtin 1981, 255). While Bakhtin argued that chronotopes are in themselves experienced holistically, performers and audiences are in a position to enter into and enact different chronotopes and to step back and contrast them, always, of course, from their own "unresolved and still evolving contemporaneity" (Bakhtin 1981, 252), This passage suggests that people can organize different aspects of their experiences and understandings according to different chronotopes, in the context of what Alaina Lemon (2009), playing off of Bakhtin's notion of heteroglossia, calls "heterochronicity": the coexistence of multiple chronotopes. It also inversely suggests that recognizing different chronotopic flavors may contribute to differentiating types—of experiences, persons, events, and things.

That is to say, contemporary performances, like the "African Trilogy" choreography described at the chapter's opening, become salient because performers and audiences compare them not only to previous folklore shows and religious ceremonies, and not only to other kinds of events including default chronotopes of everyday lived experience, but to historically distant events as well, such as the commingling of Africans brought from different places in colonial slave society, and the presumed religious and social activities of colonial-era Africans and their descendants. Performers learn which comparisons to make in their professional training, and audiences, too, pick up cues from performances and commentary that accompanies them about which comparisons they are supposed to make. That is, the chronotopic projections of events like a dance performance invite and suggest contrasts to everyday notions of contemporaneous time and space and comparisons to the chronotopes of events, from experience or imagination, that seem similar.

Through these kinds of interdiscursive comparisons, genres and other types emerge to become salient categories, available for later comparisons (Bauman and Briggs 1990). Silverstein (2005) probes the way in which such comparisons, basic as they are to social semiosis, are made, arguing that judgments about similarity between two moments in the stream of discourse require semiotic work to lift them out of the stream and momentarily suspend some entextualized representation of them in an achronic state—a frame or horizon of comparison. Out of such comparisons, we create temporal orders of what we come to see as linked events: series of earlier and later instances, examples of types, quotes, samplings, and parodies, for example. At the same time, we use and recognize myriad deictic techniques to anchor moments and events of discourse to specific temporal frames: here and now, then and there, hereafter and always. That we are all constantly and instantaneously doing such complex cognitive and interactional work is for me yet another source of amazement and a motivation for the project of this book.

Chronotope is such a basic and widely recognized semiotic phenomenon, and so often invoked in such richly diverse contexts, that it is rather surprising to see how little it has been subject to thorough theoretical treatment and how few tools for understanding it have been provided, beyond Bakhtin's own literary explorations.

One direction for expanding on Bakhtin's explorations of chronotope might be to apply musical metaphors to verbal texts and performances, to consider, for example, how to characterize the tempo and density of the chronotope created in and even across such events and contributing to our very sense of their entextualization *as* events. Tempo expressly is a musical metaphor, and this is significant because music as a semiotic system has particularly refined ways of marking time. Musicians attend to phrasing and tempo; time signatures in Western musical notation provide the basic "beat" structuring the piece; the sound of the piece can also suggest particular historical moments, for example, via stylistic indices, a kind of musical interdiscursivity.

Density of signaling, the multimodal layering of different sign systems (like orchestration choices in music), also affects our experience of chronotope through the intensity of an event and the degree to which it stands out as a definable (entextualized) event. In Cuban folk religious ceremonies, musical tempo changes combined with increases in the density of rhythmic figures and the loudness of drumming, bells, handclapping, and singing can trigger possession trances, which are construed as moments of temporal telescoping, in which beings from a time-transcending plane or spirits of deceased persons become manifest in the ritual present. In folkloric Cuban social dances, musical tempo, closely tied to particular traditional rhythms, signals activities and changes in activity, such as between marching and dancing as a display, or switching between different dance styles. Given the importance of music in the performances I examine, tempo and density are fitting tools for analyzing chronotope.

Consider as well how tempo and density shape narrative chronotopes, with corresponding effects on our biographical and historical consciousness (see, e.g., Carr 1986; Wortham 2001). The short story "The Seventh Man," by Haruki Murakami (2007), in which a narrator recounts a typhoon that was the defining event of his life, illustrates how a narrative can thicken and slow the flow of time at crucial moments, namely, when the adult narrator describes escaping a giant wave that claimed the life of his friend before his eyes when they were children. This was certainly my perception on hearing the story read aloud (on National Public Radio's *Selected Shorts*), where I felt time slowing unbearably as events lasting seconds took long minutes to recount. Indeed, when I mapped the story's internal timeline into episodes and counted the number of independent clauses of the story in each episode (as an arbitrary measure of how much narrative attention is given to each episode), about a third of the story's lines describe less than fifteen minutes of events during the eye of the typhoon, and particularly during the crucial minute or so in which the first giant wave swallows the narrator's friend and the second giant wave momentarily brings the friend's body into view before sweeping it away. The effects of this momentous event on a man in his fifties are indexed by the narrative attention given this fifteen-minute episode of reported real time. Here, the semiotic device of writing more and more dense description of shorter and shorter intervals of narrated events iconically represents the narrator's experience of how time seemed to slow at the moment of disaster, and how, even in his reported memory, the shortest interval, between when the narrating character sensed the danger and made his own escape, and when his friend was taken by the first wave and reappeared captured in the second wave, assumed its enormous impact on his biographical sense of self.

The storyteller's craft is evident in making a traumatic childhood event the gravitational center of his character's psyche, illustrating how the density of description highlights pivotal past events and their relevance to the present moment of narration. Changes in narrative density can add urgency, since we have the sense of seconds passing, but also vividness in how "fully" those stretches are remembered—as compared to the rapidity with which whole years of the narrator's life are dispatched in a few sentences. It is possible to find similar tempo and density effects across repeated events of historical recall, as in the Surinamese Saramakas' "first-time" narratives (Price 1983), which cluster around and thicken—intensify—particular moments of historical time deemed to be pivotal to Saramaka historical subjectivity, namely, their escape from slavery and their struggle to maintain independence from the colonial regime that pursued them. No matter that the Saramaka signed a peace treaty with the Dutch colonial government in 1762 and that slavery was abolished in Suriname in 1863; for the Saramaka, resistance in the present requires nourishment from stories of past resistance. Eviatar Zerubavel (2003) discusses the nonlinearity of time in memory and how memories cluster around particular nodes to make the temporality of memory bumpy, with large "empty" stretches of what was forgotten or deemed unimportant punctuated by richly remembered and frequently retold moments. One such node of remembrance in Cuba is its late colonial period of the nineteenth century, in which the brutality of slavery (and, sometimes, the brutishness of newly imported African slaves) is contrasted to the cultural resistance of African cabildos (cofraternal societies), spiritual practices, marronage, and insurrection, including Black participation in Cuba's wars for independence from Spain. Another node, often linked to these prior ones, centers on the events surrounding the Cuban Revolution of 1959: the rebels' wins and losses and the moments commemorating heroism, social progress, and external threat.

On Place

Thus far, my discussion of chronotope has focused on temporality more than on space and place, but these too must be considered, as they are in many ways mutually constituted with time. And so we must attend to the semiotics of emplacement, of what it means to situate Cuba, Spain, Africa, eastern Cuba, Santiago, and its neighborhoods in particular geographies of meaning and "topographies of memory" (Connerton 1989) that arise out of the self-same historical, national, and racial subjectivities. As Whorf described, speakers of Standard Average European languages like English and Spanish spatialize time, treating both space and time as abstract, linear entities, as substances in need of form and therefore segmentable into units that can be lined up but also contrasted based on their scale and relative position (meters and miles; minutes and millenia; yesterday, today, and tomorrow; here and there). Santiago de Cuba, the city that is the site of my research, distinguishes itself among Cuban cities as the "rebel city" and as Cuba's most self-consciously Black Caribbean location, influenced by its proximity to Jamaica and Haiti and by its proudly Black neighborhoods and rural history in the surrounding mountains.

Similar principles must apply to the semiotics of spatiality, as to temporality. And so we can ask: How is a place differentiated out of space and given meaning? How is emplacement related to a sense of "here and now"? How is a location differentiated within itself? Rather than envisioning space to be uniform and abstract, like epic time or the Newtonian universe, space takes on social meaning through differentiation into locations, just as time clusters around important nodes. Consider Keith Basso's (1990, 1996) account of Western Apache stories tied to particular places, which are thus more fully imagined than whatever "empty," unremembered spaces one crosses to reach them. Western Apache toponyms, as well as the narratives tied to them, reflect this "bumpiness" of space-as-place. Basso argues that land—place—has a mnemonic capacity: locations gain significance as sites of important events that must be remembered. Indeed, it may be that memory is constitutive of place, where a spatial location is temporally marked off as a certain kind of site. Edward Casey (1996, 36–38) ruminating on the semiotics of emplacement, argues that place, not space, is the phenomenologically primary experience, and that event is the phenomenologically primary experience that is constitutive of space-time. Rather than the abstraction of "space-time," then, there is the fully sensory experience of temporality-emplacement through which we construct our spatial and temporal deixis. And the sensuality of chronotope is imbricated with its emotional impact as well. I recall a long-ago moment as a student at Cornell, when fellow student and Diné (Navajo) poet Irvin Morris gave me food for thought when he expressed a loathing for the term "landscape" because it served to distance one from the intimately situated, emotional experience of place.

In writing about the social production of space and emplacement, it is easy to stick to what Henri Lefebvre (Lefebvre 1991; Rotenberg 2001) calls designed and conceptualized space, to the exclusion of his category of lived experiences in space, thereby privileging static, often solely visual, descriptions of space, such as maps. But if we are committed to understanding spatialization as an ongoing social process, it is important to attend to movement-through-space as mutually constituting both place and its possibilities for shaping various kinds of movement and bodily sensations of place.

The phenomenology of temporality-emplacement (cumbersome as this terminology is) is thus the realm of visual landscapes but also soundscapes, movements-across-topography, bodily sensations (starting but not ending with propioreception, circadian rhythms, effort, e.g., of walking up hills and stairs), smells and tastes, and the imagination of other place-times with differing sensations. Steven Feld, writing on church bell–defined European soundscapes as well as on rainforest "acoustemology," argues for the importance of the sonic imagination of space as well, a central but easily overlooked aspect of the religious and folklore performances I examine (Feld 1982, 2004). Visitors to Santiago as well as residents describe vividly the overwhelming sound of a conga, a type of carnival comparsa, pounding drums, banging iron, blasting Chinese coronet and attracting singing and dancing crowds, *batá* drums accompanied by singing and clapping in someone's tiny living room or patio during a Santería ceremony, or stereo systems blasting reggaeton out of doorways and cars.

Consider, too, that songs in the genres I examine may directly or indirectly evoke particular sites of historical importance: the ring of older, Black neighborhoods encircling Santiago de Cuba's colonial core that are traversed in processions on particular socially meaningful occasions, the *monte* or bush as a spiritually powerful and socially marginal location, the location of battles across the island during the wars for independence, and even Africa in whole or part. Some moments of folklore performance evoke specific locations, such as a sugar plantation or an urban neighborhood or a natural feature associated with a particular African deity, such as the ocean. Some performances are constituted by distinctive ways of moving across space—saints' day processions and carnival "visits" and "invasions"—creating distinctive soundscapes while mapping routes through physical space that define particular subjectivities and positionalities. Indeed, some performances in their totality index particular locations, such as the historically Black and poor, but very folklore-rich, neighborhood of Los Hoyos whose carnival comparsa, the Conga de los Hoyos, aurally embodies its distinctive place in the Cuban imagination. In my own imagination, to think about the Conga de los Hoyos is to recall the sound of its rhythms echoing down those packed streets as the musicians and their raucous, adoring crowd approach.

To develop the insights of Bakhtin's notion of chronotope—and Richard Bauman's playful suggestion of "sonotope"—we must keep in mind that history relates to place and emplacement as well.[9] History maps onto and thereby helps create geography; indeed, much of what we think of as geography could equally be thought of as a historical record, at many time scales (geological to biographical). As an example, let me introduce my study site in these terms of historical geography.

In Cuba, the discursive division of the island into *occidente* and *oriente*, or west and east is highly salient (map 1.1). Havana, in the west, creates a center of political and cultural gravity as the capital and by far the island's most populous city, with over 2 million residents, despite official efforts to prevent in-migration. Santiago, the island's second largest city, at almost 500,000 residents, is Havana's antipode, a provincial city that boasts of its popular traditions and Caribbean (read: Black West Indian) influences, as well as its rebellious spirit. Cuba's Oriente, encompassing the vast rural provinces that spread around Santiago and other smaller eastern cities, has the mountains, the Sierra Maestre, that have served as a "natural" cradle for resistance and revolution throughout Cuba's history, from its isolated communities of maroons (escaped slaves) to its nineteenth-century independence fighters, to its twentieth-century guerrillas. More abstractly, the eastern mountains embody the idea of the *monte* (bush) as home to deepest Cuba, filled with spiritual significance as well as with actual spirits of the natural world. For the unrepentant city dwellers of Santiago de Cuba, sitting in its steamy bowl

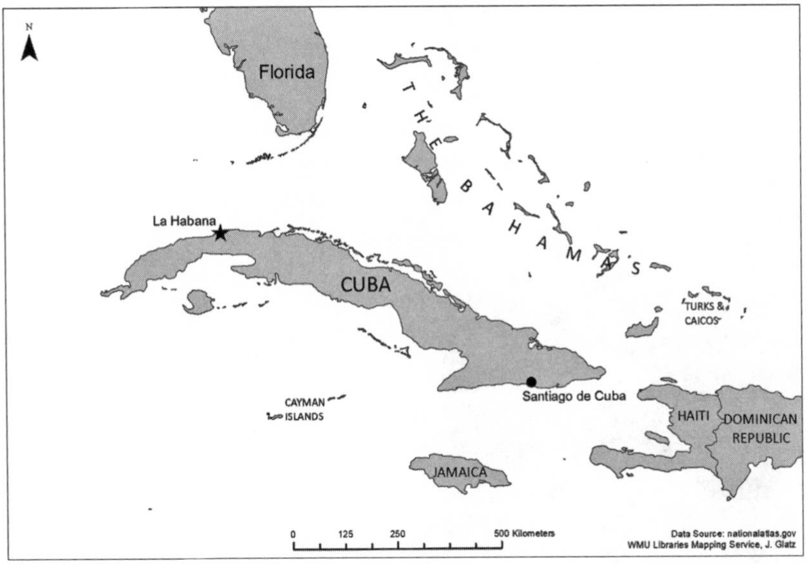

MAP 1.1 Map of Cuba by Jason Glatz, Western Michigan University Libraries Mapping Service, with data from nationalatlas.gov (open source).

of mountains on a bay that wraps around a once-fortified headland, there remains the mystique of the *monte*—the surrounding hilly countryside of small landholdings where substantial numbers of city residents still situate their agricultural predecessors—and its incursions into the cityscape: small rivers, dusty weed-choked lots where goats and horses graze, mountains enveloping the shallow horizon.

Nor is the city of Santiago de Cuba imagined to be a homogenous space: on the contrary, it is experienced by its residents as a city of neighborhoods (figs. 1.3 and 1.4; map 1.2). Up a steep hill from the bay's harbor is the city center, site of the first Spanish settlement and still anchored by the Diego Velasquez house, cathedral, historic old Casa Granda Hotel, banks, and city government building that circle the central Parque Céspedes. If one walks about ten blocks out from there in any direction, one reaches the ring of historic neighborhoods described by city historians as the "historical shell" (*casco histórico*) of the city. Most of these neighborhoods were heavily Afro-Cuban, a mix of working class, poor laborers, skilled tradesmen, artisans, and small businesses. Although the demographics have shifted, especially under the revolution's active program to desegregate White-only neighborhoods to the east and equalize housing conditions across the social classes, the "old" neighborhoods of the historical shell (and the formerly White, elite neighborhoods, too) retain their prerevolutionary resonances to a strong

FIGURE 1.3 Santiago de Cuba: Looking west down Aguilera street, past the central market, October 1999. Photo by author.

FIGURE 1.4 Santiago de Cuba: Looking northwest over Los Olmos neighborhood, Santiago, April 2002. Photo by author.

degree. Any Santiaguero knows these "popular" neighborhoods, to use the usual Cuban euphemism, and orients directions relative to them, but none actually appear on official maps. In like manner, official maps provide new (post-1959), revolutionary street names that are almost universally ignored as Santiagueros give strong preference to the older street names, many of which honor Catholic saints or an older stratum of landmarks and heroes.

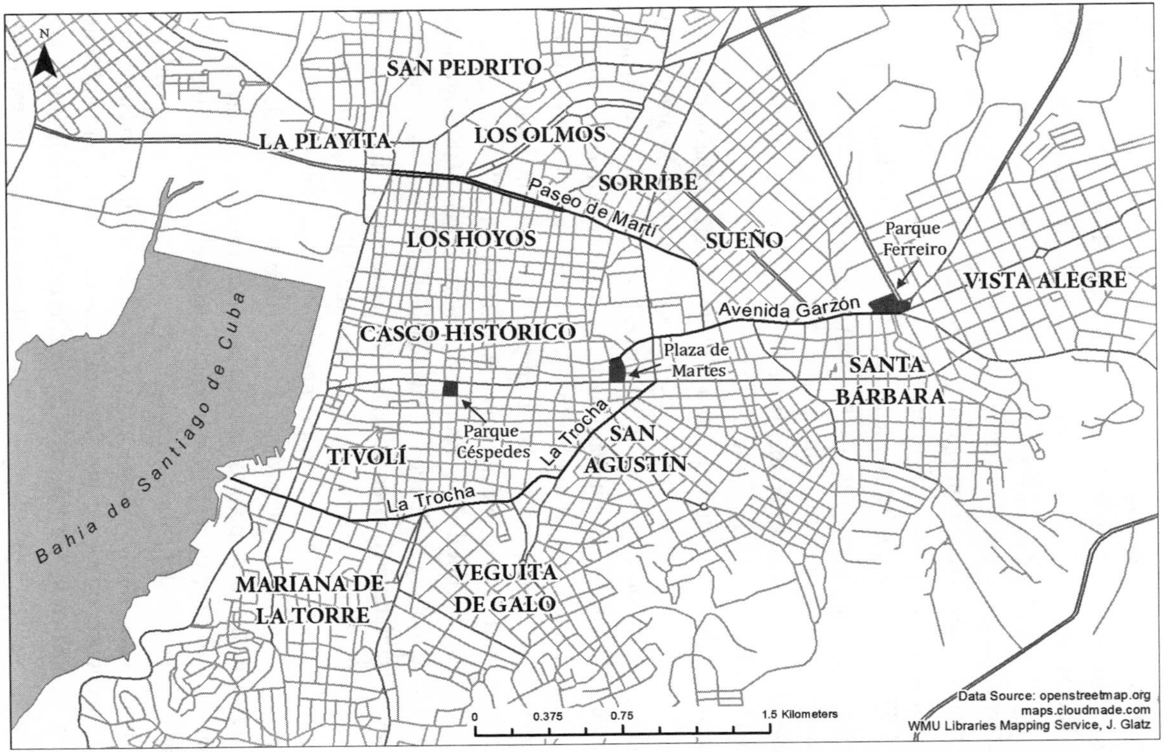

MAP 1.2 Map of Santiago de Cuba showing central neighborhoods, by Jason Glatz, Western Michigan University Libraries Mapping Service, with data from openstreetmap.org and maps.cloudmade.com (creative commons license).

Since most Santiago residents do not often encounter city maps and few have the opportunity to get an aerial view of the city from a plane (let alone GPS or Google Earth), it is by moving through the city and talking about moving through it that most of their practical knowledge about where they live comes. While residents generally develop their densest social and economic networks in their own neighborhoods, especially if they live in the same place where they grew up, most have family and friends in other neighborhoods; most are also familiar with shops, markets, and more informal locations to acquire things throughout the city because consumables of all sorts are often scarce, requiring ingenuity to locate (see Pertierra 2011). Door-to-door and street vendors walk their own routes, carrying news and gossip as well. Then, too, many other residents must travel between far-flung points across the city to get to and from work, a daily trip that at times requires herculean efforts (and familiarity with bus and taxi fixed routes, as well as fares) because of limited transportation. Hence our virtual tour is on foot and, if realized, would require several hours.

Beginning this imagined tour from the city center, to the north is Los Hoyos, typically described as a folkloric, Black neighborhood—and as poor and dangerous by those who do not live there. It stretches west to east along the Paseo de Martí, a wide boulevard starting at the northern end of the harbor (see figs. 1.5 and 1.6). On the north side of Martí is Los Olmos, and beyond that, to the north and northeast, respectively, Los Pinos and Sorribe. Due west on Martí is a lowland next to the harbor called La Playita, and north of it lies the neighborhood of San Pedrito. To the southwest of the city center, on the hill overlooking the harbor, is Tivolí, widely described as a traditionally Franco-Haitian neighborhood, where two waves of Haitian immigrants left their mark. Along the southern bottom of the hill from Tivolí stretches the Avenida Trocha, which enters the neighborhood of San Agustín to the southeast (see fig. 1.7), passing Mariana de la Torre and Veguita de Galo to the south as it stretches uphill toward the east. Returning to the city center, the main axis of elite, White development stretches east, uphill to the Plaza de Martes, then out along the commercial strip of Garzón Avenue, with the once middle-class, White neighborhood of Sueño to the north and a similar, smaller neighborhood called Santa Bárbara to the southeast, to a roundabout intersection known as the Parque Ferreiro. Beyond Ferreiro lies the once White-only neighborhood of Vista Alegre, still the site of grand mansions along its central avenue and 1950s-modern suburban ranches along the side streets, many converted to government uses and multifamily homes.

There are many other neighborhoods, too, stretching along mostly unpaved roads up the hills in all directions to the city's ever-expanding limits,

FIGURE 1.5 Late afternoon on the Paseo de Martí, central artery of Los Hoyos neighborhood, looking west from the Cultural Center of the Conga de los Hoyos, Santiago de Cuba, May 2010. Photo by author.

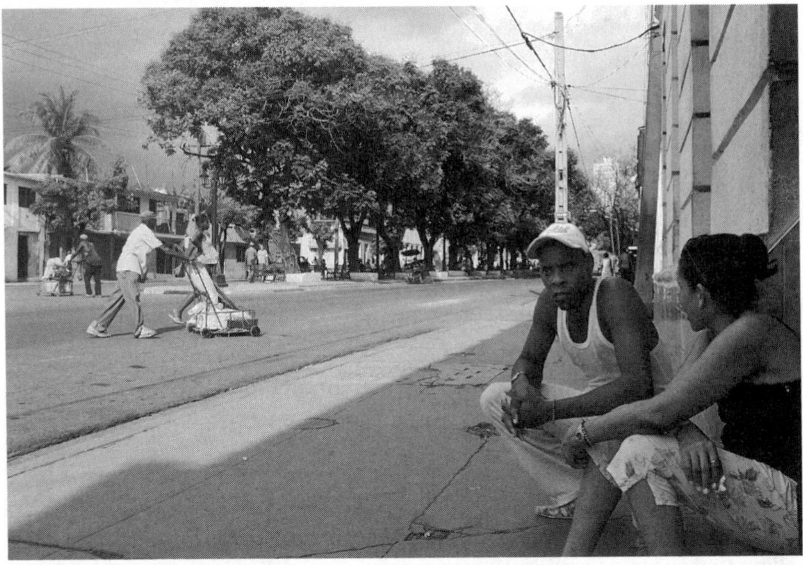

FIGURE 1.6 Late afternoon on the Paseo de Martí in Los Hoyos, looking east from the Cultural Center of the Conga de los Hoyos, Santiago de Cuba, May 2010. Photo by author.

FIGURE 1.7 Baseball game on the street in the neighborhood of San Agustín, Santiago de Cuba, May 2010. Photo by author.

but these are understood to be recent and thus not to carry the historic value of the "old" neighborhoods. Many residents of revolution-era public housing projects like the Distrito de Martí and Nueva Vista Alegre neighborhood (northwest and west of the city center) or of the still-extant slums they were to replace, like los Chicharrones to the more distant south, continue to identify with the neighborhoods of the "historic shell" and belong to their historic institutions, especially the carnival comparsas.

The neighborhoods and streets I named on my imagined tour, above, are those most frequently invoked and contrasted when Santiagueros discussed matters of race, class, and folklore in my hearing. Indeed, today's carnival route brings the various neighborhood-based comparsas up around the historic shell to a gathering and staging area at a major intersection just east of downtown, then down along the axis of Garzón Avenue, where viewing and judging stands are set up. In contrast, the grassroots event called the Invasion makes a circuit of the "traditional" Black neighborhoods beginning and ending in Los Hoyos, heart of the carnivalesque tradition of conga. It is telling that Santiago's official carnival relies on the diversity of neighborhood allegiances and their small pockets of traditional, carnivalesque resistance to order, but past a certain point and at the appointed time everyone joins the same, centralized display for, rather than of, power. The routes of Santiago's late-July carnival are, in a way, a map of revolutionary power and what lies beyond its limits, as well as a walked and danced embodied experience of history and (spatialized) identity.

On Historical Memory

The very idea of historical imagination approaches historical subjectivities as active constructions of how the past matters to the present and future, creating both trajectories and disjunctures. The term is not meant imply that some people have an "imaginary" past while others "know" the "real" past but, rather, to posit that all historicity is an act of imagination because it is about creating meaningful chronotopic contexts for recognizing signs of the past in the present. As Greg Dening (1996, 43) says, "Histories are the product of a dialectic between discovery and invention." On this basis, David Scott (1991) argues against a "verificationist" program seeking to validate subaltern historical memory by comparing it to what is taken to be the properly empirical historicity captured in archives. Rather than ask whether the historical imagination—anyone's historical imagination—is accurate, the focus should instead be on why "that event, this memory," and what semiotic traces—in narratives, objects, archives, and performances—are taken up in the service of different kinds of historicity (see also Palmié 2011). Maurice Halbwachs, speaking of collective memory, emphasized that "it does not preserve the past but reconstructs it with the aid of the material traces, rites, texts, and traditions left behind by that past, and with the aid moreover of recent psychological and social data, that is to say, with the present" (Halbwachs 1992, 119). Such take-up of the material traces of the past is selective, involving both inventions and erasures (Hobsbawm and Ranger 1992; Trouillot 1995). The costumes of Cutumba dancers in the "African Trilogy" piece I opened with were re-creations of period clothing meant to demonstrate differences among Blacks in different social strata and conditions of enslavement or freedom. The song I opened with is a different sort of material trace of the past, a replicated artifact that Cuban folklorists attribute to undated but "centenary" Carabalí society "tradition."

Historical imagination encompasses deliberate, conscious efforts at preservation, archiving, reconstruction, and commemoration as well as more implicit kinds of remembrance, of the sort once called traditions, retentions, or survivals. Recent work on historical poiesis has often emphasized embodied forms of remembering, including how "in habitual memory the past is, as it were, sedimented in the body" (Connerton 1989, 72). I will take this notion further to argue that race follows similar semiotic pathways and logics to itself become sedimented in the body—a matter of habit and memory as much as is the past. Folklore performers—the singers, musicians, and dancers of Cutumba, for example, spend long years honing their ability to replicate the rhythms and motions of Cuba's Black folk traditions—Congo, Carabalí, Lucumí, Haitian, *son*, rumba, *guaguancó*, and so forth—that are always the basis for even their newest choreographies. And yet how quick everyone is to point out that these dancers come to these rhythms naturally, as a birthright—as tradition "carried in the blood," according to some of my Cuban interlocutors. How easily habitus as memory becomes hexis as a mode of social reproduction, perhaps even losing any mnemonic function to simply become "how we do things" because of "who we are." In this view there might even seem to be a sharp distinction between history (collective notions of the past), memory (what individuals remember of their prior experience), and habit (the sedimentation of past actions into current dispositions), but the practices of history making and memory making in fact blur such distinctions, making notions such as habit and performance central to understanding the full range of imagination about the past, whether biographical or beyond.

My view is to focus on how memory is made manifest, on its public signs. These include the stories people tell via narratives and performances but also the unarticulated memories that are present because indexed by "inarticulate" actions and objects that nonetheless speak volumes: bare feet and kerchiefs, machetes, drums, and *ngangas* (Palo ritual power objects), and embodied modalities such as speech registers, modes of greeting, gestures, dance postures, and movements through space. I take these signs, encompassing material things and practices, as nodes of a web created by their invocation of previous objects, subjects, and practices and subject to semiotic ideologies that interweave history, memory, and identity.

Rosalind Shaw (2002) explores the possibility of rituals, habits, and practices whose mnemonic function remains but is hidden below the level of conscious reflection for those who engage in them, as she argues is true of Sierra Leonian memories of the slave trade. Some might interpret such situations in psychosocial terms as repression, but I find them to be more fruitfully considered as an additional modality of historical imagination. Jennifer Cole (2001), for example, proposes to investigate the "art of memory" as practices of remembering and forgetting that bring together individual memories and shared histories. She and other ethnographers of spirit possession, working in different sites in Africa, have suggested that people's interactions with the spirits and narratives about (and by) the spirits constitute what Michael Lambek calls a poiesis or crafting of colonial history (Cole 1998; Lambek 1998; Stoller 1995). Diane Taylor (2003) differentiates between an "archival" register of history, as practiced by historians and archivists, and a very different historical register of "repertoire" evident in such embodied modalities of remembering through performance (although it would not do to forget the ritual performances central to bureaucratic archive making and use; see Hull 2003).

Not just bodies and texts—the performed and the inscribed—but other material objects, too, can contribute to the poiesis of history, as Keane (1997b) suggests in arguing that objects may stabilize otherwise ephemeral processes of recall and as Routon suggests in proposing that spirit possession and the creation of ngangas, ritual power objects in Cuban Reglas de Palo, alike serve not so much to trigger "memory" as to inculcate "implicit knowledge about social relations and power" derived from a longstanding experience of marginalization (Routon 2008, 638).

Greg Dening (1996) has argued that even the academic discipline of history is performance, a notion seconded by Stephan Palmié (2011), who contrasts Trouillot's (1995) definitions of academic historicity to performed registers of immanent history in ghosts and spirits of the dead. Dening goes further to suggest that a primary function of history, even archival, academic history is entertainment, citing Northrop Frye: "People don't watch MacBeth to learn the history of Scotland; they go to watch the drama of a man losing his soul to keep his kingdom." That is, history means something to us insofar as we weave it into narratives that tell us something about who we are, and perhaps more broadly what it means to be human in all humanity's diversity.[10]

Certainly, neither Cubans nor foreign visitors watch folklore spectacles to be educated about Africans of colonial times in Cuba, and even less so do they participate in carnival to commemorate revolutionary anniversaries (despite the not-quite-coincidence of dates in Santiago's carnival and the twenty-sixth of July, date of the ill-fated attack on the Moncada garrison and rise of Fidel Castro's star). Nor do they attend religious performances and avidly listen to the spirits who descend in order to learn about their former lives and times. Audiences, rather, may seek entertainment, diversion, a playful sense of competition, maybe even fulfillment of communal pride in heritage, and perhaps, guidance in dealing with the momentous problems of the present, at least when it comes to talking with spirits of the dead. And throughout these other, divergent purposes for observing and participating in such performances, experiencing them shapes historical consciousness and historical knowledge, in ways perhaps less available to conscious reflection than reading a history textbook chapter but perhaps more powerful because entertaining and vivid.

My historical subjectivity as an ethnographer also matters to this story, especially in light of the historical subjectivities of my Cuban interlocutors. Students in my classes often ask me, "Why Cuba?" Indeed, I have no family connections, no heritage to link me to the "Pearl of the Antilles." Nor do I suspect any of my German, Polish, or Russian Cossack ancestors played much of a direct role in the making of the Atlantic world via conquest and transatlantic slavery—not to absolve them of the dirty work of history, but they don't seem to have been involved in that particular dirty work. But as a White American I am indeed entangled in the same webs of race and history as those I study among in Cuba.

In Cuba I am first and foremost an *extranjera*, foreign woman, which is a category of highly privileged outsidership. Foreigners in Cuba have money, lots of it, and have the coveted right to travel freely and thus to access more wealth and material resources abroad. Another not-insignificant part of that privilege is my Whiteness, and indeed I carry that with me, as part of me, in my own society, where I have a similar structurally determined relationship of privileged outsidership to African American communities as I do to Afro-Cubans. Moreover, in Cuba I am a *yuma*, less politely a *yanquí* or citizen of the United States in its antagonistic relationship with Cuba. I have traveled between these countries in the interstices of the U.S. embargo and travel ban, legally under the "General License" and well-known as a former foreign student and friendly cultural tourist in Cuba but nonetheless under official suspicion from both sides of the border. I become aware of surveillance mostly in those moments of passing through Customs and Immigration as I come and go.

Cuban historical subjectivities—in the plural—as manifested in folklore performance, are central topics of this book. And yet, some shared reference points are foundational to national identity. To apply Zerubavel's (2003) notion of "time maps," it is possible to point out the most salient nodes currently recognized in Cuba as essential national history. The times of Spanish colonial control and slavery spanned almost four hundred years, from 1511 to 1898 (slavery officially ended in 1886), and encompass massive sociopolitical, demographic, and economic changes, but viewed retrospectively, particular nodes stand out as prominent to Cubans today: the struggle for national independence, including wars against Spain in 1868–78 and 1895–98, in which many ex-slaves fought. Also important are the simultaneous struggles of people of color against slavery and, post-1902, for full rights as citizens in the new Cuban Republic. There were the new nation's struggles against the neocolonial power of the United States, especially as expressed in the 1901 Platt Amendment, effective until 1934 and writing U.S. rights of intervention into the Cuban constitution. Also salient are the strife and corruption of Cuba's first and second republics, ultimately leading to armed struggle led by Fidel Castro against the dictator Fulgencio Batista, including the failed attack on Santiago's Moncada barracks on July 26, 1953, and the revolution's ultimate triumph in 1959. Shortly thereafter, in 1960, the United States declared an economic embargo against Cuba that remains in effect, and then there was the failed U.S. Bay of Pigs invasion in 1961.

Taking 1898 and 1959 as moments of epic historical disjuncture and social transformation, the most recent candidate for another such moment might be 1989, when the Soviet bloc that had supported the Cuban Revolution for three decades fell apart, forcing a time of tremendous economic hardship that Castro declared to be, in 1990, "A Special Time in Period of Peace"—a time worsened by the U.S. Helms-Burton Act, which tightened the embargo. As I write this book, Cuba's revolution has survived these economic challenges and, under the leadership of Fidel's brother Raúl Castro, has embarked on a program of reforms whose profundity and effects are still unknown. The Special Period thus seems to have transformed into an Era of Reforms. This thumbnail account of Cuban history is, of course, official history. It is heavily promoted at all levels of schooling, in the media, in revolutionary propaganda such as billboards, in remembrance of national heroes, and in hosts of commemorative sites and events, including, as we will, see, in and alongside Santiago's carnival. It is the context in which enactments of the era of slavery take place in official and unofficial sites and ceremonies.

A Quick Note on Recognition

Anthropologists doing fieldwork in Cuba must navigate the ever-shifting border between official and unofficial realms of life, practices, opinions, and stances.[11] Ethical responsibilities to protect confidentiality of my field consultants exist in tension with their, and my, desire to give recognition for expertise and artistic excellence, and for their intellectual contributions to shaping this book. While I am judicious in using anonymity and disguise to protect my Cuban interlocutors from possible consequences or to avoid airing the inevitable "dirty laundry" of other people's social lives where it is necessary to advance my argument, I do identify many others. To relegate professional ensembles, venerated neighborhood associations, and locally well-known expert individuals to anonymity would be to deny their input into the writing of the book and write against their wishes, however much I must insist that I alone am responsible for the interpretive frame in which their knowledge, experiences, and performances are discussed herein. Moreover, blanket anonymity would be disingenuous because the groups would be readily identifiable, and indeed, their local and national prominence (or lack of recognition) is part of the story I wish to tell. In any case, an ethnographer can inadvertently do violence to the studied group at either extreme, in revealing too much or too little. As I navigate between the extremes, I opt to follow local Cuban sensibilities in giving recognition where it is due, thereby countering some longstanding tendencies to "folkloricize" marginalized people by making their creative production seem anonymous and traditional, rather than ongoing contributions to living culture and, yes, Culture-with-a-capital-*C* (in the sense of accomplished, virtuosic aesthetic production).

Representing Afro-Cuba: Notes on Fieldwork Methods amid Slavery Nostalgia

On Garzón Avenue, the main commercial thoroughfare connecting the old city above the harbor with the newer eastern commercial, official, and upscale residential areas like Vista Alegre, a new restaurant opened in 2007–8. This was part of a boom of new government-run restaurants, bakeries, shops, and licensed street food carts that delighted Santiagueros, who had long complained of the dearth of shopping and dining options. This particular restaurant is called El Barracón, the "slave barracks," and has plantation slavery nostalgia as its central theme, the first of its kind in Santiago although not in Cuba.[12]

El Barracón is emblematic of how highly visible representations of Afro-Cuba are in contemporary Cuba, for Cubans and foreign tourists alike. Describing it here, as I will momentarily do, poses just the quandaries of representation that I face throughout this book. The restaurant clearly represents the kind of alarmingly superficial treatments of colonial slave-society history and borderline-racist stereotypes that abound in Cuban representations of Blackness. It is, quite simply, too easy a target. I risk reducing the subtleties garnered over a dozen years of ethnographic fieldwork in Santiago to a cardboard cutout that states the obvious (or what seems to be the obvious).

This in fact is a common conundrum of scholarship on Cuba, which takes place in a highly polarized political context. For a U.S. scholar in particular, there is no escaping taking a position on the Cuban Revolution, however much I might like to balance critiques and praise, appreciation and complaint. I have the privilege to be critical in a way my Cuban colleagues, whether defenders or closet critics of a beleaguered revolution, cannot. I am also sensitive to being an elite outsider with the privilege to deconstruct other peoples' strategic essentialism (Briggs 1996). But I am far from being an apologist for racist stereotyping—my two African American children are always foremost in my mind. Nor would I claim that all representations or performances of Afro-Cuba can be explained away as instances of resistance (whether to the state and its official discourses or by the state to the U.S.-dominated, neoliberal world order). Elements of both kinds of interpretations are present, I believe, along with dynamics of what Greg Urban (1996) has called cultural inertia, where symbols of Blackness are so overdetermined and densely interconnected that they weave a thick web enveloping many aspects of Cuban life. Semiotic arguments about cultural motion and the role of metacultural or interpretive frames thus also provide a framework for analysis. Neither semiotics nor discourse analysis escapes politics, however. I cannot be what is impossible: a neutral observer.

What I can plead is great care in making and backing up my claims. My field research between 2006 and 2011 has involved seven trips to Santiago de Cuba, totaling more than four months. I relied heavily on my existing relationships with artists, performers, folklorists, religious experts, and scholars, dating back to fieldwork begun in 1998–2000 in many cases, to deepen my understanding of the role of markers of Afro-Cuban culture in their craft and to introduce me to a wider circle of individuals and groups involved in cultural production in the city. Although my life circumstances limited the length of my trips, on each one I lived in the same Cuban household, often with my daughter and later my son in tow, and kept fieldnotes on my day-to-day encounters with issues of race and representations of Afro-Cuban culture, as fluidly defined in ordinary encounters. These encounters included frequent comments on my multiracial family. I conducted formal and informal interviews with individuals and small groups, recording them whenever possible, and reinterviewing many of the same key people on each trip. I attended and recorded numerous rehearsals, meetings, social events, and performances of two professional folklore ensembles, two amateur folklore societies, and two children's carnival comparsas (one under the auspices of one of the studied folklore societies). I sought to learn about other groups and about the more general context of official administration of culture and folklore through the provincial arm of the Ministry of Culture and its subsidiary organizations such as the Casa del Caribe research institute, UNEAC (the Union of Writers and Artists of Cuba), the Municipal Office of Culture, and the *focos culturales* (neighborhood cultural centers).[13] I talked with anyone who would listen about the performances I saw, soliciting opinions from experts and nonexperts. I continued to talk with religious practitioners and to attend, even sponsor, religious ceremonies, particularly in Santería and Spiritism.

Given the sharp difference in economic status and freedom of travel separating me from even the well-to-do among my Cuban interlocutors, a word on reciprocity seems warranted. My general policy was not to pay for information, but I followed indirect cues, direct advice or requests, and my knowledge of people's economic circumstances on a case-by-case basis. Generally, I gave scholars and "culture" professionals copies of my recordings and small gifts such as bottles of ibuprofen, memory sticks, scissors, or other hard-to-find personal and household items, usually at the start or end of a trip and not as direct payment for any particular interview or access granted. For amateur participants in "culture," I generally tried to provide a public show of gratitude to the collective membership of their organization, such as by sponsoring food and drink for a party, as a way to avoid divisive jealousy in a society rife with economic need. I followed local customs of paying ritually mandated fees or gifts to the saints or spirits for religious rituals and paying experts for classes and tutoring sessions, when that was the local interpretation of what I might have called an "interview" (see Briggs 1986), trying to err on the side of generosity as befit my privileged status as a foreign guest.

Each time I returned, I would share copies of my video recordings, arrange playback interviews whenever possible, and hire Cuban transcribers and interpreters as necessary for some recordings. Back home, I wrote transcriptions and summaries and organized my mass of transcripts, photographs, video stills, and fieldnotes using Atlas.ti qualitative data analysis software and old-fashioned "find, cut-and-paste" functions. I selected stretches of discourse and performance as well as corpora of songs, dances, and images that struck me as particularly typical or rich to examine closely using techniques of discourse analysis. These techniques allowed me to tease out poetic and metrical structurings, pragmatic cues, voicing (or figuring) effects, moments of intertextuality, and other aspects of semiotic patterning that I present as my principal data here. Whenever appropriate, I provide very close readings of my data indeed.

And so, to El Barracón. I had heard about the restaurant over e-mail from a friend in 2008 and arranged to have dinner there in August 2009 with some close Cuban friends and two American colleagues; at the end of the evening, I picked up the tab, a very reasonable 40 CUC (Cuban convertible pesos, approx. US$48 with exchange fees) for plentiful food and drink for six people (but keep in mind that 40 CUC is double what most Cubans earned in a month on any kind of state salary).

The restaurant's decor and menu carried through on its slavery theme, setting a mood of nostalgia for a benevolent and pastoral imagined past animated by stereotypical Afro-Cuban figures and tropes of plantation life. Out-

FIGURE 1.8 Barracón Restaurant on Garzón Avenue, exterior with slave statues, Santiago de Cuba, February 2010. Photo by author.

side, below the large lettering of the name, two life-sized statues of a slave man and woman stand amid clumps of sugarcane (see fig. 1.8). The man wields a machete, and the woman carries a basket. Inside, a high ceiling was crisscrossed by large beams amid which were positioned an oversized spider in a web, a bat, and a jutía—a large indigenous rodent of Cuba whose meat is eaten and used in Santería ceremonies. Was this rustic-lodge decor overhead actually meant to resemble a sanitized, prettified slave barracks? My mind was reeling with historical vertigo. The walls bore pastel-toned oil paintings depicting peaceful scenes of plantation life viewed from a picturesque distance (clearly from an absentee slaveowner's or visitor's perspective), some minus any actual slaves: two oxen pull a plow; a sugarcane grinding machine sits idle (fig. 1.9). In a nook alongside the bar, a life-sized statue of an old man on a stool sat surrounded by ritual accoutrements associated with Afro-Cuban folk religions: he was the *tata*, "father" in Palo's ritual jargon, a title signaling the wisdom and religio-medicinal expertise of African elders or Afro-Cuban religious leaders. Real coins had been tossed into the bowl before him—an offering? I tried joking with the barman that someone had been tipping the *tata*, but he corrected me without a trace of humor: no, those were offerings people had left. The servers—all the restaurant staff I saw were dark skinned,

FIGURE 1.9 Barracón Restaurant interior, Santiago de Cuba, March 2010. Photo by author.

in contrast to most Cuban tourist establishments—were all dressed in white blouses and long skirts or slacks when I visited. A friend told me that when the restaurant first opened, the men working there had to wear white britches cut in a zigzag pattern at the knees: slave drag.

Already horrified at what I was participating in and even, perversely, enjoying, I opened the menu, which provided the usual Cuban restaurant fare and a few special items representing rural Afro-Cuban cuisine, with most dishes given names meant to evoke Afro-Cuban culture and its slave legacy.[14] Each item also had a parenthetical description in Spanish and English translation (see figs. 1.10 and 1.11). The overall effect of the menu on most Spanish speakers would be to convey a flavor of Africanness associated with slavery and with what was portrayed as hearty slave cuisine (rather an oxymoron).

I want to focus here on the figuration of African slave heritage in the menu's names for its offerings. Most obvious, perhaps are dishes named after types of persons. Indeed, since the menu pages bear the image of a Black woman in head wrap and long dress, holding a basket and ladle—a slave, we imagine?—the eight dishes given proper or categorical names fairly jump off the page: the *Negra Pancha* is chicken breast, and the *Doña Merced* is pork chops. The honorific "Doña" would have been denied to people of color in colonial times, and so perhaps "Mistress Mercy" is a slave owner to the rather

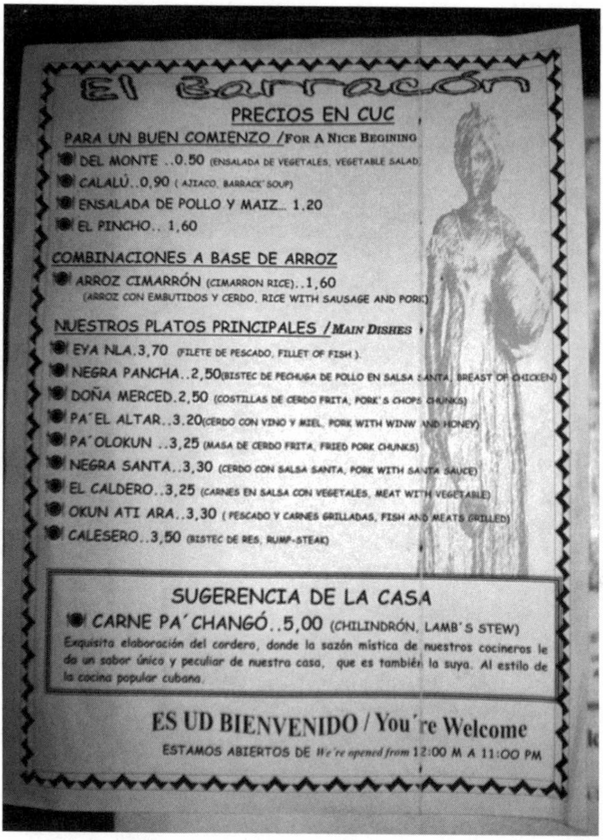

FIGURE 1.10 Barracón Restaurant menu, first page, March 2010. Photo by author.

nonhonorific "Black Pancha." The *Negra Santa*, or "Holy Black Woman," perhaps a reference to folk religious healers or santeras, is another pork dish, and the *Fuente del taita*, a pork and sausage plate, also gestures toward the figure of a revered old slave, the *taita* or "father" in a borrowed Congo word. The *Calesero*, or "carriage driver," a beefsteak dish, makes reference to a fixture of nineteenth-century Cuban literature and comic theater, inevitably a fashionably dressed Black slave bearing his master and mistress around the streets, and contrasting with the *jineteros*, literally "jockeys," of today, who make a living by hustling or offering sex to foreign tourists (in various senses "riding" them). A side of black beans and rice, a staple Cuban dish often playfully called *moros y cristianos*, "Moors and Christians," appears on the menu as *negros y amos*, "blacks and masters," playing off of the same color symbolism as the common name. Finally, there are two dishes referring to

FIGURE 1.11 Barracón Restaurant menu, second page, March 2010. Photo by author.

the *cimarrón* or escaped slave—altogether a veritable diagram of colonial Cuban social types.

Two dishes are given names in Santería's ritual jargon, Lucumí: *Eya nla*, meaning "big fish" for the fish fillet, and *Okun ati ara*, a calque of "sea and land" (i.e., "surf and turf") for a meat and fish combination plate. Three others are dedicated to particular orichas, or saints of Santería, all with the colloquial abbreviation of *para* to "*pa'*": *Carne pa' Changó* (lamb stew, a reference to an animal often sacrificed to the oricha Changó), *Arroz pa' Obatalá* (a reference to the oricha Obatalá's color, white, and preference for bland foods), and just *Pa' Olokun* (a pork dish perhaps referring to offerings made in a ceremony to the oricha Olokun).

In keeping with these invocations of popular religiosity, one of three dishes referencing locations is called *Pa' el altar*, "for the altar": pork in wine sauce. Wine is associated with altars in Catholic churches, whereas rum or cane liquor would more commonly be found on Santería altars, but the logic is loose and evocative. One other dish is named for the bush, site of agriculture, plants used for folk religion and healing, and once the site to which maroons escaped: *Del monte*, "from the bush," a salad. And there is the enormous and popular (according to Cuban friends) *Olla del barracón*, or "barracks stew."

One menu item adopts a borrowed word from elsewhere in the Caribbean, *Calalú*, as a synonym for Cuban *ajiaco*, or stew made from a mix of meats and root vegetables, where both these foods have long been symbols of the cultural and racial admixtures producing Caribbean national identities (see Khan 2004). And there are three dishes named in unmarked Spanish: the *ensalada* (salad), *pincho* (toothpick, or appetizer items like olives, cheese cubes, and ham on a toothpick), and *caldero*, or meat stew, which does have connotations of Cuban sociality, since it is often prepared by stewing a pig's head and root vegetables in enormous pots for festive events where many people need to be fed.

The Barracón's menu, in its totality, indexes a hodgepodge of loose references to colonial society and popular Afro-Cuban religiosity, and in throwing these together develops the folkloric potential of the slavery theme evident in the decor and setting as well. To borrow isolated words or phrases from Santería in this way reduces complex, contemporary ritual registers and practices to mere vocabulary lists akin to the lists of Africanisms tabulated in the era of Melville Herskovits—an impoverished view of Afro-Cuban folklore that projects such cultural forms into the nostalgic past, albeit one that serves the superficial purposes of the restaurant and the more general purposes of the Cuban Revolution (in brief, to promote tourism by marketing distinctively Cuban "culture," a formulation in which Blackness is equated with national folklore).

My visit to the Barracón Restaurant also serves as a reminder of the importance of audiences and consumers of Blackness, including me and including you, the reader, as well. Much about the menu and set-up of the restaurant clearly expects to draw foreign tourists as clientele. Neither audiences nor consumers are a monolithic group: their varied constituencies bring different frames of reference and different goals to their encounters with performances and commodifications of Blackness and history. The Barracón, like the "African Trilogy" performance that opened this chapter, evokes different kinds of historical imagination for various foreign tourists and Cuban patrons and audiences, depending on their relationships to Cuban history and larger scale Atlantic and global histories of colonialism and race. The vertigo and conflicted emotions I felt while dining at El Barracón were symptoms, I believe, of entering a historical chronotope of Blackness quite different from the chronotope of race and history I live within as a politically liberal, White American with Black children, one whose sensibilities are shaped by critical race studies and ethnographic studies of "experience tourism" and the like (Bruner 1996, 2005; Ebron 2002). Edward Bruner, for example, critiques assumptions tourists may make that their experience of something corresponds to its local meanings—what he calls "tourist realism," a flavor of naive realism—which reminds us that we cannot assume that our experience of, say, Cutumba's "African Trilogy" performance or the Barracón Restaurant will enlighten us much about what they mean to Cubans or to other foreign visitors. And yet, clearly, the expectations and responses of performers and audiences, diverse or homogenous as they may prove to be, clearly matter to the making, and remaking, of race and history. That is the story told in this book.

2

Image-inations of Blackness

I begin by bringing the visual imagination of Blackness into focus and, particularly, the "folkloric" representations of slaves, maroons, and witches that initially triggered my fascination and horror. These ubiquitous figures of Blackness in Cuba all share a certain ludic and theatrical quality, prompting questions about the relationship between performance and racial representation. The very theatricality of folkloric figurations of Blackness points to a significant characteristic of racializing processes: that, as natural and obvious as racial identifications may feel much of the time, constant cultural effort goes into sustaining racial thinking. Racial categories are notoriously slippery, even if their hierarchical logic is not. Like any cultural form, they must recirculate to remain recognized and relevant identifications for types of people, cultural practices, and social locations. As they are taken up and recontextualized in the flow of new discourses, interactions, and encounters, the potential always exists for racial categories to be challenged, transformed, repurposed. Racial logics have indeed shown a resilience and adaptability over time and space: their durability must be explained.

Indeed, I go beyond calling race slippery to describe it more technically in semiotic terms as a shifter—a type of sign whose meaning necessarily points out into the context of its occurrence. As a shifter, race does something odd: it most obviously points out its marked forms, so that talk of race often gets reduced to talk of racial *difference*—of Blackness, for example. Hence, it is significant that Blackness in particular gains meaning through theatricality, in Cuba and perhaps in other places as well.

It is especially important to recognize a wider trend in how folklore performance in Cuba (and elsewhere) tends to focus almost exclusively on only some racialized categories—namely, Blackness, indigenousness, or whatever the locally construed categories of "internal others" may be.[1] Where a nation's racially unmarked or "White" folklore gets performed, other axes of differentiation, such as region and class, will instead be foregrounded, as can be seen in various national iterations of rural, peasant, or "hick" folklorization (see, e.g., DaCosta Holton 2005; Dent 2009; Frederik 2005). What these have in common with folkloric celebrations of racialized cultural forms is the temporal projection of a folkloric figure emblematic of those cultural forms into the past, as a primordial figure, an anachronism, and a figure of nostalgia.

The figures that emerge from folklore performances gain these chronotopic values by helping shape a field of relationships of similarity and contrast with other figures representing the norms of here and now. That is, all of these figures constitute each other and gain their social significance in and through interactions, such as those among audiences, performers, and their roles in folklore performances. Through the role alignments, differentiations, identifications, and polarizations that unfold in and through such performances, figures constituted as "historical," like the slaves, maroons, and witches of Cuban folklore performance, come to have relevance for people's understandings of modern-day categories of race, class, gender, and religion. Identifications between folkloric figures and relevant modern categories of race, such as Blackness, are not automatic, and when they do emerge they may be only partial or only relevant in some contexts. Contemporary audiences of folklore performances also may make other kinds of identifications besides those of race, such as between the rebellious, somewhat dangerous character of folkloric figures like the maroon and the witch, and values of cultural resistance tied to Cubanness as national identity.

Although these figures of Blackness project a quality of permanence, of being always-already present, I seek to highlight their emergent quality and the way each performance contributes to entextualizing them alongside the chronotopes, social categories, and subject positions they help create. Analyzing static images like photographs or set types like characters in a stage show in terms of processes of emergence also illustrates how racialization occurs as a performative process that marks (and marginalizes) some social personae while leaving others unmarked. And yet, how very quickly talk of racialization in performance gets reduced to talk of Blackness in performance. This is so, I argue, because in places like Cuba Blackness has come to be associated with performance, as cultural forms and persons marked as 'African' have come to be valued primarily as signs of primordial authenticity and thus become the "stuff" of Cuban folklore, the foil even for the folkloric figure of the *guajiro* or Cuban peasant (a racially unmarked category).

I am mindful of a certain irony involved in choosing to explore the predominance of Blackness in Cuban folklore performance and thereby directing additional metacultural attention to Blackness as performance. I do so, however, thinking of Dorothy's dog Toto in the *Wizard of Oz*, in the hope of tugging back the curtain to show the workings of racialization in Oz and elsewhere as well. I ask: By what semiotic processes does race continue to exert such power over us? What are the links between the semiotic production of history and of race, and why does Blackness in particular, continue to resonate so powerfully in the historical imagination of societies like Cuba and the United States? In a broader comparative view, what can we elucidate about the images and image-ination of a society's most marginalized social personae—its internal "others"—by attending to folklore performance?

An important dynamic to grasp is how the temporal displacement of certain cultural forms—and, crucially, certain social personae associated with them—entails two seemingly contradictory orientations by audiences and sometimes performers too. These come about as effects of how the specific designation of folklore creates a performance frame and participation structure. Folklore performance frames distance participants—especially audiences, and sometimes even performers—from the performed cultural forms and figures that are marked as "traditional" and "of the past." At the same time, folklore performance frames encourage audiences to align themselves as cultural beneficiaries of the legacy of those cultural forms and folkloric figures. It will require several chapters, each taking different starting points, to show how this happens and with what consequences. My immediate goal in this chapter is to propose an analysis of how folkloric material—costumed bodies, ritual objects, music, dances, scenes, and dramas—implicate and entail categories of personhood by situating kinds of persons—more specifically, their semiotic projections as figures—in spatiotemporal and moral contexts.

To gain purchase on the phenomenon of ubiquitous Black figures in Cuban folklore performances requires a processual approach, one that examines the ongoing entextualization of configurations of images, voices, objects, and narratives in performances that become recognizable by genre and character types. That is, the figurations of "folkloric" Black figures emerge through ongoing processes of multimodal enregisterment that need to be analyzed, as do the effects of that enregisterment on the racialization of a particular category of person in Cuba. Chapter 7 provides a longer historical perspective on the enregisterment of Black figures in Cuban folklore and theatrical performance.

Asking how racialization works in this case also highlights connections between performativity in the sense of doing things with signs (Austin 1962; Derrida 1988; Searle 1969) and performance in the dramaturgical sense of a "display of communicative virtuosity" (Bauman 2004, 9), as theorized in the ethnography of speaking (Bauman 2011; Bauman and Briggs 1990; Bauman and Sherzer 1974; Hymes 1972). In this chapter, I examine Blackness as both performance and performative. As performance, Blackness is most dramatically represented in folkloric genres, which in Cuba bring colorful, socially marginalized practices to the center of national identity, showing the relevance of racial categories for historical and modern subjects alike. As performative, racial otherness continually constitutes itself through folklore as an inescapable primordial category.

While race is marked in innumerable everyday interactions in Cuba, its salience has been downplayed by official policies for most of the Cuban Revolution's half-century of governance. This officially sanctioned stance of promoting colorblindness to race and declaring racism abolished and therefore a taboo topic has made its promotion of Black cultural forms as emblematic national folklore even more striking, especially given evident continuities with racist representations of Blackness as social danger that have colonial-era precedents in fears of slave rebellion (see, e.g., Bronfman 2004). To probe these dynamics is to take a necessarily critical stance toward aesthetic forms that many Cuban artists and audiences value or hold to be harmless nostalgia, an ethically difficult position for me to sustain, made more precarious by my status as an outsider-ethnographer of Cuba and of Black Cuba in particular.

Folklore performances circulate particularly robust figurations of Blackness through common character types recognizable to Cubans and foreigners alike. The similarities among the illustrations accompanying this chapter are evident even at a quick glance and apparent even to the large numbers of foreign tourists, mainly Canadians, Europeans, and other Latin Americans, who also consume these images and performances based on notions of race and Blackness from their own national historical imaginations and from globally circulating discourses (Clarke and Thomas 2006; Gilroy 1995). This chapter's illustrations contain many different kinds of semiosis, ranging from dress and adornment to gesture, posture, and hints of choreography and dramatic action, all interacting with phenotypic markers of race, where all of these modalities are locally understood sign configurations that interact with more widely circulating—even globally prevalent—imaginations of race and of Blackness/Africanity in particular.

A key premise of my analysis is that such totalizing semiotic activity must be investigated in its multimodal glory, to understand how the visual, auditory, embodied, tactile, dramaturgical, choreographic, and musical come together to create deeply felt indexical potentialities. As a first approximation, I will consider the workings of particular modalities separately, before showing how they all work together. Visual semiosis requires special attention because images are readily treated as transparently decodable. Their referential messages—as icons *of*—are too often where analysis stops, rather than considering more fully contextualized, pragmatic functions of visual signs. Applying a basic premise of current visual anthropology that fits quite comfortably with discourse analysis, images must be considered in their contexts of production and consumption, in how what surrounds the frame gives meaning to what is visible within the frame. I propose an analysis of visual semiosis as one approach to provide a fuller account of the enregisterment of Black figures in contemporary Cuba, an ongoing process of imagining Blackness.

I suggest that racialization is deeply implicated in the kinds of participant structures and embodied stances created by folklore performances—not just the marked category of Blackness, but other racial positionings including the unmarked observer position we might cautiously gloss as "Whiteness."[2] Indeed, public performances of these figurations of Blackness help create particular racial and moral subjectivities in performers and audiences, in part through their participation structures and the stances they shape. For example, performance frames racially and temporally distance audiences from Black figures, while encouraging judgments about the authenticity and social value of these figures.

As a starting point, I wish to highlight two aspects of these performances that contribute to their racializing effects. First, Cuban folklore performances often recontextualize elements drawn from religious performances, particularly tropes of spirit possession and materializations of spiritual power in ritual objects—and particularly drawing from folk religions keyed as Black or African-derived, such as Santería and the Reglas de Palo (where the latter are often elided with witchcraft). Second, these performances almost invariably involve playful reimaginings of colonial-era history that keep Blackness at a temporal distance while reinscribing race as a highly recognizable, relevant, and time-transcending category linked to both slavery and rebellion. By tracing commonalities and intertextual connections among the many iterations of distinctive African figures, I will begin to make the book's larger argument about how Blackness is located and historicized in contemporary Cuba, and to what effect. Let us first contemplate some typical, even exemplary, images taken from folklore performances of the sort analyzed in later chapters: figures 2.1–2.3.

FIGURE 2.1 Cimarrón holding machete enters performance by the group 1802 de Orozco during the Ceremonia al cimarrón, El Cobre, Cuba, July 7, 2006. Photo by A. Abelardo Larduet for author.

Figures 1.1 and 1.2 from the previous chapter also should be considered. An initial observation is that these five images are all photographs of folklore performances, freezing static images of what were unfolding events on a stage, with only minimal and incidental visual information about the locational context and audience. In producing figures 2.1–2.3, I, or in one case, my associate, focused each photo on a primary figure commanding the stage, and so other performers—musicians, singers, dancers are visible only in the background if at all. In the three photographs, the primary figure poses theatrically, with wide, hard, even bulging eyes and a fierce stance, as does the central performer in figure 1.2, drawn from a frame of my video recording of the performance. All four performers are in costume, and despite portraying different characters in varied performance contexts, all wear what any Cuban recognizes as colonial-era clothing styles. The men performing in figures 1.2, 2.1, and 2.2 are shirtless and wear kerchiefs and loose pants reaching below the knee or to midcalf: this combination of sartorial elements is widely used in Cuba to represent slave attire (recall the statues outside the Barracón restaurant, fig. 1.8). The man in figure 2.1, possessed by a "congo cimarrón," an escaped African slave, wields a machete as he enters the performance of a folkloric rendition of a religious ceremony.

FIGURE 2.2 Final pose of Congos, with soloist Alcides Tomás dancing the role of *gangulero* or "Palo priest" in the foreground, and showing the wide-eyed, fixed stare and puffed-cheek exhalation typical of someone possessed by a *muerto*. In "El Maní," by Ballet Folklórico del Oriente, Santiago de Cuba, May 11, 2010. Photo by author.

The professional dancers in figures 1.2 and 2.2 play similar roles as male "African witches" and are marked with white makeup loosely representing facial (and chest) scarifications, or African "country marks." In figure 2.2, dancer Alcides Tomás performs the role of *gangulero*, or Palo priest, his chest painted with designs meant to evoke the esoteric cosmograms used in Palo, a religion closely associated with west Central African Congo/Bantú culture re-created in Cuba by enslaved Africans from that region. The Ballet Folklórico del Oriente is performing what the ensemble describes as a "Congo ethnic dance" called "El Maní," which features stick fighting and aggressive posturing. Although the ensemble's director and other folklorists characterize "El Maní" as an African dance, note how readily the identification is made with the contemporary Afro-Cuban religion of Palo: both are attributed to Congo/Bantú sources, and so they must be connected, or so runs the logic. The dancers' facial expressions in both figures 1.2 and 2.2, including the puffed cheeks in figure 2.2, imitate signs of spirit possession to heighten the theatrical effect.

In figure 2.3, dancer Imilce William Pinto poses in her role as *la bruja africana*, the African witch, during a performance by an amateur Afro-Cuban folklore society called the Cabildo Carabalí Olugo. She, like the other dancers

FIGURE 2.3 Soloist Imilce William Pinto poses as La Africana in performance by the Cabildo Carabalí Olugo, Santiago de Cuba, May 3, 2008. Photo by author.

behind her, is elegant in a floor-length dress and kerchief and holds behind her (just visible in her right hand) a bundle of fragrant branches, such as those used in folk religious ceremonies to purify participants. All four images represent powerful African figures from a particular, imagined past: the maroon and the African witch/sorcerer. In performance, all four performers are a bit wild, as if not entirely in control of the character portrayed but rather as if possessed by that character, manifesting the past in the present. Indeed, performers like those pictured often employ signs of spirit possession—spasmodic movements, puffing cheeks, hard, bulging eyes, and frenzied dancing—in folklore choreographies.

This much most Cubans and some foreign tourists could decode from the images I have presented, and I pause here a moment to consider the significance of their recognizability before presenting a more complete semiotic analysis of them. Pulled from varied performance contexts and examined as a set, these images show similar figures that are already entextualized for Cuban performers and observers as varied tokens of a "folkloric, Black" type. This fact makes my task—of tracing the processual in what seems already fixed—more difficult because the figural type may seem obvious, even to readers unfamiliar with Cuba.

What is so troubling to me about these folkloric representations of African witches, slaves, and maroons? First, these are highly racialized representations presenting Black Cubans and cultural forms marked as African in very particular historical contexts and always drawing on the same semiotic repertoire in dress, gesture, expression, and (as we will see in chap. 4) voice. Second, these stereotyped representations of Blackness are familiar and ubiquitous. Similar representations appear in a range of religious rituals and altar objects, carnival representations, folklore performances, tourist arts and crafts, and even occasional Cuban-produced television cartoons and historical dramas (e.g., *telenovelas*). Even when not presented as caricatures but as sincere, even reverent, evocations of the past (e.g., in figs. 2.1. and 2.3), such representations always teeter on the brink of caricature, as in figures 1.2 and 2.2, where these otherwise excellent professional companies have choreographed blatant stereotypes of savage, aggressive, "wild" Africans. Through frequent reiteration, a highly entextualized African figure has emerged, one we can describe as enregistered. Moreover, all of its iterations contribute to a durable racial imaginary concerning the importance of *lo Afro* in Cuban society. This is true even when some iterations offer alternate visions and emplacements of folkloric Blackness, as in figure 2.3, in which the group embraces a particular African and Afro-Cuban past as "Carabalí" as the basis of their solidarity within a latter-day mutual aid society. (See chap. 5 for more on the Carabalí cabildo folklore societies.)

Clearly, the stereotypes of Blackness and African cultural heritage are mundane and normalized, even expected, because Cubans, generally speaking, find them (as anthropologists like to say) "good to think with"—but to think about what? I argue that the same characterological types are ubiquitous across many kinds of media and performances because they are playful, culturally resonant, and yet ambiguous in their meanings. Instantly recognizable and, like Turner's (1967) condensation symbols, indexing a range of well-established social meanings, they come to seem more fluid and less fixed the more one traces what makes them so recognizable and what associations they index for differently positioned social actors. Different iterations in differing contexts accomplish polyvalent and sometimes even contradictory social indexical work. In the next section I provide a semiotic frame of analysis for these images.

Enregisterment in Images of Blackness

My goal in the following analysis is to indicate the general outlines of a multimodal, semiotic approach to static images, using the tools and insights developed in semiotic approaches to discourse analysis, and oriented around organizing principles such as indexicality, participation frames, contextualization, enregisterment, spatiotemporal deixis, and reflexivity (e.g., Agha 2006; Farnell and Graham 1998; Johnstone 2008; Schiffrin 1994). I begin with the metaphor of framing to examine the metapragmatic cues visual images contain about their possible interpretations. I then consider images as synchronic assemblages of signs that nonetheless have a diachronic existence. My photographs in this chapter, moreover, constitute static representations of events that unfolded in time, although those representations can also be compared across events. Among the semiotic systems evident in them are representational regimes of facial expressions, costuming, choreography, and staging, among others, all of which contribute to the overall images' intelligibility and recognizability as representations *of* certain kinds of figures and performances. I examine these representational regimes not as semantic "content" but as pragmatic markers, situating the elements of the images in sociohistorical locations via contrasts, juxtapositions, and deixis. My argument is that the enregisterment of the figures and performances I trace here happens through multimodal semiotic processes that take up static images like this chapter's figures. Considering the omnipresence of foreign visitors—and not just anthropologists—wielding cameras during Cuban folklore performances, I suspect static images like these snapshots and video stills are, in fact, a major force in mediating globally circulating notions of Blackness, including as authentic, primordial (Cuban/Caribbean) folklore. Their very muteness and seeming transparency may disguise their influence in mediating racializing representations of Blackness.

FRAMING

The first issue to consider is what kind of artifacts the images are (in figs 1.1, 1.2, 2.1–2.3). As photographs, or drawings from video stills in the case of figures 1.1 and 1.2, these images capture single instants of what were unfolding performances. All were taken in series with dozens of others of the same performance event. Each photo presents a more narrow field of vision than what an actual participant in the event would have seen, and so rather than reflecting an entire scene, they record the focus of the photographer or videographer's attention at the moment they were taken. To the extent that we can justly speak of their composition, given that they were taken by an untrained photographer for purposes of ethnographic documentation, each is bounded by a frame—the literal boundaries of the image—and a focus—here, focal figures in the foreground, with hints at the performance context as background. The notion of a frame as the boundary distinguishing an image as a bounded thing intersects in interesting ways with the metaphor of interactional "framing" introduced by Gregory Bateson (1972) and developed by Erving Goffman (1974, 1981). Both emphasized the interpretive and reflexive role of framing in how participants in an event understand the kind of event they are in and what it requires of them as participants. Bateson's charming example was of otters whose fighting and playing employ much the same repertoire of signs, requiring a cooperatively achieved metasignal—an overall framing of the communicative event—to define a given event as play or as "real" aggression.

Lest the framing of these photographs seem completely arbitrary relative to the framing of the performances they show, let me make two observations about their inclusion here and the possibilities for interpreting them. First, in all four cases, the performances were staged to be viewed by an audience separate from the performers, in the style of a proscenium, with standard orientations of upstage and downstage evident in the scenography of each performance to draw the audience's eye to particular locations and events. In figure 2.3, for example, notice that the focal figure is flanked by two rows of similarly dressed dancers, with another group lining the back of the stage area. If one peers into the darkness far upstage, one can just discern one or two of the accompanying musicians on a raised platform at the back of the room. The woman foregrounded in my photo was choreographed to be the focal point of attention at that moment of the performance. Almost the same arrangement is evident in figure 1.2, from focal figure in the foreground, flanked by a row of ensemble dancers, with singers and musicians lining the far upstage edge. This alignment between performance frame and image composition was true of all four performances.

A second point regarding the framing of the photographic images is that in all four performances the performing group had the expectation of being filmed. Other cameras are in fact evident in the background of figure 2.1, and in fact while my colleague took that photo, I was filming with my video camera, and both of us were being jostled by several other photographers and videographers seeking the same vantage point. The performance in figure 2.3 was staged for my benefit, and with the (fulfilled) expectation that I would make a video recording to share with the ensemble.

So what does a consideration of framing bring to this visual analysis? These photos and drawings, like the performances they capture, foreground particular figures that demanded the audience's attention at the time and demand the observer's attention in the still images. The rest of the image's composition reflects a narrow, rather than a complete view of the wider performance context, but what is evident is a scenography involving ensembles of performers dancing and making music.

The framing of the photographs highlights the way in which what they show relates to the larger scene at the time and how the camera's focal point and attention to depth (foreground, background; center, periphery) present a narrowed slice of an audience member's view of the performance. Moreover, the framing includes other kinds of cues of time, place, and situation: the costumes, colorful and markedly different than ordinary clothing, indicate the theatrical nature of the scene, as does the separation from the audience, even in figure 2.1, where audience members clearly form a ring around the performers, their gazes fixed on various points within the ring. The poses of the figures suggest bodies in movement, performing choreographies. The settings include indoor, outdoor, and patio locations, with tile, wood, or dirt surfaces and daylight. (During the event photographed in fig. 2.2, a passing thunderstorm had knocked out electrical power to the building, so the dance hall was lit only by daylight from windows along one side.)

SYNCHRONY AND DIACHRONY IN STILL IMAGES

Unlike the movement, speech, music, and dramatic action of the live performances they represent, these images do not unfold in time but, instead, freeze a single moment, synchronically. Within that frozen moment, we can ask about relationships of alignment, juxtaposition, and contrast among the visual elements. That is, we can take each image as an assemblage of signs combining different modalities of visual semiosis. In these images, the sartorial, the phenotypic, the gestural and choreographic, the scenographic, and the locational all must be considered. Some of these elements index particular chronotopes, embedding temporality even in a frozen moment, like a sepia-tinted photograph suggests a bygone era. We can also get a more diachronic perspective by contrasting the image with others from the same event or series and with others from different moments and events. These kinds of contrasts allow us to parse out the intertextuality of the image with other images and to recognize visual types and genres, through identifying repertoires of signs with particular indexicalities and through possibilities or constraints in the cues of particular signs or sign assemblages.

At this juncture, I will analyze figure 2.2 in these terms, as the other performances receive detailed treatment in other chapters. Three similarly clad and made-up dancers visible in this image are part of a larger group (as the hands of two additional dancers in the frame suggest), and they have struck similar poses. The two in the background hold sticks used in the mock-

FIGURE 2.4 Final pose of Congos, with soloist Alcides Tomás dancing the role of *gangulero* or "Palo priest" in the foreground, and showing the wide-mouthed inhalation typical of someone possessed by a *muerto*. In "El Maní," by Ballet Folklórico del Oriente, Santiago de Cuba, May 11, 2010. Photo by author.

fighting displays that are part of the Maní dance. In keeping with the aggressive action of the choreography, the dancers here strike fierce poses, crouching with flexed muscles and wide arms as if challenging the audience.

The two visible faces are especially important, since their expressions are part of the aggressive stance: wide, hard eyes stare out past the audience rather than at it. Puffed out cheeks and pursed lips continue facial gestures used throughout the performance, as well, in which the dancers kept their faces extremely mobile, their cheeks puffing as they rapidly drew air in and out, jaws chomping, mouths opening wide, then pursing. Figure 2.4 shows another moment of the ending poses where the wide-open mouth expression can be seen. These unusual and exaggerated facial expressions are distinctive markers of possession trance, in which spirits of the dead and orichas (deities) must operate human bodies they are alien to. Possessed bodies in religious rituals move very gracefully, even forcefully, after the disjointed spasms that mark the onset of trance, but facial expressions and movements of the head often seem to harden into a mask and take on an almost puppetlike quality, as if the agency inside was not entirely familiar with seeing the world through a human's eyes. The possessed person's eyes typically close at trance onset, then open wide into a fixed stare, sometimes with the mouth opening and closing rapidly, with cheeks puffing air (reminding me of a fish out of water). This behavior is particularly characteristic of muertos, or spirits of the dead, but can sometimes be seen in possessions by the orichas of Santería as well. These signs are often repeated, and even further exaggerated, in stage performances such as those by Cutumba and the Ballet Folklórico. As performed in this folkloric setting, then, the dancers act as if they are possessed by fierce spirits, manifesting the signs of possession in their faces.

SARTORIAL LOGICS

Now to the costumes: all the dancers in figure 2.2 wear loose pants, the abundant material of which is gathered by elastic around the waist and midcalf, a style never seen in ordinary street wear. Indeed, although the style of pants worn by male dancers in figures 1.2, 2.1, 2.2, and 2.4 varies somewhat, all are of thin cotton material and cut at midcalf or knee and so are unlike the denim, polyester, khaki, or linen full-length pants Cuban men more typically wear. Just as important is what the male dancers are *not* wearing: shirts or shoes. Dress codes for the street in Cuba required a shirt, and even while at home, everyone wore shoes, even if only sandals or flipflops. Men might go without a shirt while laboring—in a field or tinkering under a car or at home while moving something heavy or doing repairs; younger men might remove their shirts while playing baseball in the street or while rehearsing as dancers (e.g., fig. 1.7). Going shirtless was otherwise uncouth; it indexed manual labor in sites not in public view; the same man would put on a shirt to walk to the corner on an errand, leave the rehearsal, or carry to another house down the street a heavy object he had repaired. Going shirtless was, in the Cuban imagination, what slave laborers did.

Going shoeless even more tightly indexed a slave or a primitive persona: shoes were prized and required. I was often chastised for going barefoot at home, usually being warned that I would get sick because of the contrast between the cool floor under my feet and the hot air. Dancers themselves complained about this, although they did rehearse barefoot. People did not willingly put bare feet in contact with the dirt, with the notable exception being during certain kinds of ritual practice, including possession trance, where a direct connection with the earth is indexed by bare feet.[3] Folklore dancers like those in the Ballet Folklórico and Cutumba ensembles performed barefoot only in dances drawn from Afro-Cuban folk religions like Reglas de Palo and Santería or other folk traditions marked as Black or African, including Abakuá or Haitian dances like the Ban Rará.

Kerchiefs worn on the head were also part of the distinctive sartorial style indexing the African or slave persona (note the elision between these two categories) for both men and women, although taken alone head wraps didn't have the indexical specificity of bare feet or even short pants. It was common for women, in particular, to wrap their heads in a kerchief, especially when doing manual labor (including housecleaning), although some would use dressier scarves to wrap their hair on other occasions. It was rarer for men to use kerchiefs or bandannas (baseball hats or dressier cabby caps are the norm), and so these helped mark the performers' costumes as slave attire.

Also striking in figures 2.2 and 2.4 is the stage makeup: the men's cheeks are marked with lines imitating facial scarifications—the "country marks" many enslaved Africans had. The principal figure in both images instead has marks on his cheeks and chest imitating the style of esoteric cosmograms used in Reglas de Palo, even though in actual ritual practice these were typically drawn on the ground in front of an nganga or ritual power object.[4] The symbols on his body help identify him as a *gangulero*, as the ensemble describes his role—an African witch, or *brujo*, much as many Cubans regard modern-day practitioners of the Reglas de Palo. A comparison with the witch figure in figure 1.2 shows a similar costume, except that the white makeup is used to evoke scarifications and, perhaps, a theatrically skeletal face (although the emphasis on big eyes and big mouth resonates with both blackface and clowning makeup styles).

The sartorial cues for female African or slave figures are more varied than those for men. In the Ballet Folklórico performance of "El Maní," women dancers wore halter tops and short wrap skirts with lots of fringes, made of the same tie-dyed, soft purple fabric as the men's pants. Figure 2.5 captures some of the dancers relaxing during an audience question period after the performance. I especially like this photo because the "revealing rags" style of the "Maní" costumes contrasts with the colorful costume worn by a seated dancer who had just performed in a work displaying the sinuous moves of Haitian peasant social dances. Her outfit also bares the midriff and includes bare feet, but unlike the bare-headed Maní dancers, includes a dressy kerchief, heavy facial makeup to enhance "beauty," and a longer, ruffled skirt, evoking a sort of Caribbean tropical-fantasy figure like Carmen Miranda. Standing to the right, for an additional comparison, is a woman in dressy street clothes: the ensemble's director, Milagros Ramírez. When the dancers change after the show, they will depart as they arrived, in street clothes similar to hers. Some combination of kerchief, skirt, and blouse or halter, together with bare feet and, in performances of African folklore, perhaps some painted country

FIGURE 2.5 Dancers from the Ballet Folklórico del Oriente stand behind the director, Milagros Ramírez, during audience questions after a performance, Santiago de Cuba, May 11, 2010. Photo by author.

marks, evoke the African/slave costume for women. Hemlines and ruffles vary quite a bit.

The women and girls in figure 2.3 (and both figures in the pair in fig. 1.1) have rather more elegant clothes than those evident in figures 2.2 and 2.4, because they are dancing Carabalí, which is associated with colonial-era societies drawing on higher social stratum of thoroughly assimilated, urban free Blacks and skilled slaves. The women's satiny, ruffled dresses reach their ankles, and they always wear shoes (dressy flat sandals or state-provided athletic shoes for performances). In figure 2.3, only the soloist performing the character they call "the African woman" in the foreground wears a kerchief (kerchiefs appear on some of the other women in the various images, including the woman of the Carabalí pair in fig. 1.1). I will have much more to say about the Carabalí societies in chapter 5, but for now, it is important to recognize the contrasts Cuban performers make between colonial-era Africans of different backgrounds: distinctions between culturally assimilated, elegant Carabalíes and brutishly African Congos date back to the colonial era and continue to appear in the "theaters of relations" created in folklore performances. For example, the opening of the "African Trilogy" performance by the professional folklore ensemble Cutumba, discussed in chapter 1, features a "Congo" slave, shirtless and shoeless, with kerchief and loose, short pants, stealthily observing the high-stepping dance of a "Carabalí" pair, wearing a tuxedo and a long, ruffled dress and shoes (see fig. 1.1). In this sartorial logic, the revealing costumes of the "Maní" dancers index the unassimilated, primitive Africanness of the dance and the Congo people presumed to have once danced it, in contrast to the European colonial ruffles of those depicted as more fully assimilated to "civilized" Cuban society. Certainly the women's outfits in "El Maní," in particular, have little to do with historical authenticity in how Central-West Africans in Africa or Cuba would have dressed. We have here a tableau depicting an imagined historical progression, from Africans in the "savage slot" to assimilated Afro-Cubans contributing to Cuban national culture.

CHOREOGAPHY AND STAGING

Bodily movements and orientations, as much as facial expressions, comprise an important semiotic modality to consider. Although the photographs mostly capture poses, those poses were part of moving choreographies. The choreography of the "Maní" dance represented in figure 2.2 is exquisitely rehearsed to its smallest details by the professional ensemble, whose dancers have all been trained in a standard curriculum of folkloric music and dance that includes Palo and other Congo styles, like the "Maní" (see chap. 6). In a dance class I took with Cutumba members in 1998, our instructors described the basic steps as very strong and powerful. A professional folklore ensemble masters these basic steps, the side-to-side stepping, arm movements, subtle upper-torso articulations, and work with tall sticks, working them into a dramatic choreography, accompanied by live music from the Ballet's percussionists.[5]

In short, as described to me by various members of the Ballet Folklórico, the piece shows a group of African warriors (*guerreros*), led by a *tata* or elder father figure, and a (*n*)*gangulero* or Palo priest. At the opening and close of the dance, these two soloists perform before the corps. In part of the dance, the male warriors pair off to demonstrate stick fighting. In another part of the dance, two of the female warriors wrestle each other, with the rest of the group encouraging them, before the *tata* and *ngangulero* break them up. The piece is less than ten minutes long and sustains a loud, aggressive, high energy throughout, propelled by the musical score of driving Maní rhythms. The dancing is dramatic and technically impressive, with much jumping and some tumbling involved in the stick-fighting demonstrations. And yet my response to its performance was exhaustion, mostly because of its unrelentingly brutish depiction of aggressive, savage, and superstitious congos of Cuba's African past.

As figures 2.2 and 2.4 show, the scenography is quite sparse, relying almost entirely on the music, dance, and costumes to create the staging for the piece: the performers danced in their large, modern rehearsal space on the eighth floor of the grand Heredia Theater complex. They performed on the wooden floor in front of a set of platforms and folding chairs, where the audience stood or sat. The musicians and singers were lined up to the left of the audience, facing the performing area, and dancers made their entrances through the main door into the far, backstage left corner, from the elevator and staircase into the room (their dressing room is two flights up, above the performance space). The occasion of the performance was a visit by U.S.-based organizers of a major dance festival, who were auditioning various groups around the city to decide which to invite. The audience was small, made up of the U.S. organizers and their Cuban tour guides and a few other Cubans, mostly people associated with the ballet company or the facility—perhaps fifteen or twenty people in all. The director and choreographer had invited me to attend as well, permitting me to set up my video camera on one of the raised platforms next to the chairs and film the performance, which included four dances representing the ensemble's repertoire, with musical performances between each to allow for costume changes. The first piece, excerpted from a long work, used dances of the orichas to tell a legend of the orichas from Santería, and the next two depicted two very different Haitian dances, first of the *Gedé* (spirits associated with death in Cuba), then a social dance style, performed by eight women, with lovely arrangements of Haitian songs performed between each dance. The "Maní" was the finale. I was not able to talk with the American impresarios to get their impressions, but as it turned out, they did not invite the Ballet Folkórico de Oriente to the dance festival (they did invite Cutumba).

BODIES AND THE SEMIOTICS OF PHENOTYPE

The bodies of the dancers themselves are a semiotic modality apart from their costuming and adornment. Performers' bodies index gender, age, and racial ascription, in addition to conveying other information (e.g., the athleticism of the dancers is apparent in their physiques). Phenotypic indices can of course be ambiguous or misleading, and sometimes they are altered for performance (e.g., by cross-dressing or using makeup), but as signifiers they stay with the performer who has left the stage and shed costumes and props in favor of everyday street clothes, gestures, and movements. And so, following Goffman's (1959) insights about all social interaction as dramaturgy, we might ask what social identifications associated with the onstage persona remain when offstage and moving through ordinary life? The dancers depicted in this chapters' figures, whether on- or offstage remain dark skinned and phenotypically would categorize themselves or be categorized by other Cubans as of color—most likely as Black (*negro* or, in the most recent term in vogue in Cuba, *afrodescendiente*, "African-descended") in most everyday contexts. The fact of their Blackness is part of the story of why the professional dancers in some of the illustrations here became specialists in folkloric dance, as opposed to the ballet and modern dance tracks also available in Cuban dance education. Cuban professional folklore ensembles tend to be darker skinned, overall, than professional ballet ensembles. But race is not the entire story: phenotypic racial ascription is not so rigidly deterministic in Cuba. Nor, as far as I can tell, do the professional dancers of Cutumba or the Ballet Folklórico who are Black seem to claim any special connection to the African and slave characters they depict in performances. In years of informal conversations with dancers in these ensembles, the pride they take in their work is professional, and the pride they take in the traditions they perform is, by and large, about being Cuban, not being Afro-Cuban. That is, their orientation to a Black identity is what shifts between onstage and offstage, and it shifts in terms of the chronotopic quality of onstage folklore performance versus everyday lived experiences of race in Santiago.

Clearly, race matters in Cuba, and when it comes to folklore, Blackness matters: several folklorist friends commented to me that Chirri performed the role of the African witch (in fig. 1.2) because he had the proper, African phenotype for it. And other friends involved in organizing amateur music and dance societies have made frequent-enough comments about darker-skinned people (including my African American daughter and son) having Afro-Cuban rhythms "in their blood" and expressions of surprise about lighter-skinned people (including their neighbors) apparently having the rhythm, too, that I am convinced that such racialization of cultural forms is "commonsense" for many Cubans. In chapter 3 I explore some of the ideologies of embodiment that drive such common-sense understandings of race.

Afro-Cuban rhythms may be "infectious," and indeed Barbara Browning (1998) has argued that metaphors of contagion have long been constitutive of Blackness. But what of Cubans of all racial identifications who find the raw, subaltern, and mystical power of African witches and marooned slaves appealing? And how does this enthusiasm for Blackness relate to the especially stereotyped, even demeaning depictions of Africans evident in some folklore performances? What are we to make of the dark-skinned Cuban man, the one everyone else refers to as "looking African," who relishes what I cannot help regarding as his "blackface" role as an African witch because he does not identify himself as Black in the same way displayed by the witch character? If I am honest about my own reactions to these figures, it is sometimes the question of authenticity that troubles me, as with spirit possession enactments, and other times the question of sincerity that catches me off guard, as with performers' and audiences' sincere appreciation for these figures. Approaching race in my North American mode as no laughing matter, what can I make of the ludic quality Cubans infuse into depictions of Afro-Cuban stereotypes? What, indeed, does race have to do with it?

How to Study a "Social Construction": From "Race" to "Racialization"

Decades of historical, social scientific, and biological research amply demonstrate that race, rather than being biologically fixed and immutable, is a relatively recent, historically contingent, cultural invention that emerged in the context of European conquest and colonialism and that has proven durable because of what Thomas Holt (2000, 27) describes as race's plasticity and "parasitic and chameleonlike qualities as practice." In this section, I explore the implications of viewing race in terms of processes of social construction. In particular: What gives a social construction its durability? How does it come to seem naturally evident to experience? And what, if anything, distinguishes race from other durable social constructs? Race and its attendant concepts and processes—racism, racial formations, racial ideologies—seem to derive some of their staying power from appearing to be the natural order, fixed for all time, while in fact operating in highly adaptable, flexible, and downright slippery ways. Race, as Holt describes, only appears to be immutable and timeless but, in fact, "such ambiguous boundaries and seeming atemporality have characterized race and the racial for a very long time—perhaps even since its inception—but . . . these very features explain much of its staying power" (Holt 2000, 8–9). I will explore the notion that racial logics work by appearing "atemporal" at length in chapters 5 and 6. For now, the important point is that race seems immutable but endures by being very flexible. Indeed, concepts of race and racism are notoriously difficult to define, perhaps because so much of racial ideology operates as part of the normalized background of culture, not always apparent to those whose perceptions and perspectives they shape.

Moreover, race is mutually constitutive with other durable classification systems of modernity such as class, ethnicity, culture, and nationality, to the extent that there is considerable ambiguity in defining the boundaries and overlap among these concepts, and the closer we examine their workings in any particular case, the more imbricated they become. Some of this conceptual fuzziness, no doubt, derives from analytical attempts to generalize from what typically operate as very localized, context-specific discursive formations, rather than attending carefully to how such concepts are actually deployed "on the ground" in the course of real-time events and circuits of discourse. As Brackette Williams (1989) points out, it is all too easy to conflate various scholarly and local usages, ignoring underlying assumptions and overlooking, in Holt's words, the essential question of "what work race does" (Holt 2000, 27).

For example, "race," "ethnicity," and even "nationality" are labels for identifications based on primordial group membership, and as such, we can see that some contemporary U.S. discourse circuits essentially use them interchangeably, while others contrast them. Rather than ask which are the "correct" usages, as my students never tire of doing, we might instead ask what ideological work is accomplished in each case—a shift from narrowly semantic to broadly pragmatic considerations. Bonnie Urciuoli (1996) describes a specific discourse realm about and among some U.S. immigrant (and internal migrant) groups, such as Puerto Ricans and Dominicans (typically lumped into the categories of "Hispanic" or "Latino"), in which concepts of race and ethnicity are juxtaposed, with race marking some categories as inherently dangerous while ethnicity celebrates but also trivializes what it marks as exotic or quaint differences of tradition (see also Shankar 2008). It would seem that these very distinctions between racial and ethnic marking, however, all contribute to an overall racializing formation that promotes and misrecognizes systemic racism against Hispanic groups like Puerto Ricans. This racializing process, which seems to make racial versus ethnic ascriptions a consequential matter, is reinforced by the ambiguous boundaries (and corresponding anxieties) between being "raced" and being "ethnicized." Urciuoli shows how various social distinctions play out in a juxtaposition of race and ethnicity, in which emphasizing ethnicity's basis in the genealogical transmission of cultural tradition highlights how race is thought of as a natural category.

But note that ethnic and national differences, too, can slide into the realm of immutable, inherent, and dangerous differences, as in what observers of contemporary Europe often describe as cultural racism (Gilroy 1987; Mirón and Inda 2000; Stolcke 1995). "Race," "ethnicity," and "nationality" thus are deployed differently across contexts, sometimes contrastively and sometimes more or less synonymously (as anyone trying to understand the logic of official U.S. Census categories quickly realizes [Bennett 2000; Hollinger 2006; Yarnow 2003]). The conceptual fuzziness of these terms, I suggest, rather than being a definitional problem is key to their ability to function across different contexts and scales, always reinscribing naturalized differences and making them available to be sorted into hierarchies of social desirability and danger.

In other work, Urciuoli has described the productivity of concepts she calls "strategically deployable shifters," whose very ambiguity of reference gives them a certain hegemonic potential to cast a wide semantic net, meaning everything (vaguely) and nothing (specifically).[6] As one example, she discusses neoliberal higher education discourses of "diversity," often used as a euphemism referring to specifically *racial* diversity: everyone in American higher education agrees diversity is a good thing, even while its vagueness allows institutions to avoid addressing systemic exclusions and inequities that impede the participation of underrepresented groups (Urciuoli 2009). She suggests that because strategically deployable shifters have no firm reference but instead can strategically index different discursive objects with a single, purposefully vague term, they help circulate "naturalized, culture-saturating beliefs that maintain the distribution of social power" (Urciuoli 2008, 215). The constellation of signs—linguistic or visual—surrounding race in any particular local context, I suggest, can usefully be examined as "strategically deployable shifters."

Shifters are a general class of signs that point at some aspect of their context of utterance for their denotational meaning, which thus shifts each time they appear. Pronouns are a paradigmatic example of shifters (e.g., the first-person "I" indexes different people depending on who utters it in what context), as are references to relative time and space such as verb tense and aspect markers (e.g., contrastive series like "did," "am doing," "will do" indicate times relative to their moment of utterance). Shifters are but a heightened case of the more general indexical property of signs and as such draw our attention to ways in which using signs—by speaking, for example—performs a constitutive function (Silverstein 1976). We do not just reference a world already-out-there but, in pointing to what is relevant and in enacting what we want or expect to see, we shape the world. This notion of doing things with signs was described by natural language philosopher John Austin (1962) as performativity. His model was limited to a small group of metapragmatically transparent verb constructions used under properly felicitous conditions (in utterances such as "I pronounce you husband and wife" uttered by the officiant of a wedding or "You are sentenced to ten years in prison" spoken by a judge), but the idea of performativity—the power of signs to effect change in the world through the creative power of their indexicality—has been more broadly recognized as a basic function of language and all semiotic systems (Silverstein 1976).

To focus on the performativity of race, then, is to shift away from thinking of race as a system of static categories imposed on people—the structural view conveyed by terms such as "racial formations"—and toward examining racializing processes as emergent semiotic relationships including stances, identifications, and alignments that reach broader scales through uptake and circulation. In this view, what we may experience as durable "racial formations" become salient as precipitates of interaction, over time, of "practice" in Bourdieu's (1977) sense of situated human action that, even when strategic, is never entirely reflexive about how it inculcates social relationships and positionalities into embodied and felt dispositions. Racialization, then, emerges as a continuously manifest "performative accomplishment" (Butler 1999, 179).

To apply a frame of struggle between hegemonic forces and resisting agents, or an even simpler frame of racism versus antiracism would be to lose all theoretical force and subtlety. Rather we must ask who engages in what kinds of racializing discourses and performances, and how invocations of race in various contexts serve to circulate particular racial sensibilities (including the possibility of nonracial sensibilities, where race is deemed not to be relevant). That is, I advocate considering how social actors (individuals, groups) negotiate stances by drawing on available semiotic repertoires and frameworks, including those indexing racial identifications and meanings.

Of course, some racial identifications and meanings circulate so robustly that there is no avoiding their shadow. "Blackness" and "Whiteness," for example, form a similar (but not identical) powerful binary opposition in both the United States and Cuba. Thus, to investigate race as a performative, able to enact certain realities through its invocation, we must ask how powerful discourses come to saturate people's subjectivities by, in fact, constituting those subjectivities. If we start by scratching the surface to ask what qualifies as a "powerful discourse," it is clear that this means being widespread and durable, which is to say oft-cited and ubiquitous through frequent "stylized repetition of acts" (Butler 1999, 179). Moreover, we would look for evidence of its world-constituting effects, for example, in making certain sign relationships or subject positions seem self-evident, natural, or correct. Judith Butler's and Michel Foucault's extended engagements with gender and the "history of sexuality," for example, identify how powerful discourses reiterate the categories of gender and sexuality in ways banal and profound (Butler 1993, 1999; Foucault 1978). Butler's discussion of performativity, indeed, builds on Jacques Derrida's concepts of citationality and iterability, themselves derived from Derrida's critique of Austinian performativity:

> Performativity cannot be understood outside of a process of iterability, a regularized and constrained repetition of norms. And this repetition is not performed *by* a subject; this repetition is what enables a subject and constitutes the temporal condition for the subject. This iterability implies that "performance" is not a singular "act" or event, but a ritualized production, a ritual reiterated under and through constraint, under and through the force of prohibition and taboo, with the threat of ostracism and even death controlling and compelling the shape of the production, but not, I will insist, determining it fully in advance. (Butler 1993, 95)

That is, classificatory schemes like race (or gender, which is Butler's case) gain traction and come to seem the natural order because layers on layers of reiteration create configurations of racialized subject positions that, by repeatedly being occupied, create racialized subjects. Each occurrence that makes race relevant can be seen as citing past occurrences and setting conditions for further repetitions in what becomes a vast interdiscursive web of racialization. The accumulation of repeated instances recognized as repetitions entextualizes those instances into a type, a durable metacultural frame that can further circulate and "accelerate" the circulation of its object, race (Silverstein and Urban 1996; Urban 2001). This is performativity in the sense I wish to apply it to racialization processes, in which "performativity is neither free play nor theatrical self-presentation; nor can it be simply equated with performance" (Butler 1993, 95). Performances, in turn, are important for performativity in this sense because, in being highly entextualized and even ritualized events, they heighten participants' experiences of inhabiting particular subject positions.

Derrida has pointed out, in defining citationality and iterability, that once a recognizable discursive object (or token) emerges, additional copies may diverge in how the discursive object is represented and what meanings it evokes (Derrida 1988). But where Derrida plays with the seemingly endless possibilities citation offers for appropriation, reinterpretation, and parody, Butler sees intractability in social constructs: even parodic and "drag" performances are constrained to play off of normalized categories in their breach and, in any case, norm-breakers risk disciplining, or even violence. Normalization of subject positions defined by race emerges through ritualization and entextualization of particular patterns of reiteration, for example, by evoking recognized performance genres (Bauman and Briggs 1990). Hence, racial subjectivities can diverge and multiply, all the while reinforcing the existence of something real called race. Even disavowals of race must evoke its very terms to challenge them. Then, too, forces of prohibition and taboo can, violently or more subtly, enforce powerful racializing processes.

Mirón and Inda (2000), in a discussion of race as a "speech act" that brings together Austinian performativity and its further development in work by Derrida and Butler, argue against seeing race as a product of some original or baptismal event in Atlantic world history and instead posit that "it is only through the force of reiteration that the racial subject acquires a naturalized effect" (99).[7] But because iterative processes are responsible for the social construction of meaning, there is always the potential for subversion, redirection, repurposing, and even reappropriation of discursive objects and thus for the emergence of alternative racial subjectivities. Indeed, they briefly discuss the label "Black" itself as an example in its shift from denigration to pride, although it is crucial to notice that Blackness *remains* a highly marked and salient category despite the broadening (by incomplete shift) of its valences.

Blackness as Performance

In the case of the performances portrayed in figures 1.2 and 2.1–2.4, what work does Blackness do in these images? One striking common feature is their theatricality. Even without much background information, the viewer understands the image as a performance in the dramaturgical sense. The facial expressions are clearly exaggerated, almost masklike; the poses are deliberate in their aggression, as if expecting to be photographed. Their playful, theatrical quality makes it seem too big a step to ask what racial subjectivities they conjure. First, we want to know what performances they represent and perhaps also whether these are to be considered "authentic" (a loaded term I will need to unpack). In describing them above, I specified that all are keyed as folkloric performances, but in three very different settings: a (simulated?) folk religious ceremony involving possession trance, two professional folklore ensemble choreographies, and an amateur neighborhood folklore society. All of these settings are, for Cubans, paradigmatic sites for Black cultural forms.[8]

Indeed, as Duany (1988) and others have pointed out, the very category of folklore in Cuba is centered on African cultural contributions to Cuban national identity, particularly through forms of religio-magical practice, music, and dance. This is abundantly clear in the repertoires of Cuba's state-sponsored professional ensembles with "folkloric" in their titles: any Cuban dancer can tell you that in standard repertoire and among professional companies, "folkloric" contrasts with "classical" (e.g., ballet) and "modern" categories and encompasses African, Haitian, and Afro-Cuban genres but little else. I give more background on the particular Cuban history of this conflation of "Black" and "folklore" below.

In the larger context of the African Diaspora in the Americas, the association between Blackness and performance is hardly surprising, as distinctively African-inflected forms of magic/religion, spirit possession, music, dance, and speech typically capture most of the attention given to African diasporic cultural contributions.[9] Patricia de Santana Pinho (2010, 211), in her study of the cultural production of Blackness in Bahia, Brazil, calls this the "spectacularization of black culture" and shows how it contributes to essentialized conceptions of race. Indeed, Patrick Johnson (2003) suggests that both Blackness and performance are denigrated by their assumed mutual affinity. Further evidence of the pejorative nature of the association has been explored in scholarship on the history of blackface performance in the United States, where impersonations of highly stereotyped blackface characters like Jim Crow performed an intimate violence, turning as they did on the axis of hidden admiration and identification while helping solidify racialized differences between Black and White subject positions and socioeconomic possibilities. Eric Lott (1993) argues that assumptions about Black bodies, aptitudes, and innate inferiority mobilized in Black minstrelsy helped create new White subjectivities among European immigrants to the United States in the nineteenth century. White men may have been the predominant performers and audiences of blackface minstrelsy, but it was people of African descent, enslaved or free, whose Blackness was at stake in blackface performances because such performances ostensibly presented Black music, dance, speech, and humor as entertainment (more on this in chap. 7). Blackness as ludic, theatrical performance, then, succumbs to ethnic trivialization by being depicted variously as exotic, frivolous, or nostalgic folklore. And parodic depictions of Blackness as trivial, ridiculous, even laughable, further serve to obscure the workings of racism while advancing a racist imaginary of "naturally" inferior Black figures and Black culture.

Caught in the effects of these processes, those identified as Black have often been at pains to distance themselves from cultural forms and performances marked as Black, to instead assert what Franz Fanon describes as "white masks." Not only White subjectivities, but Black subjectivities, too, have been shaped by Blackness as performance (and its necessary corollary, Whiteness as performance). Self-alienation and double consciousness are the most cited effects. Fanon devastatingly describes the effects of a European child's cry, "Look! A Negro!" saying: "Here I am an object among other objects"; "I hailed the world, and the world amputated my enthusiasm" (Fanon [1952] 2008, 89, 94). Or, from a different translation: "I found that I was an object in the midst of other objects. Sealed into that crushing objecthood" (Fanon 1982, 109). In that quotidian moment, he was forced to recognize his very presence as an unintended performance of a characterological type: "Look! A Negro!"

There are numerous variations on this theme of objectification and alienation, of "Black skin" and "White masks," throughout the Atlantic world, from late-nineteenth-century African American educator Booker T. Washington's controversial support for a particular elite White American socialization project via "industrial education" said to "suit" Blacks (Anderson 1988, 33–78, 103–9; Baker 2006), to modern-day Martinique, which Richard Price describes as undergoing a process of folklorizing cultural practices formerly considered quotidian and "postcarding" its past in an ongoing project of colonial assimilation to the White metropole that is France (2006, 173–202). W. E. B. DuBois (1989) wrote most famously of the resulting "double consciousness" that comes of being forced to shift between one's own perspective and an externally imposed objectifying view of oneself (or one's actions) as a type.

In late nineteenth- and early twentieth-century Cuba, economic and social elites among people of color joined mainstream White society in condemning cultural forms marked as Black for being backward (Hevia Lanier 1996). Around the same time, in the 1920s and 1930s, predominantly White Cuban scholarly and artistic elites embraced the exoticism of Black Cuban cultural forms in the *afrocubanismo* movement (Moore 1997). There are commonalities across these cases in which cultural forms tend to fall into the "savage slot" that, whether rejected or embraced, marks Blackness as performance. Fanon, despairing at depictions of Africans by European anthropologists and Negritude writers alike, wrote: "These rites make me think twice. Black magic! Orgies, Sabbaths, pagan ceremonies, gris-gris. . . . What is one to think of all these manifestations, of all these initiations, and of all these workings? From every direction I am assaulted by the obscenity of the dances" (Fanon [1952] 2008, 105).

What is it about rituals, dances, possessions, and other such performances, whether as magic or as entertainment, as folklore or as carnivalesque, that, in case after ethnographic case, so readily allows them to mark categories delimiting the unassimilated and unassimilable other? It seems that the very frame of performance challenges assumptions about properly modern subjects and moral orders. Barbara Browning (1998), exploring the prevalent trope of "infectious rhythm" applied to African and African diasporic culture throughout the modern Atlantic world, argues that while the figure of cultural contagion takes on positive as well as negative valences—as irresistible rather than virulent—the net effect of this trope of "infectious" Black culture regularly produces fearful, even violent, reactions that reinscribe racism. The specter of the 1791 Haitian Revolution haunted slave societies throughout the New World precisely because of its potential to incite insurrections elsewhere; Browning argues that similar logics of contagion, reproduced in many discourses about African and African diasporic arts and cultural production, were evident in fears during the 1980s and 1990s about Haitian immigration and the spread of HIV, the virus that can lead to AIDS. To extend Browning's analysis, the logic of such irresistible cultural practices as infectiously catchy rhythms, or worse yet, spirit possessions, violates assumptions about modern personhood. Among the key elements of the project of modern personhood are deeply held notions of autonomy, personal responsibility, and a biographically continuous inner self that can be evaluated for its rationality, sincerity, and authentic outward presentation. Each of these are variously denied to and called into question by Blackness as performance.

Figures 1.1, 1.2, and 2.1–2.4 are theatrical moments, some of whose excitement comes from slippage between the proscenium or folklore spectacle in which they appeared and presumably authentic source contexts in which the possession trance would be real, not merely simulated. Figure 2.1, indeed, comes from what was ostensibly an actual religious ceremony, but one embedded in a state-sponsored folklore festival. This ceremony, to be discussed in chapter 6, was but the first of a sequence in which groups were invited to perform during a day of the festival dedicated to honoring the maroon as a quintessential figure of Cuban history and national character. The festival organizers, when events were running late, even insisted that this group compress its performance to save time. After them in the program came a performance of Haitian Ban Rará dance, a Burning Man–style performance in which two bonfires revealed iron sculptures hidden in the combustible material, a series of convocations and invocations borrowed from Santería, and another dance performance featuring the orichas, or deities of Santería. And indeed, the Spiritist-crossed-with-Palo opening ceremony of figure 2.1 also seemed carefully choreographed, with possession trances right on cue and a dramatic arc to the appearance of "possessed" characters like the spirit of the congo cimarrón captured in my photo.

So were these actual spirits or merely simulacra of spirit possessions? Discussing the unwanted onset of possession trances during performances by the Ballet Folklórico Nacional in Havana, Katherine Hagedorn (2001) describes how the company sought to police its dancers, in order to avoid such spiritual incursions into what were supposed to be strictly folkloric interpretations. In the context of most state-sponsored folkloric spectacles, performances must seem authentic without slipping into an overtly religious frame, which could undermine the project of folklorization as appropriation and control. In this case, however, the overtly religious displays were contained within an encompassing folkloric frame that celebrated such forms as national cultural tradition.

Authenticity and Danger in *Maximiliano contra la bruja* (1997)

I have argued that one aspect of the performativity of race is the close association of Blackness with performance, in which appearances are, at times, all that matter. And yet, my analysis above of several images of stereotypically Black folkloric figures demonstrates that Blackness, even taken as a strictly visual modality, is never *only* about skin color or physical type. What seem to be durable figures of Blackness turn out to be complex assemblages of signs contrasting with other complex assemblages of signs in an unending process of entextualization and enregisterment.

To get purchase on the visual semiosis involved in racialization, I want to offer a juxtaposition of my photographs and video stills of folklore performances by turning for a moment to paintings and prints, as a different, more formally composed visual genre. Consider the image of a Cuban family threatened by a menacing Black witch in a painting by Cuban naive painter Luis el Estudiante (Luis Joaquín Rodríguez Ricardo, b. 1966), in figure 2.6. At center is a house, inside of which a light-skinned woman with long dark hair sits in a chair cradling a brown-skinned child, while a darker-skinned man—Maximiliano—stands holding up a crucifix. On the roof of the house looms a dark-skinned woman—the darkest skinned of the figures in the painting, who holds up a large cowry shell in each hand. The stars and moon shine through trees, and the interior of the thatch-roofed house is adorned with strings of beads, an ox skull, and a turtle shell, among other details in this lush naive painting.

The painting itself presents Blackness as a kind of mask, a pigmented signifier indicating the danger that the figure on the roof—which we come to recognize as a witch—poses to the family below and, perhaps, to the viewer whom she almost seems to challenge.[10] Blackness as performance threatens the boundaries of the proscenium, or in this case, the painting's frame, and in doing so reveals the dangerous slipperiness of race. And what of the artist's positionality as evident in this image? I suggest that he simultaneously distances himself from and aligns himself with his painting's subject, as part of a tension between claiming universality as a racially unmarked Cuban artist and indexing his authenticity as a naive painter of his own rural Cuban experience.

FIGURE 2.6 *Maximiliano contra la bruja* by Luis "El Estudiante" Joaquín Rodríguez Ricardo, oil, 1997. Photo provided by artist.

In an interview with art historian Luisa Ramírez Moreira (2003, 80–81), to whom he was married at the time, Luis described his neighbor when growing up in the countryside outside of Santiago de Cuba, a man named Maximiliano. Maximiliano was Haitian and magical, a common conflation, in which, of all Cubans of color, the descendants of Haitian labor migrants and cultural forms associated with them, like Vodou are seen as the Blackest, most African, and therefore most spiritually potent and dangerous of all. Like the Cuban peasantry of earlier times, Maximiliano lived in a bohío, a small thatched hut derived from indigenous Taíno designs. Along the trunk of the giant ceíba tree in his yard, the ceíba being sacred and spiritually potent in Cuban popular religion, strange and magical things happened, things not accountable within Luis's rational, modern, nonreligious perspective—the same stance he took in our many conversations over the years.

As Luis described Maximiliano, he stands for the prototypical "folk" of Cuba, the salt of the earth, limited by his humble circumstances and superstitions, perhaps, but nonetheless possessing powerful traditions (indigenous, African) that connect him to his natural surroundings. We might say, then, that Maximiliano, the character, represents those whom the Cuban Revolution saved and served, those whom the revolution seeks to elevate to full human dignity in the model of the "new man" (Frederik 2005). And Luis el Estudiante, who represents the revolution as a "new man" committing his art to quintessentially Cuban themes, takes a complicated stance himself. He is, significantly, a naive painter and a cofounder (with his father) of the Grupo Bayate, an artists' collective promoting naive art in the rural town of Mella (Peña Montero 2012); folk and everyday scenes portraying a romanticized Cuban rural heartland are his métier. In some ways he distances himself from his subject, but he violates that distance by claiming that irreducibly magical things happened under Maximiliano's magical tree.

In figure 2.6, Maximiliano tries to protect his family (his wife and child are depicted with lighter skin) from a witch perched atop his home, depicted as a woman with markedly darker skin, holding cowry shells, associated with Afro-Cuban religion, and a broom, tool of flight for European witches. She also seems to have wings. What evil does she conjure against the family below, and is it perhaps motivated by jealousy, as Cubans often account for such magical attacks? The Black performance represented in the painting is socially dangerous because there is no proscenium to limit its reach; the witch attacks the very integrity of home and family and the very project of racially unmarked, revolutionary modernization they represent (albeit partially, as the many religious objects adorning their ceiling and wielded by Maximiliano attest). But the witch's threat seems to justify the presence of these spiritual protections. The painting is compelling for the same reason as the performances in figures 1.1 and 2.1–2.4: because the possibility of real spirit possessions and actual magical attacks lurks just offstage or on the roof—these possibilities in fact gain a certain force, a curtain call perhaps, in being depicted in the relative safety of the proscenium or painting. That is, the choreographed, photographed, and painted witches and possessing spirits, try as they might to folklorize and tame the religio-magical world, cannot help but also reinforce the presence of spiritual magic by borrowing its theatricality to bring their roles alive. This is a pitfall of authenticity: it reinscribes what it tries to leave behind or reframe as merely folkloric.

A viewer might perhaps ask whether the scene of the painting in figure 2.6 is authentic, meaning whether it accurately reflects Cuban folkways. In posing this question, one may also be asking whether the painter himself is authentic, which is to say that he paints from his own, real experience. But this very question undermines the painter's desire for distance from his folksy subjects, at least where black magic is concerned. And, proud as he is of his rural roots in eastern Cuba, as much as his life experiences interweave with those of Cubans of color, Luis embraces his identification as a White

Cuban—a product of Cuban cultural *mestizaje*, perhaps, but definitively a racially unmarked Cuban citizen. So he, too, as much as the performers in figures 1.1, 1.2, and 2.1–2.5, is entangled in the logic of authenticity. We can now, perhaps, understand that the Black Cuban dancers, as much as the White Cuban painter, are engaged in the same logic of performance, in which their everyday racial identifications are left outside the frame of performance and therefore are not directly impacted by the racializing work of the performance/image itself, except as judgments of cultural pride and authenticity that seem to hover above racial designations. That is, Blackness becomes a mask than can be donned for performances of primordial authenticity, national folklore, or cultural resistance, quite apart from everyday racial identifications and consequences.

It is an interesting exercise to situate this historically specific case in the longer duration of modern subject formation in Western societies and the ongoing challenges posed by subaltern performances of magic and spirit possession. Paul Johnson (2011) suggests that post-Enlightenment Western philosophical tradition emphasizing integral personhood, biographical continuity of autonomous individuals, and personal responsibility was intimately connected to the development of private ownership and contractual norms fundamental to capitalism. Johnson demonstrates how this regime of "forensic personhood" (pace Locke, cited in Johnson 2011, 17–18) depended on expanding notions of property and possession, where the privileges of true personhood were denied to that majority of humanity deemed unable to claim autonomous, rational agency (see also Bauman and Briggs 2003). In particular, fetishism and spirit possession emerged as recognizable comparative categories precisely because the notions of independently willful objects and subjects lacking autonomous, continuous wills precluded the proper relationship of persons to objects as that of possessing subjects and possessed things. It was thus no accident that enslaved Africans—subjects deprived of autonomy and possessed by others—provided the greatest wealth of exemplars of spirit possession and fetishism to early ethnologists (Johnson 2011; Murray 2007). And while the interpretive frames of spirit possession, fetishism, and other contradictions of the precepts of forensic personhood (ecstasy, mob frenzy, slave revolt, madness, hysteria . . .) clearly served to justify political disenfranchisement, colonial appropriations, and economic exploitation of all kinds, these same practices could also allow the possessed and dispossessed to challenge the very terms that justified their dehumanization.

Figure 2.7 illustrates just this sort of challenge, where the same man possessed by a congo cimarrón in figure 2.1 now presses his machete into his belly, a display that confirms his possession as real. Whether this is to be

FIGURE 2.7 Cimarrón with machete at belly stands before an nganga during a performance by 1812 de Orozco for the Ceremonia al cimarrón, El Cobre, Cuba, July 7, 2006. Photo by A. Abelardo Larduet for author.

taken as "proof" of the spirit or as a theatrical simulacrum of authentic spirit possession is never clear in the hybrid context of this folklore festival; indeed, the authenticity of such folkloric spectacles relies on a conjuring of real-seeming spiritual power that continually threatens to exceed its theatrical frame. In this case, the folklore festival's goal was to celebrate the cimarrón as a key cultural figure of the Cuban nation, a source of the rebelliousness that allowed Cuba to win independence from Spain, then to achieve the Cuban Revolution, and now to survive in a hostile neoliberal world.

The appropriation of subaltern power goes further, if we can pull our eyes downward from the machete to follow the man's gaze toward a complicated assemblage on the ground before him. This iron cauldron bristling with sticks and horseshoes, topped with a goat skull and lit candle and with offerings of rum and another lit candle alongside it is a concentration of raw magical power called a *prenda* or nganga and used by practitioners of the Reglas de Palo (Ochoa 2010). The construction of a prenda, including the seating of captured spirits within it, allows *paleros* (practitioners of the Reglas de Palo) to conjure what Kenneth Routon (2008, 638) aptly describes as a "kind of sorcery out of history" by materializing the exploitative relations between master and slave in this power object, where the human master binds and manipulates the prenda's spirits to serve human interests (of course, as Ochoa [2010] explains, the tables can turn if the spirit gains the upper hand). Prendas, widely respected and even feared by Cubans, are the object par excellence of those deemed the crudest and most African: cimarrones, slaves, and their modern heirs, paleros. Prendas, as objects with independent agency (i.e., the original "fetish"), together with spirits who can take possession of people, allow the subjugated and marginalized to claim a power that threatens the very precepts of forensic personhood that once justified the dispossession of their ancestors. No one asks of a prenda whether it is rational, autonomous, or sincere, but one may fairly, even apprehensively, ask whether a prenda such as the prop in the performance in figure 2.7 is authentic.

This power of the authentic has been duly noted and appropriated by the Cuban State, by Cuba's economic and social elites (who have long regarded such practices with a sort of fascinated horror and distanced admiration; Bronfman 2004; de la Fuente 2001a; Wirtz 2004), as well as by increasing numbers of privileged foreign visitors eager to experience and even be initiated into Afro-Cuban traditions like Palo and Santería (Ayorinde 2004; Ochoa 2010; Wirtz 2007e). The prenda and its prototypically "brutish" African owner (or owner who seeks to tap into the spiritual power of the "congo cimarrón") is a joint performance of Blackness-as-sorcery and Blackness-as-marronage.

No matter that actual practitioners of Palo and keepers of prendas come from all social strata and racial identifications, and no matter that all Cubans are exhorted by the revolutionary state to support its marronage in the world order (Routon 2008); the realm of maroons and paleros remains racialized as Black and African. Indeed, I argue that this racialization of particular character types—slaves, maroons, paleros—and particular cultural objects and forms—Palo, its prendas—as Black/African is necessary to the project of appropriating such subaltern power for the state and nation. In part, this is because the power attributed to the subaltern subject—in this case, these historicized Black figures—is marked as extraordinary, emanating somehow from beyond the usual regime of matter, subjectivity, and agency. Then too, relegating such challenges to a racially marked category insulates the unmarked norms of citizenship and modern subjecthood from the radical implications of spirit possessions, prendas, and the like regarding autonomy, agency, responsibility, and even the interiorities required by sincerity. After all, assumptions about the continuity of an individual's interior life are disrupted by spirit possession (Palmié 2011, 8–10) and by notions of bodies and minds infused and afflicted by spiritual forces (Ochoa 2010). Blackness, we see, must be performance under this kind of semiotic regime because, as necessary as such performances are to the national imaginary, they must not "infect" the everyday routines and assumptions of subject formation. For one, Cuban citizens must perform congruence with the revolution's rebelliousness without being rebellious themselves. And citizens must be accountable for their actions—exactly what is complicated by spirit possessions. Note too that the relegation of Blackness to certain kinds of folkloric, magical, and unruly performances functions as a "restrictive script" (Jackson 2005, 12–13) that authenticates a narrow, highly essentialized vision of being "Afro-" in Cuba.

In the final section of this chapter, I will explore these dynamics of Blackness as performance at work in figurations of "Black Cuba" in the work of Cuban artist and graphic designer Suitberto Goire Castilla.

Images of Black Cubans in the Revolutionary Zeitgeist of Goire

A lifelong resident of Santiago de Cuba, Suitberto Goire Castilla (1951–2011) had a long and productive career, having started as a graphic artist in a work unit of the Commission of Revolutionary Orientation producing propaganda posters for the Cuban Communist Party in the 1970s and 1980s (Ramírez Moreira 2012). With the collapse of the Soviet Bloc and start of Cuba's Special Period between 1989 and the early 1990s, Goire's work unit closed, and during this anxious time he reinvented himself as an independent entrepeneur. He continued to contract jobs from the state to design event posters and logos for entities such as the Casa del Caribe and to work with Cuban and foreign artists, producing, for example, silk-screened posters. He also sold his work to an international audience; like any Cuban artist or professional, he was well aware that the most lucrative opportunities came from abroad, and he successfully pursued offers for gallery exhibitions and shows in Europe and North America. I had been seeing Goire's work for years without realizing who he was, despite considerable overlap in our social circles in Santiago de Cuba, until we were at last introduced in May 2010, when I interviewed him twice. Sadly, after a sudden series of strokes, he passed away in March 2011.

Throughout his career, Goire displayed a special talent for expressing the Zeitgeist in his vibrant, straightforward style. He is a cultural broker, one who successfully interprets cultural trends to a wider audience through his ability to distill the themes and issues of the moment into images whose meanings seem transparent. I leave to others, and particularly to my colleagues Luisa Ramírez Moreira (2012) and Sarah Hill, a more complete study of Goire's life and work, since my more specific goal is to discuss some of his posters of the past decade as a lens for examining the current processes racializing Black bodies and folkloric cultural forms by linking them.

For example, Goire produced the poster announcing the thirtieth annual Festival del Fuego in 2004, a weeklong artistic and scholarly event organized by Santiago's Casa del Caribe to appreciate Caribbean culture and promote international cultural exchange. Each year, the festival's theme celebrates connections between Cuba and another Caribbean nation, which is encouraged to provide sponsorship and send delegates—Curazao and Pernambuco, Brazil, were featured in 2010. The poster, whose front side is reproduced in figure 2.8, shows a colorful tropical island of palms populated by happy, dancing, strumming, and drumming black figures dressed all in white and stylized to resemble the little folkloric dolls for sale as souvenirs from Cuban artisanal stores (see also echoes of the costumes in fig. 2.7). Clearly, the link between Cuba, Curazao, and Pernambuco is depicted as a shared African cultural heritage, one reduced to near-blackface in this image. The poster's very ordinariness of representation—nothing surprising in this attractive image of a fun Caribbean island—begs for further exegesis.

With few exceptions, revolutionary propaganda posters of the 1970s, early in Goire's career, did not regularly depict Cubans of color. Goire pointed out to me just two he had done, one for a literacy campaign in 1972 and the other recruiting for the Cuban international teaching corps at the end of the 1970s, in which one figure was darker skinned and the other lighter skinned, suggesting an equivalence of representation—the politics of equal recognition, perhaps, absent any signs of a politics of difference. Then, in the mid-1980s Goire began adapting an iconic series of images by Havana artist René Portocarrero showing the profile of a (light-skinned) woman with flowers for hair—for example, his *Cabeza de mujer ornamentada* of 1975. Goire altered the image to present a Black woman whose Afro hairstyle was made of flowers, using it in a poster for Santiago's carnaval, with a sunburst radiating behind her. He described his intent to me as trying to expand the aesthetics of feminine beauty to encompass Black women as well, an implicit critique of their absence as subjects in Cuban art.

More recently, he returned to this image in a series of approximately two dozen prints from 2007 to 2009 called *Obba la metáfora* (see fig. 2.9). All show a flat black silhouette of a woman's head and shoulders on a stark white background, with eyes as the only facial feature: red pupils on white. In many of the prints, this basic figure is adorned with hair and jewelry. The image most similar to Goire's original carnival poster of a Black woman with flowers for hair is on the lower left of figure 2.9: the forward-gazing head and shoulders

FIGURE 2.8 Poster for thirtieth Festival del Caribe, July 2010, silk screen, by Suitberto Goire Castilla.

of the woman is adorned with colorful necklaces that suggest beaded African chokers. Other images show the same figure with ribbons of colorful, long, straight hair or with tightly curly hair wrapped with a scarf evoking a Kente cloth pattern. A few show African-inspired hairstyles of hair wound into little columns, with curly puffs of hair at the ends, together with red or yellow patterns on foreheads and cheeks that recall African facial scarifications. Several prints show a more androgynous bald head with William Tell's arrow piercing an apple—or a more tropical mango—balanced on top, or full female or male bodies pierced with arrows or encoiled by an exquisitely colorful snake. Others show a silhouette behind lines as if entrapped in a spiderweb or behind a fence, or with lines radiating out from a woman's eye, as if to show she is clairvoyant. Echoes in the color and detail of adornments connect images of quintessentially contemporary Cuban styles, such as sunglasses and

FIGURE 2.9 Images from *Obba la metáfora* series, 2007–9, on side 2 of personal exhibition announcement, by Suitberto Goire Castilla.

numerous gold necklaces, with the images evoking traditional African adornments, suggesting a certain continuity in an African aesthetic of beauty.

Goire described to me his wish to present the Black figure that was largely absent in Cuban art. He also explained that his inspiration came from being fascinated by the way that bright sunlight made it hard to distinguish facial features on someone very dark skinned, so that only the eyes and silhouette were visible. He claimed to base his depictions of Black women on real women one saw in the street, so that they were very "earthy" (*terranal*) in contrast to idealized White women of classical art. When I pointed out that this polarization of Whiteness toward ethereality and Blackness toward earthiness and sexuality was a common idea in Cuban discourses about religion and culture, he simply agreed. Indeed, he named the series after an African deity (oricha) from Santería: Obba is not as popular as Ochún or Yemayá; she is associated with tombs in the cemetery, and as a wife of virile oricha Changó was tricked by Ochún into cutting off her ear and losing Changó's love. Indeed, none of the silhouettes have ears. In his vision, Obba is taken out of legend and updated, ceasing to be a "submissive, domestic captive" and coming to stand for "woman" in general and for Caribbean and Cuban women in particular (Ramírez Moreira 2009), albeit a highly sexualized vision of women. Moreover, the images with arrows suggest vulnerability in the face of violence, and the snake evokes the Christian story of Eve's temptation and perhaps also the lwa Dambala of Haitian Vodou, who is also known in Cuba. These images of entwining and penetration also contribute to the sexuality of this vision of Obba. Other images radiate beauty or suggest Obba's spiritual potency. Obba, the mythological African figure from Santería, is appropriated to represent Goire's vision of "the Black woman" as an appropriate aesthetic figure to celebrate in visual arts.

In contrast to the generally positive stylizations of Black women in his *Obba* series, Goire's earlier series of posters from the early 2000s, called *CubaNegra*, presents more ambivalent and stereotypical images of Black culture in Cuba. Most of the prints in this series present symbols of Afro-Cuban popular religiosity; for example, each oricha of Santería is depicted with its symbolic colors and implements. Some combine symbols from multiple popular religious traditions, as figure 2.10 exemplifies. In this image, the stereotypical black face of a Black religious practitioner (the *brujo* recuperated) stares out, with exaggeratedly large, broad facial features, wearing the white cap used for all ritual work in traditions of Santería, Ifá divination, and Reglas de Palo. To either side are candles, essential to all kinds of spiritual work, and behind the face is a decorative pattern of esoteric white-chalked symbols evoking the *firmas* and *vevé* cosmograms drawn to mobilize spiritual power in Reglas de Palo and Haitian Vodou ceremonies. In the foreground, below the face and candles are hands, with the foremost bearing an eye in the center, evoking the symbol commonly drawn to ward off evil eye. Around the base of the hands are cowry shells, used for divination in Santería and Reglas de Palo. Ringing the entire composition is a decorative border of green and yellow beads, such as those worn by *babalawos*, Ifá divination specialists. The Black figure is accompanied by his esoteric ritual accoutrements, just as in the performance captured in figure 2.7. To reduce Black Cubans and their cultural practices to the realm of folk religion is, as the reader by now will see, quite typical of folkloric images and performances in Cuba. Goire simply repeats a common trope with flair. It is, moreover, a commercially viable trope at a moment when Cubans have had to become very entrepeneurial to meet even their basic needs.

I find the rest of the *CubaNegra* series rather more troubling, since the other aspect of Black Cuba that Goire chose to represent was what he described as the especially crude, wickedly funny street humor associated with Black people in Cuba. His representations, however, always rely on and recirculate negative stereotypes of Blackness. In counterpoint with his later *Obba* series, one print reproduces the famous Boticelli Venus with her long hair

FIGURE 2.10 Poster from CubaNegra series, 2000, silk screen, by Suitberto Goire Castilla From author's collection and reproduced with permission of Goire's heirs.

and alabaster whiteness, standing naked in her scallop shell. But above her and leering down at her are two cartoon caricatures of Black men (with the same exaggerated facial features as in fig. 2.10, but no religious attire). He has added a caption: "Bianca te amo . . ." that carries the caricature into the voice associated with colloquial street humor. I must admit that he had to explain the joke to me, chortling as he did: what the two leering Black men are actually saying is not a profession of love but rather, "Blanca te (v)amo(s) (a violar)" or "White woman, we are going to rape you." In colloquial Cuban Spanish, and particularly in the speech ascribed to poor Black Cubans, the sounds /r/ and /1/ in many phonological contexts are often pronounced as /i/—hence, "Bianca," a foreign woman's name. Likewise, word-final /-s/ is often aspirated (as /h/) or completely dropped, and while word-initial consonant dropping is rarer, here the crude pronunciation allows "amo" to stand in for "vamos," with the rest of the phrase merely implied by ellipsis (see, e.g., Ruiz Hernández 1977, 75–77). Venus, "Bianca," is not to be admired from afar but violated by stereotypically hypersexualized Black men. The image is meant ironically—certainly this is clear in the juxtaposition of such an icon of classical white femininity with such outrageously cartoonish images of Blackness. But, as with all the images in this series, it teeters toward the edge of reinforcing rather than challenging racist stereotypes.

A few other prints in the series are even more problematic in their representations of Blackness, again mobilizing racial caricature with image and voicing. I will describe just one as an example. Accompanying the same black face with exaggerated features, this time underwater with a snorkel, is the phrase, "ñato, pero respira" (wide-nosed, but he breathes), which makes use of a derogatory term for what some Cubans see as an undesirably African facial feature. Goire attributed the saying, a reference to the supposed inferiority of a wide nose for breathing, to a religious story from Santería, called a *patakín*, in which the Creator, Olofi, was giving out noses and White people got in line first and got the best noses, while Black people only found out later and thus were stuck with what was left, until the last one in line got no nose at all (in the poster, the figure has nostrils but no outline of a nose). For Goire, this and other posters in the same vein are not meant as mockery, but as homage to the hilarity of folksy Black sayings. Certainly, his friend and colleague, art historian Ramírez Moreira (2012, 6) interprets the work as facilely portraying the "jocose dialogue" and "popular humor and charm of the black." Like Luis el Estudiante, Goire distances himself from folkloric Blackness in his work (and, in interviews with Sarah Hill, was cagey about his own racial identification), although Goire was darker skinned than el Estudiante and was described by others as more or less "mulato."

My point in examining this sampling of Goire's work has been to illustrate how racializing processes encompass images, performances, and discourse of all sorts, and how much intertextuality there is in recirculating distinctive meanings of Blackness in Cuba. Artistic merit aside, Goire's representations of Blackness are quite typical and thus reflect a more general relegation of Blackness to particular social locations: folkloric religion and magic; music and dance; street culture of the lower classes, with implications of criminality and crudity, but also humor, sexuality, festivity, and a certain liberation from social mores. In these modalities, Blackness serves as a position of cultural marronage that anyone can occupy, however temporarily and partially. That Goire dedicated his work since the 1990s almost exclusively to such "folkloric" and folklore-inspired images—work that he needed to sell to Cuban state contracts and foreigners—suggests yet another entrepeneurial dimension along which folklorized Blackness has been appropriated as what sells.

In other images, such as those from the performances I described at the start of the chapter, we see how Blackness is also historicized, located in particular chronotopes because "folklore," the primary category for cultural forms marked as Black or African in Cuba, is "traditional" by definition and thus bears the patina of past times whose ways must be preserved, for memory's sake. Moreover, as we will see in later chapters, the category of folklore of Cuba is always historically situated in Cuba's colonial past, with origins in the melding of cultures under conditions of colonization and slavery.

Conclusion

Throughout this chapter, I have argued for attending to racialization as a process, rather than to race as a static classification. An essential question to ask, in this view, is how persistent stereotypes gain their durability. To address this question for the case of Blackness in Cuba, I have sketched out an answer that relies on a broader, historicized view of a Cuban semiotic regime of morality and personhood, in and through which Blackness has gained its associations and social values. I have suggested that, in Cuba and elsewhere in the Atlantic world, Blackness has often been associated with performance; cultural forms marked as African have come to be valued primarily as signs of primordial authenticity and thus to be relegated to folkloric forms. Representative images of performances and paintings in this chapter and elsewhere throughout the book depict repertoires mobilized in the figuration of Blackness and how the multimodal signs used index the context of Cuba's colonial-era history of slaves and maroons, situating this historical vision alongside contemporary traditions of popular religiosity, and popular humor, sexuality, and unruly street culture associated with lower-classed people of color in Cuba.

To trace the connections between racialization and performativity, on the one hand, and Blackness and performance, on the other, I have argued for a conception of race itself as a "strategically deployable shifter," a denotationally ambiguous set of classifiers that act by conjuring rich fields of social meaning. Signs of Blackness (like those in the visual arts presented here) can variously convey quintessential Cubanness but also social danger, spirituality but also crudeness and earthiness, a connection to tradition but also a sense of anachronism. Moreover, *all* of these uses to which Blackness is put—the work race does in Cuba—draw on the same repertoire of signs that overdetermine Black bodies and Black culture in Cuba. Under this semiotic regime, Blackness is performed as the primordial source of Cuban culture: the folk of the conga and folklore societies who preserve the people's traditions, the cimarrones who will never admit defeat, those who are true to Cuba's patron saints who go equally by European and African names—Elegguá/Lucero, La Caridad/Ochún, San Lázaro/Babalú, Santa Bárbara/Changó—and the sorcerers who command dangerous but potent "Black" magic. In standing for heritage, rebelliousness, and cultural resistance, Black figures and cultural forms index authenticity and are judged by that standard, in contradistinction to the criteria of modern personhood in terms of personal responsibility, autonomous agency, and sincerity. The price of this bid to authenticity is precisely marginalization, banishment by anachronism, constraint to fossilizing "tradition" and blackface stereotype, labeling as spiritual and social danger, and, at times as a result, a denial of fully modern personhood.

3

Bodies in Motion: Routes of Blackness in the Carnivalesque

Racialization processes create a circular logic in which racial ascriptions seem always to be already present. Caught up as we are in "seeing" race as a natural attribute, a bodily essence, however much our critical theorizations of race say otherwise, it becomes urgent to address how physical markers of racial differences become so highly presupposed. Throughout this book, I focus on the performative effects of mobilizing particular configurations of signs in and through which Blackness emerges as a marked characteristic of some persons, bodies, cultural forms, and places, in contrast to others that, in comparison, seem racially different or perhaps racially unmarked (e.g., White). In chapter 2 my focus was on representations of Blackness in (and *as*) performance. I detailed some of the visual semiotic configurations that coalesce across repeated performances to overdetermine the primordial character of Blackness as a quintessential source of folklore and historical subjectivity and as a marker of social danger. In this chapter, I now turn to the embodiment of racial identifications in everyday interactions and, specifically, ask how Blackness as phenotypic attribute is constituted as a field of embodied experience in relation to its objectified significance. To do so will require me to make connections across very different slices of ethnographically attested social life, at various levels of scale, spanning historical discourses of race and nation and fleeting interactional moments when race-as-phenotype becomes salient. To give some coherence to the exercise, I will focus on carnival as example and as trope. If the material I presented in chapter 2 tended toward static images—freeze-frames of racial performance—this chapter will track motions and movements of raced bodies.

A premise of my analysis is that the body is constituted through social action while simultaneously providing semiotic resources for social interaction. Various strains of current social theory, particularly those influenced by Foucault, concur that there is no precultural body we can access because our experiences of and with bodies are always already mediated through fields of power relations (Foucault 1978; Turner 1997). The body—in its physical presence and experience as well as in how it is represented as an object of discourse—is a field of historically situated social relationships enacted through its roles in social action. In providing an ethnographic account of the embodiment of racial identifications in Santiago de Cuba, I want to avoid any false dichotomy between words and actions, talk and practice, since speech is a form of embodied practice, however much its potential for representation and reflexivity give it privileged status in analysis. As Charles Goodwin (2000, 1) argues, social action involves the mobilization of semiotic resources across numerous modalities that include speech, gesture, bodily orientation, and other embodied practices through which "the human body is made publicly visible as the site for a range of structurally different kinds of displays implicated in the constitution of the actions of the moment." I take this as a starting point for investigating how my Cuban interlocutors constituted racial identifications, and Blackness in particular, as relevant in and through the course of mundane interactions, including those in which people reflected on events of folkloric or artistic performance.

I pursue this angle because folklore performances and visual arts take place against a backdrop in which race already matters, although not always in quite the same ways as presented in artistic cultural production that self-consciously sets itself apart from the everyday life out of which it arises. That is, the performers and audiences of folkloric Blackness, whether it's in the context of the Slave Barracks restaurant or the "African Trilogy" dance performance, arrive at particular performances already raced (and gendered, classed, nationalized, etc.), and furthermore, we suspect that it is through their biographical accumulation of everyday interactions (both face-to-face encounters and mass-mediated encounters), as much as through their participation in specially framed events, that these identifications have gained a certain patina of stability and durability. To point this out is not to deny the potentialities always emergent across instances and the ruptures and discontinuities that can arise in performative iterations but, instead, is meant to recognize that iterability also generates inertial forces—of tradition, of habit, of identification, and so forth. Phenotypic racial markers are highly presupposed signs, available in any moment of interaction to be taken up as ready-made indices.

As an opening example, consider all the ways in which a person's presupposed identifications get mobilized in dancing to, say, the rhythms of the conga, music of carnival. To pose a sharp contrast: the conditions under which I learn to dance to the conga as an adult foreigner, whether in a class or on the street in a raucous crowd, are different than those experienced by Cubans who have grown up around a carnival comparsa, where dancing to the conga has been part of their bodily socialization over years. Our movement repertoires and bodily dispositions are "sedimentations" of past training and socialization of our bodies (Connerton 1989; Sutton 2004, 100). For someone learning a new dance, those new movements necessarily enter into a relationship with existing bodily habits that index our biographical histories in ways not readily controlled. I may find the basic steps easy but have difficulty keeping the rhythm or adding the various torso movements that depend on mastering what trained dancers call "isolations" of connected muscle groups. None of this can be reduced to "race" or any other identification: another foreigner may quickly pick up the subtleties of the dance, just as another Cuban might never get the hang of it. But it is crucial to note how each person's dancing will nonetheless be taken up as an index of identity in the interactional context of the dance. The excellent foreign dancer will be excellent in spite of his or her foreignness, while the non-dancing Cuban (and I know several) will, perhaps, be explained away as not interested or not having grown up in circumstances exposing him or her to the movements.

We, as physical presences, are moving assemblages of signs including but not limited to dance movements, and our movements will be interpreted (by ourselves and others) relative to, and saturated by, all those identifications, howsoever they are understood. And the same dance movements (assuming we could agree on what constitutes sameness performed by two different bodies) have quite different implications based on our social positioning; how each of us dance to the conga typically reinforces our preexisting identifications, rather than transforming or replacing them. And reactions to someone's dancing—including commentaries and a whole range of nonverbal responses—may directly or indirectly invoke those preexisting identifications, as when a Cuban who has grown up around the conga explains that she "carries the conga in her blood." Dancing can thus be swept up as a sign of social identification, even as the relationship between bodily dispositions and social identifications is much more complex.

So the question at the center of the tangled knot of racialization remains: How is it that we always already seem to be swept away in the inescapable tides of racialization, always already "raced" just as we are "gendered," such that even what Judith Butler (2004) describes as the abject position of those who occupy some kind of category-defying ambiguity (whether existentially or just in "passing") serves to reinforce just how important those categories remain? We who live in societies in which race seems a fact of life take it as commonsensical that race, and Blackness in particular, is a natural quality of a person's body, a reality we feel confident we can point to using some calculus of phenotypic characteristics. Certainly, racial identifications are often presupposed and perduring across interactions. But this degree of presupposition regarding the naturalness of race as written on the body begs the question of how it is semiotically accomplished. A complete account (if we can contemplate such a massive undertaking) would need to work across various scales, from moments in the interactional flow to biographical trajectories to larger movements across space and time that, I argue, implicate those very notions of personhood, subjectivity, space, and time.

In this chapter I will first describe large-scale discourses of race and nation, then examine the interactional level at which people act and sometimes reflect on their commonsense presuppositions about race as part of social identifications. I suggest an analytic attending to the everyday circulation of ideologies and practices of embodiment, governing how we understand bodies in whole or part to take on social meaning. Notice that a focus on ideologies of embodiment attacks the notion of the body as a precultural source of meaning, instead emphasizing the ways in which our experiences of and through the body are culturally mediated. In this sense, my approach considers not only what Pierre Bourdieu (1977) called habitus—learned bodily dispositions—but also hexis—the ways in which those bodily dispositions not only reflect but also enact the social order. As simultaneously physical objects and perceptual apparati taken up into semiotic activity, our bodies are socially meaningful in and through their relationality.

One key domain of ideologies of embodiment concerns the workings of genealogy and descent, through which racial identifications, marked by physical characteristics and presumed to be traits coded in genes, are passed on through a hereditary calculus from parents to children and on through the generations. The protests of geneticists and biological anthropologists aside, genetics has become a common trope to reinscribe heredity in racialized terms, giving it the authority of "science" (on this, see Palmié 2007b), but there are other tropes as well. To carry a tradition in the blood was a common idiom I heard people repeat to express the importance of heredity. Mutually imbricated ideologies of gender, class, and racial embodiment, among others, also clearly contribute to creating the body as a "natural" vessel of identity that will enact its identifications (and also, simultaneously, its individual uniqueness, a product of its particular history) in its appearance and habits of comportment.[1] It is not at some frozen level of suspended animation that

I will consider embodiment, then, but instead at the pragmatic level of bodies in motion, in relation to their social and physical contexts, asking how movements within and across temporal and physical fields of action create and re-create specifically racialized bodies and persons.

As an entry point—a heuristic for deciding where and how to dive into the mess called race—I take up the trope of movement and its traces in "routes," a popular enough metaphor in scholarship of the Black Atlantic (Gilroy 1993; Yelvington 2001, 2006). As used in such contexts, "routes" is generally contrasted with "roots," so that the physical transfer of African captives into the transatlantic slave trade serves both as the impetus and the metaphor for the movement of cultural forms "out of Africa" and in other kinds of circuits that have constituted a (Black) Atlantic world (Palmié 2007a, 2007c). I, too, will look at the effects of actual bodies in motion, and how their movements create semiotically meaningful traces we can read as ideologies and practices of embodiment that implicate the racialization of those bodies.

The physically enacted routes that interest me are local delineations of urban space in Santiago made significant by people's purposeful movement along and through them in street processions. I will take up an additional trope of movement that Santiagueros, in particular, claim as distinctively their own and express in the idiomatic reflexive verb *arrollarse*, "to roll (along)" that specifically describes dancing to the sounds of the conga of carnival (see fig. 3.1). The act of *arrollándose*, "rolling along" is closely associated with processions of congas through Santiago's streets during carnival time. Locally understood as the body's "natural" and unstoppable response to the powerful sonic environment of a conga pounding out its rhythms, arrollándose is what entire crowds of people will be drawn out in the street to do as a conga passes. As a genre of dance, Cubans evaluate arrollándose based on how much enjoyment the dancer projects, how swept away the dancer is into the conga's rhythms, and therefore how "delicious" and "rich" the movements are, as evidenced by the dancing body's fullness of movement.[2] Arrollándose plays a key role in creating the carnivalesque in Santiago's carnival, and it is fundamentally a descriptor of bodies in crowds situated in particular social spaces along particular physical routes in Santiago. The ability to arrollarse, and to produce the infectious rhythms of the conga that call it forth, are understood as markers of Cuba's African heritage and are seen to come forth more naturally from some people than others as a racialized heritage that is in the blood.

Indeed, this phrase was frequently invoked by my Cuban interlocutors in ways that resonate with widespread and historically significant discourses re-

FIGURE 3.1 After a carnival performance, a *campana* (bell) player keeps rhythm on his brake shoe instrument in the Children's Conga de los Hoyos, surrounded by dancers *arrollándose* in the street, Santiago de Cuba, July 25, 2011. Photo by author.

garding blood as the "essence" of (racial, national) belonging. Consider two very different examples from conversations I participated in with a Cuban friend on different occasions about particular children's dancing skills in the conga—the same friend who frequently repeated to me about the conga that she "carried it in the blood," and who is the director of a children's carnival comparsa. One example came in an August 2008 interview I did in which she was recounting that July's prize-winning carnival performance. She told me about a young girl, not much older than two, who had charmed the carnival jury and audience by "*arrollando* without shyness." She singled the girl out not only because she was a "natural dancer" at so young an age but also because she was "a white girl with blue eyes" who lived in the neighborhood and thus, "ya la tenía en la sangre" (she already had it in the blood). Later in the same conversation, my friend returned to this topic, emphasizing that the girl was "white, Kristina, white, white, white. You can just imagine a white girl among so many dark people . . . a pretty girl, with a lovely, lovely face, pretty." The implication was that, despite her racial ascription (where, notice, "white" gets equated with loveliness), which she contrasts to the Blackness expected of conga aficionados, the girl's exposure to the conga from living in the neighborhood had saturated her with the rhythms to be a good dancer. Notice, too, the implicit association of congas with Blackness: in this context, it is Whiteness that is marked.

During another trip, my friend taught my then seven-year-old daughter and a colleague's five-year-old daughter, both American, how to arrollarse. Talking with her and another folklorist friend about my daughter's progress, they were unsurprised and commented that of course she was arrollándose better than her friend, because my daughter was Black and, left unsaid but understood, her friend was White.[3] She might be foreign, but she had the conga rhythm in the blood because of her shared African ancestry. In this case, racial identification trumped foreignness: no matter that she had had little exposure to the conga.

In discussing similar assessments of Brazilians' aptitudes for dance or drumming as a "blood" inheritance of African-descended people, de Santana Pinho (2010, 152–56) suggests that even metaphorical usages expressed essentialized notions of race, as seems to be the case in this instance and others. By chance, as I was writing this chapter, I came across a photo essay at BBC Mundo (part of the British Broadcasting Corp.'s World Service network) on Havana's 2012 carnival, which takes place in early August (Ravsberg 2012). The caption to one photo showing comparsa dancers in their finery explains the physical demands of dancing in carnival, then continues: "Among them predominate young people, blacks and mulatos, who carry the rhythm in the blood, but also there are white men and women who move with the same grace."[4] The formulation of the caption portrays dancing in carnival—arrollándose—as "natural" to Cubans of color, while White Cubans who participate are noted as being able to dance *in spite of* their Whiteness.

I heard this idiom of "in the blood" used to express having a propensity for particular cultural forms on numerous occasions from a variety of people, and it clearly circulates more widely, as evidenced by the BBC blog site. And yet, I cannot generalize from these instances to make a claim about how deeply the idiom saturates Cuban discourses linking race and culture, nor do I think its meaning is necessarily stable across instances. Even in the two instances I described, the same interlocutor used the phrase to evoke distinct indexical orders, one privileging racial ancestry as a "fact of birth" and the other privileging neighborhood belonging as a fact of socialization, thereby illustrating de la Cadena's (2001) point that there is considerable heterogeneity even in seemingly hegemonic discourses on race and nation. But beyond this, I believe that there is a link between racialization through beliefs about facts of birth marked by physical appearance and racialization via community belonging and that these mutually constituting connections are particularly evident in some of the everyday interactions and special performances surrounding carnival.

In the next section I will briefly sketch a history of discourses about race and (national) belonging in Cuba in order to ground my further exploration of ideologies of embodiment evident in carnival practices. This is followed by a discussion of the salience of racial difference in everyday talk. Then I will introduce Santiago's carnival—or more accurately, its parallel official and grassroots carnivals. But let me first return to the notion of routes and what I think these have to do with ideologies of racialized embodiment—literally and metaphorically. There are particular moments of street procession during carnival and on a few saints' days during other times of the year, of which perhaps the most emblematic are when congas play as they move down a street, drawing residents out of their homes to watch or follow behind the conga in a growing procession. Ideally, the conga irresistibly makes everyone arrollarse, although in practice many of those who observe or follow the conga do not dance (or dance for stretches, then just walk and chat). But let me concentrate for a moment on the circuits followed by these congas: they do not travel randomly throughout the city but are situated in particular neighborhoods which, in turn, are the ones regularly exposed to their sounds. Congas and the opportunities they provide to gain familiarity with their rhythms and to arrollarse are not evenly distributed but, rather, are concentrated in older neighborhoods ringing the historic city center—neighborhoods also mostly identified as Black. So the love of the conga and the talent for arrollándose only seem to be "natural" to residents of Black neighborhoods if this spatialization of race (and concomitant racialization of space) is overlooked. But all city residents are prepared to reclaim the routes of the carnivalesque when it suits their purposes. Once, when I was interviewing my friend the children's conga director about carnival and another friend dropped by, a White historian whose involvement in carnival is minimal but whose knowledge of the city's history is vast, the two joyfully remembered a carnival song they had both heard. They recounted to me that one year a while back, when the police would not permit a crowd to gather in the street around a conga, people followed the carnival tradition of spontaneously creating a song for the moment:

> policia, déjame arrollar
> ese blanquito arrolla
>
> police, let me "roll"
> this White boy "rolls"

A Brief History of Blackness and the "Myth of *Mulataje*" in Cuba

Political scientist Mark Sawyer (2006), in a recent study of race and racism in Cuba, describes an overall situation of "inclusionary discrimination," where Blackness is central to Cuban national identity at the same time people and cultural forms marked as Black are denigrated. Note that this formulation is implied in the carnival song lyric above, a response contesting the police's treatment of arrollándose as a threat to public order, voiced by the figure of a "White boy" who "knows how to dance." Implicit in this is "common knowledge" that Black Cubans are much more likely to be in trouble with the police than White Cubans, even when Whites partake of the same cultural practices marked as Black, like arrollándose down the street in a noisy conga crowd.

This particular racial formation fits within the broader Latin American rubric often described as national myths of *mestizaje*, in which Blackness and indigenousness are projected back to a primordial cultural blending that produced today's mestizo national identity. Under these national ideologies, whitening processes and cultural forms deemed European remain privileged, while those citizens and cultural forms deemed Afro- or Indio are marginalized as insufficiently assimilated to the mestizo national norm (Godreau 2006; Rahier 2003; Whitten 2003; Wright 1990). Moreover, national myths of *mestizaje* often have had an uneasy relationship to national elite projects of whitening, under which *mestizaje* can as easily represent racial and cultural degeneracy as progress (Helg 1990).

Idioms of blood and bloodline have long been implicated in the "race to nation," taking different forms in different moments of Latin American and Caribbean history (Williams 1989). Brackette Williams invokes Keyes's (1976) notion of grounding "primordial" identifications like ethnicity, race, and nationality in what he calls "facts of birth." Such "facts" inevitably also draw on locally relevant norms of kinship and sexuality that ground determinations of "purity" and miscegenation—norms that often are advanced through racialized and sexualized imagery, for example, of "sexy mulatas" driving miscegenation through their seductiveness (Kutsinski 1993; Martinez-Alier 1989). De Santana Pinho's (2010, 2011) historical study of the body as the site of essentialized Blackness in Brazil rings true for Cuba as well. And yet, as De la Cadena (2001) points out in her comments on several studies of race and nation in Guatemala, the ways in which facts of birth and idioms of blood are taken up in discourses of national identity are and have always been messy and "heteroglossic," rather than neatly cleaving to the hegemonic model of the moment. They are, in the terminology of race developed in chapter 2, shifters in their ubiquity and ambiguous reference.

As Aline Helg (1995) and other historians document, including Alejandra Bronfman (2004), Alejandro de la Fuente (2001a), Ada Ferrer (1999), and Rebecca Scott (1985), the current state of affairs in Cuba arose out of the conditions in which Cuba gained independence from Spain at the same time that it abolished slavery. Bronfman (2004, 5) has argued that the question of "how theories of racial difference engaged notions of political equality" has been a longstanding theme that Cuban politics has addressed in different ways at different historical moments, into the present.

In Cuba, the end of slavery was a protracted and delayed affair coinciding with the rise of colonial discontent evolving into a nationalist struggle for independence from Spain, in which slaves, the plantation economy, and the promise/threat of emancipation were all tools employed by both empire and colonial discontents (Scott 1985). The anticolonial fight spanned forty years, with open warfare spanning the decade of 1868–78, the Guerra Chiquita (1879–80), and what Cubans call the Spanish-Cuban-American War of 1895–98. Cubans of color were instrumental to victory in 1898, both as military leaders, such as General Antonio Maceo, and as rank-and-file volunteers, known as the *mambí*, many of whom were escaped or released ex-slaves who fought with machetes, using guerrilla warfare techniques and living under conditions of deprivation. Slavery had been abolished incrementally over the course of 1870–86, in a drawn out legal process of emancipation.

José Martí's words of 1893 promising a Cuban nation in which "Cuban is more than white, more than mulato, more than black" were a beacon, a promissory note that Cubans of color held out for redemption in the newly formed Cuban nation, formally established with the end of U.S. military occupation in 1902 (Martí 1976, 298–300). Alas, Martí was by then dead, having been killed in action in 1895, as was General Maceo (whose body suffered the further indignity of succumbing to studies by race scientists; see de la Fuente 2001a, 38–39). And along with U.S. political domination came Jim Crow–era American notions about race and segregation that contradicted the visions of Cuban racial unity promoted by Cuban nationalists (de la Fuente 2001a; Pérez 1999).

To compress a long, sad tale: despite considerable political organizing and the recognized moral authority of mambí veterans as having earned their citizenship with blood, Cubans of color continued to be systematically, even brutally, disenfranchised, not just during the outright U.S. occupation between 1898 and 1902 but during both the First and Second Republics as well (1902–33 and 1933–59, respectively [de la Fuente 2001a; Helg 1990]). The most infamous incident was the massacre that occurred in 1912, in which thousands of Cubans of color were killed in response to a perceived threat of Black insurrection. The ostensible cause was the war of words between political elites backed by the United States and a grassroots political party with an agenda of racial equality, the Partido Independiente de Color, but the violence of 1912 was also reiterating centuries of violent reprisals against suspected slave insurrections. The result, the suppression of political organizing based on racial solidarity among Cubans of color, lasted for decades (de la Fuente 2001a; Helg 1990).[5]

Not only was political organizing by Cubans of color fraught during the decades spanning the end of the nineteenth century into the early twentieth century, but people's relationships to cultural forms seen as African were also complicated by the racial implications. This period saw a florescence of popular religiosity, out of which emerged the practices today distinguished as Santería, Reglas de Palo, and Spiritism (Brown 2003; James Figarola 2001; Román 2007). New spiritual leaders and religious affiliations emerged and moved around the island, including renowned community leader and charismatic religious figure, Mason Reynerio Pérez, who moved from Matanzas to Santiago de Cuba in the 1920s or early 1930s as a member of the Rural Guard and who is credited with establishing lineages of modern Palo Monte and Ocha (Santería) that remain prominent in Santiago today (Larduet Luaces 2001 and personal communications with Larduet Luaces, 1999–2000, 2006, 2007).

In addition, the African cofraternities of colonial times, known as cabildos, had by the late nineteenth century been reinvented as or replaced by societies of recreation and mutual aid, with some choosing to preserve and celebrate what were increasingly self-consciously recognized as African genres of music, dance, and worship (de la Fuente 2001a; Hevia Lanier 1996; Howard 1998). Even by the mid-nineteenth century, some societies of recreation and mutual aid for people of color shunned practices marked as African, instead emphasizing their creoleness and assimilation to elite White norms of culture and recreation, thereby contrasting their higher status with that of newly arrived Africans (Olga Portuondo, personal communication, May 3, 2008).

Neighborhood carnival comparsas, too, were emerging in their modern forms in cities like Santiago de Cuba (Pérez Rodríguez 1988). But these practices and associations were often challenged, declared illegal, and pointed out as evidence against the claims to equality of Cubans of color, under various mutually reinforcing logics of criminology, public health and hygiene, civic order, and social-evolutionary progress. Nor was the potential of such social and cultural organizations to facilitate political organizing lost on their participants or outside observers (Bronfman 2004; de la Fuente 2001a; Hevia Lanier 1996). For example, there was the precedent set by colonial-era cofraternities designated as of the "Congo nation" in which they organized their own hierarchies of cabildo officials, among which the leader designated the Congo king had sufficient on-the-ground authority to negotiate with local government officials on issues pertaining to the city's Congo cabildos and their neighborhoods (Olga Portuondo Zúñiga, personal communication, May 3, 2008).[6] And according to local oral history, some of Santiago's most prominent heroes of the struggle for independence, such as the Maceo brothers, used the cover of cabildos and carnival comparsas to smuggle people, munitions, and medicines in and out of the city (see Millet et al. 1997), a subterfuge repeated by revolutionaries aligned with Fidel Castro's movement in the 1950s, including the martyred Santiaguero Frank País, who used the cover of the carnival Paseo de la Placita for antigovernment activities.

Meanwhile, from the late nineteenth to the mid-twentieth centuries, many better-established, elite Cubans of color exhorted one another to reject association with practices regarded as African, lest they unwittingly provide evidence of being insufficiently civilized that would justify denying them the full rights of citizenship (Hevia Lanier 1996, 18–26). They instead sought to demonstrate their class equivalence to White Cubans of similar socioeconomic status in the face of virulent race science claims of Black inferiority. Increasingly, during the early twentieth century, they worked to distance themselves from cultural forms marked as African and align themselves with cultural forms marked as European (e.g., by forming elite associations such as the Athens Club and Fraternal Union; see de la Fuente 2001a).

Ironically enough, the period of political turmoil and building resentment toward U.S. interference from the 1920s through the 1930s also gave birth to the Afrocubanist movement, one largely although not entirely shaped by nationalist sentiments of elite, White Cubans, inflamed by U.S. imperialist and racist treatment of Cuba as little more than a "Banana republic" (de la Fuente 2001a; Moore 1997). Afrocubanism looked to aesthetic and folkloric forms marked as African to serve as a source of primordial, authentic Cuban identity. Indeed, the seminal work of Cuba's founding father of folklore studies, the venerable Fernando Ortiz, did much to create an equivalence between folklore and Afro-Cuba that lasts to this day (Bronfman 2004; Duany 1988).[7] Ortiz claimed credit for introducing the very term *afrocubano* in 1906 (in Ortiz [1906] 1973), although its circulation has remained mostly among academics and seldom as a self-ascription (Pérez Sarduy and Stubbs 1993, 28).

The emerging Cuban "myth of *mulataje*" thus acknowledged that *lo Afro* played an important role in the Cuban national imaginary, but always within the framework of a national "whitening" project that forced cultural forms marked as African into the primordial slot of folklore and permitted the ongoing marginalization of the darkest-skinned Cubans. Even when White elites participated in carnival, as they probably always had, it was through their own comparsas, which were generally characterized as more luxurious in their material trappings but without the same fiery rhythm of the poorer, Black neighborhood comparsas.[8] While middle-class and wealthy people of color feared the detriment of being identified with poor Blacks and took steps to distance themselves from the risks of being "declassed," Whites of similarly privileged economic standing could play at "blackface" or its equivalent during carnival and participate in the carnivalesque without the same risk of lasting effects from race or class misidentification.

The ironies of how ideologies of hypodescent could contradict the emerging nationalist myth of *mulataje* were not lost on Cubans of color, even when they bought into the primordialist view of African contributions to *Cubanidad.* When Afrocubanist poet Nicolás Guillén, himself a person of color, wrote his "Ballad of the Two Grandfathers" in 1934, he sketched them with images of a distant past (1972, 2:137–39):

Lanza con punta de hueso,	Lance tipped with bone,
tambor de cuero y madera:	drum of hide and wood:
mi abuelo negro.	my black grandfather.
Goguera en el cuello ancho,	Lace ruff around a wide neck,
gris armadura guerrera:	grey fighting armor:
mi abuelo blanco.	my white grandfather.

For Guillén, the black grandfather spoke of "Africa of steamy jungles" and the white grandfather of conquest through deception with beads and trinkets. To insist that "both were of the same size, shouting, dreaming, crying, singing" was to claim equal African and European patrimony for Cuba, but in doing so, *lo Afro* was firmly positioned in the past and of the past, alongside archaic images of European armor and lace. Note, too, the natural materials associated with the African grandfather: bone, wood, and animal hides, in contrast to manufactured cloth and metal symbolizing Europe's patrimony. The poem's perspective is that of a thoroughly miscegenated grandchild who embodies *mulataje* as his genealogical and cultural inheritance.

In a more colloquial and critical voice, the words of one carnival song I recorded in 2011 during a combined rehearsal of several Afro-Cuban folklore societies invokes the myth of *mulataje* to trenchantly ask "White" Cubans, "También tu abuela / ¿cómo va, cómo va?" (Also your grandmother / how is she, how is she?), as a light-skinned dancer spins away to avoid the advances of an older dark-skinned dancer—rejecting his "African grandmother," as the performers explained to me.

The Cuban Revolution, taking power in 1959, inherited these discursive and temporal frames for imagining Cubanness as what Cuban folklorist Fernando Ortiz famously called "transculturation," a product of the primordial mixing of Carib, African, and European peoples to create a distinctively new people. The revolution has consistently positioned itself as taking up the nation-building project of Martí and other independence fighters, adding a Marxist prerogative to elevate "the folk" and "the popular classes" of workers, peasants, and the very poor. Cubans of color and cultural forms associated with Cuba's African heritage, thus, have always received a degree of attention from the revolutionary state, if only as folklore and heritage of the masses, a generalized inheritance shared by all Cubans. But such attentions did not amount to a recognition of Blacks as an interest group—indeed, the revolution's stance has been to discourage racial politics on the basis that it has already abolished systemic racism (a claim that had become impossible to defend by the early 2000s; see de la Fuente 1998, 2007). Indeed, between the early 1960s and the late 1990s, anyone protesting ongoing racism risked being branded as a "counterrevolutionary" who denied the revolution's gains (Hansing 2006; Moore 1988).

Generally speaking, the revolution has approached Cuba's longstanding project of political equality through positions and policies that conform to a Rousseauian politics of equal recognition based on a "perfectly balanced reciprocity," which is predicated on leveling differences between individuals or among groups (Taylor and Guttman 1994, 47). Charles Taylor in an influential essay on the "politics of recognition" in a multicultural society that originally appeared in 1992, critiques Rousseau's vision of rejecting all social differentiation and pride in individual or group uniqueness as totalitarian in its effects, calling it one of "the most terrible forms of homogenizing tyranny" (Taylor and Gutman 1994, 47–51). Something approaching this ideal of equal recognition was the fond vision of the early Cuban Revolution once it adopted the Soviet model. Religious, racial, and class differences only divided the people and threatened the revolution, in this view, and would (must!) disappear as the ideal society emerged through the revolution, to remain only as a memory of the past contrasting with a utopian present. Thus, the myth of *mulataje*, in its various formulations, projected cultural differences into the past in a national trajectory of homogenization-through-transculturation, where folklore performances could serve to remind the public of their shared roots, rather than representing contemporary diversity.

Consider the text of a pamphlet about the recent photography exhibit, *The Orichas Descend to Earth*, by Onel Torres Roche and on display in the Heredia Theater during the 2011 Festival of the Caribbean. Despite the title's reference to the deities of Santería, a source of rich iconography (Brown 2003; Lindsay 1996), the images showed portraits of "Afro-descendants," primarily in everyday clothing and settings, suggesting an "earthy" contrast to the usual depiction of royal and mythic orichas. The accompanying pamphlet's essay by Havana journalist and critic Frank Pérez Álvarez concludes: "No more are they the old-time slaves, now they are free, in a just and solidary society that also reclaims for them a life from which have been abolished forever the remnants that can linger of discrimination and inequality."[9] Such statements, blithely ignoring contradictory evidence in the photos documenting the humble circumstances of the subjects, echo several decades of official discourse that situates racism and racialized social difference alike in Cuba's past as a contrast to the free, just, and unified society of the revolutionary present and also, to the extent the revolution is acknowledged as a work-in-progress, as a contrast to an even more utopian future to be performatively realized through these kinds of statements (as if by proclamation alone discrimination and inequality could vanish).

In declaring that discrimination of all sorts was abolished and that all citizens should strive for the same moral ideal of the self-sacrificing and solidary "new man," the revolution left political space neither for critique of ongoing problems such as racism nor for individual or organized dissent from its vision. One result has been that the racial politics of Black Consciousness and Black Nationalism in the United States and the more recent identity politics of U.S. multiculturalism and antiracism have had no sustained equivalent in Cuba (Moore 1988; Sawyer 2006). The revolution has been critiqued by outside observers such as Cuban American activist Carlos Moore (1988), in keeping with the precept, in bell hooks's (1996, 4) words, that "the absence of recognition is a strategy that facilitates making a group the Other." I might add that it also leads to the kinds of paternalistic sentiments expressed in Pérez Alvarez's essay, where humble but presumably grateful Black folk had to have society fixed on their behalf by others. Moore and hooks speak of *political* recognition predicated on an acknowledgment of just the kinds of group agency and differences in history, identity, perspective that the revolution has tried hard to erase, rather than the relegation of history to quaint folkloric tableaus aiming to unify the vision of all citizens, which is, to date, how the revolution has "recognized" Black contributions to the Cuban nation.

One good example of the official perspective objectifying "Afro-Cuban culture" is a short speech presented as the closing speech of Santiago's July 2011 Popular Religiosity Workshop, a staple of the annual Festival del Caribe that the Casa del Caribe research institute organizes. For the past few years (2011 and 2012 at least), folklore researcher A. Abelardo Larduet Luaces of the

Casa del Caribe's popular religions research team has written and presented this speech. Larduet Luaces is a practitioner as well as a researcher of popular religions and a lifelong resident of Santiago who identifies as 'African-descended," and the speech is his own. And yet, he presents the speech in an official capacity, so it is not surprising that it reflects the national ideology I have described as typical of the revolution. The speech begins:

> The Cuban nation is a lucky symbiosis in which the cult and cultural factors that comprise it have found mutual benefit through our entire history. It is worth remembering that the composition of our Cubanness [*cubanía*] was anteceded by gestures of cultural clandestinity, slave rebellion, and a noncomformist creolity before the impositions of empire: aspects that together propitiated the beginning of the Cuban Revolution in 1868, an insurrection that better achieved its quest for sovereignty in 1959. In spite of this, we still continue in combat for the same aspirations of independence in the face of the hegemonic positions that interpellate us.[10]

Here, Larduet elides slave rebellion and underground religious practices with clandestine movements and creole insurrections for national independence from Spain and, into the current era, sovereignty from U.S. domination, with all of these comprising a figure of Cubanness as a shared inheritance of feisty forebears, including Africans. The reasons for struggle in the past may have been diverse, but in the present, there can only be a shared national struggle led by the revolution. Indeed, notions of struggle and combat had special resonance during these years because of the government's slogan, "la batalla de ideas" (the battle of ideas) to promote the notion that socialist principles, assumed to be shared by all Cubans, would win the day against neoliberal and imperial forces by persuasiveness alone.

Under this requirement for national unity and adherence to a centrally imposed political ideology, young Black Cubans since the 1990s have eschewed anything overtly political and opted instead to mark cultural resistance, discontent, and disidentification through fashions and hairstyles inspired by Rastafarianism, hip-hop, and music from reggae and timba to rap and reggaeton (de la Fuente 2007; Hansing 2006; Hernandez-Reguant 2006; West-Durán 2004). As these forms of Blackness have gained popularity, each has been appropriated and brought under state control—including coming under the jurisdiction of the Ministry of Culture, being commercialized, and being located in state-controlled venues—just as fully as older cultural forms marked as Black have been co-opted as folklore that stands for a shared Cuban heritage of "clandestinity, rebellion, and nonconformity" but only in the past or as a unified stand against a common national enemy.

Overall, then, Cuba's dynamics of racialization cannot be separated from ideologies of nation, history, and descent. Contemporary Cuban racializing processes can be summarized as follows. Inclusionary exclusion, to use Sawyer's (2006) term, has relegated Blackness to inclusion in the national origin myth but in highly anachronistic ways that deny coevalness of Black Cuban identities or, as Godreau (2006) argues for Blackness in Puerto Rico, displace Black cultural forms either to the past or to "foreign import" status (as is the case with cultural forms such as reggae, Vodou, and hip-hop). But part of inclusionary exclusion as it works in Cuba, anyway, is that Black culture is sometimes seen, from some vantage points, as resistant in itself and as a powerful source of and metaphor for cultural resistance, national pride, and localized forms of cultural marronage (James Figarola 1999b, 2006b; Ramírez Calzadilla 1995). Cuban historian, folklorist, and founder of the Casa del Caribe Joel James Figarola (1999b, 2006a), exemplifying this perspective, describes Afro-Cuban religious modalities as "Deep Cuba" and Cuba itself as "the Great Nganga" (referring to the powerful, spiritually charged object at the center of Palo ritual practice).

These are tropes that his protegé and colleague Larduet Luaces echoed in the rest of his speech closing the international conference on popular religiosity: he described the religious practices many Cubans refer to as undifferentiated African "witchcraft" (*brujería*) as having "been in all processes for national sovereignty," thereby "forming an indissoluble part of our cultural identity" and ends by comparing the blood sacrifice of Afro-Cuban religious practices with the "necessary blood of our martyrs," by way of introducing the Santería ceremony that followed his speech.[11] Quite in keeping with official ideologies, Larduet has situated his racial and religious identifications and his cultural affinities, all marked as Black, as the quintessence of a shared Cubanness. And yet, as I explore throughout this book, Blackness is chronotoped to situate it in Cuba's metaphorical heartland by cloaking it with nostalgia and tradition and by positioning cultural practices marked as Black as anachronistic emblems of Cuba's roots.

Then too, not everyone agrees with Larduet's argument making Blackness essential to Cubanness. For many Cubans I have met, the "cults" and "witchcraft" he refers to are "cosas de negros," things Blacks do, and somewhat distasteful for all that. In conversations with Cubans of all hues, I have heard some profess complete ignorance about forms of culture marked as Black, sometimes expressing curiosity about what I have learned in my studies, while making clear their social distance from such practices. In contrast, the adherents and practitioners of cultural practices marked as Black also span all social groups, despite their frequent stage and media representation as the province of Black people. At the level of practice, there is no one-to-one mapping of race to cultural form.

What do these dynamics mean for Cubans' everyday experiences of being raced—to what extent does race-as-phenotype matter in day-to-day life? Although these are important questions deserving their own full-length study, I will provide a preliminary account in the section that follows.

Race as *Presupposition* in Everyday Talk

I have suggested that the performative work that creates and re-creates us as raced subjects is largely invisible to us, so that race appears as an intrinsic property of bodies and their dispositions, presupposed and so always potentially available as "already present" to be indexed for the interactional work of the moment and, precisely because of this, continually reinscribed as a natural sign rather than a performative accomplishment. Skin color and other phenotypic markers of race have salience for Cubans, as attested by abundant descriptive vocabulary, but this salience depends on whether and how race is invoked as meaningful in a given interaction. As Robin Sheriff (2001) and France Twine (1998) have shown in studies of everyday talk about race in Brazil, racial labels and ascriptions—overt forms of "racetalk," (Myers 2005)—tend to vary widely, with even the same person referring to themselves or being referred to in multiple ways, depending on the interaction. Twine argues that the lists of dozens of racial labels attested in Brazil and long fascinating to scholars should be viewed not as a static hierarchy of gradations that people are fixed into but as a set of resources people draw on for their interactional needs, a conclusion in keeping with a performative theory of racialization. She also argues that the multitude of intermediate racial categories does not soften the harsh reality of the Black-White divide that perpetually disparaged and diminished the opportunities of Brazilians of color. Cubans invoke phenotypic markers of race in similarly fluid and contextually specific ways, but almost always according to a logic recognizing White privilege over Blackness.

On the one hand, Cubans of color in particular tend to express what historian Olga Portuondo Zúñiga calls a "creole consciousness" in which people readily identify as of mixed heritage (*conciencia criolla;* personal communication, May 31, 2007). As a typical example, when I asked one very dark-skinned friend who often identifies as Black what his ancestry was, he answered that his patronym clearly was French, so his ancestry included French as well as Spanish and African predecessors, although he did not know much beyond his four Black grandparents. But when I have asked light-skinned friends—

people who generally identify as White or "wheatish" (*trigueño*)—about their ancestry, they did not mention African ancestors. One friend pointedly answered that her family was completely Spanish on both sides. Her "creole consciousness" manifested instead in her appreciation of Afro-Cuban religious modalities, which she described as practiced by people of all backgrounds.

Much as the ideology of *mestizaje* serves a certain national narrative, it is clear in people's everyday ways of referring to race that they do not see *mestizaje* as a mixing of equally valued ancestries. Phenotypic signs of Africanness are often overtly disparaged. Certainly, people employ a wide vocabulary to describe undesirable hair and facial features associated with African ancestry, and lighter skin is sometimes overtly described as preferable to darker skin. As but one of countless everyday examples in which people remark on their own or others' physical features in ways that point out racialized features and show their relative value, I think of an interchange between my then eight-year-old daughter and a middle-aged woman who worked in the house where we stayed. My daughter's thick, long, curly hair was pulled back in a puffy ponytail, a *moñito*, which the woman teased her about, saying she needed to have her hair combed properly (I was clearly an intended overhearer of this remark). Another member of the household, hearing the woman repeat this remark, coached my daughter to respond, "¡peinate tú!" (comb your own hair), which was pulled back in the exact same style. The woman then told my daughter that she would have her hair straightened for carnival and that my daughter should too, so they could go out dancing like two mulatas, where a combination of dark skin and straight hair could shift one from "black" to "mulata." Indeed, keeping curly "Black" hair "natural" was almost unthinkable for girls or women: as in the United States, braids (preferably with extensions), straightening (usually painstakingly accomplished with curlers, not chemicals), and wigs (rarer) were preferred styles for women with naturally curly hair, while younger girls would have their hair tightly pulled into little pigtails so it would stretch flat across their scalps, and bleached blond was in vogue for men and women around 2011.

The aesthetic preference for physical markers of Whiteness and the way in which phenotype is taken as a sign of social persona find expression in the descriptor *fino* meaning "refined," and sometimes used as a synonym for White physical features and/or "higher-class" taste or comportment, closely associated with Whiteness, as when an oricha possessing a santero referred to me as *gente fina* (refined people) during a ceremony. When attributed to someone Black, it is invariably contrastive, as in a prominent Santería practitioner who was described to me as "Black but refined" (*negro pero fino*). One friend born before the 1959 Revolution into a very large family that was active in their neighborhood's conga described how one of his sisters was considered "more fine" than the other siblings and so their parents forbad her to get involved with the conga and other "cosas de negros" that other members of the family participated in and instead gave her piano lessons. In such cases, for people phenotypically read as Black to reject "black things" looks to be a bid for class mobility, albeit one predicated on cultivating the properly refined bodily markers and dispositions to allow the move to be possible.[12] Such comparisons, perhaps especially within families, give preference to phenotypically whiter children over their siblings, which can be a source of anguish for those labeled blacker (e.g., de los Reyes Castillo Bueno 2000).

In a conversation I overheard between two vendors and the woman head of household who sat with them chatting over their transaction, one vendor described herself as mulata because her father was White and her mother mulata ("but he loved her," she insisted, as if a White man's capacity to love a woman of color might be in doubt). But among all four children, she was the darkest skinned, a surprise (the colonial-era term was *salto atrás* or "throwback"). She hastened to add that all her children and grandchildren were light skinned, but then lamented that the lightest-skinned granddaughter had married a Black foreigner: "What a shame to waste the opportunity of marrying a foreigner, when she could have strengthened the race" (a paraphrase recorded in my fieldnotes, surreptitiously written down as I listened from a table in the corner). This is one of the few times I heard anyone use the phrase, "strengthen the race," which refers to a strategy of upward mobility through whitening and has also been attested since the colonial era, although my friend who sat chatting with them told me later that she thought the phrase is still commonly used.

On another occasion, during a small Spiritist mass I sponsored with no more than ten people in attendance, an elderly woman did not recognize an acquaintance she had not seen for several years. She leaned over to introduce herself and ask his name. This man, the same very dark-skinned man of French, Spanish, and African ancestry mentioned above, reintroduced himself and reminded her that they knew each other. To ease the woman's embarrassment when she recognized his name, he gently and laughingly said, "We Blacks all look alike," a self-disparagement that shocked me. Looking around, it struck me that almost all the participants in the ceremony, including the elderly woman and her family members, were light skinned —phenotypically White in Cuban terms. My dark-skinned friend stood out among us, a bit of context he seemed to allude to in making the self-lowering remark. While I could imagine someone saying this ironically to call out someone else's underlying racism, his tone and affect conveyed sincerity: he was helping her recover from her gaffe, not insulting her. When the woman responded that he still looked so young, too young to be the same person she had met years before, he explained: "We Blacks don't show our age. If you see an old, wrinkled-looking Black, you know he is really old." A few minutes later, after more embarrassed apologies from the elderly woman, he repeated that he "[didn't] know what our skin is made of, but it's tough," again shocking me, but functioning to help the woman recover from her embarrassment. Indeed, the White hostess holding the ceremony, who had been listening along with the rest of us to this exchange, pointed out that she too had few wrinkles for her age, but that it was because of the fat under the skin that the two of them were lucky enough to share. The interaction then shifted to preparation for the ceremony, and the subject did not come up again.

Viewed in the context of the series of conversational moves of self-lowering and other-raising that followed from the initial gaffe of not recognizing someone, my Black friend's self-directed racial insults made a certain sense, but only against a backdrop of shared presuppositions about the comparative value of dark and light skin, where making reference to markers of one's Blackness could be construed as self-lowering. In this context, the embarrassed woman's reference to his youthful appearance and the hostess's comment about there being a similarity in their lack of wrinkles can be seen as subsequent other-raising interactional moves, respectively offering a compliment and pointing out something they share, perhaps *despite* his Blackness: a fatty layer under their differently hued skins. Valentina Pagliai (2011) describes how racist remarks can circulate without being challenged, even by people who abhor them, when they are interactionally positioned as unmarked rather than marked utterances, like talking about the weather versus talking about politics. To contest an unmarked assertion could be construed, in such a moment, to rupture the cooperatively achieved camaraderie of the interaction. In the situation I described, pointing out racial differences marked by Black skin seemed similarly unmarked, when uttered by the one dark-skinned person in the room trying to put the elderly, light-skinned woman at ease.

In other interactions, appearing Black could carry a very different weight. Years earlier, around 1999, I had met up with the very same dark-skinned friend one morning, and he recounted to me how he had been turned away from a hotel where he was supposed to meet a manager on business the night before because he had forgotten his identity card and the guards at the gate would not let him pass, despite his explanation and the fact that he was carrying a briefcase. That reminded him of another occasion when he had forgotten his identity card and been stopped by police, who took him to the station when he could not produce it. There, the commander recognized him and profusely apologized, releasing him and yelling at the officers who had brought him in for not recognizing him (my friend is locally well-known). A few minutes later, we arrived at his workplace and I moved off to the side, while he talked with several coworkers. He retold the story of being turned away from the hotel, but this time, with interlocutors who were also dark-skinned Cuban men, it was one of the bitterest exchanges about racism that I have witnessed in Cuba, in which the men raised their voices as they critiqued the constant insults from guards at tourist establishments like hotels, who routinely turned away dark-skinned people, assuming they couldn't possibly have legitimate business there. The racist dynamic they pointed out, especially surrounding tourism, was abundantly evident and much discussed among people who had experienced its impact during the 1990s (and still in the 2000s [de la Fuente 2001b, 2007]). It was knowing this background, as much as having American racial sensitivities, that triggered my shock at hearing my friend invoke the notion that "we Blacks all look alike" during the exchange at the ceremony.

Critical conversations about racism seemed more in evidence by 2011, having moved from offstage to more public forms of interactions, as for instance when a paper questioning the centenary category of "Black crime" (*deleito negro*) presented at the Workshop on Popular Religion during the Festival of the Caribbean triggered an impassioned forty-minute discussion among the mostly Cuban audience of scholars and religious practitioners. The Havana-based researcher Denys Terris Abreu (2011) critiqued the criminological association of Afro-Cuban traditions with heightened participation in drug trade, prostitution, and violent crimes using statistics and pointed out the inherent racism of the category, arguing it should be abolished. By the end of her fifteen-minute talk, the audience was as agitated as I saw it in five days of presentations, with many Black heads nodding and arms being thrown in the air in exasperation. When the microphone was opened for audience discussion, after a few comments directed at other papers in her session, several people spoke up to make eloquent statements that *mulataje* is a condition of being Cuban, or perhaps even human. One woman argued that racism is pointless because there are no pure races when everyone is mixed; pointing to a White *babalawo* from the distant province of Pinar del Río, who had been vocal throughout the conference, she said, "today I'm sincerely pleased if the Ifá priest is white, but it may be that perhaps he doesn't know that his ancestor from back there in the colony could have been black."[13] Later in the discussion, the *babalawo* took the floor to argue that the many *babalawos* he knew from his work in the Ministry of Culture who were incarcerated, mostly for drug trafficking, were of all colors. He then described descending from a prominent (White) rancher and a Guinean Black and pointed out his lovely Black wife in the audience, concluding that he lived his beliefs. As the woman audience member mentioned above observed in ending her comments, the entire discussion rendered racial categories of Black and White salient even as speakers agreed that race shouldn't matter. As she put it, even pointing out race ran the risk of making one seem racist and divisive.

Such serious moments aside, most of the occasions when I witnessed Cubans bringing up race were moments of humor that played on common presuppositions about the meaning of racial differences and especially of Blackness. There were jokes that made the rounds, including one I will retell because of an interjection during its delivery that made its key presupposition explicit, although I do so somewhat hesitantly because the joke is overtly racist. I had just explained this book project to a (White) Cuban scholar, which reminded her of this "story": "A girl tells her mother she is going to marry a Black. The mother tries to dissuade her in all the usual ways. The girl says he has a house, and the mother then says, well let's think about this. The girl says he has a car . . ." At this point in the telling, the woman's adult son, working in the next room and overhearing our conversation, shouted over, "he's whitening!" ". . . The mother says, well, maybe this isn't impossible. The girl says he works in tourism, and the mother says, well call him up and get him over here right away!"

Clearly, the joke depends on shared background knowledge: you have to know that interracial relationships are generally thought to be desired by Cubans of color (who want to "advance" or "strengthen the race" by having lighter-skinned children) and discouraged by White Cubans (who don't want any "throwbacks"—darker-skinned children). You also have to know about Cuba's housing shortage and the extreme difficulties and expenses of acquiring a house or car, unless you inherit them (until reforms enacted in 2012, it was illegal to buy and sell real estate or cars, and such transactions remain difficult). And the best houses and cars in 1959 were owned by well-to-do White families, suggesting that the girl's Black boyfriend may have White family after all. It helps to also be familiar with a gendered stereotype that women put finance above romance in choosing partners (Härkönen 2011), so that the joke manages to draw on sexist as well as racist stereotypes. And finally, you have to know that, since the 1990s, the most lucrative jobs in Cuba are in tourism because workers have access to hard currency tips from foreigners. As the Latin American saying goes, money whitens.

This sort of humor—and there are many similar jokes—serves to recirculate stereotypes and make them available for all sorts of interactional work, including more situational moments of humor. For example, I was working one morning at a computer with two friends who are researchers at the Casa del Caribe, arduous work because the machine was slow and our online connection even slower. After about an hour, one friend suddenly got up and left, excusing himself as if taking a cigarette break. The other friend and I continued to work for another hour or so, occasionally wondering where he had gone, then went outside to take a break. The balcony where we stood looked out over a garden bar, and there, at a table in the shade, sat our friend. He was sharing a bottle of rum with a few other people. We laughed and went back in to finish, and when he reappeared at last to take his leave for the day, my other friend jokingly accused him, "what disrespect: you leave us for two Black women!" All three of us laughed as we departed. Here, the humor lay in the contrasting figures of my light-skinned friend and I versus the dark-skinned women at the table in the bar, where the implicit "joke" was that our friend would leave two "respectable" (because White) women like us for the presumably "disreputable" Black women in the bar. The joke's overt racial contrast indexes an entire set of associations lining up Whiteness, virtue, propriety, and education in contrast to Blackness, licentiousness, and decadence: *we* were working, while *they* sat drinking in a bar.

The series of anecdotes I have presented can hardly present a complete picture of how notions of race get mobilized in a variety of everyday interactions, except to indicate that they do—not every time or perhaps even in most conversations, but from time to time, and inevitably they draw on shared notions about the comparative value of Blackness versus Whiteness that robustly circulate despite the national ideology privileging *mestizaje* and downplaying racial disparities. What interests me are the implicatures: the common assumptions made relevant in each instance about the social value of racialized phenotypic markers and how they are mobilized to index contrasting social characteristics that invoke moral orders. These moral orders might rely on simplistic syllogisms where White is good (beautiful, socially normative) and Black is bad (criminal, socially disruptive) or on refractions of these in Black critiques of racism (e.g., the hypocrisy of claiming all groups are equal while discriminating against one). All of this everyday racializing discourse happens frequently enough to keep racialized differences salient, even when left implicit or not invoked in some interactions.

In the racialized imaginary of casual conversation, carnival is sometimes invoked as everyone's opportunity to relax and cut loose and other times invoked as a zone of Blackness, where drunken revelers follow the congas through the streets. An implied connection is thus made between Blackness and the carnivalesque. Consider how one couplet in the carnival song, "Para que lo gocen" (So that you all enjoy it), pairs an inclusive reference to the entire city with a reference to the emblematically Black neighborhood of Los Hoyos, regarded as the epicenter of carnival spirit, thereby suggesting both contrast and equivalence:

Por todo Santiago / tio io i-o	In all of Santiago / tio io i-o
Tanto en Los Hoyos/ tio io i-o	Just as in Los Hoyos / tio io i-o[14]

Carnival songs are not known for their profundity, and this, after all, is but a fleeting moment in a silly but catchy ditty, hardly the stuff of substantial analysis. And yet it diagrams the logic of racial embodiment-through-emplacement that plays out on so many levels and in so many moments: Los Hoyos is part of us, Los Hoyos is distinct. All of Santiago is called out to create the carnivalesque by arrollándose to the sounds of the conga, and in doing so to engage in a quintessential "Black thing" that is also a "Santiaguero thing" and, if pushed, a "Cuban thing": knowing how to fully enjoy life's sensual pleasures despite its hardships. As I now turn to discussing carnival, I will especially attend to dynamics of emplacement through which bodies gain racial identifications and dispositions through their spatial movements and through which physical spaces gain racialized neighborhood identifications as people play music, process, and dance along routes through the city during carnival.

Santiago's Parallel Carnivals

Carnival in Santiago de Cuba occurs in July, centered on end-of-the-month saints' days including the July twenty-fifth day of Saint James the Apostle (Santiago Apóstol), patron saint of the city.[15] Carnival season is organized around a series of performances bifurcated between an official carnival of judged competitive displays that performing groups take months to prepare for and a grassroots carnival where the carnivalesque is more apparent. In this, Santiago's carnival demonstrates the same tensions between the "folk" and the centralizing "state" that Bakhtin wrote about for modern transformations of medieval European carnivals, in which he described a historical shift away from the carnivalesque as the state increasingly "encroached upon festive life and turned it into a parade; on the other hand, these festivities were brought into the home and became part of the family's private life" (Bakhtin 1968, 33). Rather than a complete shift from carnivalesque to parade, Santiago's carnival is constituted by the tension between these dynam-

FIGURE 3.2 The Children's Conga de los Hoyos processes between the stands to perform for the jury, Santiago de Cuba, July 25, 2011. Photo by author.

ics, where the carnivalesque did not so much move into homes as become definitive of grassroots, neighborhood-level carnival participation. As Alexei Yurchak (2005) argues for similar political dynamics during the late Soviet era in Russia, the fields of action producing tensions between "official" and "grassroots" are constitutive of these very categories.[16]

The dynamic between the official and the grassroots of carnival can be described by contrasts. If the official carnival can be metonymically described as the judged competition, the grassroots carnival metonymically is the crowd and its recreations of dancing, drinking, and socializing. The official carnival is characterized by spatiotemporal containment, restrictions on recruitment to separate roles of performer and audience, centralized official control and policing, and TV- and camera-ready virtuosic displays with costumes, choreographies, and highly focused coordination; a fair bit of ritualization is also apparent (see fig. 3.2). The grassroots carnival is characterized by a much broader and creeping spatiotemporal spread, by being multisited, and at least potentially dangerous, and by featuring very different kinds of participation frames that do not clearly separate "performer" and "audience" roles and do not have a single focus of activity or attention (see fig. 3.3). The rituals and other activities of grassroots carnival are about social inversion and "communitas" in Victor Turner's (1974) classic account; some are also portrayed as historically deep traditions.

FIGURE 3.3 Late evening on the Paseo de Martí in Los Hoyos during carnival, July 24, 2011. People carry containers, like the green plastic pitcher held by the man in the center of the photo, to purchase beer from beer trucks. Photo by author.

But these are not absolute attributes, because in fact the official is always struggling to both appropriate and contain the carnivalesque it needs for the success of its own project, and the grassroots carnival is always on the verge of overflowing the official barriers and controls to break into sheer pandemonium. Santiago's aficionados of carnival often lament how what was once a months-long season has been restricted to ever-shorter time frames, while those sharing the official opprobrium of carnival's excesses often mention the increasing danger of criminality that carnival time represents. The tensions and borrowings between centrifugal forces of control and the unfettered and cacophonous aesthetic of the carnivalesque are most evident in the organization of neighborhood-based carnival ensembles, known generically as comparsas. Santiagueros involved in carnival identify two basic kinds of comparsas, the congas and the *paseos*, which differ in their instrumentation, rhythms, and some details of their official competitive performances. Both congas and *paseos* are seen as traditional, neighborhood groups of aficionados, although all are now organized under the auspices of the city's branch of the culture ministry and its carnival commission. There are also three recognized "centenary" folklore societies using different music and dance genres, descendants of colonial-era cofraternities and societies of mutual aid that retain ethnicized African names but effectively function much like the other

FIGURE 3.4 Children's Conga de los Hoyos performs in the neighborhood, Santiago de Cuba, May 6, 2008. Instruments, from left to right, are a *bokú*, three *galletas*, and three *campanas*, all sized smaller for children. Photo by Sarah Hill used with permission.

comparsas: the Tumba Francesa "La Caridad," the Cabildo Carabalí Isuama, and the Cabildo Carabalí Olugo (the latter two are extensively discussed in chap. 6). All of these ensembles, totaling perhaps twenty-five to thirty in a given year, prepare for the official carnival competition but also engage in various social activities, and the congas, in particular, will also make forays through their neighborhoods to (quite literally) "drum up" energetic participation from their compatriots.

The conga's instrumentation includes deep, booming drums such as the wide, flat *galletas* and the elogated *bocú* that establish a low-pitched conversation to structure the rhythm (fig. 3.4). Layered over that are not only higher-pitched percussive slaps on those drums but also the ringing, fast-paced, interlocking rhythmic patterns played on the *campanas*, or bells, which are actually metal brake drums (from cars) of different sizes held up in one hand and hit with a metal rod (see fig. 3.1). Soaring melodically over the percussive core of the conga is a single wind instrument, a double reed carved from wood with a metal bell, called the Chinese coronet and attributed to Chinese indentured laborers brought to Cuba in the late nineteenth century (fig. 3.5). The Chinese coronet has a piercing sound, similar in its range of pitch to

FIGURE 3.5 Chinese coronet played in Children's Conga de los Hoyos rehearsal, Santiago de Cuba, May 6, 2010. Photo by author.

a clarinet but with a much louder and buzzier timbre that soars over the drums. The Chinese coronet often plays lead-ins to begin songs and cues the singing, which is ideally contributed by the crowd drawn out to arrollarse by the sounds of the conga—yet another example of the blurring of performer-audience roles in grassroots moments of carnival. Indeed, the volume and sonic texture of a conga can be heard blocks away, above other city sounds, giving neighbors plenty of notice to get out into the street to follow it.

The congas' forays through their own neighborhoods are in preparation for "visits" the ensembles make to other ensembles in other neighborhoods, a thrillingly agonistic endeavor in which each ensemble performs for the other in the hope of generating more crowd support and thereby "winning" the encounter. On one occasion in mid-July of 2011, the Conga del Paso Franco, situated on the south side of center city, below the historically Black neighborhood of Tivolí on the hill above la Trocha Avenue, visited the Conga de los Hoyos on the north side. I learned of the visit only because the children's *conguita* rehearsal was sparsely attended, even just a few days before the competition, and one of the directors explained the reason to me. To everyone else it was commonsensical that kids would rather join the festivities of a conga visit than be herded through a formal rehearsal. An hour or two later, in the early evening, the Conga de los Hoyos set out playing to repay the visit to the Conga del Paso Franco, which took them on a route south across the city center past the house on San Félix Street where I was staying. As we heard the conga coming up the street, I joined others of my household in the doorway to watch the conga and its growing crowd pass. As I described the view in my fieldnotes, "Tons of people, many of them young, were arrollándose. The conga itself went past in the middle of the pack, with bright umbrellas twirled over their heads. The crowd ahead and behind was singing away. A line of police, serious and stony amid the lively crowd, went just before and just behind the conga itself" (7/14/11).

After the musicians passed, and with video camera in hand, I pulled my daughter along to follow. I was about one half block behind the musicians, near the back of the accompanying crowd, some of whom walked along, while others danced or sang the refrain of the song, "Va a llover" (It's going to rain—a popular carnival song in this season of frequent downpours). One couple just ahead of us danced quite energetically, clearly enjoying the opportunity to arrollarse at the end of a long, hot afternoon. As the conga procession crossed a major intersection in the city center, the shoppers and strollers paused and became spectators to the crowd, which was now singing "La Cucaracha." Then I heard sirens and saw a police car screech to a halt at the intersection with blue lights flashing as shoppers jumped out of the way. The crowd ahead of us stopped moving forward, and as the police disappeared into the denser crowd ahead, there were the sounds of screaming, and suddenly people all around us were rushing back, away from the now-distant sounds of the conga drowned out by sirens, as several more police cars drove into the crowd ahead. Fearing my daughter would be trampled by the wave of people running past us or that we would be caught in whatever trouble was ahead, I pulled her down a different street and we left the procession. This heavy, and sometimes heavy-handed, police presence was evident throughout carnival.

The Conga de los Hoyos, as one of the oldest still-extant comparsas (dating at least from 1909 and inheriting the mantle of the nineteenth-century comparsas and their *cocoyé* rhythm; see Pérez Rodríguez 1988, 1:379) and thus certainly the most prestigious, has the honor of performing not just visits but also what is termed an "invasion" of the city, a giant, half-day affair in which the conga draws out thousands of city residents as it moves along a circular route that takes it past many of the other traditional congas of the city, who come out to play in response. The "day of invasion" marks the peak of the carnivalesque in Santiago's carnival, an enormous moving party of drumming, dancing, and drinking that occurs only with official permission and accompanied by a heavy police presence but, for all that, seems always on the brink of spinning out of control. I describe the Invasion in a separate section below.

In other moments of carnival, the judged competition and the crowd, the official and the grassroots, interpenetrate each other. A quick example is how the groups performing in official carnival's competition move from the disorderly margins of the staging area into the narrow, highly restricted space circumscribed by judging and paid-spectator stands to perform rehearsed choreographies for the competition, then continue down past the end of the stands, where, if there is sufficient energy, they may continue playing, now accompanied by a crowd that spills into the street behind them and may join them in arrollándose if the rhythms are hot, as they move toward home (a transitional moment captured in fig. 3.1). These moments of the crowd embedded in official carnival pale in comparison to the scale of the Invasion, but the nested series of contrasts between and then within events of carnival follow a fractal logic (Irvine and Gal 2000) that keeps reproducing this juxtaposition between order and disorder as a central dynamic distinguishing carnival from the rest of the year.

Not only within Santiago's carnival, but in comparisons between Santiago's carnival and apparently more staid carnival traditions separating performers from audience in other cities like Havana, Santiago is always portrayed as having a particularly raucous grassroots tradition of crowd involvement, often linked to its Black population and rebellious reputation. Nor is this a new comparison: in the late 1940s, Havana poet and journalist Regino Pedroso favorably described Santiago's "so suggestive popular force, such unbounded jubilation, that is its vernacular riches, its pure and living traditionalism, fluidly rooted in the blood and soul of the people" in comparison to the glitzy but bland carnival performances of Havana, which did not seem as distinctively Cuban in comparison.[17] To use current Havanese slang for Cuba's "Orientals": the *palestinos* are part of "us Cubans" and yet distinct from us of the capital. In this nested series of contrastive relationships, Santiago stands for "deep" Cubanness, and the congas stand for "deep" Santiago. Pedroso quotes a member of Santiago's elite, who on witnessing the eruption of crowd excitement when the Conga de los Hoyos was declared winner of carnival's first prize, declared: "One could say that it is barbaric and whatever one wants, but one would have to be dead not to feel how this thing calls to us in the blood. Moreover, it's neither black nor white. This is a people that lives what it feels!"[18]

Nancy Pérez Rodríguez (1988) has collected a decade-by-decade chronicle of historical documentation on Santiago's carnival, which is attested as far back as a suggestion in 1679 that prizes be awarded to the best comparsas. Many other references over the centuries, on the one hand to prohibitions and lamentations of carnival's dangerous chaos and on the other to efforts to celebrate, develop, control, and, by the 1920s, commodify carnival (Rodríguez 1998, 1:326), suggest that the dynamic tensions between official, elite control and the grassroots carnivalesque have always been constitutive of carnival. And, of course, the carnivalesque also has provided concrete opportunities to disrupt the social order, even in aiding armed insurrections.

Little wonder the revolutionary regime, which has converted the heart of Santiago's carnival on July 26 into one of its major national celebrations, has for half a century now been anxious to squelch the carnivalesque possibilities for political dissidence under cover of carnival. The nightly performances of official carnival are energetic and superficial, luxuriating in glitzy costumes, fancy choreography, and perhaps including some patriotic colors or figures of orichas to give a vaguely folkloric and more overtly nationalistic feel. The early evening performances of the official children's carnival seem to go further in promoting official patriotic ideology, with comparsas often choreographing small groups of children dressed in military or medical uniforms or carrying Cuban flags, or in some way elaborating a theme that makes reference to the revolution's accomplishments, however vaguely and superficially. But it is all kept very tame and controlled: in official carnival, overt politics are as absent as the topsy-turvy critiques of the true carnivalesque.[19] Little wonder, then, that most residents of Santiago seem to show little interest in attending official carnival, unless they or a family member are actually performing in it. Grassroots carnival offers much more satisfying recreation and entertainment.[20]

Let me briefly describe the unfolding of Santiago's season of *los carnivales* in July as it occurred in the years between 2007 and 2011. Many residents told me that the official start to the carnival season was marked by the Burning of the Devil, a bonfire in the park alongside Alameda Avenue next to the bay that follows a parade of folkloric and popular music and dance known as the Parade of the Serpent, and marks the end of the week-long Festival del Caribe during the first week of July and that for the past few years anyway has been accompanied by the Aquatic Carnival, in which brightly lit boats blaring music and filled with shimmying dancers skim about in the harbor like, well, floats. In 2011, the large crowds down on Alameda that night were mostly interested in walking along among the many food and beverage stands lining Alameda, although many also watched the large thatched frame of wooden poles that was burned, surging with excitement when the conflagration caught and shot several stories high. Several dozen people briefly began running around the bonfire until its tremendous heat drove them back and the entire mass of watching people began racing back, away from the fire. I felt a moment of terror as I rushed my daughter out of the way to keep her from being trampled, which for a moment seemed a real danger. This sequence of excitement then panic sweeping the crowd struck me as a rare moment where the crowd was in control of the event, rather than the officials who planned and scripted the bonfire or the many police posted everywhere to keep order.

By the time of the Burning of the Devil, the gradual build-up into carnival was already evident in the construction of temporary stalls for food and beverage vendors along some routes and viewing stands for official processions along the central thoroughfare of Garzón, along the eastern axis of the city away from the harbor. There was also increasing preparatory activity among carnival comparsas or performing groups: rehearsals and preparation of costumes and props, all of which had been under way by May and June, but were now in heightened preparations. The sounds of congas, all driving percussion and blaring coronet, were heard more and more frequently, eventually moving out of enclosed rehearsal spaces onto streets in the heart of their neighborhoods, and from there in ever-larger arcs out across the city on "visits." From the grassroots perspective of those who participate in the congas, the preparations are punctuated by the biggest "visit" of all, the Invasion, when the Conga de los Hoyos "breaks carnival" (*rompe carnaval*) in what members of that conga agree is an old, deep tradition.

Officially speaking, there are several weeks of hiatus and final preparation between the end of the Festival del Caribe and the start of carnival week, when all the carnival comparsas and floats will gather almost daily just east of the Plaza de Marte and process one at a time, down Garzón Avenue into the funnel created between the stands, where they will direct their formally choreographed, often quite elaborate performances for the jury seated in the stands on the north side of the street. In the early evening, children's comparsas gather for the processions and competition of children's carnival, and later in the evening, the adult comparsas and floats gather for carnival. The first and last days are processions involving all the performing groups, while the middle days feature a smaller list of ensembles each day that perform their full choreographies for the competition, followed by a day of prizes, in which each group processes down in front of the jury to hear the public announcement of which, if any, prizes they as a whole or their individual members may have won. This entire, carefully orchestrated spectacle is not particularly well-attended, since the stands are restricted to officially appointed jury members and those connected with them on one side and paid-admission seating on the other, and most residents of the city seem to pay it little attention, aside from the inconvenience of its disruption of traffic along a main city artery. One can watch highlights filmed from the judge's vantage point on TV and read the results in the listing of carnival prizes published in the official regional newspaper *Sierra Maestre* on the day after, in any case. Many more would-be spectators cram the crowd-control barriers at either end of the stands, leaning in for a glance at the performers as they march past, but almost none of the actual choreographed performances can be seen from this angle, since performances are directed to the carnival jury only. So the crowds at the edges of official carnival engage in more carnivalesque activities, such as drinking the plentiful beer, buying street food and trinkets, sharing draughts from bottles of cane liquor, and socializing.

Meanwhile, throughout all of July, many residents of Santiago who may not encounter the live sounds of a conga and who may only see bits of official carnival on the TV news will participate in the general entertainments of grassroots carnival by going out onto the streets and joining in the socializing, eating, and above all drinking of the season. All around the city, zones are set up with beer trucks and food vendors, and occasional outdoor stereo systems booming, like as not, reggaeton as the popular music of the moment. When people talk about the recreational opportunities of carnival, the three areas most often mentioned are the avenues of la Trocha, south of the historic city center, and Martí, on the north side, and the neighborhood of Sueño, which has kept its prerevolution status as middle class, in contrast to the lower-class neighborhoods surrounding Trocha and Martí. Of the three, Sueño's various streets dedicated to music videos or small carnival rides or the most up-to-date reggaeton seem most popular with crowds of younger people, including those who flock into the city bus station near Sueño for a night on the town. Trocha and Martí are crowded every night as well, but people's perceptions are that they are frequented mostly by their own surrounding neighborhoods, rather than drawing residents from elsewhere in the city. Certainly, my observations of Martí at various points of the afternoon and evening during carnival was that entire families would be out together, and that my Cuban companions from Los Hoyos would almost constantly be greeting people they knew.

Quite in contrast to the dire warnings Cuban friends would give me about venturing out into the carnival on Martí, the street scene I witnessed on actually going down to Martí ("me voy pa' Martí," as Santiagueros would say) during the start of the Invasion and at night several times during the height of official carnival was a calmly festive atmosphere of entire families strolling along with even the youngest of children, groups of friends sitting together in the grassy parks of the boulevard to chat, drink beer, and hail other friends as they passed, teens gathered around impossibly loud reggaeton on sound systems, and lines of people getting all manner of treats from the vendors whose stands lined the street (see fig. 3.6). Aside from sites of loud, recorded music,

FIGURE 3.6 A rainy late afternoon of grassroots carnival on the Paseo de Martí in Los Hoyos, Santiago de Cuba, July 24, 2011. Photo by author.

there was little more than a lively buzz of hundreds of people in the street enjoying themselves. Like any other urban area, I can imagine (and know from friends' stories) that a quiet, dark side street, late at night, could provide opportunities for thieves and that people who have consumed too much alcohol can sometimes become belligerent, but the feel of grassroots carnival as it unfolded around me was nothing like the juicy discourse about how dangerous things had gotten. And even on those occasions where I walked across the city returning home from late-night official carnival at 2 or 3 AM, it was calm and quiet away from the busy streets of grassroots carnival.

Not only did Cubans regard locations of the carnivalesque on Martí and Trocha as potentially dangerous in their disorder, which I interpret to be instantiations of longstanding discourses in carnival's history. Moreover, in 2011 I heard Cuban residents and frequent foreign visitors alike bemoan how things were deteriorating, with drunken men carrying knives, bolder thieves who would surely rip my camera right out of my hands, and other criminal problems they never used to see or found worse than in the past. All this to say that grassroots carnival was constructed, in discourse and other forms of social action, to be a time of heightened and possibly worsening social danger because of its unruly crowds.

Local discourses about carnival locations, activities, groups, and social dangers are generally indirectly rather than explicitly racially coded. For example, residents of Santiago draw on shared knowledge about the prerevolutionary social status of different neighborhoods in what had been a racially and class-segregated city. In largely ignoring a half-century of the revolution's interventions in residence patterns and opportunities for social mobility, Santiagueros instead give weight to the heritage of neighborhoods: certain neighborhoods have a history of enthusiastically supporting their congas. In an interview-based study about Los Hoyos, for example, Causse Cathcart (2006) found that residents most often defined their neighborhood in terms of the conga and its tradition, which certainly corresponds to how community outsiders see Los Hoyos. Other neighborhoods may have carnival comparsas that are considered more elegant, but without the mass support. And some neighborhoods have no comparsas and are not expected to be able to support one because residents are not interested. Those who do want to participate must walk to a different neighborhood to do so, thereby reinforcing the normative view of where comparsas and their festive noise belong and don't belong. In like manner, each carnival comparsa has a reputation that encapsulates and reinforces what people "already know" about that neighborhood. Individual interest and participation in carnival need not reflect racial or neighborhood identifications, but entrenched assumptions about racial and neighborhood levels of interest mark individuals coming from "outside" as interested *in spite of* coming from outside the neighborhood, just as those who live in a neighborhood like Los Hoyos will be shrugged off as atypical (or as not "really" belonging) if they are not aficionados of the conga.

To understand the racializing consequences of this sort of implicit knowledge that people acted on but only made explicit, in my experience, when my questions required them to, the notion of indirect indexicality can help explain how signs are mobilized to stand for social groups. In proposing the notion of indirect indexicality, Ochs (1992) makes an elegant argument about the relationship between language and gender, saying that it is seldom the case that a feature of speech directly and exclusively correlates with a gendered identity but, rather, it is more common that a feature or constellation of features performs pragmatic work such as taking a stance or engaging in social action that, in turn, "helps to constitute the image of gender" (343). One of her examples is self-lowering speech, for example, when a caregiver accommodates to a child's communicative capacity. She suggests that consistent patterns of self-lowering interactionally achieve a durable lower relative status for the caregiver, constituting the gendered role of "mother" in that image.

Silverstein (2003) elaborates on the relationship between different orders of indexicality at the pragmatic level, where a sign indexes a stance or attribute, and at more reflexive metapragmatic levels that take up such first-order indexical links to do additional, ideologically saturated work. Some of his examples concern the ways in which honorific forms of address (*Vous* forms) that at one level index the higher relative status of the addressee to the "humbled" speaker also serve almost the opposite expressive function at a second level of indexicality by demonstrating the *speaker's* refinement in deploying such refined language. Such honorific patterns of usage can then be taken up as the object of higher levels of indexicality, in which particular usages are read, for example, as "more democratic" or more hierarchical, as more or less modern than others, creating complex, multileveled indexical orders that, as ever-emergent structures, always have the potential for new, higher indexical levels constituting new performative effects.

To apply this notion of indirect indexicality producing entire orders of social significance to the connection between carnival and Blackness, it's not the case that the carnivalesque is Black in any direct or exclusive way but, rather, that the carnivalesque and Blackness entail one another through the mediation of indexical regimes, in which, for example, these domains overlap in their associations with both folk tradition and fun-loving personae and with unruliness and social danger. Through these intermediary indexical links and their ideological entailments, they point to and implicate one another. Arrollándose is how the body—any body—naturally responds to the conga, music of carnival out of traditionally Black neighborhoods. And through this association of place, cultural practice, and body, the quintessential body arrollándose is racialized as Black and located in Los Hoyos as part of a crowd following its beloved conga.

Another way of thinking about the workings of indirect indexicality in constituting Blackness and the carnivalesque in relation to each other concerns presupposed contrasts between marked versus unmarked categories: Cubans treat Black bodies arrollándose as unmarked and expected, while bodies arrollándose that stubbornly remain White are marked as unusual and worthy of note; Black neighborhoods are the presupposed sites of the carnivalesque within Santiago, just as Santiago is the site par excellence of carnival within Cuba. And because Santiagueros understand carnival traditions to be deepest and most fully realized by particular older neighborhoods associated with poor, lower-class, and Black sectors of the population, they expect these locations to be sites of greater potential danger during carnival (and more generally). For those living in other neighborhoods, petty crime and drunken violence are expected risks of venturing into Los Hoyos, especially during carnival—risks not associated with neighborhoods having higher social standing. To understand how the vast crowd of variously raced bodies that comes out arrollándose during carnival nonetheless comes to instantiate Blackness, as an intrinsic property of only some of those bodies and persons that nonetheless can spread to others (infectiously, as the trope is usually understood), we need to look to the workings of ideologies of embodiment and how these are rendered evident and meaningful in carnival practices.

The Invasion of the Conga de los Hoyos

I will discuss the Invasion as the emblematic carnivalesque moment in Santiago's carnival in order to show the workings of indirect indexicality in the racializing processes of carnival, through which physical locations and bodily movements through those spaces come to signify Blackness. The sensuous experience of participating in the Invasion is key: it is not a spectacle to be watched—although some of those who live along its route do stand on porches and roofs to observe the massive river of humanity that passes by—so much as an event of crowd participation. There does not seem to be another annual procession to match it; certainly May Day rallies and other official events bring out thousands, but many participate because they have to or because of incentives through their workplace, and they are assembled to spectate and to be filmed as "the masses" for TV spectators.

The Invasion is different: it is, like the revolution in Gil Scott-Heron's 1970 Motown song "The Revolution Will Not Be Televised," expressly not broadcast. It is a grassroots exercise in mass participation and historical commemoration, since it refers to a series of decisive battles across the island during the second war for independence (see chap. 5, n11). But for all that the Invasion is local in the route it takes, tracing out and reinforcing neighborhood differences and allegiances. It can also be read as a grassroots mass mobilization—certainly, that is what it *looks* like—which undoubtedly is why it does not receive the state-run media coverage of official carnival events. Interestingly, as a sort of open secret in which the populace and state both know the state merely tolerates and tries to downplay this massive, unpublicized event that everyone knows about anyway, some state-orchestrated events occasionally attempt to co-opt the Invasion's energetic, grassroots ethos by, for example, having a conga conclude the city's 2010 May Day parade, aboard a flatbed truck bearing the slogan "Unidos productivos y eficientes" (United productive and efficient) that was surrounded by a crowd marching in time, if not exactly arrollándose.[21] Such attempts at recontextualization can only partially capture the energy of the Invasion, where the conga walks (not rides) its special peregrination.

The actual Invasion is much less contained, with most people participating rather than spectating. Sometime during the week before official carnival's parades, the Conga de los Hoyos gets a government permit to "break carnival," as they say, with a massive walking tour around the neighborhoods that ring the historic city center. Once the date is set—it was a Saturday in 2011—word spreads like wildfire through Los Hoyos and other neighborhoods along the route. That weekend morning in 2011, I joined the conga's director and some other members to walk out to the city's Saint Ifigenia Cemetery ahead of the midday heat in order to pay their respects at the tomb of the conga's famous previous director, Chan, who died from injuries caused by a falling tree a decade ago, and to invoke his spirit's protection for the Invasion. After prayers, libations of sprayed and poured rum, some Spiritist prayers led by Chan's daughter, and a solo by the Chinese coronet player, Guaraní, that could have wakened the dead with its piercing beauty, we walked back to Los Hoyos ensured of Chan's beneficent presence in the day's events. As I made my way up to my house, I passed two teenagers who were discussing the afternoon's Invasion: the buzz about the event was in the air.

In the midafternoon, with the searing sun still overhead, an enormous crowd was building along the Paseo de Martí and its side streets, as conga musicians prepared their instruments inside their cultural center. Out on the street, vendors carrying trays and towers of various sweets were milling about through a swelling crowd of people meeting up with friends. As for costumes, there weren't many in evidence. A few people were carrying colorful umbrellas against the sun, and here and there were a handful of men who had dressed in women's clothing—mostly miniskirts and halter tops, some padded and others not—with head kerchiefs or garish, long-haired wigs. One cross-dressing friend, an openly gay santero, was carefully made up, stylishly outfitted in a tight red Lycra sundress, coiffed in a red-haired wig, and carrying a purse that he opened to reveal a bottle of rum. Other cross-dressing men seemed to be trying for outlandish excess or parody. Aside from this handful of cross-dressers, I came across just one elderly gentleman dressed in pink satin carnival finery of the sort that comparsas don for the official competition, wearing a Venetian-style feathered and sequined mask, topped off with a decorated umbrella.

Some people had tucked a sprig of *porsiana* behind their ears—commonly done to avoid spiritual contamination in folk religious ceremonies. A street procession, too, would activate spiritual energies and carry the risk of stirring up bad as well as good energies. A few people evidently walked the route almost as a pilgrimage that would spiritually charge them—for instance, one fellow foreigner who is a santero dressed in a vest and pants made of burlap and lined with purple on behalf of San Lázaro. And my cross-dressed santero friend, hours later and on the other side of the city, would open his purse to dispense purifications to friends and passersby, sweeping us with a *porsiana* branch, spraying us with rum (and giving out swigs from his miraculously never-empty bottle), carefully applying lipstick to a few people—discharging the positive energies accumulated by walking the route.

But at the start of the route, we milled about bumping into acquaintances and waiting on Martí with thousands of other residents. Eventually drum sounds approached where we waited on a corner: it was a set of consecrated batá drums played by initiated drummers and leading call-and-response ritual songs typical of Santería ceremonies and saints' day processions. Nonetheless, those dancing alongside them were arrollándose, not dancing the steps of oricha ceremonies. Bringing out the batá drums is a recent innovation, started only a few years ago, but the batá's owner, Pipo, is part of the illustrious Reynerio Pérez family prominent in Santería, and his drums have come to be emblematic of the neighborhood called Los Olmos, which is contiguous to and sometimes considered part of Los Hoyos. In the late 1990s, Pipo had successfully applied to the local government to restart a dormant tradition of holding a street procession around Los Hoyos in honor of Santa Bárbara on her day, December 4, so his consecrated batá drums have themselves become fixtures of street processions. Unlike the many other comparsas we passed during the Invasion, the batás walked the entire route as a sort of honor guard, rather than staying in the neighborhood's "territory" and saluting the Conga de los Hoyos as it passed.

With our Cuban hosts greatly concerned about the safety of the small group of foreigners I was with, we were urgently herded in ahead of the batá drums, hemmed in by Cuban friends determined to protect us from the many drunks and criminals they were sure would be attracted to our foreignness. Indeed, for much of the day I felt like a chaperoned virgin, with one man who was warned off from trying to approach me calling back, "you go well-protected." And we began to walk and dance the route of the Invasion, with the batá drums and their supporters following us and the Conga de los Hoyos further behind them and the crowd stretching for endless blocks behind them over the full expanse of the avenue and sidewalks, like a river at flood stage.

As we walked and danced in the leading edge, the crowd proceeded up Martí, soon passing the blowing conch shell and drum rhythms of the Tumba Francesa society and the relatively new conga called los Muñequitos, serenading us as we passed out of Los Hoyos. We walked into the Sueño neighborhood past the bright orange walls of the Moncada, long since converted into a school, and down part of Garzón Avenue, well above the official carnival stands, crossing into the southern ring of neighborhoods beginning with Alto Pino, which took us past the Conga de Alto Pino, then the Conga de Guayabito. The lead singer of Cutumba (Manolo, from the introduction) greeted us from the sidewalk then joined the batá drummers, taking over the lead singing role for a while to relieve those who had already walked so far in such heat. We passed the furiously playing Conga de San Agustín, almost as old and illustrious as the Conga de los Hoyos and with a similar degree of deep neighborhood fidelity, then started down the long hill to la Trocha Avenue, passing the Carabalí Olugo's building, which was open although no Carabalí musicians were playing. Friends there told me they would shortly have a rehearsal, presumably after the Invasion had passed.

Walking down past the Conga de Veguita Galo and the Conga del Paso Franco, we paused to look back uphill at the stream of humanity pouring along the entire length and width of the avenue above us, as far as we could see. The Conga de los Hoyos musicians were neither visible nor audible, as they were so far back. From la Trocha, having passed all the congas receiving the los Hoyos visit, we would continue toward the harbor, cutting over on Cristina Street to Alameda along the waterfront until reaching the far end of Martí across from the train station at last. From there, the Conga de los Hoyos and its loyal crowd would walk the many now darkening blocks back up to their cultural center, where a crew of women who had stayed behind had prepared an enormous pot of stew for the musicians and other members and their friends, and where the festivities would continue from their midevening return until late at night. As we passed each conga along the route, they would play and the supporting crowd around them would respond with singing, clapping, and dancing, with those of us in the passing crowd stopping to chat or commencing to arrollarse for a bit, until we would move on and the music behind us would fade into the sounds of the crowd.

The presence of police on the street, generally evident in downtown Santiago, is heightened during carnival season. During every day of "official carnival," army personnel (mostly young women doing their compulsory military service) formed a cordon across the uphill side of the judging stands performance area, challenging anyone who was accompanying the performing ensembles without a proper badge or who tried to breach the metal crowd barriers funneling down to the stands. Police were less evident, but occasionally made their presence known with noisy sirens in the midst of street festivities in other parts of the city. But most impressive was the massive police cordon set up on the Invasion's route. All along our route, police had been standing at every cross street with their cars and motorcycles forming a blockade behind them. But the massive cordon blocking the entire street was set up about halfway around the route and several hours into it, at a point when everyone had been steadily drinking rum and beer in the hot sun for a good while, and at a point along the major "grassroots" carnival site of La Trocha, forming a southern bracket around the central city core to match the Paseo de Martí's bracket to the north. The group of friends I was with, newly filled plastic bottles of rum and beer in hand, had just passed through a cordon of baton-wielding police officers stretched across the street into an area where a dozen police cars had amassed. We turned to watch more police officers join the cordon until they were standing shoulder to shoulder and facing uphill away from us and toward the multitude now streaming down Trocha like an avalanche. The locals among us pulled the curious foreigners along urgently, so we did not stay to see how well the human sieve of police officers held up to the thousands of revelers straining through while, presumably, removing any "dangerous elements."

The Invasion is a momentous annual event, a walked and danced route of "moving tradition" that builds up the communitas of the crowd to levels I never witnessed on any other occasion and that is unsurprisingly officially treated as potentially explosive even as it is tolerated only with heavy police presence. At the same time that the Invasion unites those who participate in it, it reinforces the sense of neighborhood distinctiveness and belonging as the Conga de los Hoyos and those who accompany it pass noisily through sonically defined territories of other congas. The congas who wait in their "territories" play their music to simultaneously welcome and challenge the Conga de los Hoyos. The Invasion does not encompass the entire city (much as it begins to feel that way by the third or fourth hour) but circles the "historical shell" of traditionally Black neighborhoods, circumambulating the downtown center without actually entering it. Where the Invasion passes, the regular flows of city life must stop and wait ("lock your door behind us!" declared my friend to a man whose house we had dropped by to visit and rest a moment en route). But it would be quite possible to have a normal day elsewhere in the city's more upscale or outlying neighborhoods, or indeed, in the city center, and remain oblivious to the Invasion occurring elsewhere in the city. Nor does it seem to be televised or mentioned in the papers, unlike the performances of official carnival. And yet, for those who participate in this grassroots event and accompany the Conga de los Hoyos on its route of visitations, the Invasion re-creates Los Hoyos and its conga as the focal point of carnival tradition and the carnivalesque, connecting them to the other sites most emblematic of Black carnival tradition in the city. That chain of sites *becomes* emblematic precisely by receiving the Conga de los Hoyos with their congas.

The Invasion is nothing if not a visceral embodied experience that takes those who walk it on a journey of anticipatory excitement and sensual enjoyment, then satiation, in alternating cycles of complete exhaustion and renewal, aided by conga music and plentiful drink, shared around. The route is punctuated by the sounds of congas welcoming the crowd as they announce their territory and playfully compete with the Conga de los Hoyos by playing as loudly and jauntily as they can, inciting the crowd to stop, gather, sing, and arrollarse, showing its enjoyment of the rhythms. "Winning" is judged by crowd response. The congas' music calls out to all; as that long-ago carnival observer reported, one would have to be dead not to respond to those rhythms. But the very route taken and neighborhoods called on in the Invasion preselect who will be within earshot and who will be represented in that crowd. And thus does the Conga de los Hoyos's Invasion become yet another performance of Blackness—not just because of who actually participates, since "anyone" can and does, but because the route itself traces out the carnivalesque as a set of traditions rooted in Black neighborhoods and demonstrates those traditions to be about drumming, dancing, and carousing. Even those of us—and there were many—who remained racially marked as White despite our arrollándose stood out as White against a presumed crowd of "Blacks from Los Hoyos": who else would so passionately follow their conga?

Ideologies of Embodiment, as Enacted in a Children's *Conguita*

So far, I have introduced the locations, performances, and discourses of carnival—official and grassroots—by way of providing context for all kinds of activity that occurs beyond but is constitutive of the main events of official carnival. Practices that socialize children into carnival and carnivalesque practices are one crucial site producing the indirectly racializing effects of carnival, as I will explore in this section. I have suggested that the practices of carnival and their discursive representations produce an overlapping and nested fractal series of identifications beginning with *Cubanidad* and then contrasting Cuba's *Oriente* with its West, Santiago's urban center with its historical periphery (and that with its more recent outlying neighborhoods, as a series of concentric circles). Beyond those identifications are others contrasting middle-class and White neighborhoods with lower-class and Black neighborhoods, official carnival with the grassroots carnivalesque, and Blackness itself with Whiteness. As attested in moments of discourse where various oppositions are invoked, this might seem an abstract diagram of social relationships. But these relationships also emerge in people's lived experiences and, particularly, in their movements through and orientations to the physical spaces that map these contrasts. These paired oppositions align with other pairs in the series to ground expectations about bodily dispositions and aptitudes, deeply held feelings about who will carry the conga tradition in the blood and who will "naturally" respond to conga rhythms by arrollándose fully and richly.

The nested oppositions constituting grassroots and official, Black and White, Santiago and the nation, thus also inform ideologies of embodiment, so that racial identifications exceed (and sometimes defy) mere familial descent, mere phenotype. How could it be otherwise in a society that simultaneously embraces the logics of *mestizaje* and racial exclusion, of both phenotypic and cultural Blackness? Blackness is on the one hand physically marked by phenotype but on the other hand cannot simply be reduced to phenotype, which after all may be unpredictable, with one child surprisingly dark (but still mulata) and another surprisingly White (as with a friend's grandchild whom everyone calls el Blanquito to mark how much he stands out from the rest of his family), and with complicating factors in recognized individual dispositions toward "refinement" or allegiance to place and tradition that may not be congruent with racial stereotypes. Then too, racial identifications are a question of context, and to be from Los Hoyos (or Tivolí, or San Agustín, or Veguita de Galo, or to play in the conga, any conga) is to be presumed (phenotypically or genealogically) Black or to undergo Blackening by association with Black cultural forms. Even more fleeting is to join the crowd arrollándose along with the conga and become part of a performance of (cultural) Blackness.

As a final example, I now turn to the officially recognized training ground for carnival traditions: the children's comparsas. Adult comparsas—congas, *paseos*, folklore societies like the Carabalí—have presumably always incorporated some young people to train and socialize them into their practices. But beginning in the mid-1990s, the Ministry of Culture began to develop children's comparsas for a separate children's carnival, which would precede the late-night adult carnival and provide an organized activity formally introducing children to national folklore through local tradition, as well as another telegenic event. Elian Acosta, a writer who headed Santiago's Union of Writers and Artists of Cuba (UNEAC), is credited with proposing the first children's carnival in the mid-1990s, together with local director and impresario William Ortiz. Maritza Martínez Martínez—whose father had been director of the Conga de los Hoyos and who had grown up dancing in the conga, worked as a caretaker of the conga's cultural center, and received professional training as a cultural promoter—got involved in what is widely called the *conguita* or children's conga (see fig. 6.1). Since 1995 she has served as the director of the Conguita of los Hoyos, a position that provides a (very small) seasonal supplemental salary and that she clearly holds as a labor of love.

In interviews, Maritza emphasized the necessity of the conguita and children's carnival to preserve the tradition and inculcate the sense of neighborhood belonging among youth, suggesting that today's youth were in danger of losing these connections and that the mechanisms of official carnival would rescue the traditions. In a March 2010 conversation, Maritza juxtaposed this argument about the potential for losing the tradition with the idiom of carrying it in the blood, implying that this metaphor, which might seem to be a question of genealogical inheritance, is just as much a result of early saturation in the tradition. That is, she explained the conga not as an inherently racialized cultural heritage but as one emplaced in neighborhood life: society must encourage those neighborhood-oriented ties of community for the tradition to continue. She had been explaining to me that those who step up to direct a carnival comparsa can only be successful if they love the tradition. The conversation proceeded as follows.

MARITZA MARTÍNEZ MARTÍNEZ: You carry it in the blood. That thing you carry in the blood. Because you love it. If you don't love it, Kristina—

KW: Uh-huh.

MARITZA MARTÍNEZ MARTÍNEZ: —because, li::ke, how many people . look, I've been going fifteen going on sixteen years as children's director. But I carry it in my blood, I have it from my dad, since I was a kid I thought that I am going be, be the director and told him but of course with the children's conga, and since then it has been rescuing the culture, the children's congas.[22]

A few moments later, after recounting some of the children's conga history, she continued: "The people, the majority specialize in the conga still. But the youth who go out, you have to grab those who love it and put them in a children's comparsa for the adult not to lose the tradition."[23] In describing her work, Maritza did not distinguish between what I have described as the carnivalesque, involving the Invasion, and the official, involving competitive displays before the carnival jury. I came to see the children's congas as a site connecting the two sides of carnival, channeling children's carnivalesque energy into a disciplined ensemble performance that would win a carnival prize and, in doing so, build neighborhood pride and allegiance that would find its fullest expression in carnivalesque participation in the neighborhood conga.

Let me linger a moment in describing the work of adults in the conguita, since every comparsa—and particularly, every children's comparsa—requires long hours from dedicated volunteers willing to undertake not only the training and artistic design but also the organizational effort and the additional struggle for scarce resources in order to provide instruments, costumes, and props. Maritza had an assistant director in charge of the musical ensemble and an assistant director in charge of choreography, each of whom led rehearsals of musicians and dancers, enacting the overall plan Maritza created for each year's performance. A small group of additional assistants, all of whom lived in the neighborhood and had children or grandchildren involved in the conguita, helped with bookkeeping, attendance, and discipline. During the years between 2007 and 2011, all except the young assistant director of music were women. Each received a salary supplement even smaller than the director's and participated, it seemed, more out of passion for the conga than for the extra cash. The personnel of the conguita exemplify one kind of involvement in carnival, for those few who embrace official carnival's pomp and dedicate themselves to preparing the most spectacular show they can for its competition. Indeed, each year when I interviewed Maritza, even if it was during February, she would rattle off which prizes the conguita had won in recent years (as well as which other children's congas had won the grand prize or first place, if not her beloved conguita).

She described her process of gathering ideas for each year's choreography and theme for performance as lasting throughout each year, as she watched children's TV programming, listened to pop songs, and attended to which revolutionary anniversaries were being marked that year. In February and March she would meet with the other conguita personnel to develop her ideas for a theme and its choreographic, costume, and musical elements, so that by late April and early May, when they called for auditions and rehearsals, they would have a detailed plan ready.

Carnival performances follow complex rules, as there are several expected categories of performers who each perform their own piece within the larger performance. In addition to the musicians, who must play rhythms appropriate to their kind of comparsa, there are flag carriers, who race around and around the other performers waving their banners announcing the name of the group (fig. 3.7). Right behind them are the "lanterns" or *farolas*, oversized lamps made of paper and bedecked with streamers, held on tall poles (see fig. 3.2). These might once have been actual lanterns, but in these times of

FIGURE 3.7 Banners for the Cabildo Carabalí Isuama before the opening parade of official carnival, July 21, 2011. Photo by author.

scarcity, they are merely the idea of lanterns and do not actually light up. Next comes a line of *caperos*, or wearers of capes, displaying billowing capes bearing designs they themselves have made: a sequined clown, a lion's head, abstract sparkling patterns (fig. 3.8). Then a small group of specially costumed performers will proceed down the performance area; the group may include clowns or other masked figures. Traditional characters that appear include devils and skeletons, stiltwalkers, and dancers wearing a horse costume around their waist, called "Santiago on horseback" and evoking images of the patron saint on his horse. In recent years, very young children in costumes, led by an adult, or older kids on rollerblades or in costumes representing the orichas of Santería may also perform in this initial group. Most performers, however, are part of one of the large groups of dancers that form the largest part of the performing conga. The children performers are separated by age, and some corps may consist of dancing pairs of boys and girls, while others are entirely composed of girls, as there are far more girls than boys who wish to dance. Each corps will have its own costume and choreography, and when it takes center stage to perform, the other corps will do the same dance to each side, awaiting their turn to perform center stage. The children's comparsas may also include a small float—perhaps a bicycle-taxi converted into an elegant coach for two dancers dressed as flowers or orichas, or a rolling boat bearing children dressed as navy sailors (fig. 3.9).

FIGURE 3.8 A children's carnival performer displays his cape before a performance, Santiago de Cuba, July 27, 2011. Photo by author.

Although boys and girls could ostensibly perform in any role, the roles they took reflected strong gender preferences, as was evident when I attended the Conga de los Hoyos' day of auditions: almost all the boys who showed up aspired to play conga among the musicians. Those whose drumming skills do not make the cut end up being the flag bearers, lantern carriers, cape wearers, and male pairs for the couples corps. In the years I've studied and observed the children's congas, there have not been any girls among the musicians, and the adult directors tell me that it is rare to have girls play, since they would rather dance.

As decisions were made, during auditions, one of the adults charged with bookkeeping painstakingly recorded each child's name and designated role in a small, battered school notebook that she would often consult during rehearsals, to keep track of attendance, and later, clothing and shoe sizes for costumes.[24] Being involved at this level gives children more exposure to the rhythms than they'd get simply watching, thus making it possible eventually to graduate up into the ranks of the musicians.

Some kids participate because other family members are active in the conga; others gravitate toward the conga because it is prominent in their neighborhood, and yet others are recruited by the adult personnel. Maritza has repeatedly assured me that the conguita does not need to do any recruiting because more kids than she can incorporate always show up to express

FIGURE 3.9 The Paseo La Rosa Blanca's carnival performance included this float holding two girls dressed in blue gowns representing the colors of Yemayá, the oricha of the ocean, Santiago de Cuba, July 23, 2011. Photo by the author.

their interest. Almost all live in Los Hoyos. Maritza made her expectations for fidelity to one's own neighborhood's conga clear, for example, in telling me a story about a girl who had danced in the conguita one year, then gone to a different comparsa the next, then tried to come back to the conguita. Maritza reported telling the girl she was a traitor and thus no longer welcome in the conguita, to teach her a lesson about where her allegiance should be. Since the congas compete, they strive to keep their performance plans from their competitors. As I am known to visit different groups, I have been jokingly but pointedly asked whether I am a spy when I watch a rehearsal. Maritza repeatedly emphasized, in our conversations, that allegiance to one's own neighborhood was essential. In practice, some people do cross into other neighborhoods to join comparsas. The conguita's choreographer, for example, came with her granddaughter from Tivolí to participate in the Conguita de los Hoyos, which she explained as due to longstanding participation in the cultural life of Los Hoyos.

Neighborhood belonging was also described to me by many carnival participants in terms of deep familiarity with one's own conga's sound. Maritza, among numerous others, told me that anyone involved with the conga, including many neighborhood residents in a place like Los Hoyos, could recognize a conga from far off just by hearing its distinctive *toque* or beat. Several

FIGURE 3.10 A box filled with doves waits under a sheet in the Cultural Center of the Conga de los Hoyos for its role as the *gallo tapado* or surprise of the carnival performance, in front of banners for the adult Conga's performance, July 24, 2011. Photo by the author.

times, she and various musicians tried to sing or tap out just what made the Conga de los Hoyos, for example, sound so unique. One would emphasize the deep sound of the *bokú*, and another the rapid interplay of the *campanas*, succeeding only in confusing me further about what differences they were hearing despite varying musicians and songs. Alas, I have not (yet) developed the ear that comes of long neighborhood familiarity with one's conga.

The priority placed on allegiance to the conga as a closed group is also reinforced by a longstanding tradition of official carnival, in which each group reveals a surprise, charmingly called a *gallo tapado* or "covered rooster," during its performance before the jury. The conguita's *gallo tapado* in 2011 was carried down before the jurors' stand as a large box draped with a sheet (fig. 3.10). When the sheet was pulled off, a cage full of doves was revealed, and, after a firm shake of the box, the doves flew off, symbolizing peace. A second planned aspect of the *gallo tapado*, foiled by the absence of one of the speakers, was to have the two American girls dancing in the conguita that year step up to the microphone to read a short statement about peace for World Children's Day in English that would be repeated in Spanish, where the bilingual repetition stood for intercultural diversity and understanding. The presentation of the *gallo tapado* was not rehearsed during the large-group rehearsals—the children who were to be involved were taken aside to be

FIGURE 3.11 Director Maritza Martínez rehearses a group of the youngest dancers, while the musical director rehearses the musicians of the Children's Conga de los Hoyos, Santiago de Cuba, May 10, 2010. Photo by the author.

coached, and the director herself delivered the box of doves, all to maintain the surprise.

During musical auditions and early rehearsals, such as those I sat in on during May 2008 and 2010, the conguita's choreographer, Mabel, worked on dance steps with small groups of the youngest girls—generally ages five to ten, some of whom were new participants. The juxtaposition between the two concurrent rehearsals was telling: the boys and girls had different foci of activity that were nonetheless linked because the boys' music, led by the male musical director, dominated the space and determined when the choreographer would be able lead the girls in dancing and when she would be able to explain choreographic elements she modeled for them. I suspect that the conguita was typical not just in its sharply gendered differentiation of performing roles, obvious in all of the comparsas, but also in the dual foci of activity, which I also saw in concurrent rehearsals of dancers and musicians in the Carabalí Olugo's children's group (fig. 3.11).

The boys who play in the conguita are impressively accomplished, even including two young teen-aged Chinese coronet players (many children's congas rely on an adult coronet player because the instrument is difficult and requires a lot of breath control). But those who are newer, especially in the younger of the two children's ensembles, still need help with the subtleties of

FIGURE 3.12 The musical director of the Cabildo Carabalí Olugo children's group taps a rhythm on the shoulder of a young drummer, Santiago de Cuba, May 2, 2010. Photo by the author.

rhythms and drumming techniques. A common teaching technique I have seen in the rehearsals of several different groups, and even in other settings such as batá drumming during ceremonies, is to first model the proper way to play a section and have the student repeat it, then to have one or all of the musicians play it repeatedly, while the teacher stands behind a drummer, beating out the rhythm on his shoulders as he plays until he gets it right without help (fig. 3.12).

While the musical rehearsal proceeds with these fits and starts of practicing particular rhythms, then particular songs, then transitions between songs, until the entire performance sequence is mastered, the choreographer teaches the choreographic elements needed for the dance performance. Even during auditions, I never saw Mabel need to teach even the youngest dancer the basic conga step nor the subtle array of torso movements that accompany and enrich the basic back-and-forth shifting of weight between feet and accompanying hip movements. This was different than the expectations of the Carabalí comparsas, which taught year-round classes for children to learn the Carabalí rhythms and steps, in preparation for forming their children's carnival comparsas. During an early May rehearsal, I once did see Mabel correct one girl's overly wide stance—spreading your legs apart helps accentuate the all-important swinging and gyrating of the hips, but the goal is to get that degree of movement even with a stance no more

FIGURE 3.13 Maritza Martínez shows a toddler how to *arrollarse* during a Children's Conga de los Hoyos rehearsal. The toddler, a younger sibling waiting for one of the dancers, had begun swaying to the music on her own. Santiago de Cuba, May 10, 2010. Photo by the author.

than shoulder's width apart. Even in the case of my daughter and another American girl dancing in the conguita that year, they were simply put in line and told to follow the others; the steps of arrollándose were expected to develop automatically through exposure, as they clearly had for the Cuban children (see fig. 3.13). Instead, Mabel rehearsed the girls on modifying the steps to, for example, jump rope or dance in figures with the other girls while arrollándose.

Since conga carnival performances typically present an array of song and dance genres, adapted to be played with basic conga instrumentation and rhythms, the girls also learned steps like the *pilón* or *casino* or even hip-hop, popular dance steps, or more folkloric dance steps such as rumba that would be used in their corps' particular choreography, which might run as long as five minutes and involve a series of songs and transitions. During breaks in the dance rehearsal, if the drumming continued, the girls would sometimes begin dancing the much more suggestive moves of reggaeton from music videos—an interesting counterpoint to the choreographed skipping and children's games the choreographer led them in rehearsing.

Different groups of dancers were scheduled to rehearse on different nights of the week, with older teens needing fewer early rehearsals than younger kids. By late June, the directors would begin consolidating the rehearsals to block

FIGURE 3.14 The Children's Conga de los Hoyos choreographer, Mabel Castro, rehearses one group of dancers on the street in front of the director's house in Los Hoyos, Santiago de Cuba, July 13, 2011. Photo by the author.

out larger sections of the performance, and in July, they moved to whole-ensemble rehearsals out on the street in front of the director's house. Several evenings a week, around 5 PM, the kids would arrive and be organized by the directors and various adult aides into their corps, each of which would then block out its full performance (see figs. 3.14 and 3.15). The choreographer counted and clapped the beat, called out or demonstrated moves, and issued corrections, particularly to how each dancer and group of dancers used the space of the street, sometime shouting corrections like ¡*abre*! (open!) to get them to move apart and sometimes walking among them and firmly pulling a girl by her arm into a new position. By this point, I never saw corrections of the actual movement elements, which the children had clearly mastered. The focus was on counting, coordinating with the other dancers in one's group, using the full space, and moving through the choreography properly, with timely transitions carried out in unison. As July proceeded, the ensemble's performance knit together with relatively smooth transitions as each corps learned its musical cues to move onto or off of center stage and polished its performance of each section. The beginning and end of the performance put the entire conguita in motion, as flag bearers, lantern carriers, and cape wearers ran circles stretching half a city block around the other dancers, who moved down the street arrollándose in unison.

FIGURE 3.15 The entire corps of dancers in the Children's Conga de los Hoyos rehearses on the street in front of the director's house in Los Hoyos, Santiago de Cuba, July 13, 2011.

In shaping the neighborhood kids' already honed ability to arrollarse from the dance of a jubilant and carnivalesque crowd into a disciplined and unified program of performance for an audience of spectators, the conguita rehearsals served as a nexus between the children's embodied mastery of energetic carnivalesque participation in dancing to the conga and the competitive focus on moving, not as a crowd, but in tightly choreographed unison for official carnival (fig. 3.16). Alas, 2011 was not a shining year for the Conguita de los Hoyos: on the particular day of their competitive display before the carnival jury they were well-coordinated and knew their moves but were lackluster, despite the high energy of the musicians. On prize day, the musical ensemble won a prize for best and most traditional beat, but the dancers received no recognition.

Even as participation in conguita rehearsals and practices harnesses children's already-honed bodily dispositions to arrollarse into the service of the state's officially managed carnival, the adults who dedicate hours and years to working with them hold the not-quite-congruent goal of heightening the children's feelings of loyalty to their neighborhood and its conga, of shaping and socializing them to be residents of Los Hoyos. Maritza ambiguously described this goal as "giving them a sense of belonging," which on the surface could refer to disciplining proper citizens of the nation as much as socializing neighborhood allegiance (personal communication, May 3, 2008), and

FIGURE 3.16 The youngest group of dancers in the Children's Conga de los Hoyos, dressed as butterflies, bees, and children's story characters, perform in the carnival procession on prize day, Santiago de Cuba, July 27, 2011. Photo by the author.

on other occasions emphasized the pride she tried to instill in the children and in the community at large. The conguita's actual performance at official carnival would be accessible to most Los Hoyos residents (and most people) only through the television broadcast, a sore point Maritza once obliquely referred to when exhorting the children to be lively as they processed from their meeting point in Los Hoyos up Martí to the official carnival route, telling them that this would be the only opportunity most of the neighborhood would have to see them playing and dancing in their costumes. Her fierce punishment of "traitors," her Los Hoyos neighbors' enthusiastic support in following the conga and conguita every time either comes out on the street (e.g., fig. 3.17), and the participation of thousands of city residents in their own neighborhood carnival comparsas and in events such as the Invasion suggest the grassroots importance of neighborhood pride and belonging quite apart from national sentiment.

In describing the conguita's rehearsals and preparations for its official carnival performances, I have looked to everyday practices of constituting bodily dispositions as well as practices peripheral to carnival, like rehearsals, as sites that constitute productive tensions between the official and the carnivalesque, the neighborhood and the nation. Such practices, I suggest, because they are quotidian and behind the scenes of actual official carnival

FIGURE 3.17 Residents of Los Hoyos watch and follow some young musicians in the Children's Conga de los Hoyos during a performance they organized as a demonstration for the author, led by the conga's musical director and accompanied by the Children's Conguita director, Santiago de Cuba, May 6, 2008. Photo by Sarah Hill used with permission.

performances, help naturalize social differences in bodies and their musical and movement capacities to appear to derive from such "facts" as gender and genealogy, when in fact they are mostly products of early exposure to expectations and deliberate socialization. My account can only treat a small slice of the everyday processes of embodiment through which, cumulatively, Blackness becomes a bodily fact mapped onto physical places, social locations, and cultural forms. Indeed, I have traced only a small part of the socialization processes related to arrollándose. Ideologies naturalizing the body's response to rhythm and some people's predispositions to rhythm in the blood can obscure other processes of somatic racialization-through-embodiment, such as learning local emplacement through, on the one hand, activities demonstrating belonging to one's own neighborhood and on the other walking the "routes" that map neighborhoods, and all of their social valences, in relation to one another. Subsequent chapters continue to explore different angles on the constitution of Blackness, including its voicing and its temporalization as intrinsically historical.

4

Voices: Chronotopic Registers and Historical Imagination in Cuban Folk Religious Rituals

Congo de Guinea Soy	I am a Congo from Guinea
buenas noches criollo	Good evening creole
yo dejo mis huesos allá	I leave my bones over there
yo vengo a dar caridad	I come to give charity

Ritual song calling a muerto [from James Figarola ([2006B, 138])

Distinctive voices have come to index the sound of folkloric Blackness in Cuba, through the enregisterment of forms of speech associated with African slaves and with African-derived folk religious practices. Most prominent are the prototypical voices of orichas and of muertos, spirits that speak through the bodies of those they possess in religious ceremonies. Such spiritual presences are invoked, praised, cajoled, and sometimes even threatened or insulted by religious practitioners who themselves creatively deploy linguistic resources from several complementary repertoires of ritual speech. All of this pragmatic religious activity and the reflection it provokes serve to enregister a contrasting set of speaking styles, each of which indexes a distinctive voice of Blackness.

The esoteric ritual registers called *Lucumí* and *lengua Conga/jerga palera* (Congo tongue/Palo jargon), associated with Santería and Reglas de Palo, respectively, are best known, although other *lenguas* (tongues) exist in more limited circulation.[1] These "high" registers indexing specialized religious knowledge and African source languages (Yoruba and KiKongo) interact with a "low" register called Bozal. Bozal is best described as a widely recognized archaic Cuban sociolect of Spanish heard as "African slaves' speech." In contrast to everyday, even colloquial Cuban Spanish, it sounds rustic, badly pronounced, and error ridden, the way an African captive might be imagined to speak Spanish under the less than ideal learning conditions of slavery. Bozal and the esoteric ritual registers provide a rich linguistic repertoire for folk religious practice, which itself is taken up in diverse folkloric representations and performances.

Key to the processes of enregisterment through which Lucumí, Palo jargon, and Bozal come to index particular ritual domains and voices of

Blackness are the chronotopic values each acquires through its typical patterns of use and the reflexivity inherent in speaking. By evoking particular spatiotemporal frames and categories of persons and relationships, these registers contribute to the historical and mythic imagination of Blackness.

In metadiscourses among those familiar with these registers, each indexes a different kind of speaker and domain of activity: Lucumí is associated with orichas and santeros; lengua Conga is associated with paleros, and Bozal is associated with African slaves of the past. In ritual practice, Lucumí and Palo jargon are often combined with Bozal to produce the voice of a particular speaker, whether human, spirit, or deity. From a greater sociolinguistic distance, for example, as heard by Cubans who are not familiar with folk religion or other cultural forms associated with Black culture in Cuba, the distinctions among Lucumí, lengua Conga, and Bozal apparent to religious practitioners may be lost, so that all index an undifferentiated, negatively valorized "Africanized" voice.

These dynamics can be illustrated with a song and the metacultural reflections that brought the song to my attention. My friend A. Abelardo Larduet Luaces, a professional folklorist who practices both Santería (more typically called Ocha by its practitioners) and Palo Monte (one of the Reglas de Palo) sang the following song for me to illustrate the different sensibilities between the two traditions. He had been explaining to me that Ocha practice is fixed, prizing exact replication of details. Its songs, like all of its practice, invoke the mythic plane of its deities, the orichas, which doesn't change, so its songs are set forever. In Ocha "everything is defined," he explained. In contrast, he continued, Palo has an ethos of creative adaptability and a recognition that the world is constantly in flux. Paleros (practitioners of the Reglas de Palo), in his words, "sing in order to reflect on something, to sing about an experience." He then sang:

1	Campana la Luisa	Bell of Luisa (a sugar plantation)
2	Ya se fuá	Now it's dead
3	Yo manda mi nganga a componé	I have an nganga [power object in Palo] made
4	Patico florida dime adios	Little Florida duck tell me good-bye
5	Donde manda mi nganga mando yo	Where my nganga is in command, I am in command[2]

The song's meaning was not immediately clear to me, until my friend explained that la Luisa was a *central*, or sugar plantation during the colonial era. Ostensibly, the song concerns a slave rebellion at the Central la Luisa, in which the first and most iconic act would be to smash the bell that called slaves to work and dictated their lives. Line 2, describing the bell as dead (and using an item from Palo's ritual jargon, *fuá*, meaning "killed") refers to its smashing but also perhaps suggests the violent fate of the slaveowners. Line 4, addressing a migratory species of duck and saying goodbye, suggests that the origo of the song is escaping into marronage. But lines 3 and 5 suggest that the song does not simply recount an historical vignette: in these lines, the origo invokes his nganga, or ritual power object, as a source of personal power "to command." Line 3 uses a nonstandard conjugation, *yo manda*, which is a common Bozalism and which, together with the historical vignette, evokes the persona of a Bozal speaker—an African slave strong enough to rebel and then to flee. Thus the song also describes the present situation of the singer by drawing a parallel between having once broken free of slavery and now being in control of his destiny through the power of his nganga. As Larduet summed it up, the song concerns "how I could survive then and how I can survive now."

The song creates a distinctive chronotope common to songs in Palo that gives immediacy and relevance to Cuba's history of slavery in the here and now. The voice of the song is that of a palero and maroon, achieved through its use of a first-person origo for past events and present states alike and its deployment of items from the Palo jargon and Bozal. These elements together create the temporal frame that bridges historical events and current ritual power, marked by the recognizable voice of bravado associated with modern-day paleros.

Moreover, the song performed in this example was embedded not in a ritual context but in a moment of metacultural reflection, in which a Cuban religious practitioner and folklorist was characterizing the chronotopes associated with Ocha and the Reglas de Palo. For Larduet, this song conveyed Palo's distinctive sensibility of creative adaptability, one that reflects on historical experiences to generate power in the present, in what Kenneth Routon (2008, 638) has called a "sorcery of history" and what Joel James Figarola (2006b, 41) has described as a "discipline that relates the dead to the living, not just as an act of remembrance but, at base, as a function of the work of the dead in best realizing the work of the living." In contrast, as we will see, Ocha's songs evoke a more mythic and time-transcending chronotope. Of course, as salient as such metacultural distinctions are in some contexts, they remain immanent and fluid. Nor is there a neat mapping between "voice" and register in ritual use. Like metacultural commentaries, ritual practices, from songs to speech during spirit possession, construct chronotopes and voices of Blackness out of dynamic juxtapositions of registers and other semiotic devices: the poetics of historical imagination.

Voice and Dialogicality

It is worth pausing a moment over the polyvalent meanings of "voice," which include technical uses in linguistic anthropology and literary analysis, reference to the materiality—and musicality—of human vocal sound, and metaphorical connotations of agency, as in "having a voice." While all of these usages are relevant to my analysis here, I am using "voice" primarily in the sense developed by M. M. Bakhtin (1981, 289), who argued that each form and feature of language expresses a particular point of view on the world and therefore has what he called "intentional dimensions." These expressive possibilities, he explained, derive from a complex dialogical interaction between a linguistic form's history of use and the uses to which each new speaker puts the form: "Each word tastes of the context and contexts in which it has lived its socially charged life; all words and forms are populated by intentions" such that "the word in language is half someone else's" (293). In this sense, a voice is a recognizable and sociologically (even individually) distinct marker of a person or type of person, consisting of some set of distinctive semiotic features. Some voices emerge specifically in just one text or interaction, while others have long enough half-lives across numerous interactions to become salient as registers, accents, sociolects, and other named speech varieties (Agha 2003, 2005).

"Voice" is sometimes linked to notions of biographical identity, to the extent that a range of poetic, paralinguistic, and textual cohesion devices can allow a particular speaker role to remain salient throughout an interaction or even across speaking events, as when we recognize Fidel Castro's unmistakable cadences or suspect a text to have been written by Hemingway or hear that the spirit Ma Francisca has once again joined a ceremony. But any biographically individual voice is nonetheless peopled by many other voices (Bakhtin 1981; Hill 1995).

There is no neat mapping between "individual speaker" and "voice" because, in Bakhtin's dialogical view of language, voices can mark much broader or looser social categories than individual speakers, and individual speakers can deploy multiple voices. Speaking necessarily involves roles, alignments, contrasts, quotes, and double-voicings that participants in any speech event can mobilize in using signs that are always already half someone else's. This dialogical notion of voice highlights the way in which language permits particular subjectivities to be expressed through the play of voices (Hill 1985; Mannheim and Tedlock 1995; Wortham 2001).

Discourse unfolds in time and is comprised of reiterable units and combinations replicated across events. Those replicated bits carry the "taste" of their previous contexts, speakers, and typical associations. Discourse is therefore by its nature historical and sociological, indexing temporal and locational frameworks. Bakhtin described language as "heteroglot from top to bottom: it represents the co-existence of socio-ideological contradictions between the present and the past, between differing epochs of the past, between different socio-ideological groups in the present, between tendencies, schools, circles, and so forth, all given a bodily form. These 'languages' of heteroglossia intersect each other in a variety of ways, forming new socially typifying 'languages'" (1981, 291).

Bakhtin makes a connection between the capacity of language to index sociologically meaningful distinctions and its capacity to index historical time and place. In other essays, Bakhtin further develops this insight about the interrelationship of subjectivity, time, and space in his concept of chronotope, or space-time. Indeed, I argue that the historical resonances of registers such as Lucumí, lengua Conga, and Bozal are key to their social and contextual connotations as voices of Blackness in Cuba. Each register indexes a particular idealized type of speaker, and it does so fundamentally through the chronotopic values that shape the very processes of enregisterment.

I make this argument on the basis that subjectivities—our sense of self in encounter with the world—are, first of all, necessarily constituted in and through configurations of space-time. Recognizable social entities of all kinds, from biographical individuals to broad categories of social types, are situated in and move through space and time. Some even come to typify particular locations and historical moments, like the maroon voice of the palero's song. Others, such as we ourselves and those around us, patently move through time and space even as we reflexively identify ourselves as of particular social locations in time and space (e.g., as "moderns," as citizens of particular nationalities, and so forth).

Second of all, subjectivities are always generated at the boundaries between self and other, which is to say they are dialogical (Bakhtin 1981, 289–93; Mannheim and Tedlock 1995; Wortham 2001). In this view, the self is neither reducible to interactional stances and alignments, nor is it fully isolable from intersubjective encounters, but rather, it is constructed in an "irreducible tension" with social interactions that James Wertsch (1998) likens to the pole-vaulter, who can only be described as a joint action of person and pole. Wertsch brings together Bakhtin and Vygotsky to argue that what has been compartmentalized as "mind" is more productively examined as a sociohistorical and dialogical phenomenon of situated cognition: mind as culturally and linguistically mediated action.[3] The notion that selfhood is permeable, contingent, and constituted through iterations of encounters, rather than integral, essentialized, and somehow "interior" instead of social, in fact sits well with Cuban folk religious understandings of the person as spiritually and bodily penetrable by spirits that shape one's very destiny and possibilities for interaction (see Wirtz 2013, 2014). In invoking maroon spirits, for example, Cuban religious practitioners create possibilities to develop their own rebellious spirit.

Lucumí and Lengua Conga Used in Rituals

Indeed, religious uses of registers like Lucumí, Palo jargon, and Bozal almost always presuppose spirit entities of one sort or another as interlocutors, and the character of those entities contributes to the social meanings indexed by the registers associated with their voices. In this section I compare ritual songs of Ocha and the Reglas de Palo to develop further the metacultural contrast suggested in my previous example between Ocha's historically transcendent chronotope and the Reglas de Palo's chronotope of historical immanence and magical power.

Lucumí, used in Ocha, is understood to be derived from Yoruba once spoken by West Africans brought to Cuba as slaves. Santería practitioners (santeros) treat Lucumí (and Yoruba) as the "tongue of the orichas," meaning the deities central to Ocha practice, who also made the Middle Passage as transcendent African "saints" comparable to Catholic saints. For santeros, orichas are the prototypical speakers of an idealized Lucumí language identical to Yoruba. Santería practitioners imagine contemporary Yoruba as spoken in West Africa—its dictionaries, its ritual uses today—to be entirely continuous with a "Yoruba" once spoken by Lucumí slaves in Cuba (Wirtz 2007a, 2007c). This view differs from that of historians, who have shown that the very identity Yoruba only coalesced at the end of the nineteenth century through ethnogenetic processes that unified groups who once regarded their languages as distinct into the "Yoruba" speaking a single language.[4]

Both the register and its idealized speakers, then, are imagined to be transcendently African. Santeros strive for fluency in this divine language of communication with the orichas. In their ritual practice, Lucumí serves as an honorific register to address the orichas, also called saints. Santeros evaluate their own fluency primarily in terms of the ability to use precisely replicated forms judged to be purely Yoruba in contextually appropriate ways. For example, ritual lead singers, called *akpones*, build reputations based on their command of hundreds of Lucumí songs, most of which consist of a few lines entirely in Lucumí. While these lyrics are relatively formulaic, and some song sequences are ritually mandated, the genius of a good *akpón* is the ability to select songs and hone performances to fit emerging circumstances of a ritual (see Wirtz 2007e). *Akpón* performances are virtuosic and invite—indeed, require—audience participation for the call-and-response of lines between lead singer and chorus. Most participants singing the chorus will simply repeat what they hear, since few even among initiated santeros understand the songs' words. The *akpón*, then, bears most of the responsibility for leading a proper performance.

The following Lucumí song giving praise to the oricha Changó is typical, as are the rich meanings it evokes for santeros. I recorded the version below during a religious procession on December 4, 1999, organized by members of Santiago de Cuba's preeminent religious family, descendants of Reynerio Pérez, on the Day of Santa Bárbara, the Catholic saint identified with Changó. The *akpón* sang the full verse in alternation with others in the procession, who repeated his words and melody in the call-and-response:

Aché moguó
Changó omo keke egua o
Olufina beguaó
Arabí oró
Arabí oró
Babaoke ilé soguó

While I, in common with most santeros, can at best identify and gloss just a few words and phrases in this song, knowing what a song means and how to properly sing it is a lively field of contestation among santeros. When I watched my recording almost a decade later in 2008 with another member of the Pérez family, the highly regarded *oriaté* (officiating priest) Geraldito Pérez, he pointed out that the first line had been sung incorrectly and should be: "Aye yi moguó."

Such critiques, which tacitly suggest the superior religious authority of the one making the critique, are common among santeros. Geraldito then explained that the song makes reference to a *patakín*, a parable given as a divination result. The divination sign in question reveals that someone has behaved without proper respect (to another person or to the saints and spirits), a violation of religious propriety that can result in bad fortune. Without actually translating the Lucumí lyrics into Spanish, Geraldito explained that they described a time when Changó was a child and his father, the oricha Obatalá, banished him and all his brothers from their home after an elder brother, the oricha Ogún, committed incest with his mother, the oricha Yemayá, with the complicity of the trickster oricha Elegguá. Geraldito retold the *patakín* (in Spanish), explaining how Obatalá always set the oricha Osún to guard his house when he left, but Elegguá got Osún drunk so that Ogún could have his way with Yemayá. When caught flagrante delicto by Obatalá, Ogún was so ashamed he exiled himself to the bush, but Obatalá also punished the rest of his sons, Ogún's brothers, with banishment. The story illustrates that the sometimes devastating consequences of a person's lack of respect extend to the innocent, a pointed warning to the listener. Telling this story reminded Geraldito of other accounts involving Changó, which he also related before we turned our attention back to the recording that had been playing on the television throughout our conversation.

Lucumí songs have rich pragmatic meanings, both in their context of performance and in their associations with lore about the orichas and other aspects of ritual practice, such as divinations. This is true even when the Lucumí words and phrases cannot be precisely glossed or when (as above) santeros who perhaps can translate them do not choose to share that knowledge, opting instead to focus on their proper delivery and their associations. Different opinions about the proper form of those words, as in this example, are quite common, but all agree that there *is* a proper form, and getting it right matters (lest one be guilty of committing a lack of respect, as in the story). Other ritual uses of Lucumí by santeros, in prayers, proverbs, invocations, and ceremonial exchanges like greetings, follow similar patterns: speaking proper Lucumí is ritually important but difficult and eminently challengeable because people have only partial access to what proper Lucumí should be (Wirtz 2007c).

An interesting contrast will be apparent in the next section, because when orichas speak through priests they have possessed, their speech is strikingly different from the formal, formulaic Lucumí of practitioners' songs, prayers, and invocations: orichas speak in a mix of colloquial Cuban Spanish, Lucumí, and Bozal, as if they were visiting African foreigners not entirely familiar with the local human language but trying to accommodate their hosts. Despite these pragmatic facts about the heteroglossia inherent in actual oricha speech, orichas are metadiscursively characterized—even, sometimes, quoted during the telling of stories about them—as speaking a monoglossic Lucumí (Wirtz 2007a).

Whereas Lucumí used in Ocha rituals conveys a more transcendent, mythic chronotope through linguistic forms judged against idealized (pure, unchanging) Yoruba, Palo's ritual register is regarded as a hybridized, highly improvised, invented Cuban register of Reglas de Palo, albeit one with African (specifically KiKongo) antecedents (Fuentes Guerra and Schwegler 2005; Schwegler 2006; Schwegler and Rojas-Primus 2010). While Palo practitioners (paleros) have their share of formulaic phrases, prayers, songs, and invocations, these often consist of KiKongo and Spanish and are recognized by paleros and linguists alike as linguistically hybrid rather than being idealized as pure, like Lucumí.

As an example, consider the following excerpt of a song Geraldito led, in his role as most senior palero (*tata nganga*), during funeral ceremonies for a fellow santero and palero. I made the recording in 1999 and reviewed it at long last with Geraldito in 2008.[5] He opened the song with the ritual exchange through which paleros seek and give permission for all ritual activity, where *mambé* is an invocation, a request for permission to proceed, in Palo jargon, and the response is "God" in Spanish:

GERALDITO: Mambé
ALL: Diós
GERALDITO: Mambé
ALL: Diós

Geraldito then opened by singing the chorus of a song, answered by the rest of the group in a call-and-response, with **boldface and underscoring** indicating lexical items from Palo's ritual vocabulary: "Mi **nganga** yo tengo un dolor ay Diós"

This line is in Spanish and can be readily translated as a lament invoking the nganga, the palero's ritual power object, and God: "Oh my nganga I feel a pain, oh God." After exchanging this line with the chorus several times, Geraldito began to elaborate verses. He explained to me when we viewed the recording that the lead singer has this role, while those responding continue to repeat the chorus. The main difference with the lead singer's role in Ocha ceremonies is that the palero has more latitude to improvise verses, and even entire songs, while the *akpón*'s improvisation extends only to improvising Lucumí lines to interject into existing songs as *tratados*, treatments to praise and provoke the orichas.

The next verse he sang was a reference to the burial of the newly deceased, using the euphemism *cosa buena* or "good thing" to refer to the body:

Ntoto uria cosa buena Diós
Mi **ganga** yo tengo un dolor ay Diós

Geraldito used two words from the Palo jargon: *ntoto*, meaning "the earth" and *uria*, meaning "eats," so that the first line above says "the earth will eat something good, God." The line sounds like Palo jargon because it combines lexical items from the ritual vocabulary of Palo with a circumlocution in ordinary Spanish, giving the song lyric a distinctively palero sensibility.

Geraldito's verses continued for several more minutes, in alternation with the chorus. Below, I give one more verse, indicating lexical items from Palo's ritual vocabulary with **bold underscored** type; the rest is Spanish, with one Bozalism (**bold**) in the use of the nonstandard definite article *lo* instead of *el* in the third line:

Adios mi **ganga**, adio' mi **tata**	Goodbye my **nganga**, goodbye my **godfather**
Adio' la cosa buena, Diós	Goodbye good thing, God
Adio **lo** **campo finda**, la santa noche	Goodbye **the** **cemetery**, the Holy Night
Son las horas la que está esperando	These are the hours that are waiting
Mi **ganga** yo tengo un dolor	My **nganga** I feel a pain

Geraldito's role as lead singer in this funerary ritual for a deceased palero was to elaborate the songs, expressing grief in terms of familiar Palo idioms and using ritual jargon for them, as if to hint at deeper levels of significance: the nganga and its owner (or *tata*); the cemetery, earth, and night as places, substances, and times central to Palo's ritual work.

Generally speaking, paleros prize improvisation in ritual practices, including linguistic creativity for purposes as varied as aggression, insult, placation, and misdirection, because the widespread view among practitioners and scholars is that Palo is a more cunningly adaptive approach to spiritual matters than Ocha, which emphasizes exact replication of tradition. Where santeros invoke the transcendent orichas in their mythic plane, paleros mobilize spirits to carry out their will, often working with muertos who once lived in turbulent times, like African slaves and maroons. Palo, after all, is most closely associated with denigrated and feared labels like witchcraft, magic, and sorcery. Long after Ocha has been widely accepted in the status of a religion, many Cubans still associate Palo with general magical malfeasance, an association not exactly discouraged by paleros, for whom mystery and fear are potential sources of power (Ochoa 2010). Another difference with Lucumí is that the lengua Conga is not understood as the voice of spirits or deities, per se, but is much more closely associated with the persona of the palero, stereotypified as hypermasculine, aggressive, and dangerous. The prototypical palero (male or female) manipulates language as part of controlling spiritual forces and cowing human enemies alike, and for this reason may even embrace these stereotypes. The historical trajectory of both practitioners and their ritual register is imagined to trace from knowledgeable, ancestral "Congo" Africans who used their cunning to survive slavery, through ritual lineages, from palero to palero, into the present, with much personal innovation along the way.

Bozal

Bozal, recognizably present in Palo ritual speech and often co-occurring with Lucumí in the speech of the orichas, reflects a stigmatized yet playful voice of the near historical past—that of enslaved Africans struggling to communicate in Spanish. Bozal, then, is a nonstandard variety of Spanish, drawing on some aspects of colloquial speech, such as vernacular pronunciations and colorful, earthy colloquialisms, but also peppered with phonological, lexical, and morphosyntactic variations that Cubans identify as errors of the sort poorly educated or foreign speakers of Spanish might make. Misconjugated verbs, lack of gender and number agreement, and distorted pronunciations are all perceived as Bozalisms in certain contexts of utterance. There is considerable variation in Bozalisms presented by different speakers, since any nonstandard feature or invented word could, in the context of other such features, be heard as a Bozalism. The most important contextual marker of Bozal is, in fact, that it is the voice of African-born slaves and of their spirits. If Lucumí is the tongue of the orichas and Palo is the speech of palero-"witches," then Bozal is the voice of muertos, spirits of deceased Africans. Bozal is also part of the speech of orichas when they possess devotees to speak, creating a significant asymmetry of address in which their devotees call them down with an archaic, honorific register of Lucumí, to which they answer in the earthy, even crude, accent of captive Africans.

A fascinating example of how strongly indexical Bozal is of the persona of an African of the past occurred during a sociolinguistic elicitation interview reported by linguist Luis Ortiz López (1998), a context distant from folk religious ceremonies in which African muertos typically speak. When asked to demonstrate Bozal speech, one of his Havana informants first "imitated a black woman during a spiritual session," then actually fell into trance, possessed by a muerto (140). In the following sample from his transcription, I have rendered segmentable Bozalisms in **boldface**, which in this sample mostly consist of nonstandard verb-aspect forms and lack of concordance. The translation is mine:

> Entonce ya **tá decí** pa' ti. Niño, tú **tá queré** que **lo** negro **áa decí** cuanto yo **vá hacé**, si me **tá acodá**. Cuando yo **tá vení** de **lo** tierra mí**o** sí poqque yo **tá sé** negro de nación . . .

> So already [I? he?] speak for you. Kid, you want the black man to speak as much as I will if I am willing [*estoy de acuerdo*]. When I came from my land yes because I am African-born . . .

As this excerpt illustrates, the man obliges Ortiz-López's request for Bozal speech by taking on the persona of a "negro de nación," meaning an African-born man who would still have identified with his place of origin (*nación*). He goes on in a similar register to describe life as a slave under *lo branco* (White people), living in a *baracó(n)* (slave barracks) under the "whip" (*cuero*), but still trying to maintain his religion despite being told "ovvida a lo diose de lo negro" (forget the Blacks' deities). As Ortiz-López described it, his informant "let himself get carried away until transforming into a true 'negro congo' . . . and transporting himself into that sociolinguistic past" (140) for fourteen minutes. Similar to the Palo song in this chapter's first example, speaking Bozal triggered a first-person account of colonial Cuban life from the perspective of, and in the voice of, a Bozal slave.

Voices of Blackness in Two Spirit Possessions

Much as I follow the Cuban religious practitioners who were my interlocutors in the field in emphasizing contrasting values among these three registers, the contrasts, so productive at the level of ritual practice, tend to blur and disappear altogether if we view the registers from a great enough social distance. That is to say that, for many Cubans who do not participate in or know much about popular religious traditions, all of these registers simply mark an undifferentiated "Africanized" speech, one sometimes playfully labeled "speaking Mandinga," that is socially distant from ordinary, unmarked Cuban Spanish. In religious contexts, and the folklore settings that borrow from them, the differing chronotopic values of Lucumí, lengua Conga, and Bozal, however, allow for contrasting voices of Blackness and visions of African heritage to emerge.

All of these linguistic repertoires are primarily performed rather than being recorded as textual or archival modalities of historical remembrance, and all literally give voice to various deities and spirits who possess people. Indeed, religious practitioners regard all three registers as more or less embodied practices, best learned through apprenticeship to knowledgeable godparents, and in keeping with other kinds of ritual semiotic modalities of movement, gesture, dress, adornment, materials, and manipulations that are also available to be deployed in both formulaic and improvisatory ways. Thus far my discussion has recounted metadiscourses about typical uses of Lucumí, Palo jargon, and Bozal that contribute to their enregisterment, in interaction with some examples of metapragmatic regimentation in typical ritual uses. But it is enough neither to consider the social valences of these registers in isolation from each other nor to reduce them to idealized metacultural equivalences between Lucumí and the voice of orichas, Palo ritual speech and the voice of the palero, or Bozal and the voice of the muerto. To understand how they come to have these valences—how it is that any Cuban performer can imitate these voices and be recognized as performing Blackness by any Cuban audience—we need to follow the dialogical interaction of these voices and tokens of register in use. Because tokens of Bozal, Lucumí, and Palo jargon often appear fleetingly in the stream of speech, it is necessary to look very closely at such utterances. In the examples that follow, I examine recorded interactions in great detail, arguing that it is through these minute, fleeting patterns of use that the robust metacultural characterizations and chronotopic flavors of these voices of Blackness emerge.

VOICE OF THE ORICHA: MAYENYE'S OBATALÁ SPEAKS

A *wemilere* is a ceremony held to praise the orichas, using a consecrated set of batá drums, in which the drums have undergone an initiation similar to what people undergo to receive the orichas ritually.[6] During a *wemilere* I sponsored at my godfather's house shortly before ending a long stint of fieldwork in 2000, an elderly and highly respected santera was unexpectedly possessed by her principal oricha, Obatalá. This santera, whom I will call Mayenye, was close to my godfather and had allowed me to interview her on a previous occasion. It was an honor that she attended our ceremony and even more so that she allowed her saint to possess her despite how exhausting such possessions are and how frail she was becoming. While present, Obatalá spoke to another senior santero, and then indicated that she wished to speak privately to my godfather Emilio, me, and my husband, Ed. (While Obatalá is primarily a male oricha, Obatalá also has some female avatars or "paths." I use "she" to refer to Mayenye-possessed-by-Obatalá because that was the pronoun my godfather used at the time.) So the four of us crowded into a back bedroom and as Obatalá began to speak to us, my godfather indicated that I could turn on the tape recorder I was carrying.

The resulting recording is imperfect—background noise from drums and singing in the main room, a fraying microphone cable, or perhaps the powerful *aché*, energy, of the oricha interfering with electronics—and beyond that, there is always a certain degree of uncertainty in transcribing the speech of the orichas, as it is meant to be somewhat ambiguous, indirect, and esoteric (see a fuller analysis of these dynamics in Wirtz [2005, 2007d, 2007e]).

Moreover, as in other recordings of orichas' speech during possession, I found that the transcription process often highlighted rather than diminished the uncertainties and multiplicities of meaning: my less than fluent ear aided by vivid memories gave me the gist of what had been said. Meanwhile, the Cuban transcriber I hired tended to heavily employ eye dialect—the use of nonstandard spelling for speech to draw attention to pronunciation—perhaps emphasizing her social distance from religious Black folk, while my upwardly mobile, professional godfather's transcription tended to correct Bozalisms to present, instead, more standardized Cuban speech. I would relisten to the recording with each new transcription in hand, attempting to combine the differing versions into the most complete and accurate record of what I could hear on the recording. I state all of this to dispel any illusions of a perfect or transparent transcription process. Transcription is as much a metacultural endeavor as the explicit interpretation that usually follows its presentation (Bucholtz 2000; Haviland 1996). I prefer to leave transcripts a bit messy and indeterminate to serve as reminders about all that we cannot definitively know or reconstruct about instances of interaction, even with ideal recording conditions, intact microphone cables, and countless listenings.

If these overlapping roles among transcribers and participant-analysts do not confuse matters enough, the participant structuring of events of oricha speech is in itself complex. Orichas' speech is typically mediated by an experienced, senior santero who serves as a sort of translator and whose very role indeed highlights the need for expert interpretation of oricha speech. When Mayenye's Obatalá spoke to the senior santero at the ceremony, there was no such mediation. Indeed, for each pronouncement Obatalá made, that santero promptly answered "aché, aché," acknowledging the truth of the oricha's pronouncements and at the same time silencing the oricha from airing more of his private business. But in my case, my godfather needed to translate for reasons of my comprehension and in order to expand on how we might interpret the oricha's telegraphic and often ambiguous comments in ways relevant to our situation.

Some of Obatalá's comments were directed to Ed or to both of us, adding yet another layer of comprehension issues, since Ed understood much less of the cultural performance of possession trance than even I did. My godfather's expansion on each of Obatalá's pronouncements sometimes takes into account our limited linguistic and cultural competency. Obatalá's speech uses Lucumí, Bozal, and ordinary colloquial Spanish and is characterized by indirectness, implicature, and innuendo, all of which contribute to the metapragmatic framing of oricha speech as esoteric, requiring interpretation by religious experts to be fully intelligible.

Another aspect of this interaction is that Obatalá draws attention to those who are not ratified participants in our conversation: she twice mentions her *carabela* (associate) Mayenye, whose body was host to Obatalá and who therefore could not be present in the interaction. Obatalá also expresses concern that we not repeat her comments to others who might maliciously use this privileged information against us. Indeed, Obatalá seems to be trying as hard to socialize my husband and me into the conversational norms of speaking with orichas as did my godfather and other santeros.

I here discuss two excerpts from Mayenye's Obatalá in conversation with my godfather Emilio, my husband Ed, and me. Mayenye's Obatalá had already been talking to us, directing advice to my godfather Emilio, for a minute before I asked his permission to record. Immediately after Emilio agreed with Obatalá on a final piece of advice, Obatalá turned her attention to Ed and me. In the following excerpt, Obatalá's speech heavily uses Bozal, but very little Lucumí. This was typical throughout the encounter, where Bozalisms were present in almost every utterance, with only occasional, formulaic tokens of Lucumí, such as the often-repeated first-person pronoun *emí* (*ne*). Also notice the high degree of metapragmatic reflexivity in how Obatalá and Emilio negotiate the delivery of Obatalá's message to Ed and me. It is typical of all such interactions I have witnessed for both oricha and santero interpreter to use quotatives ("I am saying"; "she says") to ensure that, whoever is speaking, responsibility for the message always is given to the oricha. It is an interactional achievement rather than a given to "voice" a manifested oricha and thereby attribute a message to a nonmaterial agency. The possibility always exists for "authorial" responsibility to slip over to the possessed person or the interpreting santero, in which case the message might slip out of its presumed divine infallibility to be judged inauthentic and challenged by other participants. In the following excerpt, Emilio is somewhat resistant to passing along Obatalá's message to Ed, which he fears could seem disrespectful, and must be prodded to do so by Obatalá.

Another important aspect of these interactions' mediated participant structure are the adjacency pairs consisting of an oricha's utterance or series of utterances and the interpreting santero's elaborated translation of that utterance or series. Some of these pairs in the excerpt below are negotiations between oricha and interpreting santero that are rich in metapragmatic content. Some conform to what Du Bois (1986) calls a "paradox of interpretability and uninterpretability": the interpreting santero's expanded, more denotationally explicit version in unmarked Spanish heightens the unintelligibility of the oricha's original utterance even as the translation anchors the original utterance's meaning in a context relevant to the person receiving the oricha's advice (my husband and me, in this case). The oricha's utterances, as "earthy" as the density of Bozalisms and colloquial Cuban Spanish pronunciations makes them, nonetheless defy complete interpretation, especially in the hectic interactional moment when the oricha speaks with urgency, allowing little space for the santero to insert his translation. Despite the lengthier exegesis by the mediating santero, some part of the oricha's message remains sublime, ineffable, because it remains uninterpreted. The copresence of Lucumí and Bozal tokens are instrumental in creating this contradictory effect of earthiness and sublimity.

In what follows, *Ob* stands for Obatalá, *Em* for Emilio, *KW* for myself, and *Ed* for my husband. **Bold type** indicates Bozalisms, underscore indicates Lucumí, and parentheses with question marks (?) indicates uncertainty in the transcription. (See n. 22 in chap. 3 for other transcription conventions used.)

1	Ob	[*inaudible—5 sec*]
2	Em	Anja [*laughs*] Uh-huh [*laughs*]
3]]	Ob	[*inaudible—4 sec*] [[para to y eso[7] [[for all that
4]]	Em	[[[*inaudible—3 sec*]
5	Ob	y tú has dejao decí que esa gente **disie** dulce **lo** pasa'o, **en decí**— [*cut in recording—1 sec*] but you have left out saying that those people **talked** sweet [in] **the** past, [I] **am saying**—
6	Em	Sí Yes
7	—	[*cut in recording—1 sec*]
8	Ob	Pero emi se **vi jocicú** se lo pasé(?)— [*cut in recording—2 sec*] But I **see a snout** it has passed(?)—
9	Em	No, yo se lo voy a explicar ahora No, I'm going to explain it to them now
10		dice ella que tú tiene [*0.5 sec*] e::h— she says that you have [*0.5 sec*] a::h—
11	Ob	—emi ne **son le** e:h tiene **jocú** —I **are** [i.e., I say] **one** has a **snout** [Sp. *hocico*]/is stubborn like an animal
12	Em	Sí sí sí [*laughs*] yes yes yes [*laughs*]
13	Ob	[*low voice*] que tiene **jocicú** con mi that he is making a snout with me [i.e., pouting or getting angry]

14 Em [*laughs*]
[*laughs*]
15 Dice [*laughs*] que tú eres una persona muy pasiva
She says [*laughs*] that you are a very passive person
16 pero que tienes un caracter que no te gusta que . abusen de tí,
but that you have a personality that you don't like being maltreated
17 que entonces te incomoda
which then bothers you
18 Enton- . . ella dice que tú tienes ese caracter fuerte cuando tratan de abusar de ti,
So. .she says that you have this strong character when they try to maltreat you
19 pero que tú eres una gente muy pasiva . . .
but you are a very passive person . . .
20 KW [*inaudible—0.5 sec*]
21 Em y que usó una jarana contigo
and that [she] teased you
22 Ed ¿Sí:?
Ye:s?
23 Em Allí, y que no te vaya a poner guapo por eso
There, and please don't get mad about it

Much of this exchange between Obatalá and Emilio concerns their negotiation of Emilio's role in interpreting Obatalá's message to Ed and me. In line 5, Obatalá points out that Emilio has neglected to convey some part of her previous message (inaudible in the recording), saying "you have left out. . . ." and repeating part of her message, to Emilio's brief acknowledgment, "yes," in line 6.

In line 8, Obatalá apparently prods Emilio to begin interpreting (in a few inaudible seconds of recording), since Emilio responds by first assuring Obatalá that he will start explaining, then, in line 10, beginning to interpret by saying, "she says that you have [*0.5 sec*] a::h—" When he hesitates, Obatalá restates her message from line 8 (in lines 11 and 13), eliciting laughter from Emilio. In lines 15–23, Emilio then delivers a softened, more fully explained interpretation of Obatalá's rather briefer, pithier message to Ed. It was not until several years later, in reviewing and transcribing the recording with me, that Emilio actually explained the teasing metaphor Obatalá had used on Ed, an idiomatic expression we had completely missed at the time. Emilio's laughter in lines 12, 14, and 15, I now think, seems to be an attempt to dispel tension and pause to rephrase in relaying Obatalá's message for Ed, as much as a jocular reaction to Obatalá's message. While orichas tend to be brutally honest, even harsh, in chastising wayward devotees in these kinds of sessions, and while santeros and orichas enjoy a robust tradition of teasing and ritualized insult, Emilio was no doubt aware that Ed and I knew little of these conventions and, always solicitous of our comfort, he might have feared that we could take offense or otherwise respond inappropriately to this unfamiliar kind of teasing provocation.

The idiom of *ponerse hocico* (making a snout) is a familiar colloquial expression for pouting or getting angry and stubborn, perhaps like an annoyed farm animal. In line 8, and again in lines 11 and 13, Obatalá changes the syntax and pronunciation of the expression with what Cubans interpret as Bozalisms, also adding a Lucumí pronoun, *emi* or *emi ne* ("I") to frame the first two repetitions as her pronouncement. While the three lines are quite similar, Obatalá makes some changes in the repetitions in line 11 and 13. In line 11, she repeats the Lucumí first-person pronoun used in line 8, which in both forms is widely used by orichas when they speak and widely recognized by santeros. It is a formulaic way of marking that the oricha (not the possessed santero) is the author and principal of utterances coming from the possessed santero's mouth. So the Lucumí-Bozal-Spanish constructions *emi se vi* and *emi ne son*, both rather garbled in denotation, should be taken as quotatives, much like the Lucumí-Bozal *en decí* (Yoruba progressive marker *ń* and Sp. *decir*—to say) in line 5, and their translation by Emilio as [*ella*] *dice* in lines 15 and 18. Obatalá also repeats a version of the expression *ponerse hocico* each time, but alternating between two Bozal pronunciations, /ho 'ku/ and /ho si 'ku/, where the latter is closer to the standard Spanish pronunciation /o 'si ko/. Her final version of the message, in line 13, is the most denotationally transparent, specifying that she sees one of us getting "snouty" (pouty) with her.

While Obatalá uses Bozal pronunciations and nonstandard, even garbled syntactic constructions, most of her utterances are composed of ordinary colloquial Spanish. And yet, those scattered Bozal flavorings cast long metapragmatic shadows over her speech (Schwegler 2006), so that a Cuban listener might, like my nonreligious transcriber, shake her head at the incomprehensibility of Obatalá's speech overall, speech her husband, listening in, referred to as "speaking Mandinga." Certainly, the Bozalisms evident in Obatalá's speech contribute to its indirectness, its vagueness of reference, if not to actual unintelligibility, even while Obatalá is making straightforward enough remarks. Obatalá's utterances in the next section of the interaction abundantly illustrate these effects of Bozal (shown in **bold**, with Lucumí indicated by <u>underscore</u>).

24	Ob	**El suyo va el suyo**
		You and you [referring to KW and her husband]
25	Em	An-jan
		Uh-huhn
26	Ob	e cuando etá ete bien
		and when you [these] are well
27		emi no está ara o
		I will not be here [in this land/body]
28	Em	Sí
		Yes
29	Ob	No para
		[I] doesn't stay
30	Em	Anja
		Uh-huh
31	Ob	así el **caramelo a el**
		so that the **shipmate** (Sp. *caravela*, "caravel" referring to a slave ship) to him
32	Em	Sí sí
		Yes yes
33	Ob	entonce a lo mejol no **ta vito** poqué **tá moí** [*inaudible*]
		so likely will not be alive because [she] will be dead [inaudible]

Obatalá's speech here is dense with Bozalisms and even Lucumí words (in line 27) that make her utterances ambiguous and indirect, requiring quite a bit of contextual information to interpret. Perhaps for this reason, Emilio did not gloss this section for us during the interaction, but let her continue for a while. In line 24, Obatalá uses a novel nonstandard Spanish construction. While *el suyo* might ordinarily indicate something that belongs to someone, as in the nominalized possessive pronoun "his" in the English construction "his is this one," Obatalá is here using *el suyo* idiosyncratically as a third-person pronoun, indicating Ed and me. This highly marked, idiosyncratic choice might be making reference to Mayenye/Obatalá's knowledge that Emilio was my godfather in Ocha and would thus likely also be responsible for my husband's spiritual needs (so we were *his* charges).

Obatalá goes on to say that she will not remain present among us, using Lucumí terms familiar to any santero: *emi* as the first-person pronoun and *ara* meaning "land" and also "body" and being used deictically to indicate the mundane plane of human existence, as opposed to the *ara taco* or land in Africa where the *ara nla* or "great beings," orichas, originated. The phrase "emi no está ara o," then, combines Lucumí lexical items into a matrix of Spanish syntax, together with the emphatic particle *o* common in Lucumí ritual songs. After this brief use of Lucumí that reminds us of Obatalá's status as an oricha and evokes the transcendent homeland of Ocha, Obatalá makes reference to Mayenye, whose body she has possessed and whose mouth gives voice to her speech. She calls Mayenye her "slave shipmate," using an archaic term for the important fictive kinship ties African captives created aboard slave ships making the Middle Passage (Mintz and Price [1976] 1992, 43–44). What makes her reference to Mayenye even less direct is her nonstandard pronunciation of *caravela* as *caramelo*, literally meaning "hard candy." Such circumlocutions contribute to the delicacy of what Obatalá wants to convey: that Mayenye is elderly, infirm, and may not live much longer.

Although the chronotopic effects of these brief lines are fleeting, they are significant in the interaction and for my argument about the play of voices deployed through Lucumí and Bozal. Obatalá uses Lucumí precisely when she refers to herself, the oricha, in contradistinction to Mayenye, whose body she possesses. But after this passing reminder of the transcendent plane of orichas, she then uses a quintessentially Bozal term of fictive kinship, "slave shipmate," an archaic term whose chronotopic flavor indexes an enslaved African's perspective. In the final excerpt below, Obatalá's voice becomes even earthier as she uses Bozalized vulgarisms (**bold**) to warn us against talking to others about personal spiritual matters, such as the initiations into Ocha that she foretells for us:

34	Ob	y tú **tá epera** que **tá** [*inaudible—1 sec*]
		and you **are waiting** for there **to be**
35		pa: que esa gente **tacén** cosa **bonite**
		so that these people **make a nice thing** [i.e., are initiated into Ocha]
36	Em	Anja [*low voice*]
		Uh-huh
37	Ob	que va a ser muy fino
		that will be very refined
38	Em	Anja [*low voice*]
		Uh-huh
39	Ob	pero no **tá jablao** mucho con to **lo** mundo
		but not **talking** much with **the** whole world
40	[[Em	No no no eso no se habla [[[*inaudible 0.5 sec*]
		No no no one does not speak of that [[[*inaudible 0.5 sec*]]
41	[[Ob	[[*inaudible*] que tá **jundi**
		[[that gets **screwed** [Sp. *jodido*, "fucked"]
42	Em	Sí
		Yes
43	Ob	que **jundi**
		that **screws (it up)**

44	Em	Sí sí sí, eso no se puede hablar mucho
		Yes yes yes, you can't talk a lot about that
45		Que lo que nosotros vamos a hacer no podemos hablarlo mucho
		We cannot talk much about what we are going to do
46	KW	Sí
		Yes

Notice the metalinguistic character of this exchange: Obatalá is warning us to keep quiet, lest we get "screwed" by others who don't need to know our business. In the ensuing section, not provided in detail here, she warns us against the "vaye vaye vaye," a Bozal-sounding neologism resonating with the colloquial Cuban expression "lleva y trae" Emilio uses to translate it, literally meaning "carry and take" and referring to the spread of gossip. In lines 35–43 above, Obatalá sets up a sharp contrast between the "refined" and "beautiful thing," her euphemisms for the event that will be our initiation into Ocha, and the vulgarity of people "fucking" us by spreading gossip. Matters of Ocha, she conveys, are secret in order to protect their spiritual potency. As for refinement, the term *fino* carries implications of wealth and Whiteness, describing Ed and me, and therefore of the lavish initiation ceremony we would be able to hold. This is a fleeting reference, and it would not do to make one instance of a word bear so much significance. That said, as described in chapter 3, *fino* often is used with these racial and socioeconomic resonances, and as a contrastive to herself, it contributes to the self-lowering this oricha achieves by using Bozalisms and colloquialisms, even vulgarity, in her speech. Obatalá, perhaps like her host Mayenye, is humble and Black as well as being wise and worldly. The oricha deploys a Bozal voice to achieve this strategic self-lowering effect.

To expand focus from these detailed analyses of less than two minutes of interaction, we can consider Obatalá's voice overall as combining the transcendent perspective of an oricha—a powerful and divine African spiritual entity, albeit imagined to have humanlike appetites and flaws (recalling Geraldito's story)—with the earthiness of a slave's humble but worldly perspective. Obatalá's voice contrasts with the voices of devotees singing praises and provocations to her and other orichas in the next room, even while she speaks to us. Those songs are almost entirely in the high, esoteric register of Lucumí, accompanied by specific, traditional rhythms on the batá drums. Obatalá's voice also contrasts with Emilio's running interpretation of her words into standard, Cuban Spanish clear as a bell to my foreign ears.

We might also ask how Obatalá's voice compares to Mayenye's own voice, when she is not possessed. Mayenye is an elderly Black woman who lives in a swampy outlying neighborhood near the harbor and whose household depends on its members' lucrative religious work in Santería. She and her household have accumulated a great deal of prestige in this limited religious sphere, however much a struggle their lives remain. Her speech is marked by the vernacular accent of poor, Black neighborhoods; Cubans frequently characterized such speech to me as "very Santiaguero" (typical of Santiago residents). Mayenye, like Obatalá speaking through her, uses marked pronunciations (e.g., pronouncing /r/ as /1/ or /i/, aspirating /s/ as /h/, all considered characteristic of colloquial Cuban Spanish) and pithy colloquialisms, as well as manifesting a certain widespread cultural preference among Cubans for conversational indirectness, implicature, and finesse.[8] But Mayenye's ordinary speech does not present Bozalisms, nor does she incorporate Lucumí terms, unless she is specifically talking about religious matters. She refers to herself in the unmarked Spanish form of *yo* (I), not with the Lucumí quotatives *emi ne* or *en decí*. Obatalá's voice, speaking through Mayenye in her possession trance, combines all these semiotic devices to distinguish itself as the voice of an oricha.

VOICE OF THE CIMARRÓN: MARÍA DEL CONGO SPEAKS

Let us now consider the speech of a religious practitioner leading a Palo crossed with Spiritist ceremony (*espiritismo cruzado*) as part of a folklore festival celebrating Afro-Cuban rebelliousness. The occasion was the annual Festival of the Caribbean, organized by the Casa del Caribe cultural research institute in Santiago. The folklore ensemble 1802 de Orozco had traveled from distant Pinar del Río province to participate in the day's Ceremony to the Cimarrón, an event described in greater detail in chapter 6. This particular performer, identifying herself at one point as the senior palera or *mariquilla* of her ritual house, led the group in invoking the spirits with a progression of Catholic, then Spiritist, then Ocha and Palo prayers, invocations, and songs. She then went into trance and began to speak in a markedly different voice, identifying herself to the large crowd as the muerto or spirit María del Congo. By this name, the spirit claimed the identity of an enslaved African given a European name that specified her place of origin as the Congo.

The outdoor site on a hill above the small mining town of El Cobre and its famous shrine to Cuba's patron saint, the Virgin of Charity of El Cobre, was filled with people, including several performing groups, busloads of festival participants from Santiago, and dozens of local people. The officiating priest, let us call her Pura, had to shout to be heard as she began the opening series of prayers, first the "Our Father" and then the "Hail Mary." Even so, her voice quality markedly changed after the concluding "Amén Jesús," becoming a much raspier shout as she launched into a third invocation in the style of the Reglas de Palo. One of my transcribers, an initiated palero and santero as well as professional folklore researcher, described her utterance as in a dialect associated with Cuba's African legacy, noting: "The priestess preaches in the dialect established by these religious practitioners of Cuba's African substrate" (my translation).

As with the Catholic prayers, she performed this Palo invocation in a monologue, at the end of which comes a formal, formulaic response from the other members of the performing group: "May it be so." But her voice now was not the voice of Catholic prayers, plaintive and holy. Rather, it was the voice of Palo, colloquial and coarse, but bristling with esoteric knowledge based on her relationships with the spirits and deities of her Palo Briyumba practice (Ochoa 2010). She spoke in the register of Palo ritual practice, thick with lexical items, phrases, and allusions from the lengua Conga register. The lengua Conga is a formal register, like the formal Spanish of Catholic prayers, but the source of its formality is an African legacy of slaves, inflected with colloquialisms, occasional Bozalisms, and often delivered in a raspy, coarse quality of voice.

Below, I note what she said, as two separate transcribers and I could best elucidate from repeated viewings of my noisy video recording. The English glosses are sometimes approximations, rather than precise word-for-word translations. In what follows, **bold type** indicates Bozalisms, **bold underscore** indicates Palo jargon, and parentheses with question marks (?) indicate uncertainty in the gloss.

1 Pura **Ta guiri** **yo** **congo**
My **congo will speak** [*or:* **Listen to my congo**]

2 **Ta guiri** yo de **ntimate**
Will speak from **the heart**

3 **Mimo** **mariquilla** que da **convite Saura**
[the] same **senior palera** who **feeds Saura** [*"Vulture"—i.e., the name of her prenda*]

4 Mamá Serafina,
Mother Serafina,

5 Con invitación de **cuadrilla** y de **to' congo soberano**
With the invitation of the **group** of **all free congos**

6 Mimo **mariquilla ndoki kalunga**
Same **senior palera of attacking spirits, sea of the dead**

7 **Briyumba Congo**
Congo of Palo Briyumba [*a specific Regla of Palo*]
8 **Kini kini bacheche**
What what resolves [i.e., resolves anything]
9 Que nace del fundamento **Zarabanda** gajo **e** loma, gajo **cheche** bejuco **nfinda**
Who is born of the prenda of **Sarabanda** (Palo deity) branch **of** the mountain, branch [of the] (**good/powerful**?) vine [*of*] **cemetery**
10 Nace de tierra **garabato**
Born of the land of **signs/hooks** (?) [*"garabato" may refer to esoteric diagrams drawn in Palo or to a curved stick*]
11 Brinca **kalunga** tierra **mambiala vence batalla**
Crosses **the sea** [**of the dead**] land of **mambiala** [mambí?] **conquers in battle**
12 Guarda fama en vuelto abajo y **cuenda** fama en vuelta abajo
Protects reputation in crossing down (to western Cuba) and **protects** reputation in crossing down (to eastern Cuba)
13 Comanda **cheche**
Governs **well**
14 Que no **son** resabio de **kriyumba congo**
That are not rancorous of the **head of the congo** [**spirit**]
15 Que no **leka**, que no tercia, que **debarata** con todo
That never **sleeps**, that does not yield, that **destroys** all
16 Que **ta güisa**
That **hears and sees**
17 Son **mimo jolongo congo**
They are the **same congo prenda**
18 Del **mimo nfumbe Ta** Magué Martínez
of the same **spirit** Father Magué Martínez
19 Mimo **Mariquilla**
Same **senior priestess**
20 Da **convite Saura**
Feeds Saura
21 Pa que no' den mucha salud, fuerza, desenvolvimiento, tranquilidad, y estabilidad
So that they will give us much health, strength, spiritual development, peace, and stability
22 según el padre celestial de los testigos
Thanks to the celestial father of the witnesses
23 Others Y así sea
May it be so

Much of this excerpt is difficult to translate, indeed would be difficult for many Cubans to understand, because of Pura's heavy use of Palo's ritual register. Some of her pronunciations and grammatical elisions might be considered Bozal, although not to the extent of Obatalá's speech in the previous section. Other paleros would find everything in her speech quite understandable and formulaic in its use of Palo jargon, even gaining information about the (public) name of her prenda (ritual power object), the powerful spirits associated with it, and her level of spiritual authority. She also followed the usual formula in her overall tenor of brazen challenge that characterizes such invocations: paleros closely identify their own spiritual power with that of the actual physical object of the prenda and its associated spirits and deities. To claim control of a powerful prenda, as she did, is to deny others the possibility of magically harming her. Her prenda works for her, she claimed, because she feeds it, where "feeding" a prenda in Palo or a santo in Ocha means providing offerings and sacrifices to spiritually charge it. But beyond her standard claims about the protections her ritual lineage's prendas and spirits provide her, she offered that power as a beneficial force that can bring blessings to everyone present. Indeed, her invocation ends by slipping back into a (formal Spanish) formulaic phrase familiar to Spiritism, Ocha, and folk Catholicism, in which the spirits are asked to provide blessings of health, peace, and spiritual development to those who worship them.

Following the Palo invocation, Pura then immediately began a Lucumí invocation to the deceased ancestors that opens all ritual work in Santería. Each time she intoned "Ibayé ibayé tonú" in the same raspy shout as the Palo invocation, another member of the group called out the name of his or her muerto (spirit), for about ten rounds of invocation. The Lucumí phrase she used usually is glossed as "rest in peace." Following the invocation, a lead singer stepped forward, taking the microphone to begin a series of Spiritist songs, all in Spanish and in a formal register comparable to the opening Catholic prayers. This Palo-Spiritist ceremony, then, opened with a series of contrasting voices and registers, where the section excerpted above stands out as the Palo voice, the palera appealing to the power of spirits who, in life, were enslaved Africans and whose occult practices and Congo speech are Palo's legacy. On this particular occasion, Pura's prayers and invocations, and the songs that followed, served to prepare for possession trances in which she and about eight other members of the ensemble would channel their muertos. The larger goal of the ceremony was to pay homage to the figure of the cimarrón, the rebellious, escaped slave.

Pura's Palo voice, then, was properly authentic, regardless of whether the ceremony was, in fact, a religious event or whether the possession trances that soon ensued were true possessions or choreographed dramatic reenactments of a religious ceremony. After several songs, Pura's muerto, María del Congo, took possession and greeted the audience, asking for a "missing congo." (**Bold** indicates Bozalisms; **bold underscore** is Palo.)

1	María	**Miserecua** pa to criollo
		Mercy for all creoles
2		Que **papá Dió** acompaña a
		May **Papa God** accompany
3		To lo **criollo** ese
		All these **creoles** here
4		Que ta **mimo** **munanso** que yo
		of the **same** **ritual house** as I
5	Others	Y así sea
		And may it be so
6	María	**Sala malekun** pa
		Greetings to
7		To **lo** **cuadrilla** que **e** congo
		All **the** **ritual families** that **is** congo
8	Other	**Malekun sala**
		Greetings
9	María	**Dici** carao
		Say damn
10		Mi falta a **uni** congo
		I am missing **a** congo
11		Donde ta **mimo** congo **lukabbo** ese
		Where is that **same** congo **lukabbo**?

When Pura's muerto, María del Congo, spoke, her voice quality remained a raspy shout, and she continued to speak in colloquial Spanish inflected by Bozalisms and lexical items from the lengua Conga. But María del Congo does not speak from the position of Pura's role as *mariquilla* or senior palera: she does not invoke Pura's lineage of Palo, her nganga, or its spirits and governing deities (*nfumbis* and *mpungus*). Instead, her stance is that of the Congo ancestors of modern-day paleros. She greets the assembled crowd, first in Bozal Spanish (lines 1–4), then with Palo's ritual greeting, borrowed from Arabic through now-forgotten processes of cultural contact. Cuban paleros have explained to me simply that the greeting was an "African greeting," and so it makes sense that paleros would have continued it. When María del

Congo says "sala malekun" (line 6), the other performers, including those also possessed by muertos, answer "malekun sala" (line 8).

Her opening words asking for God's (*Papá Diós*) mercy and protection, refers to criollo, meaning Cuban-born people of African descent (lines 1, 3), a category that contrasts with congo (lines 7, 10, 11), who are African-born. These greetings encompassed the entire audience: we are all of African descent, either criollo or congo, in María del Congo's reckoning, and she included both categories as fellow members of her ritual family, using the Palo term *munanso* (ritual lineage/house) and Spanish *cuadrilla* (crew; lines 4, 7). The categories of criollo and congo also form an implicit temporal sequence, where congos were the ancestors of criollos today, and all Cubans today are criollos—a little bit African. Her own voice was inflected with the nonstandard pronunciations that mark her as a "congo," and she called out for another muerto, a "congo lukabbo." The lead singer then began another series of songs to attract that missing muerto, beginning with the following song:

1 Si viene el mayoral lo mato
If the overseer comes I kill him
2 Si viene el mayoral lo pico
If the overseer comes I bite him

The lyrics of this song continue the ritual and temporal frame suggested by María del Congo, taking the origo of a maroon who promises to fight back if the *mayoral*, the slave foreman, tries to recapture him. As in the palero song about breaking the bell of the Central Luisa plantation in an earlier example, the song brings this particular past of slavery and marronage into the immediate present, making the maroon's rebellious aggression a stance available to all who join in the singing. The sequence begun with María del Congo's call for the maroon spirit and continued in the songs invoking him had its effect when the maroon crept in through the audience, wielding a machete and warily looking around, eventually approaching María del Congo to exchange the *sala malekun* greeting and bump elbows in the palero style (see figs. 2.1, 2.7, and 4.1).

Voices of Africans Past

The examples of Pura's muerto María del Congo and Mayenye's oricha Obatalá illustrate how juxtapositions of devices of voicing and temporality in particular ritual settings with particular interactional aims contribute to the enregisterment of Lucumí, Palo ritual speech, and Bozal. It is through register juxtapositions and contrasts that María del Congo and Obatalá emerge

FIGURE 4.1 Palo ritual greeting with elbows, Ceremonia al cimarrón, performed by 1802 de Orozco, El Cobre, July 2006. Line drawing by Jessica Krcmarik of still image from author's video recording, used with permission.

as speakers distinct from their hosts Pura and Mayenye. As with the earlier example showing how Bozal's chronotopic pull was so great that an attempt to produce Bozal in a sociolinguistic interview brought on the speaker's possession by a "muerto africano," the chronotopic values of Lucumí, Palo jargon, and Bozal serve as historical mnemonics that bring ritual participants face-to-face with the orichas of myth and the muertos of Cuba's slaving past. Such temporal telescoping permits transcendent entities and historical figures to participate in the projects of living people, allowing the historical imagination to serve as a source of ritual power.

It is not through patterns of ritual interaction alone, however, that enregisterment occurs. I have also pointed out the role of metacultural commentary—about ritual performances and about the registers themselves—in giving salience to Lucumí, Palo ritual speech, and Bozal as recognizable and contrasting styles of speaking and, in the case of Lucumí and Palo ritual speech, decomposable into lexicons. This combination of metacultural salience and poesis in ritual interaction permits Lucumí, Palo ritual speech, and Bozal to be entextualized in other ways, including being taken up and recontextualized in folklore performances. I conclude this chapter with one more example, to show how the chronotopic values and voices indexed by these registers contribute to the emergence and recognizability of Black figures in wider circuits of folklore performance. During a February 2010 interview discussing a longer series of songs planned for the 2010 carnival, the director of a folklore society called the Cabildo Carabalí Olugo sang me the following lyric, in which the **boldface** type indicates Bozalisms:

Mal cubano, nuestra jaula, el **caravelo** mío,	**Bad/mayoral** Cuban, our cage, my **slave shipmate**,
Porque yo soy carabalí, llevo los instrumentos	Because I am carabalí, I carry the instruments
Calamaná, hierba mala, cortemos por la raíz	Calamaná, bad herb, let's cut it at the root
Calamaná, hierba mala, cortemos por la raíz	Calamaná, bad herb, let's cut it at the root

Like other song examples in this chapter, the Carabalí society's song takes the origo of a slave in the moment before rebelling, but this time telescoping the immediacy of slave experience into the here-and-now moment of being a member of the Olugo cabildo, of being Carabalí. "Carabalí" is a Cuban colonial ethnonym for slaves imported from the ports of Calabar in the Niger Delta, slaves who might have been captured from any number of places over a wide region, although in Cuba today, "Carabalí" is identified with Efik and Ibibio groups of Southeastern Nigeria (see discussion in chap. 5). The very identification as a member of this Carabalí folklore society creates a continuity with a historical category of Carabalí slaves, one frequently invoked and heightened through the society's song lyrics and choreographies, as the next chapter will show.

The song begins with a play on the very first word between *mal* (bad, evil) and a Bozal pronunciation of *mayoral*, slave foreman, continuing by quickly evoking captivity (*nuestra jaula*) and the kinship created with other slaves (*caravelo mío*). The song then compares the cruel mayoral to a detested weed, the calamaná, which must be cut at the root to be killed. At this point in the planned choreography, the group of dancers with roles as "vassals" (the society's polite euphemism for "slaves") would perform attacking and carrying off the dancer with the role of *mayoral*, giving even more immediacy to the historical vignette of the song. The use of Bozalisms is fleeting in this song, but they contribute to the song's chronotope, in which Cuba's colonial past as a slave society is made relevant to the present in the first-person voice of a rebellious African slave, who becomes immanent in the moment of performance. No muerto appears in this performance; rather, the entire cabildo choreographs its legacy as proud Carabalí.

In following the often minute traces of three registers of Blackness in actual use, their very enregisterment *as* voices of Blackness becomes apparent, as does their interactional significance, which extends as far as establishing the immanence of spirits and orichas. Their fleeting appearances together and in various juxtapositions index the differing valences of Blackness—spiritual, earthy, folkloric, rebellious, sometimes humble and sometimes powerful—and invoke chronotopes juxtaposing the transcendent and the historical, present and past, Africa and Cuba. The indexical orders regimenting Bozal, Lucumí, and lengua Conga as recognizable registers do not function through static one-to-one correspondences between register and "identity," however much metadiscourse about them often proposes one-to-one correspondences between, for example, Lucumí and Santería, Bozal and slaves, lengua Conga and Paleros. Rather, more complex and emergent indexical links between register tokens and various historical and figural effects emerge in performances such as those examined in this chapter—sometimes with only a hint of pronunciation or a bit of indirectness or a single word—but with cumulative effects connecting such instances into robust voices and durable cultural logics of race and history that we will continue to explore in later chapters.

5

Pride: Singing Black History in the Carabalí Cabildos

La reina, princesa, duquesa	The queen, princess, duchess
La reina se va a coronar	The queen is going to be crowned
A la corte, a la corte	The court, the court
A la corte se va a coronar	The court is going to be crowned

Cabildo Carabalí Isuama Song, Version Cited in Pérez et al.(1982)

Queens, princesses, duchesses, and marquesas in revolutionary Cuba? They, and their partners, the kings, princes, dukes, and marquis, constitute the traditional royal "court" in Santiago's two contemporary Carabalí societies, regally dancing alongside machete-waving "vassals" who enact a more openly rebellious strain of Cuban history, as the fighters who threw off the yoke of slavery and helped free Cuba from Spain during the second half of the nineteenth century. The vassals' call is ¡*libertad*!—freedom! When the Carabalí societies perform at carnival each year, they reenact this specific, colonial-era theater of historical imagination.

In this chapter, I consider performances of Blackness in the Cabildos Carabalí Olugo and Isuama in light of their long history as neighborhood-based, somewhat autonomous domains of Black sociality and their current role as officially supported "carriers of tradition" charged with cultural preservation. So strongly are the Carabalí associated with folklore tradition that they have long been regarded as dusty, decayed, and disappearing institutions, shadows of their earlier incarnations, especially in contrast to the lively innovation associated with those other carnival comparsas known as congas, whose dancers tend to be older teens and young adults. One friend, a frequent visitor to Santiago, commented to me about the Carabalí performances during carnival: "Oh, I love to see those old people dancing!" But it is not just the Carabalí societies' membership, encompassing the elderly, the middle-aged, and the very young, that continues to regard them as essential to Santiago's sense of its history. I will give particular attention to Carabalí performances, featuring music, songs, choreography, and dramatic reenactments of what it means to be Carabalí and in ever broader concentric circles, to be Black,

Santiaguero, and Cuban. Nor can their history be understood without also considering the dynamics of gender in performance.

The goal of the chapter, then, is to understand Carabalí performances as imaginations of history that evoke the historical present of Blackness, with an eye to the uses to which the timeless immediacy of the colonial era of slavery is put in the work of racial identification, sociality, and belonging in Cuba today. I take the sentiment of pride as a focal point because my Cuban interlocutors, both folklorists and Carabalí members point out the Carabalí societies as "fuentes de autoestima" (sources of pride/self-respect). I want to understand: Whose pride? Pride about what? And why?

What better way to approach the topic of Carabalí pride—*autoestima*—than with three contrasting visions of the Carabalí princesses.

When I went to Cuba in May 2007, my then four-year-old daughter Yasmin was in a phase of wearing Disney princess dresses whenever possible. As some Cuban friends and I watched her skip around the patio dressed as Snow White one morning, I complained about the lack of brown-skinned, curly haired Disney princesses for her to identify with. We laughed ruefully about the irony of a little African American girl trying to become "snow white," then one friend, a longtime folkloric dance promoter in Santiago, said that Yasmin should see the princesses of the Carabalí. In their fancy satin gowns, stepping regally to the Carabalí rhythms, the princess, duchess, marquesa, and queen herself were emblems of pride—*autoestima*—for the city's two traditional Carabalí societies. Each female member of the "court" is accompanied by a male partner of the same rank: prince, duke, marquis, and king, all dressed in satiny, embroidered tunics with full sleeves and knee-length britches with tights, lacking only powdered wigs to look like members of the French court at Versailles (see fig. 5.1). The king, queen, princess, and prince all wear gold-colored cardboard crowns, giving an overall effect of imitating royalty to the point of parody, except that they maintain a serious and regal presence. The two Carabalí societies, Isuama and Olugo, each had a children's group as well, and over the years Yasmin and I watched the princesses of the Carabalí rehearse and perform many times. After carnival ended in July 2011, Yasmin, by then eight and still delighted by fancy frills, even got to dress up as a Carabalí princess at the house of a friend, Lidiagne, who danced in Olugo's children's group, and whose mother, Imilce, was the group's choreographer. Posed together in a series of dresses by Imilce as if for portraits for their *quinceañeras* (girls' coming-of-age celebration), the girls indeed looked like they were dressed in Disney princess gowns, but for the headscarves (see fig. 5.2).

Other Cubans pointed out the antithesis of princesses of the Carabalí in the larger corps of Carabalí dancers known as the *vasallos* (vassals), who are

FIGURE 5.1 Carabalí king and queen of the Cabildo Olugo children's ensemble in carnival performance, Santiago de Cuba, July 24, 2011. Photo by the author.

subdivided into the *esclavos* (slaves) and *libertos* (freedmen). One fervently revolutionary friend, also a folklore professional, relished describing for me, in great detail, the old-time costumes used by the Carabalí societies during the 1970s and 1980s, even locating old photographs to show me the long dresses of checked gingham worn by the women and the matching blue-and-white handkerchiefs tied around each man's throat and representing the colors of the Cuban independence fighters, with a large straw hat hanging down each man's back. All would wear a simple sandal made from a rubber strip from an old tire, held on with a strap of cloth. His nostalgic vision of the Carabalí men waving machetes and the Carabalí women waving Cuban flags and blue-and-white checked handkerchiefs evoked a very different vision of pride, expressed not in idioms of eighteenth-century European royalty but in what he saw as more properly patriotic images of what peasants and slaves might have considered their finery.[1] This, he insisted, was the traditional costume of the Carabalí, not the shiny, flouncy dresses the vassals (these days, all the Carabalí women) wear today. Photographs from the era show that the royal court, then as now, dressed in costume finery, in contrast to the vassals.

In case the colonial social order diagrammed by this opposition between court and vassals needed any further illustration, during carnival performances, a slave overseer (*mayoral*) clad in a loose white shirt, simple black pants, tall riding boots, and what Americans would call a cowboy hat strode

FIGURE 5.2 Yasmin and Lidiagne pose in Carabalí carnival costumes, Santiago de Cuba, July 29, 2011. Photo by the author.

menacingly among the rows of vassals with a whip (fig. 5.3). In keeping with these reenactments of monarchy, colonialism, and slavery, the Carabalí performances I saw always culminated with songs written shortly after Cuba won independence from Spain in 1898 by Carabalí members who were veterans of those struggles and who recounted their role in fighting for liberty and equality as well as independence from Spain. During songs with historical narratives, in particular "Libertad," and "La Invasión," the vassals brandished their machetes as the ex-slave and peasant mambí fighters once had (fig. 5.4).

One additional vision of the princesses of the Carabalí dates from prerevolutionary times and is attested by photographs and testimonies from the 1940s and 1950s, when men cross-dressed in elegant and tasteful ball gowns of the era to dance as the Carabalí princesses, partnered with other men in the male roles. Most people I asked pleaded ignorance or only reluctantly

FIGURE 5.3 The overseer watches the slaves work, with the royal court in the background, during Carabalí Cabildo Isuama carnival performance, Santiago de Cuba, July 24, 2011. Photo by the author.

discussed what one folklorist disparagingly called the "maricón princesas de la carabalí" (fairy princesses of Carabalí). But the few who could (and would) tell me something of that era emphasized that these men were proud and beautiful and that at least a few of them were highly regarded community members, despite being open or suspected homosexuals—or worse yet, in Cuban terms, effeminate men—amid rampant homophobia. Carabalí societies, which for most of the decades between 1890 and 1960 were secretive and exclusive to (Black) men, needed to have men dance the female roles that existed even then. And transvestism was and remains a robust carnival tradition in Santiago, one more variety of masquerade in the topsy-turvy performances of carnival. But what struck me in the one photograph I have been shown of a male Carabalí "princess" was the understated elegance of the dress and pose: there was no trace of the campy exaggeration—of feminine bodily curves, makeup, hair, outfit—that one sees, for example, in the crazy wigs, stuffed bras, and clingy dresses of cross-dressing carnival costumes I saw during the Conga de los Hoyos's Invasion opening carnival in July 2011 (see chap. 3). The photo, a small black-and-white full-length studio portrait, shows a slim and handsome man standing formally in his floor-length gown, looking seriously toward the camera, with just a hint of makeup perhaps, but with a man's short haircut.

FIGURE 5.4 Dancers in role of freedmen perform with cardboard machetes during Carabalí Cabildo Isuama carnival performance, Santiago de Cuba, July 24, 2011. Photo by the author.

This hidden history was finally revealed to me during an interview with folklore researcher Gladys Gonzalez, who has devoted decades to studying traditional societies like the Carabalí, when she showed me this photograph of her mentor and godfather in Ocha, José Megret Pié, a well-known local santero and palero who was among those who helped establish Santería in Santiago during the 1940s, having a close association with founding figure Reynerio Pérez.[2] The photo seems to date from the 1940s or perhaps 1950s, as José Pié, born sometime during the second decade of the twentieth century, looks no more than thirty years old. Gladys described her godfather as "very refined, very French, and homosexual without being at all effeminate."[3] Although his relationships with other men were apparently well-known, he also lived with several women during his life, and his substantial charisma made him a community leader, a central figure in the emerging Ocha and Palo religious community of the Los Hoyos neighborhood and the Carabalí Isuama society also located there. Gladys told me that the male transvestite princesses of the Carabalí were banned by government functionaries in the Ministry of Culture after the revolution, as part of the persecution of homosexuals in the 1960s. Once, probably around the end of the 1970s or early 1980s, during a decade Cuban artists and intellectuals refer to as the "gray period," José Pié showed her his photograph, which he had kept hidden. Taking hold of it as if to look more closely at it, she quickly tucked it in her bra, refusing to return it despite his entreaties because she recognized its historical value and feared he might hide it again or even destroy it, given the repressive climate of those years. Indeed, those years almost accomplished an erasure of even the memory of the transvestite princesses of the Carabalí. The historical imagination is like that: many things are forgotten in order to remember a few. The obvious question is why remember those few particular moments, and why erase those others?

Interdiscursivity, Entextualization, and Belonging

Because Carabalí performances so consistently emphasize tradition and cast a backward glance into a particular moment of history, and because the Carabalí societies themselves are viewed with nostalgia, as a tradition in need of preservation, they present an opportunity to understand the workings of chronotope in producing historical and racial subjectivities. In particular, I will consider Carabalí performances as interactional events that mobilize interdiscursive relationships to link to previous events and create recognizable genres, registers, and figures. Interdiscursivity, that basic property of semiosis that allows signs to be linked across time, is key to the reflexivity of language and its capacity to create temporal orders and time-transcending connections across them.

By allowing semiotic regularities to be discerned, interdiscursivity contributes to entextualization processes, by which certain chunks of discourse gain enough salience that they can be replicated, either in a similar context, for example, like a ritual or a story or song that can be repeated in its entirety, or recontextualized, as when a recognizable part of a ritual is parodied as a joke or when a song fragment is sampled into some new song, or when I quote someone else but bend their words to my own purpose. And entextualization, the process by which some series of signs in the stream of discourse becomes recognizable as a chunk that can be replicated, contributes to enregisterment, the process through which discourse types, speech styles, and genres become recognizable as representing particular social meanings and types of persons. Carabalí songs, as highly entextualized and therefore readily recognizable discourse events (partly because they are also musical events), are especially interesting to consider for the kinds of interdiscursivity they manifest and the temporal orders and historical subjectivities they thereby help to create in performance. I suggest that historical and interdiscursive references made in songs and indexed by their very performance create a sense of transcendent collectivity among Carabalí members, in which they reinforce feelings of belonging to the cabildo and claims about how the cabildo belongs to a proud tradition.

The major Carabalí performances occur during carnival season in Santiago, in July, when the two Carabalí societies join in officially organized parades and perform for the carnival judges. During much of the rest of the year, and particularly between May and July, the societies hold rehearsals and occasional social events. Occasionally one or the other might be called on for a performance, for example, when the Ballet Folklórico de Oriente invited both groups to join the finale of a dance performance commemorating its and Cutumba's fiftieth anniversary in November 2009, or when I or some other foreign visitor arrange for a small performance, perhaps in order to film it.

My preliminary example, however, concerns a much more informal moment of "breakthrough into performance" (Bauman 1993, 26–27) during an interview I videotaped with a small group of elderly Isuama members in March 2010, together with their young assistant director, Ricardo, known as Marimón, and folklorist Ernesto Armiñán Linares. This was a moment when historical narrative led to song and song led to a shared sense of pride in belonging. As the conversation moved from one of the elders recounting how she joined the society (around 1960) and how they did things back then, including the dresses of checked gingham, the white trousers, the straw hats, and machetes, the group began to list the names of illustrious predecessors that the Carabalí still recalled and still gave homage to in their invocations of the dead. Antonio Napolé and his wife María Antonio Rivart were mentioned, at which Marimón, a young man whose grandfather had introduced him to the cabildo as a child, reminded us that the sons of these Isuama founders were all members of the liberation army that had freed Cuba from Spanish control in 1898. In the transcription of this conversation, filmed March 1, 2010, M is Marimón and A is Armiñán.

1 M ... que eran miembros del ejército libertador. Y ocuparon, cargo dentro de aquel ejército. Y de allí uno viene que, como se dice una de la:, de las historias, [[más profundas de la carabalí.

[... that were members of the Liberation Army. And they had, responsibility in that army. And from there one comes that, as they say one of the, one of the the deepest stories of the carabalí.

2 A [[más profundas de los cabildos

[[deepest of the [Black] societies

3 M Inclusive yo he leído a veces esta investigación, y cómo los hachones han sido en un documento que daba de Antonio Maceo en el cabildo, y muchos niegan eso. Hay cartas que mencionan a Antonio Maceo como un participante más . de los cabildos, y se niegan. El mismo canto de Margarita . que habla directamente de la esclavi-

tud, que hablando de Virginia seguro que lo va a cantar, que es un canto fuerte de Virginia, es ese que dice

Including that I have sometimes read this research, and how the [redacting] hatch marks were in a document that put Antonio Maceo in the cofraternity, and many people deny this. There are letters that mention Antonio Maceo as one more participant . of the cabildos, and [they] deny it. The very song of Margarita . that speaks directly about slavery, that speaking of Virginia I'm sure she will sing it, because it is a powerful song Virginia does, and it's that [song] that says

4 Jamo te quita la vida
Master takes your life
5 Tú ya te debes cansar
You must be tired of it by now
6 Tu ve—tú misma Margarita
You see—you the same Margarita
7 que la guerra va a empezar
that the war is going to start
8 Yo amuelo bien mi machete
I sharpen my machete well
9 Que mi amo me regaló
That my master gave to me
10 Para la libertad al esclavo
For freedom to the slave
11 que Margarita llamó
that Margarita called
12 Y entonces el coro sigue
And then the chorus continues
13 La libertad, libertad, libertad
Freedom, freedom, freedom
14 Todas las campana suenan
All the bells ring
15 A [*sings, with others joining him*] Libertad, libertad, libertad, libertad
Freedom, freedom, freedom, freedom
16 libertad a la campana solís
freedom to the Solís [?] bell
17 M [*speaking*] Inclusive el final de ese canto dice, eh
Including the end of the song, which says, ah
18 [*sings*] Maceo
Maceo
19 ha guerrido
has made war
20 con su machete habló
spoke with his machete

21 negrito con el finó
little black man used it to finish things off
22 abajó el yugo del español
lowered the yoke of the Spanish
23 libertad, libertad, libertad, libertad
freedom, freedom, freedom, freedom
24 [*speaking*] y aquello tiempo cuando hacía esa manifestación, eran unas banderonas de medio metro que llevaba cada integrante, y llevaba hacía así y eran banderas [rojas and in that time when they did that performance, they were some banners of about a half a meter [*indicates size with his arms*] that each participant carried, and they raised them to here [*indicates by waving arms overhead*] and they were red [flags
25 A [[rojas
[[red
26 M [[blancas
[[white
27 A [[blancas
[[white
28 M y [[azules
and [[blue
29 A [[azules
[[blue
30 All [*crosstalk of several voices with all nodding*]

Marimón claimed that the famous Afro-Cuban general Antonio María de la Caridad Maceo Grajales, born in Los Hoyos, was a member of Isuama, a fact unspecified parties tried to conceal with censor's marks in historical documents. As evidence he began to recite a song, "Libertad." He introduced his recitation of the lyrics of the first verse with the disclaimer that it is a "powerful song" of Virginia, an elderly singer who had once sung the lead for Isuama performances and still had an operatic voice, and who had not yet arrived. Not wanting to steal her thunder or risk comparison to her, perhaps, Marimón did not perform the song as a song but rather quoted from it, in speaking intonation and with various self-corrections. But by the time he had recited a shortened version of the chorus, "Libertad, libertad, libertad / todas las campanas suenan," the song's familiar melody inserted itself. Armiñán, a talented singer, interrupted with a breakthrough into full performance, now singing that chorus, and immediately joined by everyone present, a joint performance preserving the absent Virginia's virtuosity as lead singer while giving those present the feeling of togetherness in the familiar words, like joining a round of "Auld Lang Syne." Marimón then tentatively broke into performance himself, again giving the quotative frame and discourse marker, "ah" as disclaimers of performance: "the end of the song says, ah," before singing that final verse. And, with the entire group now relaxed and animated after the stiff beginning of the interview, he and Armiñán jointly recited, in a moment of dialogic intensification, the patriotic colors of the small flags all the dancers would wave during the song, back when it was frequently performed: "red, red; white, white; and blue, blue."[4] With that, everyone in the group started talking at once, until Armiñán seized control of the floor to call for the song to once again be performed in the traditional, patriotic way. Later, Virginia of the beautiful voice did arrive, and this and other songs were sung again with her lead and the enthusiastic chorus of the other cabildo members, despite competition from the pounding reggaeton music across the street.

This moment of breakthrough into performance demonstrates an important interactional component of the Carabalí songs: they are meant to be performed by a group, with the chorus following the lead singer, and as such they creatively index group solidarity both as patriotic Cuban citizens and as cabildo members who remember and reenact their proud history—a history of slavery and of fighting for freedom. In this particular instance, the interaction itself diagrammed a build-up of energy and its channeling into the coordinated focus of jointly singing a song, thereby enacting being a proud member of the Carabalí now, then, and forever. More generally, those two kinds of belonging—the more select membership in a Carabalí society and the broader national identification—are treated as inextricable in songs such as "Libertad." And the interaction prior to the song, too, made a bid for fraternity with Antonio Maceo, as culture hero of free Cuba and Carabalí member according to an occluded history. Carabalí songs, indeed, are performative, seeking to enact the very vision of solidarity and belonging they invoke through their historical vignettes. In "Libertad," this is achieved through the song's voicing, sung from the origo of a rebelling slave and directed to "you," another slave rebel. Singing it, one can imagine Isuama's founders having the very conversation sung in the lyrics as they entered the 1895 war for independence and themselves, perhaps, taking the historical voices of enslaved predecessors—the original "Carabalí."

To borrow from Diana Taylor's (2003) metaphor contrasting the "archive" and the "repertoire" as textual versus performed modalities of historical memory, Isuama and Olugo perform a custodial role in safeguarding historical memory through their repertoire of music, song, and dance, which constitutes a repository of embodied and performed collective memory—a "repertoire" (see also Connerton 1989). My goal here is to examine the chronotopic workings of this repertoire in performance, to show how the Carabalí, in a sense, sing the historical imagination of quintessentially Cuban Blackness and solidarity.

A Brief History of the Carabalí

The term "Carabalí" is a Cuban ethnonym for what, in colonial times, were known as the various "African nations" that provided captives for the slave trade: Lucumí, Congo, Mandinga, Ganga, and many others were each traced to particular African regions and points of embarkation for particular stretches of the slave-trading era, and, in Cuban usage, were treated as seemingly stable referents for recognizable types of Africans. Slave traders and slave owners compared the relative merits of these different "nations" as slaves in terms of their relative strength, temperament, and suitability for particular kinds of labor, stereotypes that were repeated in Colonial-era travelogues written by foreigner visitors (interesting examples include Abbot 1829; Ballou 1854; Humboldt 2001; Jameson 1821; Philalethes 1856; Wurdemann 1844). These comparisons persist today, especially in contrasting stereotypes of the highly assimilated Carabalí with the brutish, rebellious Congos and the cultured, urbane Lucumí. The Cuban version of a widespread Latin American proverb about national origins hints at such comparisons even as they emphasize a shared African heritage: "él que no tiene de Congo tiene de Carabalí" (if you're not part Congo you're part Carabalí).

Slaves designated Carabalí in Cuba were those shipped from the ports of the two cities of Calabar and the neighboring city of Bonny, in modern-day southeast Nigeria, a densely populated region encompassing the Niger and Cross River deltas and their slave trade far upstream (Klein 1999, 64–64, 71–72, 195). This robust trade in slaves from a wide swath of territory across eastern Nigeria and western Cameroon would likely have encompassed many farflung societies and languages, people who would not necessarily have felt much of a common identity prior to being thrown together as slaves. On the Cuban side, those who disembarked from the Middle Passage to become Carabalí are today remembered in Cuba as the source of the Abakuá secret men's societies of Western Cuba's port cities and of the highly assimilated, urban Carabalí societies of Santiago de Cuba. Although much scholarly effort has lately gone into deciding the source societies and languages of the Cuban Carabalí (fixing usually on the Cross River societies of the Efik and Ibibio), historians have made a compelling case for these labels as products of transatlantic ethnogenesis.[5] As much as slave owners had reasons for wanting to sort (and separate) slaves, African captives and their descendants, too, had reasons for claiming particular identifications and allegiances. If adopting a clearly novel creole identity as Carabalí provided entrance into an existing network of social support, such as one of the colonial-era religious cofraternities or municipal cabildos for slaves of a particular "nation," that may have overcome obvious linguistic and cultural differences with others calling themselves Carabalí.

While early twentieth-century descendants of slaves were more likely to know that grandma was Carabalí and grandpa was Congo, specific genealogical knowledge about African places of origin has faded from family histories over the ensuing generations. Most Cubans I've asked cannot go much farther back than their own grand- or perhaps great-grandparents and seem to remember origins only when those grandparents were immigrants (from Galicia, Jamaica, or Haiti, e.g.). Even by the 1890s, when a Carabalí society called Isuama appears in Santiago's public record as a legally inscribed association, its officers were Cubans of color, creoles rather than transplanted Africans, so that its designation as a specifically Carabalí society was likely already a nod at tradition rather than a declaration of genealogy. A chronicler of the era, Manuel Palacios Estrada, cited in Pérez et al. (1982), mentions the existence of a precursor to Isuama called the Carabalizona de Santa Lucía, active between 1884 and 1887. Isuama took a different patron saint, however: San Juan de Nepomuceno. According to an unpublished oral history collected by Gladys Gonzalez, Isuama's founder, María Antonio Rivart and her husband, remembered by current members of Isuama as Antonio Baracoa, worked with a *muerto africano*, or African spirit, named Pa Ponú but identified him with (and perhaps disguised him as) the Catholic saint.[6]

Historical records attest to colonial-era "Carabalí" carnival comparsas in Santiago from the start of the nineteenth century (Pérez et al. 1982), and one supposes that some had antecedents in religious cofraternities and *cabildos de nación* specifically for people designated (or designating themselves) as Carabalí (Montejo Arrechea 1993). Religious cofraternities organized by Africans sharing a particular nation, dedicated to a Catholic patron saint and to the church where that saint's icon resided, and receiving support from wealthy White patrons were evident in Santiago de Cuba at least as early as the seventeenth century (Portuondo Zuñiga 2000). Many were designated (and perhaps came to identify themselves) as Carabalí because the Bight of Biafra, their point of departure from Africa, was a major source of captives throughout the era of the transatlantic slave trade (see Klein 1999).

It is important to keep in mind that importation of new African captives to Cuba, having reached its peak between 1820 and 1840, had slowed to a trickle by the late 1850s, long before slavery's complete abolition in 1886 and the emergence of today's Carabalí cabildos.[7] Cuban-born descendants tended to move away from any close identification with African ethnicity or language by the second generation, assimilating as creoles, some of whom preserved affinities for African-derived cultural practices of the sort cultivated in cabildos, cofraternities, and other kinds of associations. But many others, in developing a "creole consciousness," rejected things African in favor of elite, European cultural markers and forms of association that came to represent Cubanness and modernity.[8]

Creole Cubans of color were distinguished from African "Bozals" and sorted according to the Spanish colonial caste system as enslaved or free, and as morenos, pardos, mulatos, and so forth, which, in combination with their location, labor skills, and social networks, largely determined their opportunities for social advancement (Barcia Zequeira 2003; Martinez-Alier 1989; Montejo Arrechea 1993). The array of social clubs and associations mirrored the social order in being exclusive to particular social castes, although some, such as the Masons, who organized Black as well as White lodges, began to break the color barriers as the proindependence movement developed in the 1860s. These kinds of breaches, including the attempted induction of racially higher-status morenos and pardos into black *cabildos de nación*, were in turn outlawed as threats to the policy of keeping people of color divided among themselves (Montejo Arrechea 1993). Moments of social crisis erupted when people of color were suspected of working together, most notably in the elites' violent reactions to the Aponte Conspiracy of 1812, the Escalera Conspiracy of 1844, and even the much later Partido Independiente de Color (Independent Party of Color) massacre of 1912 (Palmié 2002). The specter of the Haitian Revolution haunted Cuban race relations for a hundred years.

And sometimes, one imagines, the racial order was reinforced from within, as when an elderly Isuama member and descendant of the Baracoas, Olimpo Nápoles, interviewed in the 1980s by Pérez et al. (1982), recalled that Isuama had been rejected even as late as the 1940s and 1950s as "a black thing" by mulatos who could afford to join more elite social clubs modeled on White-only clubs. According to him, in that era of racial segregation, mulatos *de verdá* (true mulatos) joined the Luz de Oriente, darker-skinned half-mulatos joined the Casino Cuba, and *negros prietos* (dark-skinned Blacks) like him joined the Sociedad de Aponte. Since anyone could join the Carabalí, only "la gente má denutrida . . . eran lo que salían en la Carabalí" (only the most malnourished people . . . were the ones to go out in the Carabalí). In that era, he avoided the Carabalí for reasons of "vanity."

By the time the Cabildo Carabalí Isuama was established, traditional cabildos and cofraternities for people of color had been outlawed because of their potential for sedition (against slavery, against Spain) and their association with the sometimes out-of-favor Catholic Church. In 1887, a new law required all such groups to convert themselves into "societies for recreation and instruction." In addition to their functions of sociality and recreation and their longstanding provisions for mutual aid in case of illness or death among members, societies like the Cabildo Carabalí Isuama also fomented political organizing (Howard 1998; Rushing 1992). The Napolés family from Baracoa, who emerged as founders of the modern Isuama in 1894, had perhaps six members who joined the ranks of officers in the Liberation Army that successfully fought the Spanish in the war of 1894–98 (Pérez et al. 1982, 12–13).

Indeed, the Baracoa brothers, as they are called even today in ritual invocations and oral histories, made their contributions to the struggle for independence central to Isuama's corporate identity. Black Cuban participation in the war on an equal footing with Whites became the touchstone for demands for equal political rights in the new Cuban Republic in the decades following its founding in 1902. And, the struggle over the place of Cubans of color in the new Republic was a defining issue during the span between 1902 and 1912, when a brutal massacre of Black Cubans destroyed the emerging Partido Independiente de Color and suppressed the political ambitions of people of color.[9] Members of Black associations like the Cabildo Carabalí Isuama and a number of other Carabalí cabildos mentioned as carnival comparsas in 1910 were marginalized by the class and color lines that governed life in the years of the Cuban Republic, but they found ways to use their societies' carnival performances as mouthpieces to broadcast their demands and critiques. The Carabalí Isuama was located in the Los Hoyos neighborhood, sometimes sharing the neighborhood with new or splinter groups that formed other Carabalí societies. The precursor of the Cabildo Carabalí Olugo in the Tivolí neighborhood also had emerged by 1910, and in 1919, according to oral history, performed a song that got it banned from carnival for forty years. As the story was separately told to me by Gladys Gonzalez and Olugo's current director, Benito Ramirez Soulary, the grandson of its founding director, the elder Porfilio Soulary led the group in singing:

O Cuba Cuba e	Oh Cuba, Cuba eh
Cuba Cuba yo	Cuba, Cuba, me
Cuba Cuba mío	Cuba, my Cuba
Blanco nos jodió	White fucked us over

On different occasions of singing the song and retelling the story, the last line varied in who it critiqued: "El gobierno nos jodió / Yanquí nos jodió" (The government fucked us over / Yankee fucked us over).

Whatever the offending line or lines may have been, and all of these would have been accurate critiques, the police seized and destroyed Olugo's instruments and banned the group from performing for decades as punishment. Carnival performances in that era before the revolution frequently had presented opportunities for veiled critique and parody. For example, in a *caracterización*, someone would dress up as a politician or other prominent figure in order to mock them or satirize their policies. Taken too far, such critiques and "characterizations" would be punished by the authorities. After the revolution, even these limited opportunities for political satire and parody disappeared from carnival, which today has a very earnest character in celebrating Cuban traditions and revolutionary milestones (see chap. 3).

As for the Cabildo Carabalí Olugo, Benito said that the society continued to exist, that members continued to pay dues and to meet clandestinely, and that they reemerged in carnival with his grandfather still the director in 1959, now leading a new verse of another song Benito sang for me:

Hace cuarenta años que yo no salí	For forty years I didn't go out
para el Carabalí Olugo de Tivolí	for the Carabalí Olugo of Tivolí
Eso es verdad, eso es así,	That's the truth, that's how it is
Olugo me trajo a Cuba a bailar carabalí	Olugo brought me to Cuba to dance Carabalí

When Benito, Marimón, and other Carabalí cabildo members and folklorists perform these songs today, whether in full performance or in momentary "breakthroughs" while talking to me or one another, the songs interdiscursively connect to the earlier performances referenced in their stories: Benito sings me the song as his grandfather once sang it, and that interdiscursivity is the very point of singing it today, now. Keeping their role as historical mnemonics in mind, one striking aspect of these songs is their first-person voicing and the immediacy of the events they describe. To sing them is to assume the voice of those Carabalí ancestors, the Baracoa brothers, the mambí heroes and outspoken men like Soulary who founded the Carabalí societies and, insofar as such manifestations of folkloric and historical Blackness index deep national identity, helped create Cuba itself. In the next sections, I examine the chronotopes enacted through Carabalí songs.

The Invasion: How Interdiscursive Comparisons Create a History of Blackness

Carabalí songs—and the performances they are part of—point back in time to a specific, historical moment, and do so in ways that make that moment, the colonial era of slavery and rebellion, relevant to the present moment of performance. They do so by enacting the speech, appearance, and actions of historical Black figures so as to create an atemporal horizon or frame of comparison with long-ago slaves, maroons, and *mambíses.* Within this frame of comparison, the colonial era of slavery is made relevant to the present moment of performance, coming to seem intrinsic to the very notions of tradition, folklore, and belonging that are central to today's Carabalí members. The effect of these performances is to create a distinctive chronotope of unchanging folkloricized Blackness that glances backward with nostalgia.

Chronotopic work inheres in interdiscursive processes as we necessarily order chunks of semiotic activity into earlier and later iterations or as instances of time-transcending types within a frame of comparison. That is, interdiscursive connections rely on chronotopic frames to become evident and, by virtue of the linkage, create temporal series that order linked events. As Michael Silverstein (2005, 7–9) argues, an indexical connection between two events necessarily creates "eval-ness" between them—an achronic state of suspension in which their similarities can be compared. He proposes that the nature of that temporal relationship determines whether the relationship is construable as between a semiotic "type" and its instantiation or between earlier and later contextually contingent semiotic events, as in reported speech (see also Dunn 2006). Carabalí songs, and indeed, Carabalí performances, are a recognized folklore genre in Santiago de Cuba: each new performance interdiscursively relates to that type. Some song performances, like Benito Ramirez's singing of "O Cuba, Cuba e" to me on several occasions, were interdiscursively framed as tokens pointing back at an earlier performance—led by his grandfather on a fateful occasion in 1919.

Silverstein (2005) specifies an additional distinction in kinds of interdiscursive connections, between sourced or targeted interdiscursivity, where "type- or token-sourced" means a general type or earlier instance is presupposed to already exist, and "type- or token-targeted" means an attempt to create a type, genre, style, voice, or the like is underway. All the Carabalí songs presented thus far are type sourced, and "O Cuba, Cuba e" is, I suggest, in addition token sourced, for which the source being quoted is the specific event of his grandfather's 1919 performance.

Benito actively writes new songs for Olugo to perform, and one of those, invoking the orichas and incorporating a brief break into *bembé* rhythms used in festive ceremonies for the orichas, was interpreted by the judges in the 2009 carnival as an attempt at type targeting the Carabalí repertoire. The judge critiqued Olugo's performance for straying from the proper Carabalí rhythms into musical territory beyond its traditional purview. Benito's attempt at innovation was unfavorably compared to Carabalí tradition because, however well performed the bembé music, it type sourced a non-Carabalí genre. His attempt to broaden the repertoire of Carabalí performance by citing (type sourcing) what he thought of as a closely related domain of folklore and tradition, an exercise in type targeting Carabalí performance, failed. As one of the Olugo musicians explained the rationale for adding bembé to the Carabalí to me: "The evolution of life, the evolution of the Carabalí Blacks, they would have done their Carabalí (rhythms and dances), and they also would have held their bembés" (Olugo group interview, February 22, 2010). This and similar explanations from Benito suggest that Olugo members viewed the failed innovation as an attempt at type sourcing "what Carabalí slaves actually did," which would have included learning from other African and creole traditions. Alas, the carnival judges, charged with enforcing genre boundaries, did not see things that way.

This example illustrates that interdiscursive links are subject to reflexive calibration: different horizons of comparison are possible, creating possibilities for divergent interpretations of what any particular event means and which temporal series of events it is part of. In describing interdiscursivity in terms of "horizons" of comparison, I am adapting Paul Johnson's (2007) notion of "diasporic horizons," which he uses to account for shifting perspectives evident among Garifuna regarding their origins and therefore their current identifications: do they look to Africa of the transatlantic slave trade era, or to the Afro-Carib maroons' banishment from their Saint Vincent island home to the remote eastern coast of Central America in 1797, or to modern-day emigration from villages along the eastern coast of Central America to cities of the global North like New York, in which they have discovered a common Blackness with other groups of the African Diaspora? Each horizon suggests a different kind of chronotope for its own distinct historical consciousness and social identifications. Note that to flatten this "heterochronicity" (Lemon 2009) into the universal, empty time of scholarly history (Trouillot 1995) can lead to the kinds of debates and confusions described above regarding what a label such as "Carabalí" (or "Yoruba" or "Abakuá" or even "Black" for that matter) might mean or have meant in any particular context, often resulting in simplistic assumptions that the primordial source of such identifications must lie in Africa.[10]

To examine the semiotic construction of chronotopic horizons, for example, in the narration of historical memories, it is essential to trace how interdiscursive links create broader spatiotemporal scenarios for the events they connect. For instance, Wilce (2009) examines how lament, iconized in women's wailing, has lately become framed as a global traditional genre, one that reflexively comments on its very endangerment and disappearance. Tomlinson (2004) examines how Fijian narratives of decline produce a "perpetual lament" for lost greatness. In both of these cases, nostalgia provides the "structure of feeling" for a retrospective chronotope of times past and things lost. In the case I examine, a romanticizing and exoticizing cloak of nostalgia is wrapped around certain figures and performances marked as African even as they occur in the present moment. This happens, I suggest, through interdiscursive webs of performances that assign Blackness to a perpetually available "historical present."

The workings of these chronotopic devices can be seen in the overall repertoire of songs from the Carabalí repertoire. As a preliminary example to sketch out the argument in a general way, consider the song "The Invasion," performed by both Olugo and Isuama and described by one folklorist as "the national hymn of the Carabalí." The song is attributed to Simon Napolés, a veteran mambí who became a songwriter (*trovador*), and it recounts the Liberation Army's famous 1895 march across Cuba to rout the Spanish.[11] I recorded this version in a May 2007 interview with Ernesto Armiñán Linares and again in a May 2008 performance by Olugo:

	La Invasión	The Invasion
1	[*estrofa 1*] Me mires en diferente	[*verse 1*] You look at me differently
2	porque soy carabalí	because I'm Carabalí
3	Me mires en diferente	You look at me differently
4	porque soy carabalí	because I'm Carabalí
5	Y en la guerra en '68	And in the war of sixty-eight
6	yo fui mambí	I was a mambí
7	Y en la del '95 a la invasión	And in the war of ninety-five, to the invasion
8	tambien yo fui	I also went
9	a defender a mi patria	to defend my fatherland
10	la tierra donde nací	the land where I was born
11	[*estrofa 2*] Cuando peleaba en Oriente	[*verse 2*] When I fought in the East
12	en la playa y en el batey	on the beach and in the grove
13	De los mangos 'e [de] Baraguá	of the Mangos o' Baraguá
14	partimos a Camagüey	we left for Camagüey
15	Se me cansó mi caballo	My horse got tired
16	y fui montado en un buey	and I went mounted on a donkey
17	[*Coro*] Y U'te lo ve camara'[da]	[*Chorus*] And so you see, comrade
18	Y U'te lo ve camara'[da]	And so you see, comrade
19	Que el negro carabalí	that the black Carabalí

20	peleó por la libertad	fought for liberty
21	[*estrofa* 3] Salimos de Camagüey	[*verse* 3] We left Camagüey
22	cruzando la trocha brava	crossing the fierce path
23	Salimos de Camagüey	We left Camagüey
24	cruzando la trocha brava	crossing the fierce path
25	Derrotando a los españoles	Defeating the Spaniards
26	llegamos a Santa Clara [Villa Clara]	we arrived in Santa Clara [Villa Clara]
	[*coro*]	[*chorus*]
27	[*estrofa* 4] Salimos de Santa Clara	[*verse* 4] We left Santa Clara
28	con honor y sin venganza	with honor and without vengeance
29	Salimos de Santa Clara	We left Santa Clara
30	con honor y sin venganza	with honor and without vengeance
31	Derrotando a los españoles	Defeating the Spaniards
32	hemos llegado a Matanzas	we have arrived in Matanzas
	[*coro*]	[*chorus*]
33	[*estrofa* 5] Y salimos de Matanzas	[*verse* 5] And we left Matanzas
34	con una gran caraván	with a great caravan
35	Y salimos de Matanzas	And we left Matanzas
36	con una gran caraván	with a great caravan
37	Derrotando a los españoles	Defeating the Spaniards
38	hemos llegado a Habana	we have arrived in Havana
	[*coro*]	[*chorus*]
39	[*estrofa* 6] Y salimos de la Habana	[*verse* 6] And we left Havana
40	sufriendo un intenso frío	suffering an intense cold
41	Y salimos de la Habana	And we left Havana
42	sufriendo un intenso frío	suffering an intense cold
43	Derrotando a los españoles	Defeating the Spaniards
44	llegamos a Pinar del Río	we arrived in Pinar del Río
	[*coro*]	[*chorus*]
45	[*estrofa* 7] Y cuando a Mantua llegamos	[*verse* 7] And when we arrived in Mantua
46	el final de la nación	the edge of the nation
47	Y cuando a Mantua llegamos	And when we arrived in Mantua
48	cayó el imperio español	the Spanish Empire fell
49	Y en el año '59 triunfó la Revolución	And in the year fifty-nine the Revolution triumphed
	[*coro*]	[*chorus*]

This song recounts the cabildo's involvement in the Cuban wars for independence from Spain. Sung as a first-person account, in simple past and then past perfect tense, it recounts the path independence fighters took across the island as they engaged the Spanish army in each place. The song thus is an aural map of the island and the war, sung from the origo of a mambí participant. As a bid for full citizenship by Carabalí members, the song revisits late nineteenth- and early twentieth-century arguments for Afro-Cubans to be accorded equal rights based on their contributions to the struggle for Cuban independence (de la Fuente 2001a; Fernández Robaina 1994; Ferrer 1999).

"La Invasión," like "Libertad," is so central to the Carabalí repertoire that I have heard one or the other, if not both, sung in every performance I have seen by Olugo and Isuama. When Ernesto Armiñán was teaching me the words of the song one afternoon as we sat on the terrace of the house where I was staying, the cook who worked there, Mabel Castro, came over to stand behind him and sing along: she had directed Isuama during the 1980s and enjoyed joining him in the chorus. After about the fourth verse, Mabel commented that the song was very long and returned to the kitchen, still humming the chorus. In performance, the vassals raise their arms and wave their machetes during this song. In a choreography Isuama performed for me in 2008, based on their previous year's carnival show, they used a dramatic vignette during the previous song to set the stage for a triumphant rendition of "The Invasion." One of the lightest-skinned court dancers—the duke, if memory serves—stepped forward alongside one of the darkest-skinned vassals, who pantomimed pleading with him, to which he pantomimed turning his back, shoving her away, then pushing her to the ground, where she lay prone, her legs twitching in death throes. Throughout this, the ensemble sang a song traditionally associated with Carabalí funerals (Gladys Gonzalez, personal communication, March 2010):

Todo el mundo sabe	The whole world knows
que eres mi nieto	that you are my grandson
y sin embargo	and yet
me negarás . . .	you deny me . . .

At her death, the vassals surged forward with their machetes, pantomiming killing the man who, they explained later, had rejected his grandmother because she was Black. They then sang "The Invasion," with its story of winning independence from Spain, bringing together themes of slavery, race, colonialism, and independence in their performance.

Carabalí songs use one of two basic rhythms played by the special ensemble of Carabalí percussion: the *obia*, used especially for songs paying homage to ancestors, and the *marcho camino*, or "moving step," used for everything else. There are a few exceptions to the general pattern of *obia* songs as ritual invocations. The "Invasión" is played in *obia*, as is another offering a commentary on the same early republican era mentioned by Marimón, the assistant director of Isuama. Referring to it as the "song of the *mambíses*," he sang me the verse and chorus:

1	Yo vine aquí carabalí	I came here Carabalí
2	a mí sí está mi nieto aquí	to me yes, my grandchild is here
3	la cosas de mi país	the events of my country
4	[*coro*] Si la enmienda	[*chorus*] If the Amendment
5	se acabara	were to end
6	o el tratado de París	or the Treaty of Paris
7	Ya somos libres y soberanos	Already we are free and sovereign
8	Ya somos libres y soberanos	Already we are free and sovereign
9	Ya mi hermano viene reclamando mi país	Already my brother comes reclaiming my country
10	Y con el machete habló	And spoke with the machete

The Treaty of Paris of 1898 ended the Spanish-Cuban-American War by giving the United States control over Spain's newly liberated colonial possessions, including Cuba. The amendment referred to in line 4 is the U.S. Platt Amendment, proposed in 1901 to guarantee the U.S. right to intervene in Cuba's governance and passed under duress by the Cuban National Assembly in 1902 and the U.S. Congress in 1903. These incursions into Cuban sovereignty were hated within Cuba, which saw its independence from one empire snatched from the jaws of victory to be claimed by another. When Marimón reached line 7, the other Carabalí members all joined in, raising their arms wide overhead: "Already we are free and sovereign!" As in the "Invasión," these songs narrate events from a hundred years ago as if they had only just happened but from a perspective after the triumph of the 1959 Revolution: "*Now* we are free and sovereign." The songs reveal a close identification with the rebellious predecessors of today's Carabalí members, who fought for freedom, independence, and sovereignty and who argued for equality with Whites on the basis of a shared identity as patriotic Cubans.

The Historical Present in the Timeless Past

In short, I argue that Blackness in Cuba is temporalized into what I call a timeless past still among us, where the relevant past is the colonial era of slavery and the struggles for independence that ended it. This chronotope has multiple inflections. For predominantly Afro-Cuban communities like the Carabalí, the chronotope of the timeless past still among us is a source of pride that explicitly claims equal commitment to patriotic ideals of independence and sovereignty as a basis for racial equality and implicitly invokes a history of independent spheres of Black sociality and cultural expression, even if within the dominant frame of nostalgia. This positionality exists in tension with Cuba's dominant racial ideology of *mestizaje*, in which racial and cultural blending in the past produced a seamlessly unified citizenry today. In this officially promoted and socially dominant view, Blackness is either viewed as an atavistic threat to modernity and progress or safely presented as national folklore that tells the story of the origins of Cubanness, of exotic others in our midst defining "us" (Bronfman 2004; de la Fuente 2001a 2001b, 2007; Hagedorn 2001). As I have argued in previous chapters, the racially marked category of Black is at the same time a necessary emblem of the primordial nation and marginalized because unassimilated to the national ideal of *mestizaje*, a state of affairs Mark Sawyer has described as "inclusionary discrimination" (Sawyer 2006). Key to this dynamic is the temporal displacement of racialized groups and cultural forms, projecting Blackness back in time to a now-completed role in national origins.

Isar Godreau has described for Puerto Rico a chronotope in which Blackness, associated with both people and cultural expressions, is displaced to the past of the nation, where it is nostalgically viewed as one of three original cultural strands that blended to produce Puerto Ricaness, thus disappearing into the mesticized mix (Godreau 2006; Godreau et al. 2008). Carabalí song performances illustrate how the Cuban case differs from her account, in which Blackness is simply distanced from the present by being, as it were, put into the past tense. Instead, in Black figures and voices mobilized in Carabalí songs and many other folkloric settings, a time-transcending or achronic past is being made forever immanent. Semiotically, this happens through modalities akin to the historical present tense in narratives, a device to make the past vivid by creating "a sense of breathless immediacy and conversational directness" (Wilson [1993] 2001). It is not just the use of the historical present that achieves the immanent timeless past: differently marked uses of the present tense co-occur with first-person pronouns and semantic (sometimes phonological) and visual icons of the slave past to construct the particular timeless, present origo of a historical African figure. The first-person origo is evident in every song I have presented thus far, conveying a shared perspective between the songs' authors in the cabildos' early years and the cabildo members now, and many other elements of performance heighten this identification that collapses time: "I am Carabalí; I came here Carabalí" as the songs repeatedly say.

The repertoires of Olugo and Isuama consist of a substantial corpus of traditional songs, some dating back to the turn of the twentieth century when these cabildos emerged in their modern form. But the repertoire is also continually being updated, with new songs and choreographies added each year in preparation for carnival, in particular. Below I present two recent songs authored by Olugo's director, Benito Ramirez Soulary, that Olugo was performing in 2008. In examining these songs as texts and in performance, I am interested in their use of similar descriptive and deictic devices to depict Black historical figures and create alignments between the performers and performed figures—or, following Silverstein (1992), between the interactional and denotational "texts" of performance.

Ramirez wrote "Rezo Nro. 2," or "Prayer No. 2," which follows, in 2007.

1	[*estrofa 1*] Yo soy negro carabalí	[*verse 1*] I am a black carabalí
2	Desde el monte yo llegué	I came from the mountain-wild [bush]
3	Vengo tocando la tumba	I come playing the drum
4	Una muela y un chachá	A muela (bell) and a chachá (rattle)
5	[*estrofa 2*] Ahi está mi Ma Francisca	[*verse 2*] Here is my Ma Francisca
6	Y lo mismo Nicolasa	And the same Nicolasa
7	Con un paño en la cabeza	With a kerchief on the head
8	Y la bemba ya pintada	And the big lips already painted
9	[*estrofa 3*] Eee, africano soy yo	[*verse 3*] Aay, I am African
10	Vengo bailando bonito	I come dancing beautifully
11	El mío es carabalí	Mine is Carabalí
12	[*estrofa 4*] Yo bailé en el monte	[*verse 4*] I danced in the bush
13	Con mi tragalegua	With my *tragalegua* drum
14	Yo soñé congo mayor	I sounded [the] big congo drum
15	Desde Africa llego	I arrive from Africa
16	[*estrofa 5*] Yo soy congo carabalí	[*verse 5*] I am a Carabalí Congo
17	Y vengo de lo monte	And I come from the bush
18	Vengo chapeando bajito	I come chopping low
19	Todo lo que yo encontré	Everything that I met
20	[*coro*] Congo carabalí	[*chorus*] Carabalí Congo
21	Yo soy hijo del lucumí	I am child of the Lucumí
22	Congo carabalí	Carabalí Congo
23	Yo soy hijo del lucumí	I am child of the Lucumí
24	Nicolasa, tú tiene callo en los pies [*se repite 3 veces*]	Nicolasa, you have calluses on your feet [*repeated 3 times*]

The following song, "Oye Oye," was written by Ramirez in 2006.

1	[*Coro*] Oye, oye, oye	[*Chorus*] Hark, hark, hark
2	Oigan los cueros sonar	Hear the [drum] skins sound
3	Oe, oe, oe	Oe, oe, oe

4	Oigan los cueros sonar	Hear the [drum] skins sound
5	[*estrofa 1*] Yo soy africano	[*verse 1*] I am African
6	Desde Nigeria soy yo	I come from Nigeria
7	Vengo a integrar mi cabildo	I come to join my cabildo
8	Olugo me llamo yo	My name is Olugo
	[*se repite*]	[*repeated*]
	[*coro*]	[*chorus*]
9	[*estrofa 2*] Yo soy nativo del pueblo	[*verse 2*] I am a native of the people
10	O primos del mismo nombre	Or cousins of the same name
11	Soy de Nigeria africana	I am from African Nigeria
12	Del pueblo del Calabar	From the town of Calabar
	[*se repite*]	[*repeated*]
	[*coro*]	[*chorus*]
13	[*estrofa 3*] Saludo al rey y a la reina	[*verse 3*] I salute the king and the queen
14	Príncipe y princesa también	Prince and princess as well
15	Saludo a toda mi corte	I salute all my court
16	Yo soy carabalí	I am Carabalí
	[*se repite*]	[*repeated*]
	[*coro*]	[*chorus*]

These two examples, like most of the Carabalí songs I have heard, are voiced in the first person to give what can be described as a timeless historical account of cabildo members as Africans and specifically as Carabalí who are now in Cuba. The first line of "Rezo Nro. 2" declares, "I am a black Carabalí," and "Oye Oye," states, "I am African" at the start of the first verse. That is, the songs' common origo is Africans of Cuba's past who are reanimated by the performers in the present, so that the songs' lyrics are deictically anchored in a subjective present, "I now am," which temporally situates even actions described in the past tense as within the experience of the narrated "I now." The "Invasión," discussed above, is an extended first-person account of participation in the Liberation Army's 1895 march across Cuba.

In these examples, the crucial poetic patterns are the repeated first-person pronoun and the present tense used to describe both historically distant situations and events of the performance. For example, line 6 of "Oye Oye" declares, "I come from Nigeria," while lines 2 and 4 state, "Hear the [drum] skins sound," and lines 13 and 15 state, "I salute the king and the queen," "I salute all the court," which index events of the performance itself. And the same pattern is evident in "Rezo Nro. 2" where line 15—"I arrive from Africa"—is juxtaposed with lines 3 and 10: "I come playing the drum" and "I come dancing beautifully." Even in the "Invasión," which describes events in the past tense, as in line 6: "I was a mambí" (indicating personal experience) there is a gesture toward a more breathless recent past of experience in the final lines of verses 4 and 5 (lines 32 and 38): "We have arrived in Matanzas; we have arrived in Havana."

In an examination of the present tense, Benjamin Lee analyzes how the "historical present" functions, using marking theory to account for three different values the present tense verb form can convey. As he says, "Its general unmarked interpretation has no time reference and indicates process in general." Present tense also has a specific unmarked value that is opposed to the marked past tense and "therefore indicates cotemporality with the event of speaking" (Lee 1997, 167). These songs contain examples of the present tense in both of these senses. In performance, the costumed dancers enact this sense of describing process in general. For example, in "Rezo Nro. 2," as the song's final lines address Nicolasa (a lame-footed mistress of the director's long-deceased grandfather), a soloist steps forward, alternately bent over with her arm holding her hip and reaching up as if to wave, and does a hobbling step around the floor: line 24, "Nicolasa, you have calluses on your feet." Recall, too, the dramatic enactment of killing the Black grandmother, which incited the vassals to wave their machetes and sing, "Libertad." Even the very beginning of "Oye Oye," uses the specific unmarked value of cotemporality to urge the audience to "hark, hark, hark / hear the [drum] skins sound."

Alongside these general and specific unmarked uses of the present are some instances of the marked historical present. Lines 5 and 6 of "Oye Oye," for example—"I am African / I am from Nigeria"—refer to some long-ago cabildo members born in Africa. Lines 11 and 12 continue: "I am from African Nigeria / from the town of Calabar," which sets up a time-transcending equivalence between the colonial-era slave port of Calabar and the modern state of Nigeria, an entity that did not exist until a century after the end of slave trade.

Note that the three separate functions of the present tense all use the very same form, and so one usage is iconic with the others, not least because of the anaphoric cohesion we expect in a chunk of entextualized discourse like a song. In the case of the historical present, in which the present tense form represents past time, the unmarked value of cotemporality between the event of the singers singing and the narrated event of the song's content continues to resonate, giving that sense of breathless immediacy in which figures from the past speak to audiences of the present through performers who seem to occupy performed past and performance present simultaneously. This effect is not unlike a possession trance performance, in which a muerto (spirit of the dead) speaks to the living.

Live performances, of course, heighten the illusion of past events unfolding before the audience's eyes, and everyone expects performers on a stage to act their roles—what Greg Urban calls the dequotative "theatrical I," which semiotically is similar to the "projective I" of possession trance. Urban argues that our ability to use the first-person pronoun in these ways beyond the strictly referential "I" is key to our awareness of "the weight of tradition" and our ability to engage the subjectivity of others (Urban 1989, 27, 36–37). He gives the example from Brazil of Shokleng narrators of an origin myth lapsing into first person to "assume the persona of historical antecedent," thereby "subjectively embodying the continuity of culture" (Urban 1989, 36–39, 45). Through these deictic cues, I suggest, the cabildo songs serve to flatten history and create a timeless "we" unifying Carabalí performers and their ancestors.

Consider also line 8 of "Oye Oye," "My name is Olugo": matching the singular first-person pronoun to the proper name of a collective violates usual number agreement (as if I said, "My name is Western Michigan University"). Here, the singular "I now" continues and completes the poetic structure of the verse ("I am . . . , I am . . . , I come . . ."). It also indexes a collective identity as a member of the cabildo. The same device was present in a song from Isuama's children's carnival performance in July 2011: "Yo mismo soy, yo mismo soy, yo mismo soy la carabalí" (I myself am, I myself am, I myself am the Carabalí).

Examples throughout this chapter have shown how the Carabalí cabildos very explicitly cultivate this continuity across time as members emphasize their cabildo's roots in colonial-era cabildos and through the calibration of today's members to the origo of the Carabalí past through dense indexical cues of many aspects of their performances: the songs, dancers' roles, costumes, and choreographies. This past is self-consciously fashioned in part as a fantasy past of royal courts and vassals, where the imagination of royalty, in particular, represents an ironic appropriation of the pomp and power of slave owners and those above them in the social structure of colonial slave society. The vassals represent a more experience-near aspect of the cabildos' history, here also fully imagined with a *mayoral* or overseer striding among their ranks while they dance (as performed by both Olugo and Isuama in the 2011 carnival), and later with arms and cardboard machetes raised in insurrection, as Olugo did for "La Invasión" during the same carnival performance. The chorus of another song used in both cabildos also takes the origo of a slave to rewrite playfully the history of the transatlantic slave trade:

Eso es verdad, eso es así
Olugo [Isuama] me trajo a Cuba a bailar Carabalí

That is the truth, that's how it is
Olugo [Isuama] brought me to Cuba to dance Carabalí

Other figures are also staples of Carabalí performances in recent years, such as the solo dancers in the roles of the African witch and the dancing Black woman. In performances by both Isuama and Olugo during July 2011, the "dancing Black woman" (*negra bailadora*) stepped out of the line of vassals to perform during a song dedicated to her and sung taking her origo:

1	Yo soy la negra la bailadora	I am the black woman who dances
2	y cuando siento mis tamboras	and when I hear my drums
3	me llamo al orden me tiro y bailo	I call myself to order, I get out there and dance
4	camará	comrade
5	ae ae ae	Ae ae ae
6	soy la negra carabalí	I am the black Carabalí woman
7	vamo a ver	let's go see
8	ae ae ae	ae ae ae

All attention focuses on the solo dancer who embodies the fun-loving character dedicated to her Carabalí, but in singing these lyrics and thus animating the voice of the character, all members of the Carabalí are principals who become dancing Black Carabalí before the drums. It is as if the *negra bailadora* is the distillation of Carabalí-ness (see fig. 5.5). There is a telling distinction I've heard friends in the cabildos make when watching others dance, for example, when reviewing a video I've filmed or watching a rehearsal at my side. Their highest compliment is that someone "enjoys their carabalí" (*goza su carabalí*), in contrast to others whose dancing is "dry" (*seco*), where the distinction can be seen in how fully committed and relaxed the movements are, with the whole body in motion responding to the rhythms, as opposed to someone whose steps might be technically correct but who doesn't express much passion or enjoyment in their movements. Members of the Carabalí cabildos aspire to demonstrate their full enjoyment of the dance, to command all eyes when they perform, just as the *negra bailadora* does (fig. 5.6).

In an Olugo performance I filmed, the dancers in these solo roles incorporated gestures and steps from Santería's ritual dances of the orichas (deities), which have also now become staples of folklore shows (figs. 5.5 and 2.3). The "dancing Black woman" danced with the coquettish moves of the oricha Ochún, deity of feminine sensuality, and the "African witch" danced fiercely, borrowing the dance gestures, lunging steps, and even the hard-eyed facial expression characteristic of the oricha Oyá, deity of the hurricane. She carried a branch of leaves in one hand that she used much like the horsetail

FIGURE 5.5 Soloist performs role of the dancing Black woman in the Carabalí Cabildo Olugo, Santiago de Cuba, May 3, 2008. Photo by the author.

broom Oyá wields as a symbol of authority and tool of purification. Their choreography, thus, type sources both Carabalí tradition and Santería, and in a way that did not create controversy as had Olugo's attempts to combine Carabalí and bembé rhythms. Danced gesture, it seems, could appropriately draw on a generalized vocabulary of folkloric Black movements transcending the usual ethnic and generic distinctions of Cuban folklore, as long as the rhythms (and basic steps) stayed within generic constraints.

Another instance of Afro-Cuban voicings and figures can be seen in "Rezo Nro. 2," where two "ancestral" Afro-Cuban figures are mentioned: Nicolasa, the lame mistress, and Ma Francisca, a popular name for spirits of Africans who serve many religious practitioners. They are described as wearing kerchiefs and having "big lips" (an offhand enough lexeme of Cuban colloquial speech that is a derogatory, racially marked description of appearance). Thus, the song unselfconsciously references stereotypical portrayals of Afro-Cuban appearances: as detailed in chapter 2, the slave "costume" is

FIGURE 5.6 Cabildo Carabalí Olugo children's ensemble with banner "I am the little dancing Black Woman," before precarnival parade, Santiago de Cuba, July 21, 2011. Photo by the author.

solidly enregistered by its repetition across these many religious and folklore performance contexts and thus is available to index metonymically an entire slave (or, by extension, Afro-Cuban) persona. In combination with speech markers such as Bozalisms (discussed in chap. 4), these embodied markers of Africanness thus form a powerful multimodal repertoire, from which any particular performance or image need only draw a few indices to invoke an entire figure.

The reference to Nicolasa with calluses on her foot in line 24 at the end of "Rezo Nro. 2" seems to quote another song about Nicolasa that I heard in a rehearsal of Olugo's children's group that ends with the same refrain (sung with the same melody line in both songs):

1	Nicolasa, la negra toma	Nicolasa, the black woman drinks
2	y le gusta bailar bembé también	and she likes to dance bembé as well
3	pero no puede	but she cannot
4	porque la tiene	because she has
5	porque la tiene callo en los pie	because she has calluses on her feet
6	porque la tiene	because she has
7	porque la tiene callo en los pie	because she has calluses on her feet
8	Nicolasa, tú tienes callos en los pies [*se repite 3 veces*]	Nicolasa, you have calluses on your feet [*repeated 3 times*]

This song, especially with a dancer performing Nicolasa's distinctive limping dance, helps make the figure of Nicolasa, the fun-loving, drinking Black woman with callused feet, a durable icon of the Carabalí.

While African origins and Black figures are prominent in the song lyrics, it is always in terms of their relevance for Cuban history. The origo of the songs is always geographically situated in Cuba (the "-tope" part of "chronotope"). The songs make frequent reference to Cuban geography, and particularly to *el monte* meaning the sparsely populated wilderness of the hills and mountains (e.g., in "Rezo Nro. 2"). The *monte* in Cuba is a powerful symbol of Africanness, rebellion, and folk Afro-Cuban spirituality: it is where maroons escaped to, nineteenth-century independence fighters hid, and twentieth-century guerrillas under Fidel mounted their rebellion. The *monte* is also the zone of fiercely independent and quintessentially Cuban small landholders who are not just *guajiros* (peasants) but *monteros* (of the bush), nestling farms and grazing pastures deep in the hills. The *monte* is also the heart of nature and, therefore, the source of spiritually and medicinally important plants, as Lydia Cabrera (1993) famously described in her book *El monte*, whose very title identified the wilderness as an African and Afro-Cuban space.

The spatiotemporal imaginary of Carabalí songs also includes the distinctive instruments and sonic environment of the cabildo, both as the musical accompaniment to the songs in full performance and as references within songs like "Rezo Nro. 2" and "Oye Oye," this latter starting with the injunction to "hear the [drum] skins sound." Most important to the distinctive Carabalí sound are three instruments, all mentioned in "Rezo Nro. 2." There is the wide, flat drum, identical to the conga drums of carnival comparsas, but called the *tragalegua* when used to define the basic bass beat in the Carabalí.[12] The *muela* is an iron bell with a *U* shape, whose two prongs are hammered to different thicknesses and therefore have different pitches. The lower-pitched, or "male," prong and the higher-pitched, or "female," prong are hit in alternation. The onomatopoeically named *chachá* is a set of two rattles (*chekeré*), made of woven strips of plant fiber (from the *guanikiki* plant), and with different-sized seeds in each, again making a pitch difference between the "male" and "female" in a pair as they are shaken in constant alternation. The *muela* and *chachá* are apparently unique to the Carabalí ensemble. When I asked a group of Olugo musicians about the lyrics of "Rezo Nro. 2," lines 3–4: "I come playing the drum / a *muela* and a *chachá*" and line 13: "With my *tragalegua*," the director Benito answered that, "if there is no *muela*, there is no cabildo; if there is no *chachá*, there is no cabildo," a phrase that set everyone nodding in agreement and repeating the phrase. How poignant, then, that

Olugo's instruments had been destroyed by police after their fateful song in 1919.

The *tragaleguas* remind Carabalí members of stories about how the hollow spaces of large drums were used to smuggle arms and supplies to support rebels from the wars of independence to the Cuban Revolution, and how the processions of the cabildos and other carnival comparsas served as cover for Cuban heroes—from General Guillermón Moncada of the wars for independence to Frank País of Fidel's revolutionaries—to gather for meetings and pass undetected in and out of the city and even to sneak in to mount their famous attack on the Moncada barracks on July 26, 1953, during carnival (a story I heard several times; also see Causse Cathcart [2006], 50). Benito Ramirez, Olugo's director, told me there had even once been special drum rhythms played to signal danger, such as approaching troops, although these apparently have been lost.

History in Place

Carabalí songs, as texts and in performances, thus animate a specifically Afro-Cuban past, as Carabalí, but they do so in a bid for claiming primordial Cubanness and, thus, a special but fully belonging role in the imagination of Cuban national identity. At the same time, it is important to recognize that the recountings of historical events and mobilizations of figurations of Blackness all take place *in* and *from* particular social and physical locations, because it is this locational deixis that helps us understand how the Carabalí cabildos engage simultaneously in supporting official history that slots them in as semifossilized patrimony to be preserved even as they maintain a subaltern presence that, while not openly resisting the official narrative, provides counterhegemonic spaces for alternate histories. Certainly the Carabalí claim a role in the origins of the Cuban nation according to officially valued history, which emphasizes comparisons between past moments of rebellion, all viewed from an idealized position of contented and quiescent present-in-the-revolution. But there is something at least latently counterhegemonic, working against complete acceptance of the present, in singing songs about liberty and the power to change society while waving machetes—and it is certainly no accident that all kinds of cultural groups, including the Carabalí and other carnival comparsas, are all supervised by the provincial and municipal offices of the Ministry of Culture (more on this in chap. 6). Moreover, as I explore in the next section, the cabildos consciously tap into a long history of *cultural* resistance, perhaps not the open forms of critique and parody once performed during carnival, and certainly not in explicitly political terms, but in quiet practices now claimed as "tradition" that perpetuate the cabildos as spaces of limited autonomy for Black sociality and cultural practices.

Colonial-era cabildos, in addition to serving the church that sponsored them, provided mutual aid to members, including support for illness, funeral expenses, and even self-purchase if enslaved, as well as limited space for expression of African-derived forms of spirituality—the precursors, presumably, of modern-day Reglas de Palo and Santería—and for self-governance (Barnet 1995; Brandon 1993; Howard 1998). Their adoption of ceremonial roles borrowed from royal courts showed some combination of a sense of irony and a desire for self-governance. Contemporary cabildo members still contribute dues for mutual aid, hold social events, and engage in understated folk religious rituals, as described in the next section and, thus, continue to carve out spaces of limited autonomy amid their recreational functions for their mostly Afro-Cuban members and the neighborhoods in which they are based.

Carabalí history in place is centered on Isuama's identification with the neighborhood of Los Hoyos and Olugo's identification with the Tivolí neighborhood, as well as their longstanding relationship of rivalry and cooperation. Isuama shares its neighborhood allegiance with the city's predominant comparsa, the Conga of the Hoyos, and with a similar "centenary" Haitian heritage society called the Tumba Francesa, which recently received recognition from UNESCO (the United Nations Educational, Scientific and Cultural Organization; a source of envious consternation for some in Isuama, which is located just down the street from the Tumba Francesa in a rather dingier, more run-down building). Isuama cannot claim to be a predominant presence in Los Hoyos, but members' sense of themselves remains that of a neighborhood-based association with deep roots there.

In the case of Olugo, the director and some of the longtime members at least are keenly aware of being in exile from Tivolí, although just up the street on la Trocha, closer to the Veguita de Galo and San Agustín neighborhoods, each of which has its own popular and highly regarded carnival conga or comparsa. Since, even walking, Olugo's building is a scant five minutes from Tivolí, I expressed some puzzlement about their unhappiness with their current location. Benito explained to me, again seconded by the musicians who sat with him, that these different neighborhoods were quite distinct and that their current neighbors felt no connection to their institution, did not come out to dance when they passed in procession, and did not even keep an eye on the building, since someone had come over rooftops to break in a few years back, stealing instruments and costumes. As Benito summed it up, "Trocha is Trocha, but Tivolí is Tivolí, and the Carabalí belongs to Tivolí" (la Trocha es la Trocha, pero el Tivolí es el Tivolí, y la Carabalí pertenece al Tivolí). It was only after Hurricane Dennis in 1981 destroyed the privately owned building they had previously used in Tivolí that Olugo moved to its current building farther west on Trocha. Even thirty years after this move, which happened before he ever became Olugo's director, Benito expressed the fond hope that they would soon find a way to move back to the neighborhood where they belonged.

The two Carabalí cabildos compete against each other in every year of carnival, but they also share much the same repertoire and danced characters and roles, such that they look very similar to anyone watching, especially in comparison with the other carnival ensembles, the congas and *paseos*, which are bigger, flashier, younger, and more contemporary in their carnival performances. During the week before carnival, the two Carabalí societies may pay visits to each other, in which one group processes up to the site of the other and they take turns playing and performing for one another in the street in a friendly competition, perhaps followed by sharing steaming *caldoso*, a rich and fragrant stew of pig's head meat or bones and vegetables, with cake, and likely some rum as well. In July 2011, they did not make this traditional visit, but instead all met on an appointed day outside the building of the Tumba Francesa, where the director of carnival led the three groups (Tumba Francesca and the two Carabalí cabildos) in a combined rehearsal for carnival, apparently an innovation that year. More typically, Olugo and Isuama maintain their own separate schedules of rehearsals and social events. For example, one Mother's Day, members of Olugo invited me to their party in honor of mothers, handing out saccharine greeting cards to each woman and serving up the inevitable caldoso stew, cake, and plenty of rum and salsa music for dancing. The calendar of social occasions waxes and wanes with the seasons and members' interest (and resources to hold a party) over time. From May to mid-July when carnival begins, the cabildos build to a crescendo of activity in preparing for the carnival competition. The days preceding carnival are especially hectic, as there are costumes to try on, shoes to distribute, props to make or fix, and final rehearsals to cram in.

This information about "offstage" activities reminds us that while Isuama and Olugo's most public performances are during carnival week, they meet and rehearse weekly for much of the year, and so most of the time they are singing and performing for themselves, whether training new members or honing their group cohesion as performers. Their external audiences during most of the year consist of neighbors passing by, overhearing their music, and perhaps stopping to peer in a window or step inside to greet someone they know. This gives the Carabalí cabildos a palpable neighborhood presence, however small their membership remains relative to the population of those neighborhoods. The physical locations of the cabildos, their members' comings and goings, and the general sphere of cabildo activities deepen our understanding of their performances as centenary societies that are considered national as much as neighborhood patrimony and that serve up a version of Black history as a Cuban national creation story.

Ancestors, Spirits, and Saints in the Carabalí

There is a mythic quality about the Carabalí enactment of a past of slavery and royalty, heroism and folksy roots. The mythic past is remembered through other Carabalí practices as well, especially those drawing on folk religious relationships with ancestor spirits and saints. Today's Carabalí cabildos may fall under the purview of the provincial Ministry of Culture's management and appear to be little more than folklore clubs with some vestigial mutual support functions, but part of the tradition they preserve relates to remembering the ancestors and paying homage to their patron saint and other saints as well. Since much of the spirituality even of colonial-era cabildos was kept secret while a version semidisguised as (and sometimes, undoubtedly, mingled with) Catholicism was presented to authorities, we should not be surprised that some present-day secrecy remains, for example, around certain spiritual practices and aspects of preparing Carabalí drums. Part of the historical memory of Black cabildos and mutual aid societies, after all, is of past waves of repression dating back into colonial times, and of course, as Walter Benjamin would have it, the oppressed have their own tradition of how to survive, including the necessity of keeping one's business to oneself. While I do not wish to cloak Olugo or Isuama in mystification, I also am quite sure that neither I nor Cuban folklorists and historians have uncovered all the quiet, secret corners of Carabalí history and practice. Then, too, practices can be polyvalent in their meanings and tradition is continually being reinvented. And yet, there is much that is readily apparent about the cabildo's attention to spirits and ancestors as part of their orientation to the past.

Both cabildos—Isuama and Olugo—regard ritual invocations of Carabalí ancestors as necessary communal practice and part of Carabalí tradition. The *obia* rhythm, in fact, is described as the rhythm to be used for songs of invocation. A folklorist and former director of Isuama who was mentored by an earlier director and elders of Isuama as a child told me that they always open their activities with a "recordatorio para los muertos y los espiritus" (remembrance for the dead and the spirits). He remembered an invocatory phrase, "O mi pa le o," that they would chant, adding the name of a cabildo ancestor, like Simón Baracoa, at which all members touch the ground and say *aché*. This Lucumí word, used here to mean something like "amen" and "power," and indeed, the whole formula of the invocation including the reverence of touching the earth where ancestors are buried closely follow Santería practice. An elderly Isuama member recalled that the Lucumí invocation *moyuba* was the term they used in honoring the cabildo ancestors. More to the point, the Carabalí attention to paying homage to the dead fits into a general concern with the dead across Cuban folk religious practices (see Espírito Santo, in press; James Figarola 1999a).

After invoking the Cabildo's eminent ancestors, the drums begin to play the *obia* rhythm, and the group sings a song that several members and folklorists described as sending off the spirits of the dead:

1	[*coro*] Ekó, ero mi tambor	[*chorus*] Ekó, ero my drum
2	Ekó mi cha cha e	Ekó my chachá [rattle] eh
3	Carabalí ya se acabó	Carabalí has finished
4	Carabalí ya se acabó	Carabalí has finished
5	Carabalí no vuelve más	Carabalí won't come again
6	Carabalí ya se acabó	Carabalí has finished
7	Carabalí ya se acabó	Carabalí has finished
8	Carabalí no vuelve más	Carabalí won't come again
9	[*estrofa 1*] Ekó, Ekó, Ekó	[*verse 1*] Ekó, ekó, ekó
10	Agayú solá	Agayú solá [oricha]
11	Agayú solá	Agayú solá
12	Ekó mi guaguancó	Ekó my guaguancó [music genre]
	[*coro*]	[*chorus*]
13	[*estrofa 2*] Ay, mi nieto	[*verse 2*] Oh, my grandson
14	mira bien a tu abuela	look carefully at your grandmother
15	como va e	how she goes, eh
	[*coro*]	[*chorus*]
16	Ekó, ekó, ekó	Ekó, ekó, ekó

The song's melody is uncharacteristically mournful among Carabalí songs (which tend to be upbeat, as befitting music for dancing and performing in carnival), and the lyrics include a reference to the oricha (deity) Agayú of Santería and several words that are in a ritual register. *Ekó* is the most frequently repeated of these words, and while I have not heard it used in Lucumí invocations, it might derive from Lucumí or from similar African source languages (the near-homophone *e kú* is, in today's Yoruba, a phrase of greeting and praise, from the verb *kú*, "to greet, salute, congratulate," which fits its use in the Carabalí song).

I have come across other Carabalí songs containing esoteric terms—what Cubans describe as being *en lengua*, literally, "in the tongue," referring to the use of African-language derived esoteric registers like Lucumí and Congo-palera speech. Neither Carabalí members nor folklorists could tell me much about the meaning of these other songs, except that they believed them to be very old, dating from when Carabalí members would perhaps still have spoken in "Carabalí" (often presumed to be derived from the African language Efik). For example, a song in the *marcho camino* rhythm says:

Seremí, seremí
Guarandaya seremí
Guarandaya, guarandaya
Guarandaya seremí[13]

And another, collected by Gladys Gonzalez, has the lyric:

Aniba barroco
Aniba barroco
Ekuenté monina
Aniba barroco

These songs must be memorized formulaically, as strings of vocables, since no one seems to remember what the words exactly are or what they once meant. Carabalí members proudly point to these songs as evidence that their cabildo, like Santería, has deep African roots and therefore is authentically folkloric.

The participation of Carabalí cabildos in folk religious practices is evident in additional ways in their buildings. In a corner of Olugo's building, near the door, sits a large, oval-shaped stone, and in the back corner of the instrument storage room sits another even taller stone in a clay bowl: these are representations of the oricha Elegguá, guardian of doorways who opens and closes the way, as practitioners of Santería say (fig. 5.7). The Elegguá stone near the door had a cigar attached to its mouth (or the indentation where its mouth would be) as an offering, and the Elegguá stone in the back room was draped in a chain and fortified with iron spikes, as working muerto spirits often are. The first time I visited Olugo, Benito took me into the back room, handed me a long, decorated wooden staff, and had me pound the floor before Elegguá as a greeting. He explained that, although he considered himself Catholic, the cabildo cared for these two Elegguás, giving them and other orichas small offerings and sometimes holding festive ceremonies called bembés to

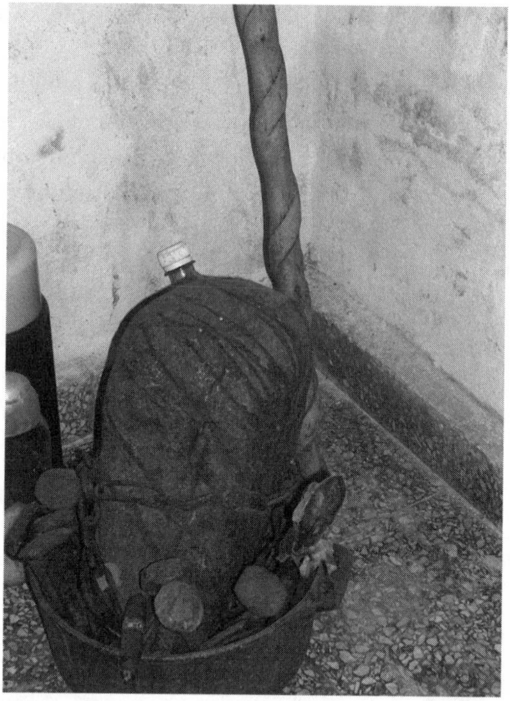

FIGURE 5.7 Stone representing Elegguá in a prenda at the Carabalí Cabildo Olugo, Santiago de Cuba, May 3, 2008. Photo by the author.

celebrate the saints' day of San Lázaro.[14] He told me that his uncle and grandfather, both former directors of Olugo, had much more actively cared for (and perhaps consulted with) muertos, including a prenda (ritual power object) his grandfather owned and two nearby graves of Carabalí he often visited, but they had taken those secrets to their own graves, and a hurricane had destroyed the prenda back in the 1970s.

Isuama, too, has its quiet spiritual traditions. Its prior location for rehearsals had been in the open courtyard of a building where the director at the time lived, and according to one account by a friend who had been a child then, the director had a room containing a number of large stones, each with a candle lit for it. My friend recalled hearing neighbors refer to "those Carabalí witches with their stones." Whatever the fate of those particular stone prendas, one such prenda had once been located in Isuama's current building, where it was kept up high and out of sight in the front of the building, and where members gathered to pay it homage and ask the spirits within it for help. That prenda, too, is apparently no longer present, but Isuama does maintain a small Elegguá figure behind the door. And one prominent younger member of Isuama described being brought as a teenager to a secret ceremony at Isuama that involved handling a prenda. He would say no more, repeating that it was secret, but he pointed out a back corner of the room where the small container had been worked on by older Isuama members and suggested the rafters of Isuama's building held other secret spiritual protections. These accounts, partial and guarded as they are, suggest familiar ceremonies in the Reglas de Palo and other folk practices influenced by Palo in which ritual power objects—variously called prendas, ngangas, or just *fundamentos*—are assembled and spiritually charged with offerings such as rum, cigar smoke, and animal blood. In Santería, objects representing the orichas are similarly prepared.

Isuama has one additional nod to folk religious practices in the form of a doll called, simply, "the doll," which is carried by a dancer in performances and represents Carabalí ancestors (fig. 5.8). Isuama members shared neither her origins nor whether she once represented a particular ancestor or spirit (and perhaps they did not know), although they agreed with my suggestion that she must represent a muerto, as do similar dolls that frequent home altars. Like the now-traditional danced roles of the *negra bailadora* and, in Olugo, Nicolasa, the dancer with the doll is now simply an expected character in the tableau that is the Carabalí in performance.

The Carabalí cabildos, thus, appear to integrate widespread folk religious practices regarding the dead, both as ancestors to be ritually remembered and as sources of spiritual power and protection. Within the cabildos, everyone participates in the invocations, but only a few with special interest and knowledge seem to participate in, or even know much about, the more elaborate spiritual practices. While today's members believe that there once were many secrets among the Carabalí and that many have been lost, it is not clear which persist today and who keeps them. Somewhere, in the transition from the very closed, male-only membership of the early twentieth century to the post-1959 opening of membership under the revolution's new management of folklore, the Carabalí cabildos seem to have given up many, if not quite all, of their predecessors' secretive ways.

In the cabildos' public performances, references to folk religion like Isuama's doll are currently prominent, but they seem to be important only as performances invoking folkloric tradition, not because of the religious allegiances or spiritual practices of the cabildos. For example, during an interview with Benito in summer 2008, he told me he was working on writing a new song that would pay homage to the major orichas of Santería and hoped Olugo would develop a choreography involving flags in the orichas' colors and solo dancers in costumes depicting each of the orichas. When I asked

FIGURE 5.8 Carabalí Cabildo Isuama's *muerta* doll is carried in children's carnival performance, Santiago de Cuba, July 24, 2011. Photo by the author.

about progress on the song during an interview with Benito and some of Olugo's musicians in late February 2010, they performed it for me. Benito proclaims rather than sings the opening of the song, accompanied only by the *din-dun* rhythm of the iron *muela:*

Esos son los fundamentos	These are the fundamentals
Obatalá	Obatalá
Yemayá	Yemayá
Changó	Changó
Ogún	Ogún
Ochún	Ochún
Elegguá . . .	Elegguá. . .

He then began to sing the chorus, now with full musical accompaniment:

Olugo me llama	Olugo calls me
A Olugo responde	To Olugo answer
Yo soy Olugo	I am Olugo
de Tivolí . . .	of Tivolí . . .

Subsequent verses repeated the list of orichas, and at the end, Benito closed by calling out: "¡Virgen de la Caridad, danos tu bendición!" (Virgin of Charity, give us your blessing!).

With great enthusiasm, he described how this song would open their 2010 carnival performance, followed by a choreography among the vassal dancers, who would act out being "plantation slaves at work," while singing "Olugo brought me to Cuba to dance Carabalí," with the slave overseer character striding around shouting at them to work. They would then converge on the slave overseer and kill him, while singing "Mal cubano, Nuestra jaula / Yo soy carabalí" (see chap. 4's conclusion), then reveal Cuban flags hidden in their baskets. In the finale, the "dancing Black woman" would step out to dance her solo, accompanied by the song "yo soy la negra la bailadora." As he laid this out, he and the musicians discussed how to present the orichas and invoke the music of the bembé, the folk religious ceremony feting the orichas, without straying from "the Carabalí"; my recording has moments of intense crosstalk, with voices urging, "one has to be careful with this . . ." while Benito argues that the choreography has to show the orichas in a bembé and assures everyone that "I maintain the Carabalí faith" (mantengo la fé del carabalí).[15]

Conclusion

Carabalí cabildo songs and performances draw on a rich repertoire of linguistic and embodied markers of Blackness and Cuban history to align performers with historical figures of Africans and create a seamless link between the past and current cabildo and its activities. The time-marking linguistic features of the songs, the historically and religiously inflected embodied cues of the dancers, music, and props, and the cabildos' allegiances to particular neighborhoods known as centers of Blackness work together to create the chronotope of the immanent timeless past, which tells Cuban audiences not only who their national ancestors were (as in Isar Godreau's [2006] case of Black cultural forms indicating the origins of Puerto Ricaness) but also who they are now. The complex effects of this semiotic work of temporal and racial emplacement are a product of competing historical subjectivities, defined by different chronotopic horizons. One predominant historical narrative is rooted in dominant Cuban ideologies of racial and cultural contact in the past producing modern Cuban hybridity or *mestizaje*. Another different historical narrative is apparent in religious and social domains marked as Afro-Cuban and covertly celebrates a separate and distinctive Afro-Cuban cultural sphere, a counterhegemonic inflection embedded in the cabildos' seeming acceptance of their current status as bearers of national patrimony who cannot innovate but only preserve tradition.

I have discussed Carabalí cabildo activities, and particularly, performances of their songs, in terms of their conscious interdiscursivity with past Carabalí performances, the early days of the cabildos' founders, and a less-defined past populated with African slaves, overseers, and masters who appear as royalty. In mobilizing indices to point at and reenact these particular strands of history, the Carabalí engage in enregistering their own contemporary performances into a genre of folkloric tradition. Their performances also contribute to the enregisterment of durable figurations of Blackness as folkloric tradition, always present but as history to be preserved, not as innovation pointing into the future.

Asif Agha (2003) has developed a model of enregisterment as an accretive historical process, in which judgments of social value move across speech chains from one interaction to the next. Through this accumulative but dynamic and nonteleological process, particular metapragmatic evaluations that map social stereotypes onto ways of speaking can circulate along with actual tokens of those ways of speaking. Although this circulatory model of enregisterment allows multiple, competing judgments of social value or "metaculture" (Urban 2001) to circulate (the Carabalí as fossilized tradition, the Carabalí as culturally resistant), the robustness of certain pathways of discourse dissemination and replication permits broad consensus about the social and characterological value of a register to emerge, even if such consensus is never complete and always remains challengeable. I have shown how this model, applied to performances of Blackness as history in the Carabalí, demonstrates the racializing potential of these performances. Carabalí songs, especially in performance, create a distinctive chronotope of Blackness as the timeless past still among us, a matter of history and folklore rather than an identification to be made in contemporary cultural politics. It is through interdiscursive connections with particular imagined sources that this chronotope of Blackness emerges.

Rather than chains of interdiscursivity, which carry the implication of an almost teleological genealogy of interactional events from some "original," I prefer the metaphor of interdiscursive webs connecting professional and amateur, traditional and interpreted, folkloric and religious performances of historicized Black figures within semiotic horizons of coevalness that allow for complex source and target relationships among performances and their (imagined) precedents. In tracing a few of these connections, I have focused on semiotic devices of temporality and performer-performed figure-audience alignment in giving these performances the force of racializing discourses (and in linking to other spheres of Cuban racializing discourses, as other chapters illustrate).

I have attended to three levels of the semiosis of temporality. First, I addressed the temporal work accomplished through interdiscursive connections comparing imagined colonial-era events, figures, and acts with various religious and folklore contexts of performance. Second, I traced how this fine-grained level in turn produces a particular chronotope of Blackness as a form of historical imagination that circulates through the linguistic and embodied markers of historical African figures who populate such performances. And third, I considered the robustness of racializing discourses themselves, including these sorts of performances and the racial subjects and objects they create. As with Irvine and Gal's (2000) examination of the role of semiotic processes of iconization, fractal recursivity, and erasure (all of which are present in the materials presented here as well), the discourse history of these dense, intertextual webs of performance has generated a rich repertoire of signs of Blackness, which is so overdetermined that only a few need be invoked in a given text or performance to conjure up an African figure.

Some of the staying power of discourses of racialization thus resides in the rich, multimodal characterization of racialized historical African figures, which circulate widely across many kinds of genres and events via dense webs of interdiscursivity and which are concatenated with other sorts of discourses—of history, nation, locale, and certainly others beyond the scope of this particular analysis. The semiotic production of a chronotope of Blackness as a timeless past still among us is absolutely central to the role of the performances examined here in simultaneously advancing both a dominant racial ideology of *mestizaje* that folkloricizes Blackness as a representation of a shared Cuban national past and a counterhegemonic and more covert and localized racial ideology that celebrates Cuba's long history of independent Afro-Cuban spheres of sociality and cultural expression—cultural marronage, if you will. But, following De la Cadena's (2001) understanding of hegemony as something fractured and unstable, rather than easily separable into dominating and resisting modalities, I suggest that each ideology relies on different sets of links in the interdiscursive web to trace a different kind of relationship from performers and audiences back to the imagined "originals" of the various African, slave, maroon, and religious figures reiterated in modern-day performances. Because these interdiscursive webs have nodes in both public, state-controlled folklore representations and more private and local religious and social spheres beyond direct state control, my analysis leads me to question top-down explanations of how dominant racial ideologies are reproduced and suggest a more complex interplay of dominant and counterhegemonic discourses that comes into focus when we carefully examine the interdiscursive web. The next chapter probes the interface of state folklore and culture management and grassroots folk religiosity in performance, and the final chapter traces the deeper discourse histories of this web connecting moments of performative performance.

6

Performance: State-Sponsored Folklore Spectacles of Blackness as History

Spectacles of race and history and, more specifically, of Blackness *as* history, are a commonplace of folklore performance in Cuba. Having examined the semiotic processes at work in figuring Blackness through performance in previous chapters, I now situate folklore performance in its revolutionary context in contemporary Cuba, where aesthetic cultural production receives substantial government oversight. To investigate the uptake of folklore into state-sponsored spectacles, I analyze the participation frames and chronotopic work of two particular performances. One performance, by one of Santiago's two major professional folklore ensembles, took place amid the graceful arches of a colonial-era building in the old city center. The other, by a small amateur ensemble selected to travel from a distant province to take part in Santiago's Festival del Caribe, unfolded on a hillside in the town of El Cobre outside of Santiago, below the national Monument to the Cimarrón.

To describe such events as spectacles requires attention to performance as a coproduction of performers and audiences of spectators because spectacles are characterized by a clear distinction and separation between roles of performer and audience. As Goffman (1959) points out in exploring the dramaturgical metaphor in interaction more generally, performances involve (indeed create) "onstage" in contradistinction to "backstage," "offstage," and, key for our purposes, audience response as interactional frames structuring events. Even passive audiences who merely watch attentively and clap politely at the end are vital coparticipants in creating a spectacle, as too are mass-mediated audiences of televised spectacles, for example. Then, too, what audiences do afterward with what they have seen, how they choose to discuss the spectacle and therefore give it metacultural momentum (or not), also matters to its effects as a spectacle.

The appearance of apparently un-ironic, caricatured congo and witch figures, often performed in folklore shows by people who identify as Black at least some of the time, raises additional questions about the alignments between performers, performed figures, and audiences. Understanding how these alignments arise out of (and across) interdiscursive webs of these performances is also key to specifying the racializing functions they serve. A related question, then, is how particular spectacles fit into larger discourse histories. Here, I approach this question by exploring how state-sponsored folklore spectacles mine cultural practices, including other folklore performances, from various settings, thereby creating an interdiscursive web—or better yet, a genealogy—of "authentic" folk sources, mediated by authoritative professional culture interpreters and supported by bureaucratic state practices, such that these folklore spectacles contribute to the ideologies of nationhood that legitimate those state practices of authorization and authentication.

All states produce spectacles intended to help create or re-create national and nationalist sensibilities in their audiences, presumed to be citizens and subjects but sometimes also intended to include international audiences—Olympic Games opening ceremonies, for example, are inevitably of this sort. Some regimes perfect the spectacle of nation, as did Nazi Germany, for example, of which Lennie Riefenstahl's controversial film of the 1936 Berlin Olympics, *Olympia* (1938), is a dramatic example. Robin Sheriff (1999) has argued that Rio de Janeiro's carnival has become the defining spectacle of the Brazilian nation, in part because of its idealized depiction of tropical racial harmony and distinctively Brazilian culture. And Kate Ramsey (2011) has shown how Hollywood spectacles of "voodoo" drew on longstanding Haitian legal and political treatments of popular folk practices of *sèvi lwa* or "serving the spirits," thereby advancing the objectification of *vaudoux* as Haiti's defining national folklore. Alongside such internationally visible spectacles of nation are many smaller-scale spectacles of more modest scope that nonetheless serve as what David Guss (2000) describes as sites of cultural performance, where cultural performances are highly visible, ritualized, and reflexive events (see Bauman 2011, 715–16). For example, Guss documents how local festivals celebrating racial, regional, and religious identifications are taken up and renegotiated in light of state-promoted narratives of national identity in Venezuela.

Cuban folklore performances are generally more modest spectacles, although they may occur as part of festivals that draw wider attention. During the past decade, they have occurred in such proliferation that Cubans and foreign visitors alike are hard-pressed to avoid encountering them, however shallowly and peripherally, at a minimum in TV broadcasts of announcements and event footage, in lobbies of airports and hotels, or on the streets during carnival season in particular. Cubans and foreigners making up the mass audiences may not be familiar with the folklore genres they view, and what they do know is likely to be mediated already by official folklore categories gleaned from a history of such encounters. Only those who intimately know folk religious or dance practices might offer critiques of their folklorized versions, and even then they often cleave to what folklore professionals have set as the proper criteria. But such distinctions are lost on many others in typical audiences of folklore spectacles. Watching one of my videos of the second folklore performance I describe, an elderly Cuban friend saw performers going into possession trance and commented that this was "Africa, pure Africa," that they were demonstrating. The idea that some of her neighbors might regularly be possessed by spirits of the dead seemed almost as foreign to her as it likely is to the average Canadian or European tourist.

The Revolutionary Bureaucratization of Folklore in Cuba

Folklore is an official, bureaucratically managed category of cultural production in Cuba. Fidel Castro famously announced, in a 1961 speech to artists and intellectuals, "within the Revolution, everything; outside the Revolution, no rights at all"—an articulation of the role arts and academy were to play in advancing the agenda of the revolution's transformation of Cuban society (Castro 1961). While one reading of this pronouncement is ominous, presaging repressive policies toward artists and intellectuals that reached a low point during the 1970s and early 1980s (Navarro 2002), another equally valid reading, in Cuban terms, is evident in the incredible state support of the arts and cultural production as an essential component of the revolution.[1] The very category of folklore came to be considered part of the arts and as such was brought under the bureaucratic oversight of the National Council on Culture, an institution created in 1961 whose mission was to cultivate cultural production as an ideological vanguard of the revolution, inculcating its values into the general population.

The development of the revolution's policy toward culture and aesthetic production is a story of a massive bureaucratization of cultural production not only to promote revolutionary ideology and ensure it saturated the arts and intellectual life but also to democratize access to the means of cultural production. Additional important goals evident in the National Council on Culture's work were to elevate folk forms to receive recognition as the patrimony of the people and to elevate Cuba's international standing by demonstrating excellence in elite forms of culture (e.g., ballet, classical music, literature). Schools of the arts, including the National School of Art, developed normalized curricula. Dancers, for example, would become proficient in three tracks: ballet, modern, and folkloric, eventually specializing in just one (Daniel 2002; John 2002). Folkloric dance was thus officially set on par with ballet and modern, although in practice the forms carried and still carry rather different levels of prestige, with ballet the most prestigious and folkloric dance still looked down on as Black and low class by many Cubans ("popular" is the usual euphemism), particularly those from whiter middle-class and elite backgrounds (see Hagedorn 2001; Moore 2006).

The revolution's goal was for artists, musicians, writers, performers, and all other cultural workers to be state-supported, rather than depending on the tastes of capitalist consumption for support. The first three decades of the revolution correspondingly saw the development of a government infrastructure to support and control artistic production, from the identification and training of future talent to the organization of its artistic workforce in ensembles, theaters, galleries, labor unions, festivals, and so forth, a massive project that included registering and often reorganizing existing amateur and professional groups as well as creating new ones. The National Council on Culture also oversaw distribution of limited resources and instituted methods of evaluating groups, organizations, and programs to determine where those resources went and who got which opportunities and recognitions. The early 1960s saw a tremendous outpouring of creativity, including the establishment of professional ensembles, such as the Conjunto Folklórico de Oriente in Santiago de Cuba, whose founding members embarked on field research projects to identify the most authentic forms of folk music and dance traditions, including many that had never received any recognition for their cultural or artistic merit beyond the community of participants.

In the 1970s, for a number of reasons not detailed here, the revolution became more repressive and controlling, even turning on some of the very artists and intellectuals it had celebrated a few years earlier (Loomis 1999; Moore 2006; Mousouris 2002; Navarro 2002). As Katherine Hagedorn (2001) and Robin Moore (2006) describe, folkloric music and dance in some ways escaped the worst repression but nonetheless suffered suspicion and neglect because of their association with Afro-Cuban religious practices and with a forbidden identity politics of racial separateness (Moore 1988), both of which contradicted increasingly rigid Marxist-Leninist doctrine. And yet many folklore ensembles continued, new ones were started, and the efforts to standardize and thereby stabilize the folklore genres continued. The ideological role of folklore in the revolution was simply too important to discard completely, especially when it came to continuing to win the hearts and minds of the masses, for many of whom some "folkloricized" forms were daily practice (Ayorinde 2004). Professional ensembles like Cutumba (which along with the Ballet Folklórico de Oriente resulted from the fissioning of the original Conjunto Folklórico de Oriente) kept up a schedule of performances during neighborhood public health campaigns, festivals and trade fairs, and commemorations of revolutionary anniversaries.

These schedules of public service performances have continued into the present. In 1998, I accompanied Cutumba into a muddy and marginal distant neighborhood of Santiago, where they performed after speakers from the public health department had promoted the latest campaign against dengue, a mosquito-borne disease that can thrive in those conditions. A more recent example was the monthly events calendar posted in the Ballet Folklórico de Oriente's dressing room in March 2008, which listed one performance at the medical school for a celebration of the Day of Health, a show on the big stage of Santiago's Teatro Heredia and three others in the smaller venue of the Cabildo Teatral, and several shows to be scheduled as part of the Festival of Books at the end of the month. And in 2011, on the twenty-sixth of July anniversary of the Moncada attacks, I watched a central Cuban folklore ensemble perform a peasant dance on national television right after a long series of speeches by government officials. The camera captured President Raúl Castro and other top officials in the audience, nodding and smiling along with the music.

In 1976, the earlier National Council on Culture became the Ministry of Culture, organized into national, provincial, and municipal offices, all referred to simply as "la Cultura," and whose web site in 2011 described its mission as: "To direct, orient, control, and carry out . . . the application of the cultural politics [*política cultural*] of the state . . . as well as guarantee the defense, preservation, and enrichment of the cultural patrimony of the Cuban nation."[2]

In its role of ensuring the preservation of cultural patrimony, Cultura recognized and administered not only prestigious professional ensembles but also amateur or aficionado folklore ensembles, many of which were organized in particular work or school locations. For example, during this period, construction worker–turned-choreographer Ernesto Armiñán Linares started a folkloric dance ensemble with students in the University of the Oriente's College of Construction (in 1975) and another called the "3 de diciembre" with students in the College of Medical Sciences in Santiago (in 1976).[3] Existing traditional societies and comparsas were also brought under the direction of Cultura, often being designated *grupos portadores* meaning groups "carrying" cultural patrimony. Other amateur groups, as well as professional folklore ensembles, were and are designated *grupos interpretantes*, or interpreters of tradition. Although Cultura ensured and continues to ensure that all groups are accurately performing folklore genres, interpreters are not as tightly bound to "tradition" (as defined by Cultura's army of folklore professionals) as are "carriers" of tradition, like the Carabalí cabildos discussed in chapter 5.

To receive the status of a traditional culture carrier, groups must successfully claim primordial status; patrimony is, after all, "discovered," not "created." It does seem that the heyday of discovering culture carriers evident during the 1960s has long since passed (cf. Viddal 2012 on the ongoing folklorization of Haitian-Cuban cultural forms). To be recognized in this way was a double-edged sword: certainly, few associations of any sort exist in Cuba without government permission, and even entities that are somewhat autonomous must conform to stringent ideological controls. Although revolutionary recognition elevated humble, ignored, and even despised cultural practices and associations to the status of national patrimony, receiving this status has also served to appropriate culture carriers for their symbolic importance and roles as nodes of community involvement in neighborhoods. The price of recognition and support has been to cede control to a centralized (and impoverished) government ministry, with endless bureaucracy.

For example, the Conga de los Hoyos carnival comparsa and the two Carabalí cabildos (described in previous chapters) are all recognized as culture carriers with centenary traditions—designations their members are quick to share with interested foreigners. The spaces where they rehearsed went from being privately owned arrangements to state-provided and, nominally at least, state-maintained *focos culturales* or "cultural foci" (community centers). A longtime participant in the Conga de los Hoyos described the earlier space as tiny and open air, requiring the directors to store the instruments in their homes. In contrast, the state built a spacious rehearsal and storage location in the Foco cultural de Los Hoyos, a prominent building on the Paseo de Martí in the heart of the Los Hoyos neighborhood. To protect this investment, Cultura's department of *focos culturales* (cultural centers) even provided a salaried caretaker who cleaned the space and kept an eye on it, as well as training and employing a small army of "cultural promoters" to identify, nurture, and organize new talent and ensure that these community spaces are lively and thoroughly used by the community (fig. 6.1). Of course, buildings age with the wear and tear of use, and so the groups who feel most ownership in particular *focos culturales* are constantly lobbying the department for renovations or even new, more desirable locations (as in the case of the Carabalí Olugo cabildo recounted in chap. 5, whose older members

FIGURE 6.1 Maritza Martínez, caretaker of the Foco Cultural de Los Hoyos and director of the Children's Conga de los Hoyos, in front of a wall of mementos in 1999, Santiago de Cuba. Photo by the author.

desired a return to the Tivolí neighborhood, if a suitable space could be prepared for them there).

Professional folklore ensembles like Cutumba and the Folklórico de Oriente, too, felt the bureaucratic and ideological constraints on their work. A choreographer involved with one of these groups recounted a choreography the group had presented during the late 1980s based on legends (*patakines*) from Santería about the oricha Babalú Ayé that used the festive rhythms of bembés, popular drumming ceremonies to fete the orichas. He told me that the work was tremendously popular, attracting large Cuban audiences, who treated it as an actual bembé, dancing in the aisles and, in some cases, even succumbing to possession trances. As I recorded the choreographer's story in my fieldnotes, the government then prohibited further performances of this piece because it promoted religion. Things changed later, but the ensemble has never reinstated the work. He concluded that this piece could now be performed because it would be interpreted as "un hecho folklórico para rescatar las tradiciones" (a folkloric act to rescue traditions). The proper framing of performances as "folkloric" was essential, and audience reframing of this particular piece to highlight its religious significance ruptured its presentation as salvaged tradition by revealing that in fact bembés are living tradition. While this is an indisputable fact, the revolution's professional folklorists sometimes framed folkloric genres as dying traditions or, at the very least, as doomed traditions once revolutionary gains in the population's level of education and culture rendered them irrelevant (e.g., Argüelles Mederos and Hodge Limonta 1991). Folklore performances needed to maintain this chronotopic frame projecting cultural forms into the past and narrating their trajectories as threatened or disappearing traditions.

To return to the historical outline, there were few opportunities to commercialize the arts during the decades between 1960 and 1990, and in any event, cultural workers received a state salary like everyone else, freeing them from the burden of having to seek commercial success to continue their work. Instead, folklore ensembles of all designations, professional and aficionado, *portador* or *interpretante*, all aspired to be selected to participate in festivals and competitions, especially national and even international events (generally within the Soviet bloc) that afforded rare opportunities to travel. Until the 1990s, folklore groups measured their success not monetarily but in terms of performance opportunities, recognitions, and prizes won. Ideological conformity was at times as important as artistic merit in achieving success.

With the fall of the Soviet bloc and corresponding crash of Cuba's economy after 1989, the situation dramatically changed. Although the schedule of festivals continued (and continues today), the economic transformations that wracked Cuban society opened up new opportunities for commercialization and for travel to capitalist countries. Today, folklore ensembles of all designations aspire to success at least partially in economic terms, where opportunities come mainly from foreigners, as tourists who pay to see folklore shows or more rarely aficionados who might pay or contribute gifts in return for learning the music or dance or as impresarios with the means to arrange foreign tours. These new audiences and potential sponsors bring different expectations about authenticity, living tradition, and tropical "color" that sometimes create uneasy tension with revolutionary bureaucratic prerogatives and sometimes have shifted those prerogatives as the state pursues foreign capital. For example, Cultura now actively encourages groups' efforts to score international tours as a source of state income and a boost to the artists' otherwise low salaries. Of course, such opportunities are not equally available to all kinds of ensembles, favoring the prestigious professional ensembles. And my experience has been that those groups least able to find opportunities to generate revenue, such as the "carriers of cultural patrimony" like the tradition carnival congas and Carabalí cabildos, tend to cling most desperately to the increasingly outdated notion that the state should provide for all their needs.

During the current decade, the Ministry of Culture continues to play a dominant role in administering folklore as cultural production, despite the plethora of new opportunities for entrepeneurship and the economic pressures behind recent efforts to shrink the presence of the centralized state. Cultura continues to oversee (and pay salaries, albeit nominal ones in the case of nonprofessional groups) to artistic directors, keep lists of participants, and have final say in decisions about when and where groups can perform, including in local, national, and international festivals, tours, or other kinds of events. Cultura also determines the level of funding provided for costumes, equipment, instruments, staging and sound, travel costs, and technical support, and so exerts enormous influence on the possibilities open to various groups. The general scarcity of funds and materials means that Cultura directly and indirectly encourages groups to use nongovernmental resources, at least within certain bounds. Groups like the Carabalí cabildos continue to collect dues from members to fund social activities, as their antecedents have always done. Ensemble directors may develop contacts with foreigners willing to donate or bring materials from abroad or, more rarely, foreign institutions willing to sponsor an international tour or make a donation, perhaps in return for filming the group. As with so much of life in Cuba, talk of the government providing everything and of socialist ideals of collective sacrifice and betterment is made possible by the high reliance on private efforts, often secret and illegal entrepeneurship, quiet deals with foreigners, theft of state resources or, inversely, commitment of private resources of group directors, and other such arrangements that take place despite the high degree of bureaucratic oversight.[4]

In local venues, the status that Cultura assigns a given group determines whether it can generate income, or commercialize, in which case Cultura oversees the quality of performers and authenticates the accuracy of performances through a system of periodic evaluations that determine whether a group can maintain its designation. Amateur aficionado groups don't automatically receive this kind of oversight to the degree professional and commercialized groups do, but Cultura officials and professional folklorists do sometimes intervene if a group seems dysfunctional or if the quality of its work declines too greatly. Even among those folklore performers who might simply like to earn some extra cash performing at a local tourist hotel, the Ministry of Culture places firm controls on commercialization. And the guiding principles of Cultura's direction of *cultura* continue to be to promote the revolution's values and to preserve cultural patrimony by enforcing a standardized, professionally developed set of criteria for what the folklore genres are and how they should be performed.[5]

Prestigious, fully professional groups like Cutumba and the Ballet Folklórico de Oriente, themselves under Cultura Provincial's authority, exert a strong normative influence on amateur groups, including the culture carriers that were once their sources of authentic forms. An important effect of fifty years of the bureaucratization of folklore has been the development of just the kind of professionally developed criteria for folklore genres called for to preserve those forms as authentically as possible. The extent to which professional folklorists serve a prescriptive role was finally made apparent to me in a recent conversation with a naive painter in Santiago. On hearing I was an anthropologist who had written a book about Santería, he passionately declared that what Cuba needed was more anthropologists, because anthropologists could dictate to artists what the proper representations of Santería were and put a limit on those who did not adhere to the proper conventions for depicting the orichas and their symbolism. Rather startling me out of my American notions of being an anthropologist, he explained that anthropologists (like folklorists) had the knowledge to tell the people, "stop right there" and correct their mistakes about folk cultural forms. When I asked him what sources he drew on in his own paintings of folk religious themes, he listed off books about Santería by prominent Cuban folklorists like Miguel Barnet and Natalia Bolívar and showed me art catalogs of Haitian folk art brought from the United States, from which he learned how to represent the *lwa* of Haitian Vodou properly. He himself was not particularly religious and not a practitioner, but rather an admirer of the richness of folk religious visual imagery, and he was not shy about critiquing other artists whose representations strayed from the verifiably authentic. Indeed, visiting traditional culture carriers with a professional folklore choreographer like Armiñán, I frequently witnessed the prescriptivist stance professionals took in "educating" and sometimes correcting members of traditional groups about dance steps, rhythms, lyrics, costumes, choreographies, pedagogical methods, and other "traditions."

Not only Cultura, but even other kinds of state organizations, from those under the auspices of Cultura, like UNEAC, the Casa del Caribe, or the carnival commission, to completely separate institutions, like the neighborhood

Committees in Defense of the Revolution or the school where a group is based, may intervene in aesthetic cultural production of folklore, for example, in recruiting members or requesting that a group perform on a particular occasion or even stepping in to replace directors if groups seem dysfunctional.[6] In the case of the carnival commission, consisting of various artists, promoters, and other culture professionals appointed to serve each year, it determines the schedule of carnival performances, selects judges who will award prizes and recognition to the best groups, and sets other policy related to carnival, always in the spirit of affirming or improving on past practices.

In sum: officially speaking, there is no recognition of primordial folklore outside the sphere of the state because the revolution has made a point of fully appropriating folklore in its mission of elevating the masses. Folk practices and other popular cultural innovations that inevitably emerge around the edges of the state are, often sooner rather than later, subsumed into the machine that is institutionalized Cultura. This is so because of the politics of the revolutionary state, in which folklore, together with all of the arts and the academy, are mobilized to promote the revolution and ensure its survival. This is true even in moments of apparent "folk" ruptures of performances, as when an audience treats as stage performance an actual spiritual event, in which case the show might be discontinued, or, offstage and beyond folklore venues, where there is wide participation in ceremonies celebrating the saints. Consider, too, my example in chapter 3 of the invisibility of that major grassroots event of carnival called the Invasion in the media, despite the heavy-handed bureaucratic and police control that permit the Invasion to occur. Even in the sphere of private religious devotions, the state requires permits for ceremonies involving groups of people, and its cultural agents stand ever ready to mine—and folkloricize—such folk effervescences for new talent and aesthetic ideas.

The state's success in objectifying certain domains and practices as folklore also relies on its creation of spectators for folklore spectacles, not just before live performances but in the television coverage about folklore genres or specific folklore events as well. With the limited channels available through state-run television, it is fair to say that the Cuban viewing audience gets relatively homogenous exposure to the short clips of folklore performances that appear as ads for upcoming shows or in news coverage of local and national events. Some TV viewers, like my elderly friend above, may have understandings of Cuban folklore as patrimony that are heavily mediated by television coverage. Others, accustomed to participating in practices deemed folkloric, may also become accustomed to seeing those practices objectified as folklore and patrimony on TV. Those who perform in carnival ensembles or other amateur or professional groups become used to being filmed for television, so that they and those who know them may look forward to catching a snippet of their performance on the evening's televised news, thereby learning to become spectators to, as well as performers of, folklore and to see folklore expertise as an important form of social capital.

One could be tempted to give a strictly Machiavellian interpretation of the state's interest in maintaining control of the arts as a source of powerful expressions of ideology and in keeping tight controls on all forms of assembly in this one-party state—the list of duties on the Ministry of Culture's website provides ample evidence. However, folk effervescence has other uses as well: Fidel and his rebels made their famous early attack on the Batista regime, on July 26, 1953, by using the cover of Santiago's carnival to sneak into the city and mount an assault on the Moncada Barracks, just uphill from Los Hoyos, in the wee hours of the morning, after the soldiers and everyone else would be sleeping off the night's carnival excesses. And they themselves were following in the footsteps of Cuba's Liberation Army, who, as tradition has it, used the big *tragalegua* drums of the Carabalí to smuggle arms and medicines in and out of Santiago during the 1895–98 war for independence. Folklore, apparently, can serve more material needs of the resistance than simply being an ideological tool.

But folklore is not simply appropriated for outright ideological manipulation. That would be a shallow analysis indeed. Instead, I have argued throughout this book that folklore performances are taken up as constitutive of Cubanness itself, giving shape to figurations of race, history, and national identity. These are the stuff of revolutionary governance, yes, because they are also the condensations and reflexive "celebrative occasions" (Bauman 2011, 715; after Goffman 1981) of everyday identifications and alignments, sources of social danger and pride, and emblems of "us" and of the (racialized) "others" who define "us" at the profoundest levels of "Deep Cuba" (James Figarola 1999b).

However totalizing the revolutionary project of centralized control of cultural production has been in intent, it has never achieved complete control (if such a thing is even possible), and folklore groups of all sorts have latitude in their creative endeavors, at least within certain parameters, and in negotiation with the bureaucratic machinery and prescriptivism of state folklore under Cultura. In the two performances examined in this chapter, full artistic credit goes to the groups themselves, and to the vision of their choreographers and directors in particular, whose creativity is of course also shaped by the general ferment of cultural practices around them, including other state-recognized groups and more informal religious, neighborhood, and family practices and sensibilities. My analysis thus considers negotiations between official state oversight of Cuban "culture" and grassroots identifications, affiliations, and agendas.

Cutumba's "African Trilogy"

Santiago de Cuba's Ballet Folklórico Cutumba emerged as one of two folklore brigades born of the fission of the original Conjunto Folklórico de Oriente, founded in Santiago de Cuba in 1959 by Manuel Marquez. The fission happened in 1975 due to differences between then-director Antonio Pérez and assistant director Aldo Durados, who then directed the "1st brigade" which took the name Isomba. In 1985, his brigade was renamed Cutumba, a neologism with an African flavor (see chap. 4) that combines "Cuba" and *tumba*, a word meaning "drum" and, metonymically, "party" or "festive celebration with drumming."[7]

Among the first generation of Cutumba singers, musicians, and dancers were many who had helped found the original ensemble in the 1960s and had studied traditional forms by doing field research with religious and ethnic (Haitian) "carrier" communities, generally under the supervision of Havana's emerging folklore intellectuals. Many, like sisters Berta and Nereidys Armiñán Linares, both singers, had family ties or had grown up in the communities they later studied, giving them an especially insightful insider's view of the traditions (see also Viddal 2012). Their brothers, Wichi Armiñán and the much younger Ernesto, had grown up playing and singing in bembé ceremonies and brought that firsthand religious experience to their work as folklorists (Wichi was a percussionist, and Ernesto became a choreographer). That said, their professionalization involved adapting to the "salvage and preservation" framework of the state folklore machine.

The ensemble's primary work after those early years of collecting culture shifted to presenting aestheticized interpretations of these forms on the stage for national and international audiences: its members describe Cutumba as an artistic institution. Like other major folklore ensembles, including the flagship Conjunto Folklórico Nacional in Havana, Cutumba's repertoire followed the emerging canon of Cuban folkloric dance, including the standard fare of dances of the orichas, rumba, Palo dances, and so forth, as taught in the dance curriculum of arts schools.[8] The current generation of professional interpreters of folkloric dance and music do not need to consult culture-carrier sources: they learn all they need from the educational canon. Despite stylistic and interpretive differences between Cutumba and its sister, the Ballet Folklórico de Oriente, I am also struck by how closely their repertoires mirror one another, a result of the workings of such bureaucratic standardization, professionalization, and genre purification as described above. It seems that each ensemble has developed its version of a standard list of folklore genres: oricha dances, rumba, Tajona, sinuous Haitian women's dance, fierce display of Palo dance, and so forth.

As part of the competitive polarization between Cuba's capital, Havana, and the provincial hinterlands, Santiago's folklore ensembles set themselves apart early on by specializing in what they claimed as the Oriente's distinctive folklore traditions, particularly those genres deriving from Haitian-Cuban traditions. This includes the Tumba Francesa, the Ban Rará, the dances of Vodou, the Tajona (an acrobatic version of a maypole dance), and the Haitian-influenced folk representations of spirits or *lwas* like the Gedé. The Carabalí, too, is a local tradition, whereas the Abakuá influence, particularly in the emblematic figure of the *diablito*, an Abakuá masquerade figure, is local to western Cuban port cities such as Matanzas and Guanabacoa (on the Bay of Havana). Efforts to claim regional folklores, however, did not gain much traction against the prevailing centralizing tendencies of the revolutionary state, and so all of these local traditions are now part of the canonical repertoire taught and performed across Cuba. Of course, each ensemble claims its specialties, and both Cutumba and the Ballet Folklórico del Oriente insist that they give especially authentic interpretations of local forms because of their proximity to the cultural roots. Some of their members also complain that "Havana" (i.e., the capital and by extension the national government) does not respect or care about eastern Cuban traditions, part of a general disdain for the provinces on the part of the capital. But such arguments do not, for them, contradict their inclusion of genres emblematic of other regions: Cutumba, too, performs the Abakuá dance of the *diablito*.

Many of the founders have retired, and some, like Wichi Armiñán, have passed away. The current generation of musicians and dancers are children (and grandchildren, generationally) of the revolution, and most were professionally trained in the standardized curricula of art schools, although a few developed their talents in aficionado or *portador* groups and were then recruited into the professional ensemble, where they are evaluated by the same standardized criteria for each folklore genre. The dancers, in particular, are trained in ballet, modern, and folkloric dance, and so are encouraged to think of themselves as dancers, not as specifically folkloric dancers. Most aspire to the more prestigious appointments to national ballet and modern dance ensembles, so working in a folklore ensemble may not have been their first choice, nor would it necessarily reflect a connection to or identification with folklore genres and the religious communities, neighborhoods, or social strata they come from. Moreover, folklore provides a fount of Cubanness to inflect internationally recognized genres, like ballet and modern, with quintessential Cubanness.[9] The situation for musicians is similar. Professional folklore performers, therefore, tend to take a distancing stance to the traditions they perform: in my interactions over the years with many of them, the most typical stance they take is that their knowledge is complete and authoritative and that it comes from their training and professional experience, not from their personal lives.

I opened my introduction to this book with a description of the first part of a performance by Cutumba of a work called "African Trilogy," as performed in the colonial architecture and slightly shabby elegance of the Casa de Estudiantes. This work caught my eye because of its juxtaposition of Carabalí, Congo, and Haitian music and dance traditions to present what Cubans call a "theater of relations" involving figures of slaves, Carabalí cabildo members, and paleros. In my first viewing, I was especially struck by the caricatured depiction of the "witch" (fig. 1.2) and of popular religious practices, like possession trance. The theaters of relations that sets social types into dialogue on the page or the stage has had a long trajectory, being a staple of nineteenth-century Cuban *costumbrist* (quaint customs-focused) and comic theatrical and literary traditions, as will be explored in chapter 7. Here I am interested in its modern instantiation as folklore spectacle and, especially, in how the elements present in grassroots culture-carrier performances are transformed in being transposed to the professional folklore stage. My particular focus will be on how these imagined historical tableaus contribute to the enregisterment of Blackness as folklore and history, with attention to the participation structures and resulting alignments between stage characters, performers, and audiences that inculcate particular racial and historical subject positions.

The choreographer of the "Trilogy," Licenciado Juan Teodoro Florentino, professor of folklore and choreographer for Cutumba, is a longtime member of Cutumba, having begun in various children's groups organized by his mentor, Ernesto Armiñán, been subsequently recruited as a dancer into Cutumba, developed as a choreographer, and in 2010 completed his Licenciatura in folkloric dance at the Instituto Superior de Arte in Havana. I begin with his description of the work, which does not exactly align with my interpretation, since he disputes any hint of historical imagination, arguing that every detail of the "Trilogy" is carefully researched and accurate (which I would generally agree with without changing my interpretation). What follows is his account of the work, as transcribed in my fieldnotes of our most recent conversation on July 30, 2011:

> Florentino intended the "African Trilogy" as a history, with every aspect having meaning. It makes a *recorrido* [route] of the island of Cuba, from east to west, and shows the history of *africanía* [Africanness], of domestic slaves and slaves of the *centrales* [sugar plantations]. It starts with the French influence, with *gente de color* [people of color] dressed in the French style of that epoch, yes, dancing Carabalí. The *esclavos del campo* [field slaves] watch and learn from the domestic slaves, who have learned all the contradances and such from the French, who came to Cuba and brought their Haitian slaves. He rejected my term "theater of relations," saying that his work was based on research, and everything had its meaning as a custom of Cuba, if you look deep enough.

As I have seen and recorded it in several performances, the piece opens with two songs adapted from the Carabalí cabildos' repertoire. The first song follows.

1	Señores, hasta aquí llegamos	Gentle folk, we have arrived here
2	Al compás de este vaíven	At this point in our journey
	[*se repite líneas 1 y 2 dos veces*]	[*repeat lines 1 and 2 two times*]
3	Saludando al territorio	Greeting the territory
4	Y pa' la Isuama también	And for the (Cabildo) Isuama as well
	[*se repite líneas 3 y 4 dos veces*]	[*repeat lines 3 and 4 two times*]
	[*Coro*]	[*Chorus*]
5	Ae cantadore' respóndanlo bien	Ayy, singers respond to this well
6	Ae cantadore' respóndanlo bien	Ayy, singers respond to this well
7	Que la reina del cabildo, ja ja ja	That the queen of the cabildo, ha ha ha
8	es la que se va coronada	Is the one who is wearing a crown
	[*se repite líneas 7 y 8 dos veces*]	[*repeat lines 7 and 8 two times*]

And these are the lyrics to the second song:

1	Yo soy africano, pariente del lucumí	I am African, kin of the Lucumí
2	Olugo me trajo a Cuba a bailar carabalí	Olugo brought me to Cuba to dance Carabalí
	[*Coro*]	[*Chorus*]
3	Eso es verdad, eso es así	That is the truth, that's how it is
4	Olugo me trajo a Cuba a bailar carabalí	Olugo brought me to Cuba to dance Carabalí

I have described the opening choreography in chapter 1, in which an elegantly dressed couple promenades around the dance floor, then demonstrates Carabalí dance steps, watched by a stealthy figure enacting the iconic role of a congo slave, who somersaults in behind them, creeps back out, then returns leading a line of fellow congos to admire and imitiate the pair (figs. 1.1 and 6.2). Indeed, this is precisely how another Cutumba choreographer I asked explained it, saying that the group of men was made up of congos who were impressed by the elegance of the creole cabildo members. He also described the choreography as replicating the distinction between the Carabalí cabildo's elegant "court" and rustic "vassals," as we saw in chapter 5, although Cutumba's congos were depicted far more rustically than the Carabalí vassals, who dress in elegant, satiny long dresses (checked gingham, in former times) and dance regally, with erect postures, not crouched close to the ground with bowed shoulders, as the corps of congos does in the opening sequence of "Trilogy." During this scene enacting African transculturation, the witch figure briefly enters to place a tall, hollowed-out wooden vessel center stage—a prop that is half drum and half prenda (power object of Palo) but entirely Afro-Cuban in its resonances. He gestures to "throw" magic into it, and then exits.

As the second song begins, the group of congos takes center stage and performs an eclectic combination of Carabalí dance steps and moves imitating agricultural work of slaves: cutting cane and bearing loads (fig. 6.3). They perform the slave origo of the song, and their representation of slave labor highlights the intentional parody of the song: "I am African . . . Olugo brought me to Cuba to dance Carabalí." One folklore expert, watching my recording during an interview, critiqued this section of the piece because the dancers were combining Carabalí steps with other steps and movements that were unrelated to the Carabalí, rather than properly performing pure Carabalí steps to the Carabalí rhythms. Others, including members of the two professional folklore ensembles, have commented that the high, jumping step used to represent the Carabalí on stage is a transformation wrought by professional dancers to heighten interest, whereas Carabalí cabildo members never jump, but dance much more sedately. In asking around about this change and even arranging a dance lesson with members of the Ballet Folklórico, I was told that the jumping step is now standardly taught, alongside the traditional stationary and marching steps. Everyone I talked to took care to mark the distinction between the traditional and theatrical steps. Some transformations are unavoidable with recontextualization as staged theater, but that does not render them uncontroversial in the ongoing work of genre purification.

FIGURE 6.2 Carabalí dancer is admired by Congo slaves in *Trilogía africana*, by Ballet Folklórico Cutumba, Santiago de Cuba, July 2006. Line drawing by Jessica Krcmarik of still image from author's video recording, used with permission.

Changes in musical instrumentation, in contrast, are uncontroversial, as long as the proper rhythms and sonic textures are present. The Carabalí songs are played with a *tumbadora*-style upright drum serving as *tragalegua*, a regular iron cowbell playing the *muela* part, albeit without the distinctive alternation in pitch, and a regular *güiro* (*chekeré*) providing the rattling texture of the *chachás*, again without the alternation in pitch. Three additional tapered *tumbadora* drums fill in the rhythmic textures, as the *quinto* and *requinto* might in a Carabalí cabildo ensemble. But most strikingly different is the use of the *catá*, a drum made from a hollowed chunk of log set horizontally on the floor and played by hitting the wood with sticks—an instrument that does not appear in the Carabalí and is more associated with Haitian musical influences. It adds a distinctively sharp, knocking sound to the music, and yet no one reviewing my recording commented on this or any of the other adaptations of the Carabalí sound to the set of instruments used for this folklore performance. Indeed, the same instruments (minus the *chekeré* for some songs) were used throughout the "Trilogy," even as they changed musical genres.

The wild-eyed witch then makes another entrance, wearing painted "country marks," chomping on a cigar, and shaking two maracas as he cir-

FIGURE 6.3 Dancers combine Carabalí steps with movements of agricultural slave labor (carrying loads) in *Trilogía africana*, by Ballet Folklórico Cutumba, Santiago de Cuba, July 2006. Line drawing by Jessica Krcmarik of still image from author's video recording, used with permission.

cles around the other male dancers who have frozen into poses (see fig. 1.2). The music then shifts dramatically into one of the traditional Carabalí songs in *lengua* or "African tongue," with short lines that shorten the call-and-response alternation between lead singer and chorus and accelerate the pace, a musical technique masterfully used in festive drumming ceremonies to build the energy necessary to bring down the saints and spirits. Here, the accelerated rhythm builds momentum in the dramatic action. Having little denotational meaning, the "Africanized" lyrics index the African otherness of the congo slave characters, as in the third song:

1 Iyá sanfaranfá iyá
2 Batibao
[*repeated*]
3 Yo tiro un pie
I kick out a foot
4 Carabalí
[*repeated*]

The next song, played with an intense, percussive energy, shifts from the Carabalí repertoire to the Gagá repertoire, derived from transplanted Haitian processions during Holy Week known as *Ban Rará*, from which the term *Gagá* is derived.[10] I present the presumably Kreyòl-derived lyrics, here in the fourth song, as written by a Cutumba singer without any attempt at translation, since none of the singers could tell me what the song said, simply describing the lyrics to me as in a "patois" of Kreyòl and Spanish.

1 Eti malanga te
[*two times*] [*repeated by the chorus one time*]
2 Feyo elepé soyí malé
[*two times*] [*repeated by the chorus one time*]
3 Feyo, Feyo piti piti piti soyí malé

During this song, the witch mimes doing magic inside his wooden prenda. His actions frighten the other dancers into a corner, and when they return, he casts them into writhing convulsions of possession trance with what the choreographer Florentino described as "bad spiritual energies." Another dancer enters waving a flaming frying pan, which he waves all around the possessed dancers, purifying them of the bad spiritual influences. Florentino described this use of purification by flame as a folk ritual practice to cleanse the house, akin to practices I have seen in people's homes, like lighting a candle or rolling a coconut around, then casting it out the door. Purified of their possessing spirits, the corps of dancers performs Haitian-style dances.

The combination of African-sounding songs with these danced images is not subtle in conveying Blackness as exotic, superstitious, theatrical, and impenetrable, nor is it coincidental that the most African-looking dancer in an ensemble dedicated to Afro-Cuban folklore, most of whose dancers identify as Black or mulato, performs the "witch" role. As a Cuban folklorist put it when I asked him, Chirri had the right phenotype for the role.

The piece suddenly and dramatically slows its pace, as the musicians abruptly begin to play Palo rhythms, accompanied by a fierce call-and-response song from the ritual song genre called the *llamada*, in the Congo-palero ritual register and used in Reglas de Palo to perform palero spiritual potency and bravado. I present a sampling of the fifth song here, in which the lead singer's lines can be repeated in any order, with glosses where I can provide them, and with **<u>bold underscored</u>** type marking words from the Palo ritual jargon:

Lead	Te con é, ago tintero
Chorus	Te con é
Lead	Con mi **<u>yumba</u>** de acero
	With my **<u>Briyumba</u>** [lineage of Palo magic] of steel

Chorus	Te con é
Lead	Con mi **yumba nganga**
	With my **Briyumba ritual power object**
Chorus	Te con é
Lead	Con mi cuento que yo **emboa**
	With my story that I **serve** my prenda [ritual power object]
Chorus	Te con é
Lead	El mimito Siete Rayas
	The same Seven Rays (deity)
Chorus	Te con é
Lead	Con cuchillo de Palo
	With the knife of Palo
Chorus	Te con é
Lead	Con mi **ganga** de Palo
	With my **ritual power object** of Palo
Chorus	Te con é
Lead	Juramento no me pesa
	Swearing allegiance [being initiated] does not weigh on me

With the impressively deep voice of Manolo (Rafael Cisnero Lescay) booming out the lead, the song radiates power, as do the strong steps of the dancers beginning the Palo dance. The song, with its refrain of "te con é" (*t* with *e* [?]) that no one in Cutumba could gloss, alternates with the lead's lines that boast of his ritual power and offer an implicit challenge. Manolo told me he can improvise, as paleros do when singing *llamadas* during festive ceremonies called *juegos*, "games," in which paleros invoke the spirits of their prendas and compete for dominance through the claims they make about their prenda's power (see Ochoa 2010).

In this choreographic and musical route from assimilated Carabalí to slave laborers to Haitian rhythms to Palo rituals, a time-transcending link is made, as if to say that the legacy of slaves is Haitian cultural forms and Reglas de Palo ritual practices. This elision, of course, disregards the more recent source of Haitian culture in Cuba—from early twentieth-century labor migrants—and the modernity of Reglas de Palo as a relatively recently codified, contemporary religion. Haiti and the Reglas de Palo instead are made coeval with a primeval, African era, in which African-born field slaves admired and imitated assimilated creole domestic slaves. The characteristics of one of these figurations spreads to them all, especially because the corps of six male dancers, the original "congos," remains the same. The other elision that happens is that the witch character, working with evil spirits, smoothly transitions into a palero, a common stereotype of paleros that they sometimes even encourage.

But the performative effect of this witch/palero character is to portray Afro-Cuban religious practices as the work of superstitious, evil-intentioned, and sometimes aggressive people.

Indeed, the choreography during this section involves aggressive displays of Palo bravado based loosely on the Palo ceremony of the *juego*, in which paleros from one or more ritual lineages gather to sing boasting songs about their spiritual power in friendly competition with each other that can still have a dangerous edge: to sing about one's prenda is to awaken and provoke that prenda, and of course there is always the danger of spiritual attacks mounted by enemies using their prendas. All of this ritual complexity is compressed in the folkloric representation of Palo, which depicts it as aggressively, even violently, masculine and magical. During the *llamada* song, the corps of dancers exchange the Palo ritual greeting motion of bumping elbows, then freeze in a head-to-head pose as the witch slowly carries in a prenda: a large, flat, metal bowl, bristling with iron spikes and other implements, wooden sticks, and leafy branches (fig. 6.4). He sets it at the front of the stage, then gives it the elbow greeting used among paleros. The music stops, and the dancers call out a call-and-response *llamada* invoking God:

<u>**Mambé!**</u>
Diós!
<u>**Mambé!**</u>
Diós!
<u>**Mambé!**</u>
Diós!

They then perform a dialogue in congo-palero register in which two paleros, the original witch and another dancer, challenge each other to spiritual warfare between their prendas. As I described in chapter 4, the register brings together tokens of African-derived vocabulary from Palo ritual jargon (<u>**bold underscore**</u>) with Bozalisms (**bold**) in a matrix of Spanish, including some specialized phrases.

1	Challenger:	¿Quién **son** <u>**mayombe**</u> que da cuenta arriba <u>**en toto**</u>?	Who **are palero** who acknowledges before the prenda
2	Witch:	<u>**Ekuá mayumbelá**</u>	<u>**Ekuá palo priest**</u>
3		Yo **soa** <u>**molonkisi bisuami viramundo**</u>	I **am** <u>**Molonkisi Bisuami Viramundo**</u> [ritual name]
4		¿**Que** quién <u>**vela molenén toto**</u>?	**What** who <u>**cares for this**</u> prenda?

FIGURE 6.4 The witch carries a prenda as other dancers pose in combat in *Trilogía africana*, by Ballet Folklórico Cutumba, Santiago de Cuba, July 2006. Line drawing by Jessica Krcmarik of still image from author's video recording, used with permission.

5		Yo **batiendo** lo que mando	I **breaking** what I command
6		¿Quién **son** tu **guariguari**?	Who **are** you **blabbing too much** [a Cuban colloquialism with African flavor]
7	Challenger:	Ajá ja ja ja. Yo soy **mulungo quintadele ntada**	Aha-ha-ha-ha. I am **Mulungo Quintadele Ntada** [ritual name]
8		**Ma** rayo parta mi centella	**Bad** ray splits my lightning [you have insulted me]
9	Both	**¡Changaná!**	**War!**

Although this dialogue is entirely intelligible to practitioners of Palo, it would be quite denotationally opaque to most folklore audiences, Cuban or foreign, who would have to rely on the pragmatic and paralinguistic cues to understand what this interaction is about. As the two dancers speak, they circle each other, point accusingly, slap the floor, and posture aggressively (fig. 6.5). Their tones are harsh: clearly a fight is brewing. The challenger's laugh in line 7 is full-throated, with head thrown back: a derisive laugh. The two freeze shoulder to shoulder, erect, and with chests lifted and arms back, then tremble and begin to dance as the music begins again, this time with songs of insult or *pulla* that provoke people and spirits to display their force, as here in the sixth song (with Bozalisms again in **bold**):

Lead	Juey con juey tarro **va topá**	Ox with ox horns **will clash**
Chorus	Juey con juey	Ox with ox

At a fast and furious pace and immense, reverberating volume, the song describes the choreography, in which the dancers, including both paleros, circle the prenda and wooden vessel that form an altar at center stage. The witch bends before this altar, pulling out plastic snakes (only rarely associated with Palo practice), and the rest of the dancers' movements become jerkier and more frantic, as if they were being possessed by spirits to do the work of ritual warfare.[11] One moves to the center and falls to the ground, writhing back toward the witch who holds the plastic snakes, then rising and lurching around with the writhing snakes in his arms, lunging toward the audience, then contorting his face in the signs of spirit possession.[12] Another, the former challenging palero, does a virtuosic and athletic solo, speeding up the sharp arm gestures of Palo dance almost to a blur. Meanwhile, the witch moves forward with a burning torch in each hand that he first runs up and down each arm, demonstrating to the audience that he is not burned, His face twitches in the hardened, puppetlike way of people possessed by spirits: the fact that he is not burned seems to suggest that his trance is real. Dancing back to the wooden vessel, he uses a bit of stage magic to blow streams of fire over the prop. Then he again moves to the edge of the stage, before the audience, and extinguishes each torch in his mouth, another bit of theater that has no basis in any folk religious practice. The piece ends with more powerful Palo dancing, including dancers jumping up to bump chests in midair, then the dancers strike a final pose around the stage altar of prendas.

Thus far, I have described the performance itself and some of its interdiscursive references to various genres of folklore but have not linked it to the larger frame including not just stage roles but performers and audiences as well. In a stage performance such as Cutumba's, the alignment between performers and performed personas, reinforced as it is by having Black Cubans perform the roles of historical African figures, is clearly framed as a theatrical conceit. The professional performers give a compelling show, but it is clearly just a show. The "Trilogy" was performed as one piece in a longer program, in which the same dancers returned in different costumes, animat-

FIGURE 6.5 The witch and another palero trade ritual challenges, with the prenda on the ground between them in *Trilogía africana*, by Ballet Folklórico Cutumba, Santiago de Cuba, July 2006. Line drawing by Jessica Krcmarik of still image from author's video recording, used with permission.

ing different folkloric genres and narratives. Also clear is the performance's invitation to audiences to position themselves in contradistinction to the caricatured historical African figures in the performance and to regard the entire performance, and indeed the folklore ensemble itself, as the timeless African past still among us but not as "us." In one performance of the "African Trilogy," the audience watched and listened attentively and gasped in reaction to the witch's stunts with fire, but otherwise was seated quietly throughout. In another, the audience seated in a darkened theater was silent and undemonstrative throughout the performance, saving more enthusiastic clapping for other pieces.

Watching the video with educated, White friends who are socially quite distant from Afro-Cuban cultural forms and "popular" neighborhoods where these forms are more visible, they were not entirely sure what traditions they were seeing, turning to me for an explanation of the piece. An elderly friend who was clearly fascinated hastened to assure me that she had never seen these kinds of performances before and, while interested, considered herself Catholic. Indeed, many whiter, better-educated Cubans not involved in folk religions like Palo or Santería tend to regard these religions as superstitious vestiges of less-enlightened times, present only among Blacks in popular, less cultured/educated (*cultos*) neighborhoods, and bound to disappear when those populations become better educated, a view belied by the obviously growing popularity of these religions even among those same Cuban elites.

These metacultural perceptions, I believe, demonstrate the pervasiveness of the chronotope of Blackness as timeless past still among us to apply even to entire Afro-Cuban genres of performance, societies, and religions. That is, the indexical order of folkloric Blackness encourages Cubans to look on Black cultural forms in popular neighborhoods as vestiges of the past, as if those contemporary practitioners were not entirely coeval with the rest of Cuba (or were simply playing roles from the past, like the Carabalí cabildos do). Other manifestations of cultural practices marked as Black that are not so neatly contained in the chronotope of vestigial traditions to be preserved tend to be treated as unruly, even posing social danger, revealing potentially criminal, unhygienic, or atavistic tendencies—religious traditions like Santería and Palo, Abakuá societies, and even the older carnival congas receive special police (and other official) attention and are commented on in these ways by Cubans unfamiliar with them, for example, in warning me not to risk getting robbed or worse by going to a bembé.[13] As a whole, then, these performances play into dominant notions of Cubanness in which "Blackness" has been (or must be) diluted and transculturated into racially blended modern citizens, who view Blackness from a distance, as audience members experiencing something colorful and exotic.

Of course, audience responses are not monolithic because audiences themselves are diverse and can occupy different kinds of roles and role fractions *as* audiences (Goffman 1981); their reactions are shaped by background experiences with the folkloric forms being presented and choices about the stance they wish to take toward those forms, as well as by the context of performance. The spectator-spectacle frame creates a distance between audience and performance roles, in which the audience is meant to watch across a chronotopic gap separating spectators from music and dance forms marked as Black and characters marked as African/slaves/Black witches. Blackness on stage means something distinct—condensed and heightened—from phenotypic Blackness of audience members, who watch as Cubans (or foreigners), not as principals of the stage action (Goffman 1981).[14] And yet, interactional roles aside, all Cubans have a stake in the enactments of Blackness as primordial Cubanness. Unlike in religious ceremonies or even Carabalí invocations of the ancestors in prayers and songs, no spiritual power is activated by this performance, nor is an example set for action in the present. Neither do the spirits really manifest themselves nor does anyone present truly believe they even could, not on this stage.

The choreographer of "The African Trilogy," Teodoro Florentino, described his intent as showing a panorama, a "route" of Afro-Cuban traditions. Another Cutumba choreographer, discussing the piece with me, suggested that the objective of the "Trilogy" was to show how three different African cultural strains—Carabalí, Congo, and Haitian—came together in Cuba, as well as to illustrate what he called "the evils of witchcraft." For all the skill and attention to detail, "Trilogy" is not a history lesson and is not taken up as one. *MacBeth*, after all, is not the history of Scotland (see Dening 1996). And yet the "Trilogy" and performances like it do animate a particular, historical vision of Blackness and its contributions to Cuban art and identity, all projected into the past tense.

This, then, is how such performances, through the interdiscursive links they make to other genres and imagined historical events, serve as tacit racializing discourses: they draw on source types from contemporary Afro-Cuban religious and neighborhood-based cultural expressions like the Carabalí cabildos, Haitian heritage groups, and Reglas de Palo for their material, which they frame as timelessly representing colonial-era African figures and cultural expressions. The source materials, from religious practices like Palo and neighborhood folklore societies like the Carabalí cabildos, lend themselves to these reinterpretations because they already cast a backward glance at colonial-era figures and events, making the spirits of the past coeval with themselves through the kinds of chronotopic devices and alignments I have examined, including an overabundance of embodied markers, props, voices, and rhythms of Africanness, slavery, and witchcraft. Every performance points back at earlier ones that carry the weight of unbroken tradition because each seemingly replicates some "original" African figure, activating what Urban (2001) calls a metaculture of tradition.

The "Ceremony to the Cimarrón"

To illuminate further the state's role in institutionalizing and objectifying the proper subject of folklore through spectacles and the additional effects of interactions among performers and audiences, I turn to an annual event in Santiago that began in the early 1980s and has grown into a citywide festival, called both the Festival of the Caribbean and the Festival of Fire. In recent years, the festival has taken place over a week in early July, and I have participated in 1998, 2006, and 2011. Organized by the Casa del Caribe, a cultural research institute in Santiago under the jurisdiction of the Ministry of Culture, the festival's program involves academic conferences, art exhibitions, musical performances, parades, and religious ceremonies. The festival generally opens with a convocation in the city's largest theater, the Heredia Theater, with a program of speeches, musical numbers, and, in recent years, presentation of a prestigious award, the José María Heredia Plaque awarded by Cultura Provincial for lifetime achievement in culture. The festival closes with a parade through Santiago's old historic downtown, with each group stopping to perform before VIP seating set up on the front steps of city hall on the oldest plaza, the Parque Céspedes. Downhill on Alameda Boulevard, along the harbor front, food stands, children's rides, and other vendors line the boulevard, brightly lit boats filled with dancers move through the harbor in the Aquatic Carnival, and a giant bonfire called the *quema del diablo* or "burning of the devil" draws the largest crowds and marks the start of the carnival season (see chap. 3). The Festival del Caribe is a big deal for city residents and is also intended to stimulate tourism and international scholarly and cultural exchange. Foreign visitors do come for the festival, although few are traditional tourists.

The festival has, for at least the past decade, dedicated particular days to particular religious traditions or folklore genres, celebrated by special afternoon events. In recent years, one such event has been a Santería ceremony dedicated to the oricha Yemayá, deity of the littoral ocean, and held on an idyllic beach outside of town. Other afternoons or evenings have featured Palo or Vodou ceremonies, rural *bembés de sau*, or peasant *décima* poets. The character of these events varies but generally invites skilled aficionados to enjoy camaraderie while performing for an audience. In the case of religious ceremonies, these are framed (and experienced by insider participants) as real and serious ritual events, but their religiosity takes place in a larger frame of spectatorship, creating a certain dissonance between religious leaders calling for proper participation at the same time that a nonreligious audience chats and drinks beer on the fringes, like spectators at a baseball game.[15]

During the 2011 ceremony for Yemayá on the beach, my daughter and her friends, all in bathing suits, frolicked in the waves right next to where santeros were sacrificing a goat and two ducks, surrounded by a gawking crowd of sightseers. They left their play and stood to watch for a time only when the santeros moved closer to them to rinse the blood from their sacred stones, briefly staining the water where they had played. Vendors hawked Virgin of Charity tchotchkes and cold drinks, while initiated drummers prepared to play the cycle of ritual songs on their consecrated batá drums and one santero, in the water with the kids a while later, administered large streams of honey onto the bodies of anyone wanting to be purified by "the two waters," Yemayá and Ochún. After a while, he began anointing the children, whose water play while washing off the honey defied any separation between religious ritual and recreation.

One long-running event during the festival takes place outside the city, in the nearby old mining town of El Cobre. The event, called Ceremony to the Cimarrón, brings visitors to El Cobre to visit the national Monument to the Cimarrón at the top of a hill above town and pay homage to this heroic figure of African heritage and Cubanness. In the late afternoon, a program of music, folkloric performances, and semireligious observances begins, drawing crowds of visitors uphill from the town square. I have participated in the event twice and heard accounts of other years, and clearly the program varies somewhat from year to year. In comparing 2006 and 2011's events, the Casa del Caribe's researchers created a much more elaborate and condensed event in 2006, whereas in 2011, even with about the same number of participating folklore ensembles, events were spatially more spread out and more leisurely. I will discuss what happened in 2006 in greater detail because it so clearly illustrates how religious and state-folklore imperatives can come together in the same performances.

The gathering point in 2011 was the town square, where recorded pop music was playing through loudspeakers. From there, the crowd walked through the streets following a Gagá ensemble, which stopped at the foot of a long staircase up the mountain and played music as people filed up the stairs. After a short, steep climb, the stairs brought people to a flat area halfway up the mountain, where, later on, another folklore ensemble dressed in bright colors of the various orichas of Santería performed each oricha's dance, until the whole pantheon was spinning across the space cleared by the watching crowd. Before this started, there was time to hike further up to the summit of the hill, passing a small cabin that was set up as an altar, to the sculpture representing the cimarrón, a work by Santiago artist Alberto Lescay that depicts an abstract human figure, arm outstretched toward the sky, rising out of a huge cauldron like a prenda, again eliding historical African figures with folk religious symbols. The sculpture overlooks a steep view with copper-blue lakes from hundreds of years of mining shimmering far below, serving as a reminder of El Cobre's history of the successful insurrection of royal mining slaves whose protests eventually won their freedom (Díaz 2000; Franco 1975). The cimarrón is tall enough that its upper third, and especially the raised arm, are visible from vantage points far below. There had apparently already been a small ceremony up there involving invocations of the ancestors and small offerings, although I had missed it.

In 2006, the buses bearing registered festival participants from Santiago drove up to the flat area halfway up the hill, and loudspeakers were set up to play recorded music. There had been a small ceremony beforehand at the monument, described to me as a religious invocation of the cimarrón. All the rest of the events would take place on that flat area of the hill below the monument. Those events were structured like a theater of relations, presenting a tableau of many manifestations of Cuban national folklore, all expressly Afro-Cuban. And yet the larger goal of the day was a nationalistic one: to celebrate the figure of the cimarrón as a national character. According to the printed schedule of festival events, the event was a ceremony for the "rebel slaves." Although not expressly compared to Fidel's revolutionaries, the implicit recognition of their similarly rebellious heroism is lost on neither Cubans nor foreign visitors.

First on the program was an aficionado group invited from distant Pinar del Río province, in western Cuba, the 1802 de Orozco, who performed a Spiritist-crossed-with-Palo ceremony that blurred the boundaries between religious ritual, in which spirits regularly appear and speak, and folkloric spectacle, in which simulacra of these spirits of the past are performed, dressed to play the part of congos of Cuba's past (see chap. 4). Since the day's events had gotten off to a late start, the organizer in charge of the program, an official from UNEAC (Unión Nacional de Escritores y Artistas Cubanos), told the group's leaders to hurry things along and keep their performance short. When it was still going after forty minutes, albeit winding down, the next group, a Gagá ensemble, simply started their performance nearby. The noise of blowing conch shells and energetic Haitian rhythms, and the group's energetic spinning of colorful flags drew the crowd to this second performance. As the Gagá group concluded its performance, the organizers set fire to two giant brush piles, and the bonfire revealed an abstract iron sculpture underneath. As the excitement of the bonfire quieted, several Casa del Caribe researchers who are also initiated santeros, together with several additional local and visiting santeros, led a series of Lucumí invocations on a raised area opposite the bonfires, and then the day's final ensemble sounded its batá drums and Lucumí songs, and dancers dressed as orichas climbed down from the raised area where they had waited in order to dance in a long clearing the crowd made between the stage and the bonfires.

During this rather long performance, several dancers showed the effects of possession trance, although none fell deeply into trance. But the spiritual effects of the performance refused to be contained in the official folkloric frame of the event. One local *muertero*, a folk practitioner who works with muertos, did succumb, and his cimarrón spirit refused to depart, despite repeated efforts to send it away by several santeros. He alternately joined the dancers in the performance space, sometimes to their annoyance as he got in their way and called attention to his own antics, and wandered through the crowd to stop and stare back at spectators. When the official performances had ended and dusk was turning to night, as my bus descended the hill into El Cobre, we passed the man, still possessed, heading down the long staircase and leading a contingent of people trying to keep him safe until his muerto would depart.

Structurally, the two years' programs were similar in presenting folklore performances to celebrate the cimarrón's legacy. The events in 2006 more overtly combined secular and religious commemorations, with Spiritist, Palo, and Santería invocations all occurring in the course of the public ceremony. In neither year was there any explicit linkage to either the mambí fighters for independence or the revolutionaries or people of today. The cimarrón was held at a historical distance, so to speak, on display as a source of Cuban character but not necessarily a role model for today. The cimarrón spirit who insisted on manifesting itself during the 2006 event did so by transgressing the entire frame of the performance, exceeding and violating the folkloric effort to keep such presences safely contained in the past. One might read into this the implication that Cubans don't need to be maroons today because their state provides for them and inculcates different roles, as loyal, dedicated citizens ready to sacrifice for Cuba-the-cimarrón-nation. Audiences, foreign and Cuban, participate in their distancing from the folkloric figures being performed: they jostle for good views, take photos, spectate, chat, and share rum rather than joining in the singing, dancing, and clapping.

The program's overall frame, then, was of national commemoration not of a biographical individual or group but, rather, of an emblematic figure from the colonial past: the rebel slave. To examine how the cimarrón figure was both invoked and contained (for the most part) within this folkloric spectacle, I return to the performance by the 1802 de Orozco folklore ensemble. The group cleared stones and smoothed the ground in a small area, setting up a small altar of banana leaves, on which they placed a doll dressed in blue, with leafy branches, a coconut, and a vase of flowers arrayed before her as offerings. A bottle of rum was poured into numerous small coconut shell or gourd cups, which were also set out along the leaves, each with a cigar next to it. The three drummers lined up behind this altar, with several singers at a microphone next to them, and about a dozen dancers formed a U shape around the altar. The crowd gathered in a ring around the ensemble, including foreigners and Cuban TV crews with cameras. An older woman, Pura, in a knee-length blue dress and kerchief, wearing an apron, took the microphone. As I describe in chapter 4, she began a series of prayers and invocations from several religious traditions, in Spanish, Lucumí, and lengua Conga, after which the singers performed four Spiritist songs, all in Spanish and sung without drums. I present two here as examples.

La luz, la fe, la unión	Light, faith, union
Radia la luz poder divino	The light radiates divine power
Ay Dios	Oh God
Radia la luz para este ser	The light radiates for this being

Lead	[*sings*] Séase el santísimo	May it be the holiest of holies
Response	[*shout*] Sea	May it be
Lead	[*sings*] Séase el santísimo	May it be the holiest of holies
Response	[*shout*] Sea	May it be
Lead	[*sings*] Madre mía de la Caridad, ayúdanos, ampáranos	My Mother of Charity, help us, give us aid
Response	En el nombre de Diós, ay Dios	In the name of God, oh God

The singing did not spread to the crowd of spectators. Pura tapped her staff on the ground in time to the song, and the other dancers stood with heads bowed. With the third song, "Séase el santísimo,"the drums began a rapid, constant tapping, and with the fourth song, called "Si la luz redentora te llama buen ser" (If the redemptive light calls you good being), Pura moved around the group of dancers, blowing cigar smoke in each one's face to encourage the spirits to come. The drums began to play a Cuban *guaguancó* (a type of *son*) rhythm and the dancers began to move to it, as they began to sing the melody of an old popular song on the syllables, "Na Na na-na-na. . . ." They then joined hands into a ring and, swinging their arms, sang a song in the Spiritist *cordonero* tradition—a version of Cuban Spiritism "of the cordon" in which participants join hands to dance and sing the spirits down. In what follows (here and below), **bold** type indicates Bozalisms and <u>underscoring</u> indicates Lucumí.

Lead	Ya llegó cordón florero	The praising cordon has arrived
	Amo a ver cordón florero	**Let's** see the praising cordon
Chorus	Na-na-na, ya llegó cordón florero	Na-na-na, the praising cordon has arrived
	Amo a ver cordón florero	**Let's** see the praising cordon
Lead	Vamo' a ver	Let's see

Chorus	Cordón florero	Praising cordon
Lead	Con un cordón **yo congo**	With a cordon **I congo**
	Jala viente un mil congo	**Pulling wind a thousand congo**
	Con un cordón	With a cordon

The lead singer used Bozal in her ending improvisations, invoking the lengua Conga register in her call for spirits that she called "pulling wind a thousand congo." At this, Pura, who had seated herself on a chair just behind the banana-leaf altar, fell into trance. The music stopped, and she shouted, but now in the voice of an African muerto, calling on the spirits of other congos to possess the rest of the dancers:

1	Yo **dicí** y si [i]bodú bodó	I **say** y sí bodú bodó
2	y **congo alabe di congo yorú bodó**	and congo **praise of congo yorub-odó**
3	Vamo' **congo derechito**	Let's go, **good congo**

This voice, thick with tokens of Bozal and even parodic appearances of Lucumí, is the voice of a congo, a *muerto africano*. She used a Lucumí ritual greeting of santeros when entering the house of a *babalawo* (divining priest, senior to santeros), but she mispronounced it: *sibodú* instead of *ibodú*. She then repeated it as a pun with "Yoruba," creating the clever neologism "*yorubodó*." As her voice raised to a ragged shout in line 3, the other dancers in the circle responded by falling forward to their knees on the ground and going into trance convulsions. After writhing on the ground, they clapped, rising up onto their knees and back down to crouch low, bending forward to sip rum from the coconut shells on the altar of leaves and to light and puff on cigars. Some made a hissing sound, "ssss," that often signals spirit presence in Spiritist ceremonies. Their bare feet and positions on the ground around the leaf altar, together with their behaviors using the props, indexed Africanness in demeanor and taste: the congo spirits had arrived.

To this point, the ceremony conforms to similar religious rituals, even if it is rather compressed, but it is never clear whether the trances are real or simulated. They were certainly performed to seem real, and only the accelerated timing of the ceremony, and particularly the next series of actions, suggested that the performance might be a theatrical rendition of a ceremony, realistic but perhaps with rather too neat a dramatic arc. It is true that, even in performances clearly demarcated as folklore presentations, religious performers have been known to succumb to actual spirits (Hagedorn 2001), and this aura of authenticity adds to the thrill for folklore audiences. In the end, it does not really matter whether either the performers of 1802 of Orozco or their audience believed they were truly possessed or whether they were really just acting: the possibility of real spirits arriving is always latent in performances of the ceremonies that attract them, even when those performances occur in folkloric rather than religious settings. And the setting of the Ceremony to the Cimarrón was ambiguous, clearly incorporating both religious invocations and folkloric demonstrations to create an event of spectacle commemorating the cimarrón.

Pura then issued her greetings to the assembled congos and criollos, calling for a missing congo. The next song called for the congo cimarrón, taking the origo of one who threatens to kill any slave catcher coming after him (see chap. 4). Before long, the missing congo cimarrón entered, watchful and wielding a machete, then announcing his presence with the inarticulate cries common to possessions by spirits whose human hosts have not learned how to let them talk: "Eh! Eh! Eh!" (see fig. 2.1). Holding the crowd's attention and attracting a shoving mass of cameras and film crews, the cimarrón greeted Pura's muerto with the Palero elbow-bump and exchange of <u>**sala malecum**</u>, then joined the other muertos seated on the ground, while Pura's muerto made additional pronouncements in the same register as before. I give an excerpt here (with Bozalisms again in **bold** and Palo jargon shown <u>**bold underscore**</u>), in which she declared the success of the ceremony and described the presence of an entire palenque or maroon settlement of spirits. In Spiritist ceremonies, the medium will usually channel one spirit who serves as a conduit for messages from spirits who are present but do not possess anyone. The muerto then departed with the hissing of spirit presence.

1	(Pura's Muerto)	**Dici** cara'o que **dici** cara'o	**I say** damn that **I say** damn
2		mucha fuerza y mucho desenvolvimiento en ese lugar	much energy and much spiritual evolution in this place
3		en este **areda'o**	in these surroundings
4	(Response)	Y así sea	And so be it
5	(Muerto)	Y si hay un cimarrón derecho	And if there is a good maroon
6		**dici** que cara'o	**I say** that damn
7		**dici** atrás que estaba un <u>**llumbí kichada**</u>[16]	**I say** behind that there was a <u>**spirit**</u> [??]
8		El <u>**lumbi**</u> de cara'o para el palenque	The damn <u>**spirit**</u> for the settlement

del cimarrón	of the maroon
dici hay un cimarrón	**I say** there is a maroon
Sss Ssss Ah! Ah!	Sss Ssss Ah! Ah!

At this, all the other muertos departed and the dancers rapidly dissembled the altar and stood once again, except for the cimarrón (in fig. 2.1), who strode around calling out "Eh! Eh!" until a man began as lead singer with a new set of songs from Palo, starting with the familiar opening *llamada* invoking God: "**Mambé!** / Diós!" After elaborating on the call and response, he ended with the repeated exchange: "**Mpungo!** [**War!**]" During the *llamada*, the cimarrón carried out a prenda or Palo power object to place in the center, just in front of the "muerta" doll, now seated on the small chair Pura had been using. Throughout this section of the performance, the cimarrón tended to his prenda, sitting on the ground with his legs straddling it and arranging bundles of herbs in it, then pacing around and spraying rum on it, and so forth.

The Palo songs began with the gentle greeting and lament (see chap. 4): "Ooo, una buena noche, congo **awé** . . ." (Oh, a good night, congo **awé** . . .). As this and the next songs continued, the cimarrón continued to perform, tending to his prenda, then dancing vigorously, then demonstrating the veracity of his possession trance by pressing a machete into his stomach (see fig. 2.7). Just as in the "African Trilogy," the masculine aggressiveness associated with Palo practitioners was performed when another of the male dancers stepped forward to lean over and greet the prenda with elbow jabs, then stood before the cimarrón. The original cimarrón dancer slapped his chest with one hand, and then they greeted each other by bumping elbows then clasping right hands and pushing back and forth as if testing one another s strength. Their contest ended with the original cimarrón bringing their clasped hands to his crotch to ostentatiously brush his genitals, then releasing the other s hand. With this, the drama ended and the performance wrapped up with a few more songs, again led by the original woman lead singer, while the assembled dancers waved their arms in the air, another gesture taken from Spiritist *cruzado* ceremonies. As the drums of the Gagá ensemble began to sound, the crowd still gathered around this performance gave a thin smattering of applause and turned to watch the next event. The participation frame of performers and spectators remained intact: no spectators joined in singing or dancing or fell into possession trance. Show over, the spectators turned to the next source of entertainment.

As with the "African Trilogy," the 1802 de Orozco ensemble's ceremony for the cimarrón brought together a tableau of genres, including many of the same multimodal cues of Blackness, from costumes to bare feet to ritual register, music, dance, gestures, and props. Both ceremonies made clear references to contemporary folkloric sources, and to the Reglas de Palo in particular, as the strongest markers of primordial African otherness, setting representations of Palo practices and objects like the prenda into an imagined past of African slaves and maroons. The feel of the two performances was quite different: the "Trilogy" never diverged from being a masterfully choreographed stage performance, whereas the 1802 de Orozco's ceremony blended religiosity and theater so completely that one could never be entirely sure whether the spirits might really have possessed the performers. Such folklore performances demonstrate a knowing familiarity with folk religious practices polished up by a theatrical presentation. And yet both performances created interdiscursive frames of comparison expressly encouraging audiences to recognize references to the "typical" speech and actions of long-ago slaves and contemporary religious ceremonies as type sources for the current performance.

In chapter 7 I will unravel the logic of these interdiscursive links, tracing out a discourse history of Bozal, as one robustly enregistered marker of historical Blackness. I will argue that animations of "Bozal" slave speech help create Bozal as a register rather than simply reproducing actual slave speech (see Lane 2005, 48). Thus the performances are type sourced with regard to folklore and religious performances and type targeted in creating the imagined speech and behavior of historical African figures (Silverstein 2005). Performance like "African Trilogy" and the Ceremony for the Cimarrón, like countless other Cuban folkloric spectacles, serve to link historical figurations and cultural expressions associated with primordial Blackness to people and cultural expressions marked as Afro-Cuban in the present, where the same markers of Blackness too often serve as markers of cultural backwardness and social danger. The Reglas de Palo are perhaps the starkest example because of how they continue to be treated as either dangerously divisive and atavistic superstitions or as witchcraft.

The Cultural Politics of Race in Folkloric Spectacles

As much as race, and particularly Blackness, are globally circulating discourses (Clarke and Thomas 2006; Gilroy 1993), racializing processes do not necessarily play out the same way everywhere. I have focused my attention on folkloric performances of Blackness as history in order to gain purchase on the specific semiotics of racialization in these encounters of theater and audiences, while also tracking how these performances interdiscursively link to other kinds of events and event types, such as religious practices. I have also situated these performances in the wider context of the revolutionary bureaucratic and ideological control of folklore as a category that advances the revolution's agenda for social transformation, now entering its sixth decade of improvisation in the face of changing national and world circumstances.

While the politics of race and norms of acceptable public and explicitly racializing discourses in Cuba are quite different than in the United States, there is a shared predilection for avoiding denotationally explicit racist speech and critiques of racism alike in public discourse.[17] As Carlos Moore (1988) has perhaps most passionately argued, in Cuba these patterns of avoidance were at least partly a product of government claims to have abolished racism after the 1959 Cuban Revolution, making it counterrevolutionary to point out any ongoing racism. Racial pride, or any attempt at an overt identity politics of race, have also been forbidden as seditious in a system as highly centralized, with such concentrated power, and perpetually feeling externally threatened as revolutionary Cuba is. In contrast, the revolution encourages, and constantly models, revolutionary pride as a unifying patriotic attitude, on billboards, in slogans, in broadcast and print media, and in every possible domain of society. Pride in the revolution is consistently framed as national pride: to be Cuban is to love the revolution. Racial pride—what one friend described as Black self-esteem—can find expression and receive recognition most fully as a link in the discourse chain producing Cuban national pride. The exoticized portrayal of primordial Blackness at the origins of the nation is one such link, currently expressed as being a cimarrón nation that was created out of a tradition of rebelliousness tracing from rebel slaves and maroons to independence fighters to the revolutionary army itself. Folklore, in its ideological capacity, dramatizes that tradition as Cuba's history.

And yet, despite the overwhelming folkloric framing of Blackness as Cuba's "past still among us," even in that folklore are hints of other kinds of clandestine pride and racial identification. Folklore researcher Abelardo Larduet Luaces, who is also a religious practitioner with lifelong ties in neighborhoods like Los Hoyos, recounted to me an oral history interview with an elderly santera in his ritual lineage. Pointing to an old picture on the wall that he knew was of a long-deceased relative who had been born in Africa and whose family had helped establish Santería (from western Cuba) in Santiago in the 1930s and 1940s, he asked for confirmation that the woman had been African. "Africana de pura cepa" (Pure African from the source) came the quick reply, and she added that the woman was rich and came to Cuba to rescue her brother from slavery. Asked whether the woman had succeeded, the santera said, "Well of course: she was rich!" Furthermore, she was a shapeshifter (*cajuera*), able to turn herself into anything. The santera concluded that luckily the woman had died without sharing her occult secrets, which was a good thing, or else the santera would not be able to finish her story because she would have turned into a bicycle!

This story, passed from a quick-witted elderly santera to her successful, well-respected godchild and on to me, suggests that stories and memories of African heritage can serve as a source of pride: wealth, power, determination, and enigma are all attributed to this remarkable African woman who clearly was the agent of her own destiny. But this is not the usual public figuration of Africans in Cuba's past, who more typically are figured as barely intelligible Bozal-speaking slaves or maroons, doubly enslaved to their fetishes (Palo prendas as depicted in folklore performances). Thinking about this, in the course of my long conversation with Larduet that day, I asked whether he thought that people identified as African like the woman in the story (and several others he had described from his oral history study of early santeros in Santiago) would, in the 1930s, still have been regarded as "Bozals," some sixty years after the end of slavery. He thought so, explaining that while African ethnic identities—*naciones*—had started to fade by the time of the 1895 war for independence and the 1902 founding of the Cuban Republic, an overall sense of African heritage remained strong, even amid the racial discrimination, which distinguished degrees of Blackness, from mulato to negro. In sum, he explained, "Cuba es el pais más blanqueador y el más africano" (Cuba is the most whitened nation and the most African). I now turn to the "most African" of African voices: Bozal.

7

Brutology: The Enregisterment of Bozal, from "Blackface" Theater to Spirit Possession

CRISPÍN: Esos escollos que exasperan su fantasía solo se encuentran en esos desgraciados séres de los estranjeros climas de Africa.

ANICETO: No hablemos de esos ignorantes individuos !......... ¡Lástima me dá su incultura y el grado de brutología en que se encuentran, en comparancia de nuestros conocimientos científicos!

CRISPÍN: Those pitfalls that exasperate their fantasy are only to be found in those disgraceful beings from the foreign climates of Africa

ANICETO: Let us not speak of those ignorant individuals!......... It pains me so their lack of culture and the degree of *brutology* in which they are found, in *comparativization* with our scientific knowledge!

from *Los negros catedráticos* (FERNANDEZ 1868, 5)

One form that racial disparagement has taken in Cuba (and elsewhere) is stereotypification and mockery of the denigrated race's speech. The chapter's epigraph gives an example from the nineteenth-century Cuban teatro bufo, or comic theater, in which two Black characters disparage Africans, from whom they clearly distance themselves based on their superior education, but they do so in such ridiculously overexalted terms that the farce reveals them to in fact be just as ignorant as other Black characters in the play who demonstrate appropriate humbleness by delivering their lines in Bozal Spanish. These sorts of comic dialogues, typically performed in blackface by White actors and employing a stock of character types that became familiar to audiences, helped to enregister these voices of Blackness that have superceded and outlasted the bufo theatrical genre.

Bozal is a Cuban sociolect understood to derive from the speech of African-born slaves once called Bozals to differentiate them from creole (Cuban-born) or ladino (Spanish-born) slaves of African descent. Bozal, like many other markers of Blackness in Cuba, relies on a distinctive chronotope of Cuba's past as a slave-holding Spanish colony. Its modern instantiations in folk religious and folklore performance settings speak to how Cubans make this aspect of their national historical imagination relevant to current negotiations of postcolonial national-linguistic orders. As explored in chapter 4, Bozal today indexes the presence of Africans from the past, for example, as spirits and African deities who possess the bodies of devotees to speak during ceremonies or as part of ritual registers used by religious practitioners—practitioners of the Reglas de Palo, in particular.

It has long struck me that there is something uncomfortably like racist caricature in the bulging-eyed, savage performances of spirit possession—and even more so in folkloric renditions—as much as Cuban interlocutors insist to me that such behaviors signal authenticity and veracity. Consider an unexpected spirit possession during the 2006 Ceremony to the Cimarrón described in chapter 6, in which a well-known medium was possessed by his African muerto, a congo cimarrón. Wandering through the crowd of onlookers on the fringe of the scheduled performance of oricha dances from Santería, the possessed man was confronted by a skeptical Mexican tourist, who stood directly in front of him, arms folded, gazing intently at him. Gazing intently at the tourist, the muerto explained to him: "Yo son bruta"—I are brutish—where the misconjugated verb and the lack of gender agreement marked his utterance as Bozal and confirmed him as a Bozal from Cuba's colonial, slaving past. His claim to brutishness echoes the denigrations of Africans' "degree of brutology" voiced by two of the nineteenth-century Cuban theater's best-known characters. Such parallels have led me to ask how the racializing imaginaries of the nineteenth century might continue to be relevant in the speech of brutish African muertos of today—an instance of what I described in chapter 5 as a Cuban chronotope of Blackness as the timeless past among us.

Examining the historical record, exemplars of and commentaries on Bozal appear in many genres of written text and performance, contributing to the multimodal symphony of signs that overdetermine figures of Blackness and markers of Afro-Cuban culture in Cuba, producing multiple genealogies of Bozal as a "voice of Blackness." In this chapter I will focus on a sampling of prominent scholarly and theatrical sources not because these are the only possible archival traces of Bozal but because they overwhelmingly compose the corpus cited in current scholarly discussions of Bozal, particularly in the context of Afro-Hispanic literature, linguistics, and creole studies.

Given how ideologically saturated Blackness is, and has perhaps always been, in the Cuban historical imagination, and given the various contexts of Bozal's appearance, from comic theater type to voice of the muertos, it seems premature to treat exemplars of Bozal as what they might seem to be: transparent and decontextualizable tokens of a time-transcending register of African slave speech that can be extracted for comparison of their linguistic features. Linguists such as Lipski (2005, 145; see also 5–8), while sensitive to the possible inaccuracies and exaggerations of some texts, argue that the "high degree of consistency" in their representations of Bozal points to a "common denominator" in actual slave speech. I argue that another explanation is possible if we consider the reflexive and performative effects of what linguistic anthropologists call metalinguistic (and by extension, metacultural) attention, or practices that reflect on other practices (in short, speech about speech is metalinguistic; cultural attention to cultural forms and practices is metacultural [see Silverstein 1993; Urban 2001]). If we instead focus on the metalinguistic and metacultural effects of the historical corpus of "Bozal," and on how earlier instantiations may have influenced later ones—through a process known as intertextuality or interdiscursivity—the "common denominator" might be at the metacultural level of those interdiscursive comparisons.

Consider how the comic theater character Aniceto ventriloquates condescending and mocking views of African "brutology" common in Cuban slaveholding society, even as his own overreaching turns of phrase put the joke on him, so that these figures of comic theater are parodies, doubled-voiced from the start and, therefore, conveying more information about the White Cuban playwrights and audiences of the time than about enslaved Africans. And yet, I suggest that this is precisely what too many scholars have done, despite recognizing the parody, in accepting this chronotope of unchanging Blackness and mining nineteenth-century texts for evidence of enslaved Africans' Bozal speech. I will even go so far as to suggest that, rather than discovering evidence for or against various theories regarding the Caribbean's "missing Spanish creole languages," such efforts have instead contributed to the enregisterment of a time-transcending category of Bozal, as something recognizable in literary traces of the past and ritual performances of the present alike. In many ways, this chapter should be read as a preliminary exercise in asking what different insights we might gain in this case by treating Bozal speech and its written traces in archives and literature as Bakhtin would have it: a nontransparent medium through which social orders are not simply reflected but actively constructed.

In this chapter I trace some of the moments involved in how Bozal has emerged as a voice of Blackness, suggesting an alternative to the predominant view of Bozal, as enregistered *not* along a speech chain originating in actual slave speech but, *rather*, through an interdiscursive web centered on the metaculturally powerful and highly racialized persona of the African slave. The stage characters of Crispín and Aniceto are also part of this web, along with other figurations of Blackness from theater, literature, folk religious practices, and possibly other discourse domains not considered here as well.

The enregisterment of Bozal as the voice of Blackness, of course, is part of a much larger story of racialization of Africans that has unfolded across half a millenium and the world brought into being during that span. In the nexus of Western epistemic, economic, and moral orders that "invented Africa" and created the racialized category of Africans (Appiah 1992; Mudimbe 1988, 1994), one small but significant contribution has been the circulation of a distinctive, usually parodied, African voice. From Cervantes, through the early nineteenth- to early twentieth-century heyday of "blackface" entertainments such as minstrelsy, to modern instantiations of mock Ebonics in the United States, there are countless instances in which a voice of "Blackness" has been ventriloquated, caricatured, and denigrated according to what, borrowing from Cuban blackface theater, I ironically call a trope of brutology. In this chapter I focus narrowly on the trajectory of one such voice, Bozal, in Cuba, but in doing so I do not mean to suggest that Cuban Bozal is or has ever been isolated from racializing currents across the Atlantic World. While a more fully comparative analysis must await another occasion, I do wish to point out some connections that promise deeper insight into the dynamics of racialization at work in the Cuban case and, likely, elsewhere as well.

Lately, a variety of contemporary mocking registers have received serious analytical attention. Jane Hill's pioneering work on mock Spanish laid out the basic premises of subsequent work on other racializing mock forms (1993). Most important is the parodic voicing of mock forms, in which speakers use an ironic, humorous, or disparaging stance to distance themselves from identification with a marked social voice they deploy. Related to this are the linguistic features framed as tokens of the disparaged register, which tend to be a few widely recognized forms that often do not accurately reproduce actual (nonmocking) speech practices of the disparaged group. These socially charged tokens are recontextualized by association with negative, or at least extremely limited, personal or group attributes drawn from widely circulating racial stereotypes. Ronkin and Karn's (1999) example of mock-AAVE (African-American Vernacular English) in overtly racist websites shows how stigmatized tokens taken to represent AAVE, such as double negatives, are associated with ugly stereotypes—as, for example, lack of education and criminality—to create what most Americans would recognize as an explicitly racist caricature of African Americans. Contrast this to Hill's mock Spanish examples, in which the racializing consequences for Latinos are much less explicit and more deniable because more or less stylized tokens of Spanish are associated with what she describes as a light-hearted, humorous, and fun-loving, even cosmopolitan Anglo, English-speaking persona. And yet, the way in which mock Spanish recirculates associations between Spanish and a laid-back or lazy, trivialized, party-loving, and even law-breaking persona, often through intertextual series of implicature, accomplishes much the same racializing work as do more overtly racist mock forms (Hill 1993, 2001, 2005, 2008).

Recently, more complex voicing effects have been described for mock forms. Chun (2009), for example, explores critical reappropriations of mock Asian by an Asian American comedian. Roth-Gordon (2011) examines the inevitable leakiness across even the most robust attempts to distance a (white) speaker from the (nonwhite) persona of a mock form he or she voices, arguing that such disorderly discourses are inherently asymmetrical, since Whites apparently suffer only momentary linguistic "contamination" in using mock forms, while nonwhite speakers who linguistically "discipline" themselves can never lose the taint of their bodily nonwhiteness. In the same journal issue, Gaudio (2011) argues that in linguistic appropriations of stigmatized voices where speakers align with, rather than distance themselves from, the marked voice can subvert some of the disparaging associations even while making use of the racializing effects—for example, using AAVE forms in association with Nigerian pidgin to index shared claims to transatlantic Blackness through broken English. For that matter, White British youth and young White American hip-hop fans have been shown to claim alignment with Blackness (and by association, a working-class or culturally resistant status) through their admiring, rather than mocking, appropriations of what they construe to be "hip" markers of Black speech (Cutler 2003; Rampton 1995), and groups identified as nonwhite, such as Dominican American and Laotian American teens, strategically deploy AAVE and mainstream U.S. English features to negotiate their own, nonwhite racialized positionings (Bailey 2001; Bucholtz 2009).

Although the rich scholarship on Anglophone, and particularly American, blackface minstrelsy has rarely attended to the workings of language, it has provided abundant examples of all of these forms of voicing, albeit sometimes too quickly describing texts such as song lyrics, characterizations, plays, and even advertisements as imitating what is at face value assumed to be Black dialect or West Indian English (e.g., Mahar 1999; Nathan 1962). Eric Lott (1993) has compellingly argued that mid-nineteenth-century American blackface entertainments reveal moments both of social distancing from Blackness (part of immigrant efforts to assimilate to the privileges of Whiteness) and of desire for and admiration of Blackness, in a context combining extreme racism and racial intimacy. While Mahar (1999) has critiqued Lott's analysis as giving a psychological reading too far from the social contexts of blackface performance, he has also argued that White performers used blackface (and voice) as a disguise and vehicle for social critique of dominant views and parodies of a much wider range of social types than just African Americans. And Chude-Sokei (2006) has developed the theme of disguise and masking to describe the use of blackface by Black performers as a medium for heightening and critiquing the "double consciousness" imposed by a racist society, in his biography of the early twentieth-century Black superstar Egbert Austin Williams, whose blackface virtuosity on the eve of the Harlem Renaissance ensured his erasure from theater and pop culture history. Chude-Sokei's focus on black-on-black minstrelsy highlights both the distinction between and the interpenetration of processes of self-identification and interpellation, subjectivity and subjectification.

The range of uses and effects of racial parody clearly show the significance of metalinguistic awareness in stylistic choices of speakers and perceptions of their interlocutors—for example, in the very identification of a parodic theatrical style as "the speech of plantation slaves." The recent body of work on contemporary mock forms also demonstrates the larger point that language styles cannot neatly be matched to social identifications and that the normal state of linguistic affairs is complex in its heteroglossia (Agha 2006; Coupland 2007). Meek (2006) gives a telling example of subjectification through what we might call a conative projection of identity from a recent Hollywood film, in which one character's Native American identity is crudely established for film audiences in part by another nonnative character's use of Hollywood "Injun" English in addressing him (just before inflicting unspeakable violence against him), and in part by his silent response (construed as an index of stereotypical Indian stoicism). When a recognizable linguistic style does come to index tightly a particular social persona, as AAVE and mock AAVE index different takes on the meaning of Blackness, or White-invented Hollywood Injun English indexes a stereotyped figure of Native Americans, we must investigate how this happens. But in doing so, we must take care not to collapse representations, mock forms, and actual speech of members of these groups into each other, looking instead for moments of interdiscursivity: citation, imitation, appropriation, and reappropriation, whether acknowledged or not.

Building on these insights, the modal use of Bozal in Cuba today, to voice the presence of a historical African figure during spirit-possession ceremonies, is clearly not a mock form (nor, for that matter, are most of the staged folklore performances of Bozal). In these cases, Bozal does mark a distancing between animator and author/principal speaking roles, but for the purpose of manifesting a spirit's presence in the body of a human host (Du Bois 1992; Irvine 1992; Keane 1997a), where the relationship is one of power and respect, not of irony, parody, or disparagement. And yet, by tracing the historical context of these contemporary instantiations of Bozal, I aim to show that Bozal's trajectory includes genealogical links to the quintessentially and overtly mocking form of blackface comedy that give it complicated indexical effects in the present. A consideration of the discourse history that gave rise to Bozal raises questions about how we should model interdiscursivity across larger scales of time and space, in light of longstanding questions about the effects of metalinguistic awareness and the indeterminacy of contextualization (Cameron 1995; Gumperz 1992; Silverstein 2001). Our answers to these questions have implications for how we go about defining a register like Bozal.

Bozal, Metacultural Awareness, and Webs of Interdiscursivity

The earliest canonical Spanish writers in the age of Cervantes were already representing parodied African speech, influenced by an emerging Portuguese literary genre of *fala de preto* (Black speech [Lipski 2005]). African "types" joined in the dialogic play of voices in popular comedic theater and song, both secular and religious, at the dawn of the Atlantic world. The "father of Spanish theater," Lope de Rueda (1510–65), featured Africans speaking a distinctive register in his comic dialogues. Scarcely a generation later, the poet Quevedo (1590–1645) mocked the established comic formula of representing "the Guinea tongue by changing the r's into l's and the l's into r's, thus Francisco = Flansico" (Stevenson 1994, 485–86). Numerous popular religious songs of Iberia and the New World colonies, the *villancicos* of the seventeenth century, were called *negros* or *negrillos* because they animated rustic African voices. Sor Juana Inés de la Cruz, of late seventeenth-century New Spain, employed a kit of dialectal markers and invented "Africanisms" that would, as we will see, be as recognizable among twentieth- and twenty-first-century purveyors of Bozalisms as to Cervantes and his era. Her Africanisms, vocable expressions like "gurugú" and "he he he cambulé," mark one moment in a history of characterizing African voices with nonsense words, semantically empty but pragmatically rich.[1] Even in making a case for mining these texts as "sources of evidence on earlier Afro-Hispanic speech," Lipski (2005, 93) sums up these Golden Age Bozal characters as "frozen stereotypes." Centuries later, twentieth-century Cuban poet Nicolás Guillén employed similar sounding vocables in poems like "Canto negro" from 1931 (Guillén 1972, 1:122; Stevenson 1994):

¡Yambambó, yambambé!	Yambambó, yambambé!
Repica el congo solongo,	Rings the congo solongo,
repica el negro bien negro;	rings the very black black;

congo solongo del Songo	congo solongo from Songo
baila yambó sobre un pie.	dances yambó on one foot.

While Guillén's vocables speak to a specific early twentieth-century context of developing a distinctive national culture rooted in the transculturation of African, European, and other roots, they continue what had become a several-century tradition of voicing the African as primitive, if musically inclined, other. Through the trajectories of colonialism and postcolonialism, including genres of theater, literature, and scholarship, African figures and Bozal speech have circulated widely. Bozal voices continue to circulate not only in Cuba but even in sites where other traces of the African Diaspora have been otherwise scrubbed from the national historical consciousness. In Peru, for example, despite a century and a half of attempts at whitening, containing, and erasing, forms of folk and popular music continue to breathe life into the stereotypical figures and voices of otherwise absent Africans (Moore 1997, 248n5; Stevenson 1968). Similar dynamics are afoot in Montevidean carnival troupes known as *comparsas de negros lubolos*, featuring blackface performers in a nation that defines itself as a product of European immigration (and in contradistinction to Black Uruguayan troupes known as *llamadas* that specifically perform an alignment to Blackness in Black neighborhoods [Andrews 2007, xiv, 59; Remedi 2004]).

Bozal thus emerged and in some usages continues to serve as a parodic voice. Parodies require a doubling of voices—a ventriloquation, as Bakhtin says—where one voice evaluates a copresent voice. The comic dialogue in the epigraph is a good example, especially considering that the (White) playwright himself first performed the role of Aniceto (in blackface, of course). Although linguists seeking the "missing Spanish creole" have sought to reconstruct original slave speech from today's Bozal and from nineteenth-century sources like comic plays, I suggest they are on the wrong track, and we must attend to the less obvious evaluative voice, which implies an alternative interdiscursive trajectory, not necessarily exclusive of actual African voices, but certainly troubling any straightforward reading of the latter in historical Bozal texts. As an analogy, I think of Mudimbe's analysis of late fifteenth- to early sixteenth-century European paintings of Africans, where he remarks on the double representation through which European painters imagined so-called black bodies based on White models (Mudimbe 1988).

The analysis I develop in this chapter moves between the microdiscursive scale of communicative events and the *longue durée* of historical-cultural movement to consider the enregisterment of Bozal as a racializing process. The very term "enregisterment," which I have put to use throughout this book, refers to the reflexive social processes through which "cultural models of speech" emerge and can be traced historically (Agha 2003, 2006). Enregisterment, I argue, occurs at the interdiscursive level, when events in the stream of discourse become recognizable instances of a social voice indexing a particular social persona. When the indexical link between type of person and manner of speech becomes tight enough at the metalinguistic level (if not necessarily in practice—see Ochs 1992), we can call that manner of speech a register, whether or not it goes by a particular label—legalese, baby talk, Bozal.

There are two issues I wish to explore in particular. First is the recognition of resemblance required for a generic type to become salient. To attend to this issue of iconicity is to raise questions about how the conditions of interdiscursivity are shaped by different degrees or different types of metalinguistic awareness of the similarities linking disparate moments of discourse, with or without complete metacultural awareness (i.e., recognizing a cultural form *as* a form in order to make it available as an object of reflection and commentary). Consider the process of tracing out discourse histories to link events across time and genre: What are the ramifications to social actors' ability to recognize when interdiscursivity occurs? What are the limits of awareness in determining that two separate instances of discourse are iconically linked (Silverstein 2001, 2003)? I start from the premise, described in earlier chapters, that discourse circulation necessarily involves relationships of interdiscursivity across speaking events (including intertextuality across written texts).

To speak of processes of entextualization and enregisterment, then, is to posit that a fundamental similarity or set of similarities is recognized in comparing two semiotic events. The *recognition* of a "family resemblance" links disparate discourse events to each other (and, if the entextualization is robust, to an abstractable "type"—e.g., to a recognizable social persona, interactional trope, code, genre, or register). That is, the similarity that serves as the basis for an interdiscursive link must be culturally meaningful within some interpretive frame in order to be recognized (Agha 2006, 78; Irvine 2005, 24; and others in the same special issue). It follows that some degree of metalinguistic (or, more precisely, metapragmatic) awareness is required for the recognition of any particular case of interdiscursivity, but of course we know that metapragmatic function often does not require fully articulated (metadiscursive) awareness that would allow for conscious reflection on the phenomenon. We also know how fickle, incomplete, and misdirected metalinguistic awareness can be, precisely because it is saturated by ideologies, linguistic and otherwise (Agha 2006; Irvine 2008; Irvine and Gal 2000;

Silverstein 1993, 2003). For this reason we can describe many racializing discourses as covert or tacit: their racializing functions in replicating signifiers of racial difference and danger go unacknowledged or even unrecognized by those participating in their circulation (Dick and Wirtz 2011).

There is something fundamentally open-ended about interdiscursivity: iconicities linking two discourse events can be discovered at any moment, and likewise, such similarities can also be disavowed, ignored, or erased, depending on the chronotopic frame in which discourse events and types are being compared. In previous chapters, I have demonstrated how Cuban signifiers of Blackness in folklore performance index a chronotope of colonial nostalgia that expressly links Blackness in the present to colonial-era figurations of Africans. Scholars, too, in our role as metaculture specialists pointing out and commenting on cultural forms, also engage historically specific metacultural frameworks in our analyses of interdiscursivity: we may find that some interdiscursive links form historical chains, thus allowing us to reconstruct discourse histories—histories of uptake and circulation, for example, through which particular speech registers emerge and become salient.

But what of the shifting metacultural awareness of those who reproduce features indexing a recognizable register? How are they negotiating (by expanding or narrowing) the inevitable "intertextual gaps" (Bauman and Briggs 1990)? I want to focus, for now, on the dynamics connecting interdiscursivity to the creation of event-internal metacultural models of discourse history. Asif Agha (2006, 72–73) discusses how some interactional events formulate "virtual models" of their own sociohistorical situation, pointing out that such models may or may not bear much resemblance to empirically verifiable discourse histories. One such virtual model I have explored in this book is the chronotope relegating Blackness to the timeless past, wherein emblems such as Bozal speech, slave dress, and even movements and gestures seem to be unproblematic icons of *actual* slave speech, dress, movements, and gestures. Just how has this time warp linking signs of Blackness to this particular imagined slave persona become so overdetermined?

This brings me to the second issue I wish to explore here, which is to reconsider the metaphor of speech chains and offer, instead, the more complex metaphor of interdiscursive "webs." Quite apart from their eerie resonances with the topic of slavery, speech chains are a powerful idea in a semiotically informed, diachronic study of discourse, and one traceable to Saussure (in linguistic anthropology's own discourse history), who provided the famous basic diagram of what he called the "speech circuit" (1996, 11; fig. 7.1). He pointed out "the linearity of time" inherent in linguistic signals (70) and introduced a theoretical apparatus for delimiting the semiologically meaning-

FIGURE 7.1 Saussure's basic unit, the speech circuit, from Saussure (1996), *A Course in Linguistics*, 11.

ful divisions in sound sequences, including his argument for the necessity of "compar[ing] series of phrases in which the same unit occurs" in order to segment the flow of speech sound (103). Recognizing similar units separated in time is fundamental to our ability to segment the stream of speech into meaningful chunks. Figure 7.1 illustrates the basic unit of his "speech circuit" consisting of a speaker and receiver, with the two perhaps alternating roles.

The contemporary idea of discourse chains, deriving also from Saul Kripke's (1972) and Hilary Putnam's (1977) work on meaning and reference, allows us to shift scale from the temporality within unfolding interactions to that across interactions comprising longer-term discourses and even across the *longue durée*, thereby tracing how semiotic objects—names, for example—are constituted across sociohistorical chains of reference. An example of the speech-chain model is Agha's (2003) study of the enregisterment of British Received Pronunciation. Figure 7.2 shows that Agha's diagram is in essence an elaboration of Saussure's diagram. I suggest that the metaphor of a chain is misleading, however, in being too linear for the multiple reticulations that produce what look more like interdiscursive *webs*. Metaphors matter as models, and the kinds of rich analyses of unfolding discourse that describe multiple cultural movements, indexical orders, and scales of context are better described using the less linear, less teleological, more open-ended metaphor of a web.

But even the metaphor of a web has its limitations: it may be too static a structure to capture the open-endedness of real-time contextualization processes, in which new juxtapositions (such as those I propose for spirit possession speech in this chapter) invoke new orders of indexicality. Perhaps "configuration" or, current favorites in popular discourse, "clouds" and "crowds" are terms that might better capture the dynamic quality of interdiscursivity, but they bring other unnecessary baggage and to my mind simply confuse

```
[S--->R]      [S--->R]      [S--->R]      [S--->R] ......
       |_____|       |_____|       |_____|
time→→→→→→→→→→→→→→→→→→→→→→
S= 'sender'
R= 'receiver'
```

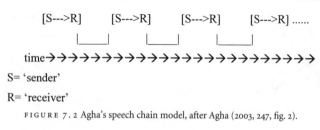

FIGURE 7.2 Agha's speech chain model, after Agha (2003, 247, fig. 2).

matters. As a different option for replacing the metaphor of speech chains, I also play with the notion of discourse genealogies. Ideologies of lineage direct our attention toward only particular lines of descent, but of course, with each subsequent generation, the number of ancestors doubles (two parents, four grandparents, and on). To apply the genealogy metaphor to the Bakhtinian "echoes" of prior speech in each subsequent speech event, this tension between the potential number of earlier speech occurrences that could influence a current speech event and those that actually are recognized as relevant is precisely what my metaphor of discourse genealogies seeks to point out.

Bozal's Enregisterment in Cuba

Bozal, characterized in Cuba today as "how African slaves once spoke," is derived from the Spanish word for "mouth." Its meanings include "wild" and "untamed," "ignorant," and also "dog muzzle" and "bridle bit" (as instruments of control). This was the label applied to African-born slaves (as opposed to Iberian- or creole-born slaves), and it seems to have been in use in Spain and the colonies at least from the sixteenth century (Alonso 1958; Covarrubios Orozco [1611] 2006). Early on, the term also came to refer to the way that such Africans would have spoken Spanish, which has been consistently characterized (over hundreds of years and into the present) as "mal hablado, defectivo, enreda'o, feo, . . ." (badly spoken, defective, mixed up, ugly . . .).[2]

The first mention of Bozal in Cuba's historical record may be a call by Havana's new bishop in the 1750s for Catholic priests to learn Bozal, if not African languages (cited in Castellanos 1990, 71). Bozal received increasing metacultural attention with the vast growth in Cuba's slavery economy due to the sugarcane agriculture boom on the island after the 1790s. Whereas in 1792 slaves made up about 31 percent of the population (87,000 out of 270,000), in 1827 the slave population alone had increased to 287,000, or about 41 percent of the total population of 700,000 (Bergad 2007, 17–18 ; Bergad et al. 1995, 39). Over time a substantial free colored population had arisen, and by the

1862 census there were some 370,000 slaves and 200,000 free people of color, making up 44 percent of Cuba's total population of 1,400,000 (Bergad 2007, 10; see also: Curtin 1969; Kiple 1976; Murray 1971). Abolition came late and gradually to Cuba, finally being completed in 1886.

A catechism published in Havana in 1797, the *Doctrina para negros: Explicación de la doctrina cristiana acomodada a la capacidad de los negros bozales*, advises priests to speak slowly and to teach African slaves to enunciate words correctly.[3] The author, Havana priest Nicolás Duque de Estrada, refers to "that language that they use without cases, without types, without conjunctions, without agreement, without order" ([1797] 1989, 66, 118; my translation). These characterizations of non-European language are, of course, all familiar enough from countless other cases of European colonial linguistics (for an early critique, see Boas 1889).

Another elite commentary comes from Cuban geographer Estebán Pichardo y Tapia, who in 1836 published a dictionary of Cuban Spanish that included examples of Bozal, which he characterized as consisting of "grammar defects and sound changes" that created a "disfigured Castilian" (Pichardo y Tapia [1836] 1977, 85). Below is a sampling of his textual representation of Bozal, together with my attempt at a more standard Spanish gloss, in the second line, to indicate what is marked as disfigured in his version, and my English translation in the third line). Pichardo y Tapia did not himself provide a gloss of his example, suggesting that he might have thought its denotational meaning to be clear to readers despite the many nonstandard orthographic forms he deploys to represent this speech style. I thus indicate uncertainties in my glosses:

1 yo mi ñama Frasico Mandinga, nenglito reburujaoro, crabo musuamo ño Mingué
yo me llamo Francisco Mandinga, negrito [reburujador?], esclavo mi su amo Don Miguel
my name is Franscisco Mandinga, little [out of place?][4] black, slave, my master[5] Don [honorific] Miguel

2 de la Cribanerí, branco como carabon, suña como nan gato,
de la [carbonería?], blanco como carbón, las uñas como un gato,
of the [coalyard?], white like charcoal, nails like a cat,

3 poco poco mirá oté cribi papele toro ri toro ri,
hace poco miro a Usted escribiendo papeles torori torori [nonsense vocables]
for a while I watch you writing papers la-ti-da[6]

4 Frasico dale dinele, non gurbia dinele, e laja cabesa,
Fransisco le da dinero, [está agobiado?][7] dinero y raja la cabeza,
Francisco gives him money, the money [is not sufficient?], and breaks his head,

5 e bebe guariente, e coje la cuelo, guanta qui guanta
y bebo aguardiente, y me coge el cuero, aguanto aquí aguanto
and I drink cane liquor, and get the whip, I endure here I endure[8]

We don't know how Pichardo y Tapia produced this sample, nor from what source or sources, but note that the marked phonological, lexical, and grammatical features of this passage, as represented orthographically, anyway, are in keeping with later representations of Bozal. He provides examples of phonological substitutions, including *r* for *l* and *l* for *r* (already noted in Spain, we've seen, and today described as typical of colloquial Cuban speech), phonological elisions, nonstandard verb conjugation and a few other syntactic "errors" and innovations, like reduplication for emphasis. Note, too, that this is presented as a first-person account by a Bozal speaker, in which markers of Bozal speech co-occur with stereotypical semantic indications of slave existence: his surname, Mandinga, is an ethnonym describing his presumed place of origin in Africa; he seems puzzled by "written papers" and mentions needing money and drinking cane liquor; and if my interpretation is correct, he seems to end on a note of misery. A crucial observation is that Bozal is always tightly linked to a slave persona, to the extent that even these early scholarly renditions of Bozal can't help but deploy it in a projected "first-person" voice of a slave. I will return to this point later in my discussion of spirit possession, as it contributes to the chronotope of Blackness as the timeless past among us.

If this text and its accompanying characterizations represent elite, educated, White recognition of Bozal as African slaves' distinctive way of speaking, other texts indicate how Bozal was being represented in popular entertainment for middle- and lower-class Whites. Vernacular musical theater, popular literature like comic verse and costumbrist (or quaint-customs) scenarios, and newspapers began to represent Bozal through blackface characters on the stage and in print, first evident in the *negrito* performances of Covarrubias in 1812–15 (who is described as blackening his face, but whose texts have not survived). The trend accelerated in the 1830s and 1840s, thanks to writer and performer Crespo y Borbón and his African persona Creto Gangá, and again in the late 1860s, with the teatro bufo. Cuban comic theater presented skits called *negritos* derived from French, Italian, and Iberian comic theater and was well-established long before U.S. blackface performers brought the character Jim Crow and the like on tours to Cuba during the U.S. Civil War (Leal 1975,1:21). Today we have access to numerous libretti and song lyrics from these vernacular theater genres, as well as advertisements and accounts of performances in newspapers. In these, we see a personification of Bozal speakers in what becomes a set character type, the *negrito*, with the diminutive ending on *negro* reflecting condescending White attitudes toward Blacks.

To illustrate briefly the early theatrical Bozal, I present a sample of an influential characterization by Bartolomé José Crespo y Borbón, a Galician immigrant to Cuba who famously inhabited his invented alter ego, Creto Gangá, in live performances and even in what were considered hilariously illiterate letters he penned to newspapers during the 1840s. Crespo y Borbón had already published comic dialogues and collections of poetry featuring the interplay of various "Cuban" voices including Bozal, often under pen names. But once he created Creto Gangá, this became his best-known authorial persona. Mary Cruz (1974) documents how Creto Gangá's biographical details slowly emerged over numerous publications and newspaper announcements. In the persona of Creto Gangá, Bozal once again is used to voice a projected first-person account by a putative African whose last name is also his ethnonym, although Creto Gangá could represent either a slave or a freedman. Creto Gangá's 1846 poem's title is itself an exemplar of his Bozal, which I follow with the opening phrase of this play-in-verse (Cruz 1974, 50):

1 Laborintos y trifucas de Canavá
(Los) Laberintos y trifulcas del Carnaval
Labyrinths and commotions of Carnival

2 veraero hitoria en veso de lo que pasá en la mácara
verdadero historia en verso de lo que pasó con la máscara
true history in verse of what happened in the masquerade

3 a yo Creto Gangá y nengrita mío Frasica lucumí, cuentá po yo memo
a mi, Creto Gangá, y la negrita mía Francisca Lucumí, cuenta para mi [mismo]
to myself, Creto Gangá, and my woman Francisca Lucumí, told by myself

4 Domingo de Canavá / yo vití de macarita
El domingo del Carnaval / yo me vestí de mascarita
The Sunday of Carnival / I dressed myself in mask

y me fue con mi nengrita / po todo pate a pasiá
y me fui con mi negrita / para todas partes a pasear
and I went with my woman / to walk all over

Similar kinds of phonological substitutions and elisions, nonstandard verb conjugation, and other syntactic errors of agreement and case are evident in this sample as in others. Note, too, that this character's concerns—with frivolous pursuits of carnival—are in keeping with negative characterizations of slaves. And finally, note the playful contrast between the attempted pretentious register of the main title, "labyrinths and commotions" and subsequent versification, and the Bozalisms throughout, finding comedy in this presumed dissonance of social indexicality, perhaps akin to reciting a Shakespearian sonnet in a Cockney accent.[9]

At that moment in Cuba's history as a Spanish colony, Cuba's literati and theater were still oriented toward the genres, fashions, and opinions of the metropole—Europe, after all, was clearly the seat of political as well as cultural authority. Unsurprisingly, then, Bozal enregisterment continued along the lines already laid down in Iberian literature. As the logic went, African-born slaves were denigrated in part for their inability to speak properly, which served as proof that they belonged in their low status, and Africans in Cuba who aspired to higher economic and social status were ridiculed as rising above their station—that was why Creto Gangá's verses and letters to newspapers inspired hilarity among the predominantly White reading public. Things were poised to change, however, with the emergence of a proto-national Cuban identity that would layer a new, rebellious metacultural frame onto the existing one concerning the social significance of Africans, as I will describe.

Two additional trends emerged. First, Cuban vernacular theater produced a whole set of stock character types, standing for Cuba itself, and no marked racial, internal, or foreign group was left out: peasants, Galicians, Canary Islanders, and even Yanquis, like the loud and abrasive "Míster Smith" were parodied in comic dialogues between characters representing two or more "types." Initially, Cuban peasants and Bozal Blacks were represented with similar voicing devices—grunts, slurred words, and nonstandard phonology and grammar, only being differentiated over time. Second, amid this costumbrist proliferation of what Cuban theater scholars have called Cuba's own, homegrown "comedia dell'arte" (Leal 1975,1:17), the prototypical *negrito* character itself, emblemized by Creto Gangá, proliferated into distinct types of black characters, who could be played against one another to heighten the comic effects. Innovations included juxtaposing Bozal-speaking Congo Blacks to *Negros catedráticos* or "educated Blacks" (where this term was meant to convey a humorous oxymoron).[10] The teatro bufo also created scenarios depicting stereotyped mulatas, Black carriage drivers or *caleseros*, and *negros curros*, an urban subculture of free Blacks who resisted White authority through fashion, speech, and economic independence (nineteenth-century predecessors of zoot suits and Harlem street culture).[11]

Amid the proliferation, Bozal Blacks would continue to be represented as crude-sounding brutes, for comic effect, but increasingly as honest, earnest, and authentic brutes, even as audiences that had begun to think of themselves as Cubans could identify with such brutish resistance to the polished hand of Spanish imperial power. To illustrate, consider the interplay of stock character types in an example from the later teatro bufo of the 1860s: Francisco Fernández's one-act "comedy of Cuban customs," titled *Los negros catedráticos*, builds its humor by juxtaposing the humble Congo, José, with the pretentious *catedráticos*, Aniceto and Crispín (see the epigraph to this chapter), who envision a perfect match between one's daughter and the other's son and disdain José as a suitor, until it turns out that José, ill-speaking *Bozal* though he is, makes a lot of money as a stevedore. Compare the following self-descriptions by José and Aniceto, which occur within a few lines of each other, early in the play (Fernandez 1868, 10; italicized words in original):

José (*negro congo*):

1 Yo só congo trabajaore la muelle. Yo no toma güariente.
Yo soy congo trabajador de los muelles. Yo no tomo aguardiente.
I am a Congo dockworker. I do not drink cane liquor.

2 Yo só libre. Yo ganá do peso tuitico lu día.
Yo soy libre. Yo gano dos pesos todos los días.
I am free. I earn two pesos every day.

Aniceto (*negro catedrático*):

1 Escúchame negro *hidrógrafo.* ¿Tú sabes el crímen que has cometido con tu atrevida petición?
Listen to me *hydrographic* black. Do you know the crime you have committed with your cheeky petition?

2 Si no fuera por que soy un hombre *instruío y metafísico* que reconozco
If it weren't because I am a *well-instructed and metaphysical man* that I recognize

3 tu inadvertencia é ignorancia, ya te hubiera elevado a las *raíces cúbicas.*
your lack of caution and ignorance, I would already have elevated you to the *cubic roots.*

In this brief juxtaposition, we can see the emergent differentiation of Afro-Cuban voices, where the malapropisms, register infelicities, and silly locutions of the ridiculous, overreaching "black professor" are counterposed to the steadfast, authentic, dumbed-down Bozal of the Congo laborer, who sounds humble as befits his low social position (what Americans might call an "aw shucks" persona).

Bakhtin's (1981) exploration of the carnivalesque roots of the novel highlights precisely what we see in Cuban teatro bufo, which is a dialogic play of voices that allows for experiments with new social alignments and identifications. All nineteenth-century Cuban theatrical representations of Black speech were double-voiced by White actors and writers interested in representing Bozal and its prototypical speakers in particular ways. For vernacular theater, as Laurie Frederik (1998) has argued, building on the work of Rine Leal (1975, 1982) and Robin Moore (1997), the agenda of such actors and writers included reinforcing the social order of slavery and dealing rhetorically with political and social tensions, including those arising from the presence of a large class of free Afro-Cubans in a slave society. Scholars of Cuban vernacular theater agree in characterizing its representations of Black speech as what Jill Lane (2005) calls a "literary register of bozal as discursive blackface" intended as an "inherent parody" and what Rine Leal (1975,1:22) describes as an effort to "aurally define" and ridicule the figure of the Bozal Black.

But it is also noteworthy that theatrical Bozal in the 1860s comes to be the register of the more sympathetic Black character, the one who recognizes, as José says in the sequel play, that "¿tó no só negro?" (aren't we all black? [Montes Huidobro 1987, 11]). Theatrical Bozal thus also came to mark the popularization of a notion of Cubanness, one ventriloquated through blackface characters and thus increasingly establishing Afro-Cuban culture as a basis for Cuban national identity (Frederik 1998). At the same time, proimperial and proslavery political rhetoric was heightening the sense of racial otherness and danger that Blacks represented (Ferrer 1999).

Above all, Cuban teatro bufo, with its interspersed dialogues, songs, and verses, was, as Matías Montes Huidobro says, "meant to be superficial and subversive through a heightened awareness of language" (1987, 23–24; my translation). Indeed, he argues that the Cuban teatro bufo, arising at a moment of increasing political tensions and censorship in the 1860s, amid nascent social awareness of the potential for an independent Cuban nation, can be compared to twentieth-century theater of the absurd in its emphasis on facade, word play, parody, and mockery—including the famous Cuban *choteo*, or witty insult, which nonetheless could slip past censors as innocent of political subversion. He asks whether the teatro bufo, with its heavy theatrical artifice, is best understood as White people mocking Black people, or White people using blackface to mock themselves (Montes Huidobro 1987).

Given this analysis, it would stretch credulity to assume that Bozal as it appears in these theatrical libretti even attempted documentary accuracy in representing how enslaved Africans actually spoke, except insofar as it mocked errors common to many foreign learners of Spanish. Indeed, commentators at the time, such as the antislavery writers and activists of the Del Monte group, critiqued costumbrist depictions of Bozal as exaggerated (Williams 1995).[12] And Afro-Cuban elites of the late nineteenth and early twentieth centuries took pains to distance themselves from such false depictions (Lane 2005; Morrison 2000). Lorna Williams (1995) argues that the shifting, often contested portrayals of White and Black Cubans, whether distinguished by speech or speaking a common "Cubano," were tied to shifting models of national identity. Language ideologies and, particularly, notions about how different social groups spoke Spanish were certainly intertwined with racial and national imaginaries, creating mutually reinforcing notions about accents and social identifications (Gal and Woolard 2001, 10). I agree with Jill Lane's (2005, 48) suggestion that what was enregistered in these nineteenth-century "literary" representations of Bozal in written text and performance was not the actual speech of Africans struggling to learn Spanish but an increasingly entextualized, imagined speech style associated with the caricatured *persona* of the African slave. I therefore suggest that the Bozal spoken today shows the influence of this discursive history of "blackface" Bozal.[13]

Let me now take a moment to summarize the first strands in the interdiscursive web linking Bozal instances into a discourse history of "brutology," to again borrow the *negro catedrático* character Aniceto's neologism directed at Bozal Africans. I have outlined what, for shorthand, I will call scholarly and theatrical metadiscourses offering representations of Bozal. My intention with these labels is to condense a lot of detail into what I am broadly labeling metadiscourses of Bozal in order to be able to focus on interdiscursive relationships across entire genres and contexts. Clearly, both scholarly and theatrical metadiscourses of Bozal could each be expanded into their own interdiscursive webs constituting those discourses as recognizable and even nameable types (e.g., across events, authors, texts, and performances). Moreover, as I have indicated, when examined in greater detail, each of these discourses has its own distinctive and often complicated stances toward the Bozal voices ventriloquated through that discourse, which are so often juxtaposed to other voices in classic Bakhtinian heteroglossia. Each followed its own circuits, with theatrical Bozal likely finding a wider audience than the catechisms and dictionaries.

Both scholarly and theatrical Bozal presupposed and further enregistered a certain persona of the African slave, the alleged original speaker of Bozal, but in neither case is *actual* slave speech a particularly necessary "source." The influence of actual slaves' speech on the persona of the *Bozal* represented in these metadiscourses is uncertain—indeed, it may even be doubtful—but in any case, it is overshadowed from the start by other metacultural concerns driving the producers and audiences of scholarly and theatrical Bozal, including an overwhelming marginalization of Africans in the racial order. Notice, too, that because Bozal as a way of speaking linked to the figure of the Bozal come to have their own metacultural life as objects of discourse we can see that the specific intentions of various authors and performers are beside the point in tracing uptake and further circulation of Bozal as a type. Lipski's (2005) and others' very careful efforts to delineate which historical sources give more or less authentic representations of Afro-Hispanic speech, based on their apparent intent to parody, denigrate, celebrate, or uplift do not—and cannot—dispel our doubts about the impact of circulating metacultural models of Bozal on even the most careful ears of the most astute and sympathetic observers of Afro-Cubans. And the pervasiveness of even just scholarly and theatrical instantiations of Bozal in nineteenth-century Cuba, leaving aside additional possible journalistic, literary, musical, religious, juridical, and other pathways for Bozal's enregisterment, suggests that few in Cuban society would be unaware of the social indexicality of Bozal as "the speech of African slaves." The intertextual webs enregistering literary and theatrical Bozal are robustly attested.

In the early years of the Cuban Republic, Afro-Cubans struggled for equal rights as full citizens of a nation whose independence many had fought for. Even as the heroic figure of the mambí fighter—the uneducated rural Black ex-slave who fought the Spanish imperial forces armed only with a machete—took on national political importance, the crude and countrified speech attributed to poor, rural Blacks had become a new source of Bozal (Lipski 2005, 167–70). This expansion meant that Bozal significantly overlapped with vernacular Cuban Spanish but carried all the negative racial associations it had by then long since accumulated as the speech of Bozal African slaves, becoming a weapon against Afro-Cuban political claims. Cuba's founding folklorist Fernando Ortiz himself, in the early twentieth century, elaborated an equivalence between Africanness, witchcraft (understood as superstition), and criminality in a series of influential books and articles delineating Afro-Cuban social types and cultural forms starting with *Los negros brujos* (The black witches [Ortiz (1906) 1973]), which had the parenthetical subtitle, *Apuntes para un estudio de etnología criminal* (Points for a study of criminal ethnology). Afro-Cuban elites of the late nineteenth and early twentieth centuries took pains to distance themselves from such false depictions and to align themselves instead with nationalist political rhetoric of racial brotherhood and equality epitomized by José Martí's writings and enacted as a goal of the multiracial insurgency (Ferrer 1999; Lane 2005; Morrison 2000).

In the struggle over the role of Blacks in the new Cuban nation, the nineteenth-century scholarly and theatrical representations of Bozal were taken up by twentieth-century scholars as if they were transparent records of slave speech. Ortiz wrote about the *negro catedrático* (Black professor) as if this character reflected a real social type, rather than a theatrical parody (Lane 2005, 76–77). His study of an infamous nineteenth-century social type called *los negros curros*, representing a resistant subculture of free, urban Blacks, relied on characterizations of their speech by nineteenth-century Costumbrist writers, such as novelist Cirilo Villaverde. For example, to illustrate the *curro*'s "affected, insolent, and defiant" speech with its "special jargon" and "peculiar pronunciation" mixing up /1/ and /r/ and substituting /i/, he cited an 1848 poem by José V. Betancourt called "El Negro José del Rosario." As illustrated in the first stanza below, the poem voices the persona of a *negro curro* using eye dialect, such as "nasí" for "nací" (/s/ for /θ/, written as unvoiced *th* in English) and "Manglai" for "Manglar" (/i/ for /r/), as well as terms from urban jargon (Ortiz 1986, 66–70):

Nasí en Jesú María	I was born in Jesus María
En el famoso Manglai	In the famous Manglar [neighborhood]
Fui perico no hay dudai	I was a *perico* [ruffian] no doubt
Y a ningún cheche temía	And of no *cheche* [tough guy] was I afraid

Comic and costumbrist texts thus became the ethnohistorical evidence of later generations (Lane 2005, 78–79). Scholarly and theatrical representations of Bozal not only survived the end of slavery and birth of the independent Cuban Republic at the turn of the twentieth century, they also outlived African-born Cubans themselves. The legacy of nineteenth-century scholarly and theatrical representations of Bozal is evident in twentieth-century literary and theatrical genres, including novels, poetry, early folklore studies, song lyrics, and *zarzuelas*, or light comic operas, that together created the many facets of the new nation's literary and aesthetic culture, including the Afrocubanism movement of the 1920s and 1930s (Moore 1997; Williams 1995). Indeed, *zarzuelas*, often in blackface, were enormously popular right up to the 1959 Cuban Revolution (and reappeared in nostalgic revivals of the 1990s [Moore 1997; Thomas 2009]). In sum, my analysis thus far suggests that the enregisterment of Bozal as a metacultural object of attention had taken on a life of its own, with comic theater becoming a source type not only for new theater but for other, seemingly unrelated genres such as the emerging "criminal ethnology" and "folklore studies" as well.

Ortiz's sister-in-law Lydia Cabrera contributed groundbreaking folklore scholarship from the 1930s through the 1980s, including influential literary representations of Bozal in her short stories and ethnographic studies (see Castellanos 1994; Rodríguez-Mangual 2004). Her work, even more than Ortiz's, has been and continues to be directly taken up by practitioners of Afro-Cuban religion as an ethnographically and religiously authoritative source, constituting an interdiscursive link between comic theater typifications and folk religious practices. Her entextualizations of Bozal were ostensibly grounded in how she heard her elderly Afro-Cuban informants speak, most of whom would by then have been at least at one generation's remove from their African-born predecessors. But Cabrera, herself elite and White, would not have been "innocent" of earlier and cotemporaneous literary and theatrical instantiations of Bozal any more than Ortiz was. Moreover, she was certainly aware of the production of fellow members of the Afrocubanist movement, such as poet Nicolás Guillén and novelist Alejo Carpentier, caught up as she was in Paris's "primitivist" craze when she lived there during the 1930s. Cabrera's work attests to her ethnographic sensibilities but also to her equally excellent literary gifts. It is important to remember, too, that she was initially working without recording technology and that the youngest of any African-born informants would already have been at least in their seventies by the late 1930s, when she began her ethnographic investigations in earnest (and that the importation of captive Africans had diminished to a trickle of illegal shipments during the final decades of Cuban slavery, so most of her informants would have been Cuban-born, not "Bozal").[14] It is a dubious assumption, indeed, that the Bozal-inflected voices through which she conveys the wise and funny stories, the herbal and magical lore, are transparent records of actual African-born Cuban speech (see Lipski 2005, 163–68).[15]

Cabrera's Bozal examples demonstrate a similar range of features to those evident in previous cases, as can be seen in this small excerpt from a story recounted in *El monte* ([1954] 1993, 183), a book that, in turn, has been mined by creolists seeking evidence of Afro-Hispanic speech. These lines are from a song embedded in a story she attributes to an informant called R. H.

> Pavo Real, tá bucán palo / pa pará bien, bien, bien / yá pará rriba jagüey
>
> El pavo real está buscando un palo / para pararse bien / ya se paró arriba en el jagüey

The peacock is looking for a branch / to perch well / now it perched high in the liana vine.

Thus far, I have brought the White scholarly and theatrical blackface representations of Bozal into the twentieth century. But what of actual African-born slaves who would have spoken to their children, creating a completely separate circuit for African-inflected Spanish? Indeed, there are two related metadiscourses of Bozal with sociologically distinct patterns of circulation among Afro-Cuban descendants and cultural heirs of slaves, who also produced (and produce) a fully oral register of Bozal, both as a recollection of how elderly African-born or second-generation relatives spoke in the early decades of the twentieth century (Ortiz López 1998) and as a register of religious performance. When in trance, many folk religious practitioners (of all racial backgrounds) are possessed by spirits of deceased Africans and African deities like the orichas of Santería, who are often characterized as speaking in Bozal. Bozal thus continues to demand a first-person voicing in which the speaker performs the persona of an African speaking Spanish, whether as deity, free person, slave, or religious authority.

Recall from chapter 4 that this indexical connection is so powerful that an informant of the linguist Luis Ortiz López, when asked to demonstrate Bozal speech in a sociolinguistic interview, first "imitated a black woman during a spiritual session," then actually fell into trance, possessed by a muerto (Ortiz López 1998; see Wirtz 2007b). I repeat here part of a sample as transcribed by Ortiz López, with my standardized gloss and translation below each line:

1 Niño, tú tá queré que lo negro áa decí cuanto yo vá hacé, si me tá acodá
Niño, tú quieres que el negro diga en cuanto yo voy a hacer, si estoy de acuerdo
Kid, you want the Black man to speak as much as I will if I am willing.

2 Cuando yo tá vení de lo tierra mío sí poqque yo tá sé negro de nación
Cuando yo vine desde mi tierra es porque yo soy negro de nación
When I came from my land it is because I am African born

The spirit describes himself as a *negro de nación*, a more polite colonial-era label than *negro bozal* for someone born in Africa.[16] In his speech we see features characteristic of theatrical and scholarly Bozal, including the presence of protocreole verbal aspect markers similar to those that Germán de Granda (1971) identified in Cabrera's voicings of her elderly Black informants. Indeed, Cabrera's work has been tremendously influential among folk religious practitioners, with her book *El monte* becoming something of a religious source-text alongside Santería practitioners' tradition of keeping religious notebooks, sometimes published as manuals (Dianteill and Swearingen 2003; Duany 1988; Rodríguez-Mangual 2004). All of Cabrera's writings have become a source of Bozal as well as other specialized religious language and knowledge and are treated as a transparent, written record of orally transmitted knowledge passed from Bozal slaves to their genealogical and cultural heirs. This is but one case of a more general point that some later-appearing discourses in the interdiscursive web now mediate the metacultural interpretation of earlier discourses, such that contemporary representations of Bozal are interdiscursive with multiple antecedents.

Interdiscursive relationships can exist between cotemporal discourses as well, even when the discourses follow quite different sociological circuits, because even actors in separate social positions are nonetheless aware of each other and of more socially distant discourses (if only in a vague and general way). It seems likely that Lydia Cabrera was influenced by *both* literary "blackface" Bozal and elderly Afro-Cubans and folk religious practitioners, although she explicitly type sourced *only* the latter. Likewise, it is evident that Afro-Cuban descendants of slaves were aware of, and even performed in, consumed, or critiqued, some of the ubiquitous blackface Bozal saturating popular theater, music, and literature at the same time that they partook in folk religious practice or other circuits of Bozal.

In actual religious contexts, Bozalisms and biographical details of an African or slave persona usually co-occur with markers of one or another religious register, Lucumí used in Santería or the Congo jargon of the Reglas de Palo, and the entire combination is often referred to as *la lengua* (the tongue), a shorthand for "the African tongue." Among religious participants, virtuosic displays of ritual jargon from those working with or possessed by African deities or muertos index ritual knowledge and religious community belonging. This code mixing changes the flavor, too, for those who are not religious experts, in ways reminiscent of the invented Africanisms of Sor Juana and Nicolás Guillén alike, adding an exotic or esoteric flavor as African speech. The same range of phonological and syntactic features still mark Bozalisms, as is evident in my transcriptions of the ritual performances of spirits and saints in previous chapters (see, e.g., chap. 4). There are today many such folklore performances drawing on and metaculturally refracting earlier literary and other contemporary oral instantiations of Bozal, particularly from religious performances.

Analyzing a corpus of ritual speech recorded during Palo Monte ceremonies in western Cuba, Armin Schwegler (2006) catalogs Bozal features that appeared, including:

- morphological reductions (e.g., *yo te llama*, "I call you")
- phonetic alterations (*riba* instead of [*a*]*rriba*, "on top")
- grammatical simplifications (e.g., elimination of articles)
- grammatical overextensions (e.g., use of genderless article *lo* instead of *el* or *la*)
- reduplications (e.g., *tiempo tiempo*, "a long time ago")
- omissions of syntactic complementizers (e.g., *tiempo tiempo* —— [*que*] *te llama*)
- deletion of prepositional "of" (e.g., *cuarto* —— [*del*] *fundamento*)
- uninflected *ta* + INFINITIVE
- archaic Spanish-derived vocabulary (e.g., *agüé*, "today")

The parenthetic examples are Schwegler's, but examples of all of these features have appeared in the examples presented in this chapter as well. Balga Rodríguez (2000–2003) mentions many of the same features but characterizes them as, for the most part, typical of the mistakes any nonfluent speaker of Spanish might make, rather than anything exclusive to Bozal slaves.

Alongside religious and folklore representations of Bozal, there is a new generation of scholarly metadiscourses about Bozal. Linguists studying marginalized Spanish dialects and seeking evidence of possible Spanish creolization (McWhorter 2000) bring together examples culled from all of the earlier and contemporary representations of Bozal as a single, unitary register that they characterize as the speech of African slaves. Granda (1994) describes two approaches to collecting exemplars of Bozal: one focused on written historical sources and the other directed toward oral traditions. He and other creolists have of course pointed out the caricatures evident in some literary sources, even as they start with the telling assumption that all represented speech of colonial-era Africans belongs to the category of Bozal (Castellanos 1990; Granda 1988; Lipski 2005). That is, they make a secondary distinction between sources deemed authentic or spurious because contaminated by stereotypes but retain Bozal as a totalizing category. Overall, by virtue of finding historical linguistic value in Bozal exemplars, creolists have initiated a whole new, positive metacultural reappraisal of previous Bozal discourses. But in doing so, they also do the metacultural work of arranging neat, linear discourse chains that point back to *actual* slave speech as the original "baptismal event" of Bozal.

We should be wary of assuming that the enregisterment of Bozal as it has come down to us tells us much at all about how African-born slaves once spoke Spanish and whether their speech could even be collectively characterized as a unitary register (except retroactively). Instead, this analysis tells us volumes about how they were viewed and how these simultaneously overdetermined and compressed representations of Blackness and particularly of

Africanness have served a variety of ideological ends over the decades and centuries, and how claims to represent Black speech authentically (usually staked on having heard actual slave or ex-slave speech) at some nodes of the web serve to authorize those ideological ends. There are reasons for caution: Balga Rodríguez's (2000–2003) linguistic study of costumbrist and bufo Bozal concludes that there is much variability, very little evidence of creolizing features, and a great deal of evidence that authors were deliberately creating comedic and derogatory effects.

The twentieth-century examples of Bozal include textual *and* oral commentaries and representations. We can note the consistency in how the register is characterized (even as elite scholarly metadiscourses have shifted their stance from early denigration of Black speech to today's self-consciously neutral linguistic account of the degree of phonological and morphosyntactic deviation from unmarked colloquial Cuban speech). But what comes out of this web of distinct nodes of metalinguistic activity is a clear sense of a unitary register under the label Bozal. I have focused here on the broadest interdiscursive connections across these entextualized types of discourse because it is at this macrolevel, I argue, that Bozal is enregistered, enabling it to transcend the ebb and flow of popularity (and thus replication) of discourses instantiating it. For example, the relative decline of blackface vernacular entertainment has not prevented exaggerated visual and aural cues of blackface from reappearing in other kinds of performances, such as in folklore and religious ritual examples discussed in previous chapters.

For that matter, North Americans certainly have had exposure to Cuban Bozal, although most have not had the Spanish linguistic sensibilities to differentiate an African slave voice and persona out of an undifferentiated Cuban or overall Latino voice, which in the United States is already so often characterized as a foreign and uneducated-sounding code. Thus, breakthrough Cuban performers Desi Arnaz's and Miguelito Valdes's popular renderings of a song like "Babalu" in the late 1940s and 1950s, where the singer assumes the persona of a superstitious and backward Black man praying to the deity Babalú Ayé, contribute to a very different racializing project of Latinos in the United States than what I have described for Bozal in Cuba. That said, the ongoing enregisterment of Bozal in Cuba itself connects into a spatially broader and temporally deeper web giving the racializing construct of Blackness its durability across the Atlantic world, a world that Blackness in all of its valences is partly constitutive of.

Babalú / Babalú	Babalú / Babalú
Babalú Ayé	Babalú Ayé

Babalú Ayé / Babalú	Babalú Ayé / Babalú
Tá empezando lo velorio	The night vigil is beginning
que le hacemos a Babalú	that we do for Babalú
Dame diez y siete velas	Give me seventeen candles
pa' ponerle en cruz	to put them in the shape of a cross
Dame un cabo de tabaco Mayenye	Give me a cigar, Mayenye
y un jarrito de aguardiente	and a small jug of cane liquor
Dame un poco de dinero Mayenye	Give me a bit of money Mayenye
pa' que me dé la suerte—yo	so that I'll have luck—I
quiere pedí	wants [*sic*] to request
que mi negra me quiera	that my black woman will love me
que tenga dinero	that I will have money
y que no se muera	and that she won't die
Ay, yo le quiero pedí Babalú	Oh, I want to request of Babalú
na negra muy	a black woman very
Santa como tú que no tenga	Saintly like you that she has no
otro negro	other black man
pa' que no se fuera	so that she won't leave

In the lyrics of "Babalu," written by Margarita Lecuona in 1941, and reproduced above, there are only three Bozalisms, and they are single tokens in each instance. In line 4, *lo* substitutes for the standard masculine definite article *el* in *el velorio* (literally, "wake," but here used in a second, more specialized sense to mean an all-night ceremony held on the eve of a saint's day) and in lines 11–12 the verb conjugation does not agree with the subject, producing the nonstandard *yo quiere* for the standard *yo quiero*, "I want." In line 17, *na* substitutes for the standard feminine indefinite definite articles *una* or perhaps *la* in *na negra*. The latter Bozalism, *na*, sounds African in Cuban ears (more specifically, what Cubans would identify as Congo-Bantú) and so is what Schwegler (1998) calls an "Africanized word," a neologism that indexes African origins. Alongside fluently used complex grammatical constructions of unmarked Spanish, such as subjunctive conjugations and use of object pronouns with verbs (e.g., line 7: *pa' ponerle en cruz*), these tokens of Bozal are no more than flavorings indexing a Bozalized voice already enregistered and known to Cuban listeners, whether in 1941 or 2012.

Other linguistic markers of Blackness in the lyrics include the invocation of the oricha Babalú Ayé, more commonly referred to by the corresponding saint, San Lázaro, and so indexing the specifically Afro-Cuban religious orientation of the song's origo. There is an implied self-reference to this origo's race in lines 18–19, in hoping "na negra muy Santa" won't have another "negro." The lyrics describe what in folklore performances would appear as stage props of the scene: candles, cigars, cane liquor, and a small monetary offering are all necessary components of altars to spirits and saints across Cuban folk religious practices. And there is the colloquial character of the Spanish—not Bozal, but familiar, informal, everyday speech in which a humble character makes modest requests of the saint. Bozalisms and other linguistic markers of Blackness, like the oricha's name, have what Schwegler (2006) describes as a "spreading effect" on the surrounding speech, making entire clauses sound Bozal to a Cuban ear and helping create the overall voice projected by the lyric. This origo is thus marked as Black, but in the song's being racially marked and yet performed by racially diverse singers who did not necessarily identify as Black, it also stands for the Cuban everyman: anyone who has ever offered a small, fervent prayer to the spirits and saints that saturate the Cuban national imagination.

The "Black" voice of "Babalu" thus both marks race and permits its transcendence into Cubanness, much as the nineteenth-century teatro bufo characters like José, the *negro congo* character in *Los negros catedráticos*, were sometimes sympathetic in their humble aspirations and thus came to stand for a distinctly Cuban national character, at least for some audiences in some moments. José the Congo poses this identification as a question, asking incredulously in one scene, "¿yo so bruto?" and in the previous scene (Fernandez 1868, 11):

> ¿Tó no só negro?. . . . . . nó?. . . . . . Criollo, lucumí, carabalí, gangá, arará, congo, toitico, toitico so negro! negro toito!
>
> Aren't we all black? No? Creole, lucumí, carabalaí, ganga, arará, congo, all, all are black! Black all!

But even at such moments of transcendent identification among character-performer-audience, the potential for racializing mockery and denigration remains in the marked linguistic forms used to create the character.

An Interdiscursive Web of Bozal

I have suggested that the enregisterment of Bozal is an enormously detailed story, especially in tracing links between nineteenth-century literary blackface caricatures and present-day uses of Bozal in popular religious ceremonies. In presenting my model of the interdiscursive web through which Bozal has emerged as a register, I am mindful of a warning Kit Woolard provided as discussant of an early conference paper based on this material (2009). She invoked Jorge Luis Borges's story of a "Cartography that attained such Perfection that . . . a Map of the Empire . . . was of the same Scale as the Empire and . . . coincided with it point for point. . . . Succeeding Generations came to judge a map of such Magnitude cumbersome and, not without Irreverence, abandoned it to the Rigours of sun and Rain" (Borges 1975). To this cautionary tale, I respond with Foucault's statement: "discourse in general . . . is so complex a reality that we not only can but should approach it at different levels and with different methods" ([1966] 1973, xiv, see also Mudimbe 1988). And given my argument about the interdiscursive web that has enregistered Bozal as "African slave speech" and more broadly as "Black speech," it is intriguing that this Borges citation itself involves embedded interdiscursivity, not just in Woolard's and my shared familiarity with the text (in my case, with an English translation of the original Spanish), but with the way that Borges and his coauthor were themselves playing with citationality in attributing this quote to a fictitious 1658 text, "Travels of Praiseworthy Men," while in fact elaborating on a similar map of 1:1 scale about which Lewis Carroll had written. Clearly, we cannot but approach discourse as history if we are to make sense of its constitutive force in, at times, creating history.

I would suggest that both uptake and metacultural reevaluation are central to enregisterment, such that a robust and durable African slave persona is created and tightly linked to a recognizably "disfigured" way of speaking that unites all of the disparate discourses in the web I have described as instances of a unitary type called Bozal. The full interdiscursive web traced out in this brief discourse history is an elaboration of what Judith Irvine (2005, 78) describes as triadic interdiscursivity, where "discourse A is linked to discourse B, but also each of these is linked to (say) person P." For the case of Bozal, the persona of the African-born slave, rather than any specific set of linguistic features, can be envisioned as the central axis around which enregisterment of Bozal has occurred, as it is always implicated in Bozal voicings. Irvine (2005) poses a general question about how the various kinds of interdiscursive relationships are "picked out" to be linked within a chronotope that allows for their comparison as somehow the "same." This is a fundamental question, and one touching on the issues I raised at the start of this chapter about how to categorize the various kinds of interdiscursive relationships I have described. What, precisely, is being taken up and carried forward with each link? How do newer discourses presuppose the "voices," personae, and interactional configurations of older discourses or challenge them with new entailments—entailments that may metaculturally reinterpret the older discourses?

And what of this hidden (or at least hitherto unacknowledged) history of blackface scholarly and theater traditions influencing religious and folklore genres of performance? Certainly, my argument about these influences flies in the face of Cuban scholarly and religious understandings about Bozal as the primordial, unmediated voice of Africans in Cuba that generations have "heard" and therefore accurately reproduced. The implications of understanding that the enregisterment of Bozal included not only religious, folkloric, and scholarly settings and imperatives but also the settings and imperatives of blackface theater challenge the scholarly work of linguists reconstructing how African slaves spoke Spanish and the authenticity of voices of African muertos and *santos* in ceremonies and folklore spectacles. At the very least, my argument requires acknowledgment of a more complicated story of Bozal in Cuba.

Evidence of the linkages and differentiations reticulated across this interdiscursive web consists of a heavily overdetermined and consistently portrayed African slave persona but also contains the similarities and differences in the linguistic features of each representation of "Bozal," for example, as summarized in lists of Bozal features by Balga Rodriguez (2000–2003) and Schwegler (2006), as described above. Taken together, these analyses not only contribute to the enregisterment of Bozal but also help to tease out subtleties in how Bozal's features and framings vary across the different kinds of Bozal metadiscourses, as well as commonalities, such as marked phonological changes, that allow for the metapragmatic regimentation of Bozal across genres. For example, while lack of concord in subject-verb and subject-adjective pairs is present in all metadiscourses of Bozal I have examined, uses of the nonstandard verbal aspect marker *ta* with an infinitive do not appear in nineteenth-century Bozal texts, although it seems common in Lydia Cabrera's texts and in possession trance speech. And the heavy use of discourse markers (what Schwegler calls "fillers") such as *mimo* and *cómo son* is apparent in many (but not all) instances of spoken Bozal in ceremonies, but, as one might expect, it is not present in any of the literary versions of Bozal.

To consider a particularly interesting example briefly, hypercorrection is not present in literary or theatrical Bozal samples, although I have recorded instances of hypercorrection as a Bozalism, for example, in the possession trance speech of one santero possessed by his oricha Ochún, who used nominalized forms of verbs to create nonstandard conjugations as shown in table 7.1.

These hypercorrections were pointed out to me by two different Cuban transcribers as Bozalisms, even though hypercorrect forms are not characteristic markers of Bozal in any other written or oral samples I have found. Hypercorrections exaggerated to the limit of silliness, however, were the defining characteristic of the *negro catedrático* voice in comic theater characters

TABLE 7.1 Instances of Hypercorrection in the Possession Trance Speech of a Santero (recorded in Santiago de Cuba in 2000)

Infinitive (Standard)	*Nominalized (Standardized Form)*	*Hypercorrect Bozalism(s) Used by Ochún in Ceremony*
acompañar (to accompany)	*acompañamiento* (accompaniment)	"quien lo acompañamienta . . ." (who accompaniments him)
cumplir (to fulfill)	*cumplimiento* (fulfillment)	"vamos a cumplimentar . . ." (let's fulfill [things promised]) "Ud. ya cumplimentó con emi ne" (You [V.] already fulfilled [promise] with me)
aconsejar (to counsel)	*consejo* (advice)	"lo aconsejamiento" ([she] counsels you)

such as Aniceto and Crispín. I can only speculate about whether any particular interdiscursive web might connect these robust nineteenth-century theatrical tropes of ridiculously overreaching Blacks and the appearance of hypercorrect forms in Bozal speech of an oricha at the turn of the twenty-first century.

Conclusion

Clearly, Bozal is a robust metalinguistic category enregistered to index a distinctive voice. It has existed as a metalinguistic category in Cuba for well over two centuries, largely on the strength of its ability to ventriloquate the social persona of African-born slaves and its metacultural value as distinctively "wrong, bad, and ugly" Spanish—consisting of utterances not conforming to unmarked, everyday Cuban speech. And, here's the rub: it appears to be a linguistic *invention* of *White people*, one perhaps as constitutive of their Whiteness as of the Blackness of African-born "Bozals."

Americanists will recognize parallels with recent scholarship on U.S. blackface minstrelsy, for example, in Lott's (1993, 18) argument that such nineteenth-century entertainments of the working classes imitated what they imagined to be Black aesthetic forms to help construct their Whiteness and class status through a dialectic of intimacy, desire, and distancing, thereby constituting "a peculiarly American structure of racial feeling." Or consider examples traced by Lhamon (1998), who, even as he contests Lott's assertion that White performers would have known little of Black folkways, instead depicts northeastern U.S. states in the late eighteenth through mid-nineteenth centuries, in places like New York City and along the Erie Canal, as sites of considerable cultural intimacy, miscegenation, and "cross-racial affiliation" (1998, 17–19, 151). And yet Lhamon details the paths of cultural transmission where enslaved Black performer Bobolink Bob Rowley's 1820s imitations of bird whistles were borrowed into Thomas Rice's Jim Crow performances, and that "strange whistle," by the 1840s understood to imitate train whistles not birds, became a staple trope of blackface (elided with Black?) authenticity, until again appearing in Al Jolson's twentieth-century performances (Lhamon 1998, 90–102). That a Black slave's performance anchors this particular interdiscursive history does not change the enregisterment of the whistle (together with any number of additional gestures, songs, steps, and voicings) through multiple reticulations imitating and adapting not just authentic "Black folk" but any number of influential performers of all racial backgrounds. A "verificationist" agenda disregarding the complexities of Black performance in light of blackface minstrelsy in order to link Bobolink Bob directly to Al Jolson (for example) seems rather to miss the point (see Scott 1991). As in the case of Cuban Bozal as form of speech and figure of the Cuban national imagination, blackface theatrical representations generated their own trajectories of invention and imitation.

The question guiding my analysis of the interdiscursive web of Bozal has been to ask: What are current representations of Bozal speech, especially those in folk religious ceremonies, interdiscursive with? My answer has contradicted the usual characterization of Bozal as directly type sourcing once-upon-a-time slave speech via a linear speech chain that presumably would trace actual (and ritual) genealogies. I have instead proposed that we understand contemporary performances of Bozal as deriving from a tradition of "discursive blackface" as much as (or rather than) from a tradition of Black speech. In this case, contemporary religious performances of Bozal (and some folklore performances) would constitute a reappropriation from discursive blackface and elite folklore studies, rather than continuity with an African and slave past, on the part of Cubans identifying (however partially) with Blackness and/or with cultural practices marked as Afro-Cuban.

A parting thought, to return to the other issue with which I began this chapter: Does it matter whether these interdiscursive links are reflexively recognized in some way, or can interdiscursivity mean something purely as an analytical discovery by the observer? For a closer-to-home example, if filmmaker Spike Lee makes an interdiscursive link between American blackface minstrelsy and contemporary hip-hop artists, as he does in the final scenes of the film *Bamboozled* (2000; see also Lhamon 1998), is an actual, demonstrable and preexisting historical connection required, or is it enough that *Bamboozled* has made the connection? And, to pose the inverse question, if there are demonstrable, or at least likely historical connections, what if the contemporary artists nonetheless reject them? Cuban religious practitioners readily describe the speech of African muertos and deities as Bozal, but they explain similarities to blackface Bozal as a result of a common origin in actual slave speech, not in a more direct influence of theatrical stereotypes on spirit possession speech. Given that racializing discourses are so often propagated through a refusal to recognize them as such, the stakes of my question are high. As of yet, I am not sure what recognizing an interdiscursive history of blackface would mean for Cuban religious invocations of Bozal—maybe a lot, maybe nothing. What greater reflexivity about our participation in enregisterment processes means for linguistic attempts to "reconstruct" Afro-Hispanic speech through Bozal is, I hope, clear from my argument. So, to conclude not with a declarative but with a question: How do all of us entangled in a particular racializing web evaluate potential interdiscursive links in creating discourse histories—and to what ends?

These questions speak to the larger argument of this book, which has described the profoundly entangled, mutually constituting processes connecting racialization and historical imagination in Cuba, where folkloric performances of Blackness contribute to more broadly circulating discourses about race and nation. Many of these discourses have endured through—even been heightened by—moments of historical disjuncture stretching from Cuba's struggles for and achievement of independence from Spain, its (partial) enfranchisement of former slaves and their descendants and discovery of the Afro-Cuban roots of national identity, and its 1959 Revolution. These historical nodes are the very ones that constitute the chronotopic imaginaries (re)created by and through folklore performances since the revolution and throughout the post-Soviet period of the last two decades.

To investigate the ongoing work of making race and history in Cuba, as I have done, is to speak to social scientific questions of broad importance about what race is, how it works as a central principle structuring inequality globally, and why it has such peculiar staying powers, despite occasional, not entirely convincing protestations of entering a "postracial" era, based in part on a post–World War II scientific consensus rejecting a biological basis for race and in part on the increasing visibility and power of historically disenfranchised people (and peoples) of color in public life and globally circulating media of all sorts. Of course, given the long history of Blackness as performance, success in entering public life and visible contributions to public debates even at the highest levels, while crucial steps in the "arc of history," are no panacea for the destructive racial logics that continue to structure inequality in racialized societies such as Cuba and my home, the United States.

My approach to this ethnography of performance that strives also to be an anthropology of history has relied on semiotic analysis, sometimes of processes most evident at a detailed, even microscopic level of interactional events and textual signs, although I have sought to link these to discourse processes at wider scales of circulation and impact. It is at these wider scales across events that enregisterment processes operate to populate our discursive lives and "structures of feeling" with durable figures, voices, cultural forms, and social types. Given the central role of temporality, historicity, and locality in the discourses of identification and affiliation, belonging and exclusion that are mobilized through folklore performances, I have pushed hard to develop the conceptual apparatus of Bakhtin's notion of chronotope, showing how emplacement, embodiment, participation framing, interdiscursive horizons, and temporal marking work together to create subjectivities national, racial, gendered, classed, and historical. And not only are these subjectivities interconnected: they complicate analytical distinctions between habit, memory, bodily hexis, and reflexivity. Race functions simultaneously as object of discourse, theme of performance, and performative of/in lived experience: it is a totalizing indexical order. And yet, caught in its web as we are, we may think we know what it is *not*, but we have more difficulty articulating what it *is* and how it works. Making its semiosis visible, tangible, traceable has been a major goal of this book.

My story is necessarily incomplete; my field of focus has necessarily been narrow. Even within my chosen field site of Santiago de Cuba between 1998 and 2012, I have chosen some foci for analysis, while passing over others. Then, too, were I beginning research for this book now—in your, the reader's t_0—no doubt the story would change to fit ongoing events and shifts. Semiosis is always open-ended, which gives me hope for the future of our racial and historical imaginaries. And yet, it is with mixed feelings that I conclude that the Black spirits haunting Cuba's historical imagination—the victims of slavery but also the stubbornly independent maroons and *mambises*—will continue to speak to us in our present moment for some time to come. Will our ears and hearts be open to them? Whose voices will we hear? What will we say in reply?

Notes

Chapter One

1. The choreographer of *Trilogía africana* is Licenciado Juan Teodoro Florentino. The soloists mentioned in the text are Maura Isaac Álvarez, Sergio Hechavarría Gallardo, and Roberto (Chirrí) Nordé LaVallé. Rafael Manolo Cisnero was the lead singer. Cutumba's director is Idalberto Bandera Guerrero.

2. A good overview of policies and processes of whitening that diminished the salience of past slavery and African ancestry in some Latin American societies is in Andrews (2004). Helg (1990) and Knight (1996) provide comparative studies of how concepts of race, class, and citizenship developed in Latin America. Price (1983) describes the relevance of historical memory of slave times among Saramaka of Suriname, as do Jones (1997) and Smitherman (2000) in elucidating community and racial identity among African Americans. Ongoing commemorations of Juneteenth, e.g., in my city of Kalamazoo, Michigan, attest to the continuing relevance of slavery in these identifications, as do racial healing initiatives designed to bring Black and White Americans together to address the collective trauma of slavery (see DeWolf and Morgan 2012). See Walter Rodney's (1982) influential argument for the slave trade's ongoing, if largely unrecognized, relevance to Africa and the Atlantic world.

3. Consider, e.g., the much-told tales of Fidel Castro's affinity for Afro-Cuban folk religious practices, from the dove that famously alighted on his shoulder during a speech, symbolizing for some that he was a child of the oricha Obatalá, to whispers of his secret prenda, or ritual power object in Palo (see Ayorinde 2004; Routon 2010).

4. Consider for example that *raza* (race) referred to people's religious genealogy in the anxious times after Spain's Christian reconquest from the Moors and only later developed new meanings as a result of exploration, colonialism, and transatlantic slavery.

5. Hegel's influence is also evident in phenomenological understandings of the self, e.g., Merleau-Ponty ([1962] 1989).

6. A few exemplars include Bauman (1986); Bauman and Briggs (1990); Friedrich (1986, 1991); Hill (2008); Mannheim (1986); and Urban (1991, 1996). The effects of linguistic reflexivity and, particularly, of conscious metalinguistic reflection are also important to consider; on this vast topic, see especially Cameron (1995); Irvine and Gal (2000); Lucy (1993); Silverstein (1979, 1993); and Urban (2001).

7. I have examined this dynamic in related work on esoteric ritual speech in Cuban Santería; see Wirtz (2007a).

8. For a brilliant historical exposé of the creation of this privileged, "scientific" subject position in light of language ideologies of modernity, see Bauman and Briggs (2003).

9. Bauman offered this term as discussant of the "Sound Politics" session during the thirteenth Annual Michicagoan Graduate Student Conference in Linguistic Anthropology, Ann Arbor, May 7, 2011.

10. See Frye's (1963) discussion of the Aristotelian contrast between poetry and praxis, where the former fixes on the universal rather than the actual.

11. On differing boundaries and expectations of public and private in other centralized Socialist states, see Gal (2005). For Cuba-specific discussions of these negotiations, see Henken (2002, 2007) and Weinreb (2009).

12. Another slavery-themed restaurant located on a former sugar plantation in central Cuba is shown in the film *Traces of the Trade* directed by Katrina Browne and Alla Kovgan ([San Francisco]: California Newsreel, 2008), DVD.

13. UNEAC, or Unión Nacional de Escritores y Artistas Cubanos, is the national writers' and artists' labor syndicate, administered by the Ministry of Culture. Trade unions in Cuba, like virtually all organizations, are part of the state, rather than independent of it.

14. The menu may have promised too many items not available on a regular enough basis, or perhaps it was too hard for customers to understand: when I revisited the restaurant in July 2011, there was a new menu renaming many of the dishes more simply, albeit keeping to the slavery-nostalgia theme with names such as Mama Inez for the broiled chicken plate.

Chapter Two

1. Ramsey (1997, 2011) describes a similar case of folklorization of Vodou in Haiti; Guss (2000) and Whitten (2003) discuss examples from Latin America; Lemon's (2000) case is of Roma in Russia.

2. The category of Whiteness as construed in U.S. critical race studies does not quite fit Cuban notions of Whiteness, which play across lines of racial unmarking—as creole products of Cuba's history of miscegenation—and Whiteness as a categorization of Cuban elites and foreigners. Compare Frankenburg (1997) and Hartigan (1999) on Whiteness in the United States to Knight (1996) and contributors to Knight and Martínez-Vergne (2005) on racial categories in Cuba.

3. Todd Ochoa (2010) discusses the significance of bare feet on the ground in Palo ritual practice.

4. See James Figarola (2006b) and Ochoa (2010) for discussions of Congo cosmograms. I have also seen these drawn on a coffin during Palo funerary ceremonies.

5. The original choreographer of this particular work was the ensemble's former director, Antonio Pérez, with modifications by the current director, Milagros Ramírez.

6. Although Urciuoli's term expressly draws on Roman Jakobson's notion of "shifters" in a strain of linguistics informed by Peirce's semiotic theory (see, e.g., Jakobson 1970), it is undoubtedly also informed by Claude Lévi-Strauss's distinct structuralist anthropological line of thought regarding the "floating signifer," which he applied to seemingly magical concepts, like *mana*, where the exuberance of the signifier creates a highly productive nonequivalence or "in-adequation" between the signifier and any possible referent, allowing the potentially endless proliferation

and shifting of signification (Lévi-Strauss 1987). Cultural studies theorists such as Stuart Hall have described race as a floating signifier to highlight its performativity and fluidity of meaning (see, e.g. the film *Stuart Hall: Race, the Floating Signifier*, directed by Sut Jhally [Northampton, MA: Media Education Foundation, 1997], DVD). The notion of race as a "strategically deployable shifter" differs first in taking the much wider purview of indexicality than just the referential relation of the Saussurean sign and second in emphasizing agency and "strategy" rather than universal cognitive structures. I thank Matt Tomlinson for proposing the comparison.

7. The notion of links between a sign and its referent originating in some "baptismal event" comes from Saul Kripke's (1972) work, in which he began with the paradigmatic case of proper names that become permanently attached to particular individuals (see discussion in Lee 1997).

8. One might ask what other sites index specifically Black positionality. Aside from the folkloric, the other social location indexing Blackness would be youth (particularly male) aesthetic culture, and especially its importation of fashions and musical genres including rap, hip-hop, reggae, and Rastafari fashion and reggaeton (see Hansing 2006 and West-Durán 2004). Hernandez-Reguant (2006) argues that homegrown *timba* music also indexes a resistant young Black male stance. Alongside these musically defined stances are other genres, like *rock*, and especially *feeling* (a kind of pop music in Cuba) and a mania for Beatles songs, that index White (or racially unmarked) Cuban youth positionality (see Borges-Triana 2009).

9. Melville Herskovits (1945), for an influential example, claimed to have found much greater evidence of African "survivals" in aesthetic forms, such as religion/magic, music, and dance than in domains such as technology or agriculture (see Apter 1991).

10. Her gender, too, seems significant, especially since jealousy is seen as a particularly feminine vice in Cuba, as in the United States, and I have often heard presumptions made in Cuba that Black women would have more reasons for envy than anyone else—certainly, the jealous Black woman willing to resort to Black magic has appeared as a character in more than one story I've been told over the years.

Chapter Three

1. Think, too, of the rich information about heredity, diet, nutritional history, habitual usages, disease, injury, and even geographical location that biological anthropologists routinely read out of even partial remains. Our bodies become material records of our histories, thereby giving nonbiological social constructions like race real biological consequences, e.g., in measurably differential patterns of health and mortality.

2. The Spanish verb *arrollar* suggests an overwhelming force rolling, crushing, or sweeping away everything before it, just as flood waters race through an *arroyo*.

3. Although it was my interlocutors' view that "of course" the Black girl was "naturally" dancing better than the White girl, I hasten to add that their certainty in this judgment was part of how race was being presupposed as relevant to the situation. Even if we accept their evaluations as accurate, other interpretations are possible, such as that one child was more interested, more focused, had more prior exposure to Cuban dance, or was just plain older than the other.

4. Original Spanish caption: "Entre ellos priman los jóvenes, los negros y los mulatos, quienes llevan el ritmo en la sangre pero también hay blancos y blancas que se mueven con la misma gracia."

5. See Rafael (2009) for a comparative case in the Philippines during the same historical moment of the Spanish-American War, in which racialized notions of "conspiracy" and "conjuration" coalesced in suppressing Philippine anticolonial resistance.

6. I also heard much the same information about the Rey Congo from other Santiago-based folklore scholars, although I have not located written sources about this office or its occupant(s). Santiago's Emilio Bacardí Moreau Museum has artifacts attributed to the Congo King Juan Gongorá on display. It is possible that this figure primarily had authority with regard to carnival or saints' day processions, rather than broader everyday political authority.

7. In dozens of volumes that remain influential, Ortiz systematically explored Afro-Cuban religion, music genres and instruments, dance, speech, social types, and influences on Cuban vernacular culture.

8. The parallels to racial divides between carnival associations in New Orleans's Mardi Gras are strong. In Santiago, one of the most elite comparsas was La Kimona, distinguished by the elaborate kimonos and general Asian theme of its performances.

9. The exhibit flyer, a trifold 8½ x 11 sheet with the exhibit title (*The Orichas Descend to Earth*) and photographer's name (Onel Torres Roche), is dated Havana, June 21, 2011; original Spanish: "Ya no son los antiguos esclavos, ahora son libres, en una sociedad justa y solidaria, que también reclama para ellos una vida donde han desaparecido para siempre, los restos que puedan quedar de discriminación o desigualdad."

10. Speech given July 8, 2011, at the Playa Juan Gonzalez ceremony for Yemayá; unpublished text shared with permission. Quoted section: "La nación cubana es una suerte de simbiosis donde los factores culturales y cultuales que la integran, han sacado provecho común a lo largo de toda nuestra historia. Vale recordar, que para el dibujo de nuestra cubanía, antecedieron gestos de clandestinaje cultural, de rebeldía esclava, y de una criollidad inconforme, ante las imposiciones del imperio; aspectos que en su conjunto propiciaron, el inicio de la Revolución Cubana en 1868, acto de insurrección que tiene una mejor definición de sus ansias de soberanía en 1959. A pesar de ello, aún seguimos en combate por las mismas aspiraciones de independencia frente a las posiciones hegemónicas que nos interpelan."

11. The quoted parts of the speech read, in the original Spanish: "Todo indica que la brujería ha estado en todos los procesos por la soberanía de la nación, de ahí el que esta forme parte indisoluble de nuestra identidad cultural."

12. Puerto Rican literary scholar Rafael Ocasio (2012) similarly positions himself as a *negro fino* using just these oppositions between phenotype, *cosas de negros*, and refinement. He suggests that the figure of the *negro fino* has historical precedent in the mocking nineteenth-century stage persona of the *negro catedrático*, or "Black professor," a figure I examine in chap. 7.

13. Original Spanish: "Hoy a mi me place sinceramente que el sacerdote de Ifá sea blanco, pero es que él quizás no sepa que su ancestro de allá de la colonia pudo haber sido negro."

14. "Para que lo gocen" appears on the CD *Congas Santiagueras* (date and publisher unknown).

15. The other saints' days most frequently mentioned as defining carnival's timing are San Juan and Santa Cristina (July 24), Santa Ana (July 26), and San Pedro (July 29).

16. Similar tensions between public and private are evident in other domains of everyday life, although it would not do to draw too tight a parallel to the late Soviet era in Russia, as Cuba's revolution is quite distinct, and prophets of its imminent demise have been proved false for five decades and counting. *Cuidao con eso*, as Cubans would say.

17. Pedroso (2005, 138–39), originally published in 1947; Spanish original: "Tan sugestiva fuerza popular, tan debordante júbilo, es su riqueza vernácula, su pura y viva tradicionalidad, enraizada jugosamente en la sangre y el alma del pueblo."

18. Pedroso (2005, 139): "Se podría decir que es bárbaro y todo lo que se quiera, pero hay que estar muerto para no sentir cómo esa cosa nos grita en la sangre. Además eso no es negro ni blanco. ¡Eso es un pueblo que vive lo que siente!"

19. Such political and social critiques were once part of carnival, as Pérez's (1988, 1:133) documentation of *relaciones*, or spontaneous street theater, suggests. One folklore scholar described to me the kinds of parodies of political figures that occurred in prerevolutionary carnival, and as discussed in chap. 6, the director of a Carabalí comparsa described his grandfather's use of song lyrics to critique the political situation of the 1920s, which got his group banned from future carnivals.

20. One might draw a parallel to the ways in which citizens of other authoritarian regimes elsewhere demonstrate noninvolvement in the required civics of participation—e.g., Yurchak's (2005) work on the late Soviet era in Russia and Skidmore's (2003) account of mass rallies in Myanmar.

21. See the video posted from an official Cuban e-mail address: "Congas santiagueras cierran desfile por el Primero de Mayo," uploaded on April 23, 2011, http://www.youtube.com/watch?v=KKyJffr_Glg.

22. Interview, March 1, 2010, original Spanish: "Tú la traes en la sangre. Esa cosa tú la traes en la sangre. Porque te gusta. Si no te gusta, Kristina, [KW: Anja] porque, como:: . cuántas personas . mira, yo llevo 15 años que van para 16 años siendo directora del infantil. Pero que yo la traí en la sangre, que yo le tengo de mi papá que desde niña que voy a pensar que yo voy a ser directora y yo le dije pero por supuesto con la conga infantil, y ya entonces se fue rescatando la cultura, las congas infantiles."

A note about transcription is in order. I have used certain symbols to represent vagaries of speech as follows. Two open double brackets lined up vertically indicate overlapping speech:

Speaker A: [[text

Speaker B: [[text

A colon next to a vowel indicates elongation:

te:xt (pronounced *teeext*, where the *e* is short in each case).

A hyphen at the end of a word indicates interrupted speech. When another speaker immediately talks without a pause between turns, a hyphen will begin their first word, to indicate that there was no break in speech:

Speaker A: text--

Speaker B: --text

And free periods—that is, periods floating in the middle of a sentence—indicate pauses, such as when someone hesitates midsentence. Each free period indicates a beat pause, such as might occur between phrases, but in mid-phrase, as when a speaker briefly hesitates:

text . text (a beat pause)

text . . text (a two-beat pause)

Pauses at the end of phrases or intonational curves are represented with regular punctuation. Longer pauses are timed.

23. Continued: "La gente la mayoría especializan en la conga todavía. Pero la juventud que va saliendo hay que coger los que le guste y ponerlos en una comparsa infantil para la adulta, para que no se pierda la tradición."

24. The government provides a selection of fabrics that carnival ensembles get to chose from, based on a lottery system. If a director pulled a low number, she would get a better selection, whereas those stuck with high numbers in a given year might find, e.g., that only dark colors are left. Directors then take their material and ideas to a government sewing shop, where a professional seamstress will produce the actual costumes. Directors do a lot of informal trading and often use their own resources to scrounge additional supplies for more beautiful costumes. All performers also receive a pair of athletic shoes from the government—while these are seldom high-quality shoes, a free pair is a major perk for performers.

Chapter Four

1. Other registers with more limited distribution include *Iyesa*, associated with songs and rhythms related to Ocha in Matanzas, *Makawa*, described by Testa (2004) in a cabildo of the town of Sagua la Grande, *Carabalí* in Carabalí cabildo songs in Santiago (see chap. 5), and of course the Abakuá ritual register sometimes also called *Carabalí* (or *Efik*) used in Abakuá lodges of Havana and Matanzas. Valdés Bernal (1986, 1996–97) presents an overview of their lexical contributions to Cuban Spanish, a topic of longstanding interest to Cuban scholars.

2. Song of Palo Monte, A. Abelardo Larduet Luaces, personal communication, May 22, 2007.

3. See also Volosinov (1973) for a cogent early argument for reconceptualizing the psyche itself as already and always an ideologically saturated outcome of semiosis.

4. See Law (1997). Some traces of these prior "ethnic" distinctions remain in Cuban Santería, when drummers and singers differentiate between *Arataco*, *Iyesa*, and *Arara* songs and rhythms from what were once separate groups (see CIPS 1998, 13–14; Hagedorn 2001, 124–25). See Palmié's (1993) discussion of ethnogenetic processes under New World creolization.

5. Tragically, Geraldito Pérez passed away suddenly in 2009 after a stroke. I am grateful for all the assistance and advice he shared with me over the years and dedicate this chapter to him, *ibayé ibayén tonú*.

6. Drums are dedicated to the oricha of drumming, called Aña in Cuba (see Vincent 2006 and Vaughan and Aldama 2012). At the time of my fieldwork in 1999–2000, there were just four consecrated sets of batá drums in Santiago de Cuba (a number that has probably tripled since then), and each one's owner had trained and initiated a cadre of drummers who had undergone a ceremony to become *omo aña*, "child of the drum," and to allow them to play the consecrated drums. The drums and their dedicated players would be hired by anyone wishing to hold a *wemilere*.

7. See chap. 3, n. 22 for an explanation of transcription conventions.

8. Alas, I know of no sociolinguistic studies of Cuban communicative norms and make this claim based on my own cross-cultural experiences learning appropriate norms of demeanor and interaction, usually discovering these in my breach of them.

Chapter Five

1. See photographs in Perez et al. (1982).

2. Born to Haitian immigrants in Cuba as Pierre Jacobin (father's patronym: de la Nieves Negrel de Megret), he changed his name several times during his life, writing and pronouncing "Pierre" as "Pié." He was the first santero dedicated to the oricha Elegguá who was initiated

in Santiago, in 1944 (A. Abelardo Larduet Luaces and Gladys Gonzalez, personal communications in 2007 and 2010). For more on Reynerio Pérez, whose ritual practice, according to local oral tradition, fiercely excluded effeminate and gay men, see Larduet Luaces (2001) and Schmidt (2011).

3. In Santiago, to describe oneself or someone else as French is understood as a euphemism for Haitian origins or a way of highlighting European over African heritage and tastes, by way of French colonial ancestors—see chap. 3 discussion of the category of the *negro fino*. Indicating French heritage usually implied an association not with the early twentieth-century labor migration of very poor Haitians to Cuba, until recently a highly stigmatized and marginalized population, but the early nineteenth-century influx of "cultured" French refugees from the aftermath of the Haitian Revolution of 1791.

4. Greg Urban (1986) argues that the poetics of formal dialogicality through repetition, present in many ritual contexts, may serve as a semiotic model for social solidarity and agreement, as seems to be the case here.

5. Ivor Miller (2005) and Armin Schwegler (Schwegler and Rojas-Primus 2010), e.g., exemplify current efforts to identify African origins for Cuban ethnonyms and esoteric lexicons associated with them, while Stephan Palmié (2007a) and Ken Routon (2005) offer trenchant critiques of these efforts, based on work by historians such as Robin Law (1997), Paul Lovejoy (2003), and J. D. Y. Peel (1989), who have shown the degree of fluidity in cultural identifications and ethnogenetic processes at work as Africa was drawn into the emerging Atlantic world (see also Palmié 1993).

6. The idea that African *cabildos de nación* disguised their African deities and spirits as Catholic saints is a robust part of the origin story of religions like Santería. Of course, by the 1890s, the era of Catholic Church–sponsored religious cofraternities had passed, but it is possible that people still preferred to hide practices widely regarded as primitive superstition or witchcraft behind more socially acceptable veneration of Catholic saints.

7. The overall slave population, however, reached its peak in the 1860s, a time of unprecedented growth among all sectors of the Cuban population. See Klein (1999, 39–40, 46).

8. I thank Santiago city historian Olguita Portuondo Zúñiga for generously sharing her insights about the Cuban *conciencia criolla* in conversations with me during 2007.

9. The other defining issue of the era, and indeed, of the entire twentieth century, was U.S. intervention in Cuba starting in 1898, which shaped the context of Cuban racial politics in profound ways between 1898 and 1959, when the Cuban Revolution finally achieved autonomy from U.S. control. Excellent historical work on issues of race, equality, and nation during Cuba's First Republic, encompassing various perspectives, has been done by Bronfman (2004), de la Fuente (2001a), Ferrer (1999), Helg (1995), James Figarola (1974), and Serviat (1986).

10. For somewhat differently framed arguments mobilizing similar critiques, see Palmié (2007a, 2007c) and Wirtz (2007a).

11. After the Protest of Baraguá, when Cuban rebels decided to fight the Spanish for independence, General Antonio Maceo led the Cuban liberation army on a ninety-day, 1,965 km trek westward across the island from Mangos de Baraguá in Oriente on October 22, 1895 to Montua in Pinar del Río on January 22, 1896, encountering Spanish forces all along the way. This information comes from the Museo de Antonio Maceo in Santiago de Cuba.

12. Along with the *tragalegua*, which is the largest drum, another similar flat drum plays the role of *respondadora*, or respondent, and the conical *tumbadora* drums called the *quinto* and *requinto* (where the latter is a smaller version of the former) fill out the drum section's sound.

It is important to distinguish what Americans call conga drums with Cuban usage, where these tall, barrel-shaped drums with tuners are known as *tumbadoras*. And the same large, wide, shallow drums held with shoulder straps that are called *tragaleguas* in the Carabalí ensembles are known as *galletas* in congas. The percussion terminology can be confusing, because it varies even for what looks like the "same" instrument depending on the genre of music and the specific role it is playing among other drums.

13. See also the version in Pérez et al. (1982, 42): "Ceremí ceremí / Guaranchara ceremí," where *guaranchara* resembles *guaranchar*, colloquially meaning "to party or dance," and derives from a once-popular music genre. Such variations in the lyrics of songs in ritual registers are common, given the near-absence of fixed referential meanings.

14. San Lázaro's day, December 17, and the evening before it, are widely celebrated in Cuba, as this saint is revered. San Lázaro, depicted as a leper and beggar, is associated with the oricha Babalú Ayé, whose domain includes infectious diseases.

15. Recall from earlier in the chapter that Olugo had been critiqued by a judge in a previous carnival for inserting bembé rhythms into the Carabalí, and thereby mixing what should be kept separate.

Chapter Six

1. The full text of the speech is a fascinating blend of justifications of censorship and descriptions of grand plans to improve Cuban arts, culture, and education, all amid discussion of the limits of artistic and intellectual freedom.

2. Regional Office for Culture in Latin America and the Caribbean, "Directory of Institutions," www.lacult.org/institucion/showitem.php?lg=1&id=2, accessed September 20, 2011; my translation.

3. Ernesto is a beloved friend with whom I have talked often about his life, which is also chronicled in Florentino (2010). Born into poverty in 1949, his life has followed the revolution's arc, and his entry into folkloric dance choreography was initially as an aficionado, although by the mid-1970s he had transitioned into working in the arts (following several older siblings who had founded the Conjunto Folklórico de Oriente), eventually joining Cutumba in the 1980s and receiving his Licenciatura degree from the Instituto Superior de Arte in 1995. By that point, he had become a widely recognized and prominent figure in Santiago's folklore scene.

4. Sean Brotherton (2008) argues that Cuba's much-touted universal healthcare system in fact has come to rely on privatization in the informal economy as a mainstay of its "life support," despite rhetoric that continues to promise socialism as the solution to the economic crisis. I think the same case can be made for the realm of culture and the arts, education, and probably most spheres of life officially managed by the centralized state.

5. See Ramiro Guerra's (1989) influential discussion of the parameters for presenting folklore on the stage, where he emphasizes that generic boundaries must be maintained in order to preserve tradition. Cuban folklorists sometimes cited this book when discussing folklore performance with me.

6. I have gleaned from many conversations that those proposed to become directors of professional groups and traditional culture carriers must be approved by the Communist Party as well. In most realms of work and education, ideological control remains the prerogative of the party, and part of the role of any workplace supervisor is to maintain discipline, including by promoting the party's messages.

7. I thank Ernesto Armiñán Linares for providing this history (in April 2002).

8. See Hagedorn (2001) for a parallel account of the development of the Conjunto Folklórico Nacional.

9. See John (2002) and Mousouris (2002) for perspectives from modern dance.

10. See McAlister (2002) for a broader perspective on Rará in Haiti and its diaspora.

11. Todd Ochoa (2010) does describe a palero keeping a snake amid his prendas, but no one I asked in Santiago had heard of this and when pushed would at most suggest that there once had been a cult of snakes in colonial times. Florentino himself explained the snakes as a reference to Damballah, a lwa of Vodou.

12. His movements briefly recall possession trances of devotees of the Haitian lwa Damballah and their uptake into Haitian folklore performances, including in pieces choreographed by Katherine Dunham.

13. I discuss some of these interpretations of Afro-Cuban culture as social danger in Wirtz (2004) and (2009).

14. Goffman delineated different fractional speaking roles, such as "animator," "author," and "principal," where the latter role refers to who has the major stake in the utterance.

15. It is true that Santería festive ceremonies are never solemn, quiet affairs, and chatting and drinking rum are as much a part of them as dancing, singing, and clapping. But these contrasts between formal ritually determined behaviors at the center of the ritual and a looser, party-like atmosphere on the fringes were heightened in the religious performances during the festival. These were truly intended as spectacles, to be observed as much as or more than participated in.

16. I am not familiar with this phrase, although it is clearly in the Congo-palero register. I gloss *llumbí* and what I take to be a variation, *lumbi*, to be related perhaps to *nfumbi*, "spirit," or to *Briyumba*, a branch of Palo magic, and so to tentatively mean "spirit." I have not encountered a possible gloss for *kichada*.

17. Compare, e.g., de la Fuente (2007), Hansing (2006, 188–95), and Sawyer (2006) on Cuba to Dick and Wirtz (2011), Myers (2005), and especially Hill (2008) on the United States.

Chapter Seven

1. Nathan's (1962) study of nineteenth-century English blackface entertainments gives numerous examples of vocables characterizing African voices in songs. David Samuels (2004), describing a very different historical moment of vocables in doo-wop, situates this popular music genre in a longer history of modernity in which nonsense words, marking a contrastive nonmodern stance within modernity, have systematically been attributed to marginalized groups, from children to slaves to colonized peoples.

2. Early sources giving these characterizations are discussed in the text; Ortiz López (1998, 129) reports a very similar list in how his elderly Cuban informants described the speech of slaves in the 1990s: "enreda'o, tragiversa'o, extraño, distinto, feo, mal habla'o, extranjero, bozal, cruzado, al revés" (mixed up, twisted, odd, distinct, ugly, badly spoken, foreign, bozal, crossed, and backward), and Testa (2004)'s informants also described Bozal speech as "mixed up."

3. I am not aware of documentation showing whether this advice was systematically implemented, nor indeed, what discussions of Bozal might have occurred among Catholic clergy beyond this text.

4. The colloquialism *reburujado*, meaning disordered or out of place, was not familiar to Santiagueros I asked, one of whom suggested that *reburujaoro* might be *revoliquero*, an archaic colloquialism meaning "life of the party."

5. The use of variants such as *suamo* and *misuamo* for *mi amo* (my master) are attested in other instances of Bozal, including a folk etymology I was given for Isuama in Santiago de Cuba (for much older instances, see Lipski 2005, 79).

6. According to Cuban folklorist María Isabel Berbes Ribeaux, the reduplicated vocable "torori torori," sometimes still used into children's stories, conveys the sense of nonsense, as in "who knows what you are writing."

7. This gloss of *non gurbia* as *agobiado* is tenuous at best; María Isabel Berbes Ribeaux also suggested that this phrase sounded very much like modern-day "Congo" speech in Palo ceremonies, although I have not encountered a likely meaning for *gurbia*.

8. The last phrase could also be a repetition for emphasis: "Aguanta que aguanta." I thank a reviewer for pointing out this and other alternatives in my gloss.

9. One might also consider connections to various Caribbean and African American traditions of "fancy talk," which often achieved comic effect and "signified" on dominant society using hypercorrect and grandiloquent forms (Abrahams 1983; Lipski 2005, 151–52; Ortiz 1986).

10. In U.S. blackface minstrelsy, the basic character types juxtaposed Jim Crow the "plantation slave" to Zip Coon the "dandy," who affected being "larned," and both of these to the (crossdressing male) "wench" (see Nathan 1962).

11. See Noreña's (1881) dialogue between two *negros curros*, or Bachiller y Morales's (1883) argument about the "disfiguration" of Spanish, based on analysis of published caricatures. Ortiz's classic study of *negros curros* (1986) drew almost entirely on costumbrist literature and comic theater—secondary representations at best.

12. It is worth pointing out, however, that the limited Afro-Cuban literary production encouraged by the Del Monte circle, e.g., Juan Francisco Manzano's *Life and Poems* ([1840] 1981), contained uncorrected writing errors (poor Spanish, not Bozalisms) because the editors felt that "sloppiness" conveyed greater authenticity (Lane 2005, 49–56).

13. As further evidence, Balga Rodríguez's (2000–2003) linguistic study of costumbrist and bufo Bozal concludes that there is much variability in linguistic features, very little evidence of creolizing features, and a great deal of evidence that authors were deliberately creating comic and derogatory effects.

14. There is some evidence that as a teenager Cabrera was already attending Afro-Cuban religious ceremonies, but clearly her closest informants, including family servants who gave her entry into these ceremonies, were Cuban-born Blacks, steeped in what was already, and perhaps always, a profoundly Cuban, rather than African, folk religious domain (Rodríguez-Mangual 2004, 8–10).

15. Even as some practitioners of Santería, a major Afro-Cuban folk religion, have consulted Cabrera's works as sources for religious practice, others have critiqued Cabrera's claims to accuracy and authenticity on the basis that an outsider could never penetrate closely held religious secrets and that *El monte* in particular demonstrates confusion in mixing distinct jargons and traditions. An important example was the introduction to a published Santería manual and glossary of religious terms, dated 1955 and signed by a Dr. Roque de la Nuez, who expressly disparages *El monte* (Angarica 1955, 3–4). I thank Stephan Palmié for this observation and the suggestion that the impassioned doctor who also identifies himself by his initiated name in

Santería, Efún Yomí, might have been inadvertently inhabiting an updated *negro catedrático* persona (see Ocasio 2012).

16. The term also applied to Cuban-born and ladino Blacks who belonged to religious cofraternities organized by *nación* and thus retained a genealogical or corporate identification with a particular African origin.

References Cited

Abbot, Abiel. 1829. *Letters Written in the Interior of Cuba.* Boston: Bowles and Dearborn.

Abrahams, Roger. 1983. *The Man-of-Words in the West Indies: Performance and the Emergence of Creole Culture.* Baltimore: Johns Hopkins University Press.

Abreu, Denys Terris. 2011. "Mestizaje de religión y cultura." Paper presented at the thirty-first Festival del Caribe, Taller de Religiones Populares, Santiago de Cuba, July 6.

Agha, Asif. 2003. "The Social Life of Cultural Value." *Language and Communication* 23: 231–73.

———. 2005. "Voice, Footing, Enregisterment." *Journal of Linguistic Anthropology* 15 (1): 38–59.

———. 2006. *Language and Social Relations.* Cambridge: Cambridge University Press.

Alonso, Gladys, and Ángel Luis Fernández, eds. 1977. *Antología de lingüística cubana.* Vol. 1. Havana: Editorial de Ciencias Sociales.

Alonso, Martín. 1958. *Enciclopedia del idioma.* Vol. 1. Madrid: Aguilar.

Anderson, James D. 1988. *The Education of Blacks in the South, 1860–1935.* Chapel Hill: University of North Carolina Press.

Andrews, George Reid. 2004. *Afro-Latin America, 1800–2000.* Oxford: Oxford University Press.

———. 2007. "Recordando Africa al inventar Uruguay: Sociedades de negros en el carnaval de Montevideo, 1865–1930." *Revista de Estudios Sociales* 26 (April): 127–28.

Angarica, Nicolas Valentin. 1955. *Manual de Orihate: Religion Lucumi.* N.p.

Appiah, Kwame Anthony. 1992. *In My Father's House: Africa in the Philosophy of Culture.* New York: Cambridge University Press.

Apter, Andrew. 1991. "Herskovits's Heritage: Rethinking Syncretism in the African Diaspora." *Diaspora* 1 (3): 235–60.

Argüelles Mederos, Anibal, and Ileana Hodge Limonta. 1991. *Los llamados cultos sincréticos y el espiritismo.* Havana: Editorial Academia.

Austin, John. 1962. *How to Do Things with Words.* London: Oxford University Press.

Ayorinde, Christine. 2004. *Afro-Cuban Religiosity, Revolution, and National Identity.* Gainesville: University Press of Florida.

Bachiller y Morales, Antonio. 1883. "Desfiguración a que está expuesto el idioma castellano al contacto y mezcla de las razas." *Revista de Cuba* 14:97–104.

Bailey, Benjamin. 2001. "The Language of Multiple Identities among Dominican Americans." *Journal of Linguistic Anthropology* 10 (2): 190–223.

Baker, Lee D. 2006. "Missionary Positions." In *Globalization and Race*, edited by K. M. Clarke and D. A. Thomas, 37–54. Durham, NC: Duke University Press.

Bakhtin, Mikhail M. 1968. *Rabelais and His World*. Translated by H. Iswolsky. Cambridge, MA: MIT Press.

———. 1981. *The Dialogic Imagination: Four Essays*. Edited by Michael Holquist. Translated by Caryl Emerson and Michael Holquist. Austin: University of Texas Press.

Balga Rodríguez, Yohanis. 2000–2003. "El habla bozal y su representación en una muestra de la literatura costumbrista cubana: Un acercamiento a la problemática del supuesto criollo cubano." *Anuario L/L: Estudios Lingüísticos* (Havana) 15–18:17–24.

Ballou, Maturin M. 1854. *History of Cuba*. Boston: Phillips, Sampson, & Co.

Barcia Zequeira, María del Carmen. 2003. *La otra familia: Parientes, redes y descendencia de los esclavos en Cuba*. Havana: Fondo Editorial Casa de las Americas.

Barnet, Miguel. 1995. *Cultos Afrocubanos: La Regla de Ocha, la Regla de Palo Monte*. Havana: Artex y Ediciones Union.

Basso, Keith H. 1990. *Western Apache Language and Culture*. Tuscon: University of Arizona Press.

———. 1996. *Wisdom Sits in Places: Landscape and Language among the Western Apache*. Albuquerque: University of New Mexico Press.

Bateson, Gregory. 1972. "A Theory of Play and Fantasy." In *Steps to an Ecology of Mind*, 177–200. New York: Ballantine Books.

Bauman, Richard. 1986. *Story, Performance, and Event*. Cambridge: Cambridge University Press.

———. 1993. "Disclaimers of Performance." In *Responsibility and Evidence in Oral Discourse*, edited by J. H. Hill and J. T. Irvine, 182–96. Cambridge: Cambridge University Press.

———. 2004. *A World of Others' Words*. Oxford: Blackwell.

———. 2011. "Commentary: Foundations in Performance." *Journal of Sociolinguistics* 15 (5): 707–20.

Bauman, Richard, and Charles L. Briggs. 1990. "Poetics and Performance as Critical Perspectives on Language and Social Life." *Annual Review of Anthropology* 19:59–88.

———. 2003. *Voices of Modernity: Language Ideologies and the Politics of Inequality*. Cambridge: Cambridge University Press.

Bauman, Richard, and Joel Sherzer, eds. 1974. *Explorations in the Ethnography of Speaking*. Cambridge: Cambridge University Press.

Bennett, Claudette. 2000. "Racial Categories Used in the Decennial Censuses, 1790 to the Present." *Government Information Quarterly* 17 (2): 161–80.

Bergad, Laird. 2007. *The Comparative Histories of Slavery in Brazil, Cuba, and the United States*. Cambridge: Cambridge University Press.

Bergad, Laird W., Fe Iglesias García, and María del Carmen Barcia. 1995. *The Cuban Slave Market, 1790–1880*. Cambridge: Cambridge University Press.

Boas, Franz. 1889. "On Alternating Sounds." In *The Shaping of American Anthropology*, edited by G. Stocking, 72–77. New York: Basic Books.

Borges, Jorge Luis. 1975. "On Exactitude in Science." In *A Universal History of Infamy*. London: Penguin Books.

Borges-Triana, Joaquín. 2009. *La Luz, Bróder, la Luz: Canción cubana contemporanea*. Havana: Centro Cultural Pablo de la Torriente Brau.

Bourdieu, Pierre. 1977. *Outline of a Theory of Practice*. Translated by R. Nice. Cambridge: Cambridge University Press.

Brandon, George. 1993. *Santería from Africa to the New World: The Dead Sell Memories*. Bloomington: Indiana University Press.

Briggs, Charles L. 1986. *Learning How to Ask: A Sociolinguistic Appraisal of the Role of the Interview in Social Science Research*. Cambridge: Cambridge University Press.

———. 1996. "The Politics of Discursive Authority in Research on the Invention of Tradition." *Cultural Anthropology* 11 (4): 435–69.

Bronfman, Alejandra. 2004. *Measures of Equality: Social Science, Citizenship, and Race in Cuba, 1902–1940*. Chapel Hill: University of North Carolina Press.

Brotherton, P. Sean. 2008. "'We Have to Think Like Capitalists but Continue Being Socialists': Medicalized Subjectivities, Emergent Capital, and Socialist Entrepeneurs in Post-Soviet Cuba." *American Ethnologist* 35 (2): 259–74.

Brown, David H. 2003. *Santería Enthroned: Art, Ritual, and Innovation in an Afro-Cuban Religion*. Chicago: University of Chicago Press.

Browning, Barbara. 1998. *Infectious Rhythm: Metaphors of Contagion and the Spread of African Culture*. New York: Routledge.

Bruner, Edward M. 1996. "Tourism in Ghana: The Representation of Slavery and the Return of the Black Diaspora." *American Anthropologist* 98 (2): 290–304.

———. 2005. *Culture on Tour*. Chicago: University of Chicago Press.

Bucholtz, Mary. 2000. "The Politics of Transcription." *Journal of Pragmatics* 32:1439–65.

———. 2009. "Styles and Stereotypes: Laotian American Girls' Linguistic Negotiation of Identity." In *Beyond Yellow English: Toward a Linguistic Anthropology of Asian Pacific America*, edited by A. Reyes and A. Lo, 21–42. New York: Oxford University Press.

Butler, Judith. 1993. *Bodies That Matter: On the Discursive Limits of "Sex."* New York: Routledge.

———. 1999. *Gender Trouble: Feminism and the Subversion of Identity*. New York: Routledge.

———. 2004. *Undoing Gender*. New York: Routledge.

Cabrera, Lydia. (1954) 1993. *El monte*. Havana: Editorial Letras Cubanas.

Cameron, Deborah. 1995. *Verbal Hygiene*. London: Routledge.

Carr, David. 1986. *Time, Narrative, and History*. Bloomington: Indiana University Press.

Casey, Edward S. 1996. "How to Get from Space to Place in a Fairly Short Stretch of Time: Phenomenological Prolegomena." In *Senses of Place*, edited by S. Feld and K. H. Basso, 13–52. Santa Fe, NM: SAR Press.

Castellanos, Isabel. 1990. "Grammatical Structure, Historical Development, and Religious Usage of Afro-Cuban Bozal Speech." *Folklore Forum* 23 (1–2): 57–84.

———. 1994. "Introducción." In *Lydia Cabrera: Páginas Sueltas*, edited by I. Castellanos, 11–66. Miami: Ediciones Universal.

Castro, Fidel. 1961. "Palabras a los Intelectuales." Latin American Network Information Center, University of Texas at Austin. http://lanic.utexas.edu/project/castro/db/1961/19610630.html.

———. 1975. *Discurso pronunciado por el comandante en jefe Fidel Castro Ruz, primer secretario del comite central del partido comunista de Cuba y primer ministro del gobierno revolucionario, en el acto de masas con motivo de la clausura del primer congreso del partido comunista de cuba: Plaza de la Revolucion, 22 de diciembre de 1975, "año del primer congreso."* Havana: Departamento de Versiones Taquigraficas del Gobierno Revolucionario.

Causse Cathcart, Mercedes. 2006. "Los unificadores culturales como expresión de identidad en los Hoyos: Un estudio desde la teoria sociolingüística tesis" Doctoral thesis. Facultad de Letras, Universidad de Oriente.
Chude-Sokei, Louis. 2006. *The Last "Darky": Bert Williams, Black-on-Black Minstrelsy, and the African Diaspora.* Durham, NC: Duke University Press.
Chun, Elaine W. 2009. "Ideologies of Legitimate Mockery." In *Beyond Yellow English: Toward a Linguistic Anthropology of Asian Pacific America*, edited by A. Reyes and A. Lo, 261–87. New York: Oxford University Press.
CIPS, Centro de Investigaciones Psícologicas y Sociológicas. 1998. *Panorama de la religión en Cuba.* Havana: Editorial Política.
Clarke, Kamari Maxine, and Deborah A. Thomas, eds. 2006. *Globalization and Race: Transformations in the Cultural Production of Blackness.* Durham, NC: Duke University Press.
Cole, Jennifer. 1998. "The Work of Memory in Madagascar." *American Ethnologist* 25 (4): 610–33.
———. 2001. *Forget Colonialism? Sacrifice and the Art of Memory in Madagascar.* Berkeley: University of California Press.
Connerton, Paul. 1989. *How Societies Remember.* Cambridge: Cambridge University Press.
Coupland, Nikolas. 2007. *Style: Language Variation and Identity.* Cambridge: Cambridge University Press.
Covarrubios Orozco, Sebastián de. (1611) 2006. *Tesoro de la lengua castellana o española.* Pamplona: Universidad de Navarra.
Cruz, Mary. 1974. *Creto Gangá.* Havana: Instituto Cubano del Libro.
Curtin, Philip D. 1969. *The Slave Trade: A Census.* Madison: University of Wisconsin Press.
Cutler, Cecilia. 2003. " 'Keepin' It Real': White Hip-Hoppers' Discourses of Language, Race, and Authenticity." *Journal of Linguistic Anthropology* 13 (2): 211–33.
DaCosta Holton, Kimberly. 2005. Performing Folklore: Ranchos Folclóricos from Lisbon to Newark. Bloomington: Indiana University Press.
Daniel, Yvonne. 2002. "Cuban Dance: An Orchard of Caribbean Creativity." In *Caribbean Dance from Abakuá to Zouk*, edited by S. Sloat, 23–55. Gainesville: University Press of Florida.
De la Cadena, Marisol. 2001. "Comments: Ambiguity and Contradiction in the Analysis of Race and the State." *Journal of Latin American Anthropology* 6 (2): 252–66.
de la Fuente, Alejandro. 1998. "Raza, desigualdad y prejuicio en Cuba." *América Negra* 15:21–39.
———. 2001a. A Nation for All: Race, Equality, and Nation in 20th century Cuba. Chapel Hill: University of North Carolina Press.
———. 2001b. "Recreating Racism: Race and Discrimination in Cuba's 'Special Period.'" *Socialism and Democracy* 15 (1): 65–91.
———. 2007. "Racism, Culture, and Mobilization." Commissioned Reports, Cuban Research Intitute, Florida International University. http://cri.fiu.edu/research/commissioned-reports/racism-fuente.pdf.
de los Reyes Castillo Bueno, Maria. 2000. *Reyita: The Life of a Black Cuban Woman in the Twentieth Century.* Translated by A. McLean. Durham, NC: Duke University Press.
Dening, Greg. 1996. *Performances.* Victoria: Melbourne University Press.
Dent, Alexander Sebastian. 2009. *River of Tears: Country Music, Memory, and Modernity in Brazil.* Durham, NC: Duke University Press.
Derrida, Jacques. 1988. *Limited Inc.* Evanston, IL: Northwestern University Press.
de Santana Pinho, Patricia. 2010. *Mama Africa: Reinventing Blackness in Bahia.* Durham, NC: Duke University Press.

———. 2011. "Gilberto Freyre y la bahianidad." *Del Caribe* 55:3–13.

DeWolf, Thomas Norman, and Sharon Leslie Morgan. 2012. *Gather at the Table: The Healing Journey of a Daughter of Slavery and a Son of the Slave Trade.* Boston: Beacon Press.

Dianteill, Erwan, and Martha Swearingen. 2003. "From Hierography to Ethnography and Back: Lydia Cabrera's Texts and the Written Tradition in Afro-Cuban Religions." *Journal of American Folklore* 116 (2): 273–92.

Díaz, María Elena. 2000. *The Virgin, the King, and the Royal Slaves of El Cobre: Negotiating Freedom in Colonial Cuba, 1670–1780.* Stanford, CA: Stanford University Press.

Dick, Hilary, and Kristina Wirtz. 2011. "Introduction—Racializing Discourses." In "Racializing Discourses," *Journal of Linguistic Anthropology* 21 (S1): E2–E10.

di Leonardo, Micaela. 1998. *Exotics at Home: Anthropologies, Others, American Modernity.* Chicago: University of Chicago Press.

Duany, Jorge. 1988. "After the Revolution: The Search for Roots in Afro-Cuban Culture." *Latin American Research Review* 23 (1): 244–55.

Du Bois, John W. 1986. "Self-evidence and Ritual Speech." In *Evidentiality: The Linguistic Coding of Epistemology,* edited by W. Chafe and J. Nichols, 313–36. Norwood, NJ: Ablex.

———. 1992. "Meaning without Intention: Lessons from Divination." In *Responsibility and Evidence in Oral Discourse,* edited by J. H. Hill and J. T. Irvine, 48–71. Cambridge: Cambridge University Press.

DuBois, W. E. B. 1989. *The Souls of Black Folk.* New York: Bantam Books.

Dunn, Cynthia Dickel. 2006. "Formulaic Expressions, Chinese Proverbs, and Newspaper Editorials: Exploring Type and Token Interdiscursivity in Japanese Wedding Speeches." *Journal of Linguistic Anthropology* 16 (2): 153–72.

Duque de Estrada, Nicolás. (1797) 1989. *Doctrina para negros: Explicación de la doctrina cristiana acomodada a la capacidad de los negros bozales.* Edited by Javier Laviña. Barcelona: Sendai ediciones.

Ebron, Paulla. 2002. *Performing Africa.* Princeton, NJ: Princeton University Press.

Espírito Santo, Diana. In press. *Developing the Dead: Cosmology and Personhood in Cuban Spiritism.* Gainesville: University Press of Florida.

Fabian, Johannes. 1983. *Time and the Other: How Anthropology Makes Its Object.* New York: Columbia University Press.

Fanon, Franz. 1982. *Black Skin, White Masks.* Translated by C. L. Markmann. New York: Grove Press.

———. (1952) 2008. *Black Skin, White Masks.* Translated by R. Philcox. New York: Grove Press.

Farnell, Brenda, and Laura R. Graham. 1998. "Discourse-Centered Methods." In *Handbook of Methods in Cultural Anthropology,* edited by R. Bernard, 411–57. Walnut Creek, CA: Altamira.

Faulkner, William. 1951. *Requiem for a Nun.* New York: Random House.

Feld, Steven. 1982. *Sound and Sentiment: Birds, Weeping, Poetics, and Song in Kaluli Expression.* Austin: University of Texas Press.

———. 2004. *The Time of Bells.* Vol. 1. (Liner Notes for CD.) http://voxlox.myshopify.com/products/steven-feld-the-time-of-bells-1.

Fernandez, Francisco. 1868. *Los negros catedráticos: Absurdo cómico en un acto de costumbres cubanas en prosa y verso.* Havana: Comercio Obispo.

Fernández Robaina, Tomás. 1994. *El negro en Cuba, 1902–1958.* Havana: Editorial de Ciencias Sociales.

Ferrer, Ada. 1999. *Insurgent Cuba: Race, Nation, and Revolution, 1868–1898*. Chapel Hill: University of North Carolina Press.

Florentino, Juan Teodoro. 2010. "Un acercamiento a la labor artística integral de Ernesto Armiñán Linares, Danza Folklórica." Masters Thesis, Instituto Superior de Arte, Havana.

Foucault, Michel. (1966) 1973. *The Order of Things: An Archaeology of the Human Sciences*. New York: Vintage Books.

———. 1978. *History of Sexuality: An Introduction*. Vol. 1. New York: Vintage Books.

Franco, José Luciano. 1975. *Las minas de Santiago del Prado y la rebelión de los cobreros (1530–1800)*. Havana: Editorial de Ciencias Sociales.

Frankenberg, Ruth, ed. 1997. *Displacing Whiteness: Essays in Social and Cultural Criticism*. Durham, NC: Duke University Press.

Frederik, Laurie Aleen. 1998. "The Contestation of Cuba's Public Sphere in National Theater and the Transformation from Teatro Bufo to Teatro Nuevo; or, What Happens When el Negrito, el Gallego, and la Mulata Meet el Hombre Nuevo." University of Chicago Hewlett Foundation Working Papers Series, HWPS-001.

———. 2005. "Cuba's National Characters: Setting the Stage for the *hombre novísimo*." *Journal of Latin American Anthropology* 10 (2): 401–36.

Friedrich, Paul. 1986. *The Language Parallax: Linguistic Relativism and Poetic Indeterminacy*. Austin: University of Texas Press.

———. 1991. "Polytropy." In *Beyond Metaphor: The Theory of Tropes in Anthropology.*, edited by J. W. Fernandez, 17–55. Stanford, CA: Stanford University Press.

Frye, Northrop. 1963. *Fables of Identity: Studies in Poetic Mythology*. New York: Harcourt, Brace, Jovanovich.

Fuentes Guerra, Jesús, and Armin Schwegler. 2005. *Lengua y ritos del Palo Monte Mayombe: Dioses cubanos y sus fuentes africanas*. Madrid: Iberoamericana Vervuert.

Gal, Susan. 2005. "Language Ideologies Compared: Metaphors of Public/Private." *Journal of Linguistic Anthropology* 15 (1): 23–37.

Gal, Susan, and Kathryn A. Woolard, eds. 2001. *Languages and Publics: The Making of Authority*. Manchester: St. Jerome Publishing.

Gaudio, Rudolph P. 2011. "The Blackness of 'Broken English.'" *Journal of Linguistic Anthropology* 21 (2): 230–46.

Gilroy, Paul. 1987. *There Ain't No Black in the Union Jack: The Cultural Politics of Race and Nation*. London: Hutchison.

———. 1993. *The Black Atlantic: Modernity and Double Consciousness*. Cambridge, MA: Harvard University Press.

———. 1995. "Roots and Routes: Black Identity as an Outernational Project." In *Racial and Ethnic Identity: Psychological Development and Creative Expression.*, edited by H. W. Harris, H. Blue, and E. Griffith, 15–30. New York: Routledge.

Godreau, Isar P. 2006. "Folkloric 'Others': Blanqueamiento and the Celebration of Blackness as Exception in Puerto Rico." In *Globalization and Race*, edited by K. M. Clarke and D. A. Thomas, 171–87. Durham, NC: Duke University Press.

Godreau, Isar P., et al. 2008. "Lessons of Slavery: Discourses of Slavery, Mestizaje, and Blanqueamiento in an Elementary School in Puerto Rico. *American Ethnologist* 35 (1): 115–35.

Goffman, Erving. 1959. *The Presentation of Self in Everyday Life*. Garden City, NY: Doubleday.

———. 1974. *Frame Analysis*. New York: Harper and Row.

———. 1981. *Forms of Talk*. Philadelphia: University of Pennsylvania Press.

Goodwin, Charles. 2000. "Action and Embodiment within Situated Human Interaction." *Journal of Pragmatics* 32:1489–1522.

Gordon, Edmund T., and Mark Anderson. 1999. "The African Diaspora: Toward an Ethnography of Diasporic Identification." *Journal of American Folklore* 112 (445): 282–96.

Granda, Germán de. 1971. "Algunos datos sobre la pervivencia del 'criollo' en Cuba." *Boletín de la Real Academia Española* 51:481–91.

———. 1988. *Lingüística e historia: Temas Afro-Hispánicos.* Valladolid: Universidad de Valladolid, Secretariado de Publicaciones.

———. 1994. *Español de América, Español de Africa, y hablas criollas hispánicas: Cambios, contactos y contextos.* Madrid: Editorial Gredos.

Guerra, Ramiro. 1989. *Teatralización del folklore y otros ensayos.* Havana: Editorial Letras Cubanas.

Guillén, Nicolás. 1972. *Obra Poética.* 2 vols. Havana: Instituto Cubano del Libro.

Gumperz, John J. 1992. "Contextualization and Understanding." In *Rethinking Context: Language as an Interactive Phenomenon*, edited by A. Duranti and C. Goodwin, 229–52. Cambridge: Cambridge University Press.

Guss, David M. 2000. *The Festive State: Race, Ethnicity, and Nationalism as Cultural Performance.* Berkeley: University of California Press.

Hagedorn, Katherine J. 2001. *Divine Utterances: The Performance of Afro-Cuban Santería.* Washington, DC: Smithsonian Institution Press.

Halbwachs, Maurice. 1992. *On Collective Memory.* Translated by L. A. Coser. Chicago: University of Chicago Press.

Hansing, Katrin. 2006. *Rasta, Race, and Revolution; The Emergence and Development of the Rastafari Movement in Socialist Cuba.* Münster: Lit Verlag.

Härkönen, Heidi Kristiina. 2011. "Love, Jealousy and Gender in Post-Soviet Cuba." Paper presented at the annual meeting of the American Anthropological Association, Montreal, Canada, November 17.

Hartigan, John. 1999. *Racial Situations: Class Predicaments of Whiteness in Detroit.* Princeton, NJ: Princeton University Press.

Haviland, John B. 1996. "Text from Talk in Tzotzil." In *Natural Histories of Discourse*, edited by M. Silverstein and G. Urban, 45–80. Chicago: University of Chicago Press.

Helg, Aline. 1990. "Race in Argentina and Cuba, 1880–1930: Theory, Policies, and Popular Reactions." In *The Idea of Race in Latin America, 1870–1940*, edited by R. Graham, 45–69. Austin: University of Texas Press.

———. 1995. *Our Rightful Share: The Afro-Cuban Struggle for Equality, 1886–1912.* Chapel Hill: University of North Carolina Press.

Henken, Ted. 2002. "'Vale todo' (Anything Goes): Cuba's *paladares.*" *Cuba in Transition* 12: 344–53.

———. 2007. "*Dirigentes, Diplogente, Indigentes, and Delincuentes*: Official Corruption and Underground Honesty in Today's Cuba." Commissioned Report by the Cuban Research Institute of Florida International University. http://cri.fiu.edu/research/commissioned-reports/dirigentes-henken.pdf.

Herskovits, Melville J. 1945. "Problem, Method, and Theory in Afroamerican Studies," *Afroamerica* 1:5–24.

Hernandez-Reguant, Ariana. 2006. "Havana's Timba: A Macho Sound for Black Sex." In *Globalization and Race*, edited by K. M. Clarke and D. A. Thomas, 249–78. Durham, NC: Duke University Press.

Hevia Lanier, Oilda. 1996. *El directorio central de las sociedades negras de Cuba (1886–1894).* Havana: Editorial de Ciencas Sociales.

Hill, Jane H. 1993. "Hasta la Vista Baby: Anglo Spanish in the American Southwest." *Critique of Anthropology* 13 (2): 145–76.

———. 1995. "The Voices of Don Gabriel: Responsibility and Self in a Modern Mexicano Narrative." In *The Dialogic Emergence of Culture,* edited by D. Tedlock and B. Mannheim, 97–147. Urbana: University of Illinois Press.

———. 2001. "Mock Spanish, Covert Racism and the (Leaky) Boundary between Public and Private Spheres." In *Languages and Publics: The Making of Authority,* edited by S. Gal and K. A. Woolard, 83–102. Manchester: St. Jerome Publishing.

———. 2005. "Intertextuality as Source and Evidence for Indirect Indexical Meanings." *Journal of Linguistic Anthropology* 15 (1): 113–24.

———. 2008. *The Everyday Language of White Racism.* Chichester: Wiley-Blackwell.

Hobsbawm, Eric, and Terence Ranger. 1992. *The Invention of Tradition.* Cambridge: Cambridge University Press.

Hollinger, David. 2006. "Race, Politics, and the Census." *Chronicle of Higher . Education* 52 (28): B6.

Holt, Thomas. 2000. *The Problem of Race in the Twenty-First Century.* Cambridge: Harvard University Press.

hooks, bell. 1996. *Killing Rage: Ending Racism.* New York: Henry Holt & Co.

Howard, Philip A. 1998. *Changing History: Afro-Cuban Cabildos and Societies of Color in the Nineteenth Century.* Baton Rouge: Louisiana State University Press.

Hull, Matthew. 2003. "The File: Agency, Authority, and Autography in a Pakistan Bureaucracy." *Language and Communication* 23 (3–4): 287–314.

Humboldt, Alexander von. 2001. *The Island of Cuba: A Political Essay.* Translated by J. S. Thrasher. Princeton, NJ: Markus Wiener.

Hymes, Dell. 1972. "The Contribution of Folklore to Sociolinguistic Research." In *Toward New Perspectives in Folklore,* edited by A. Paredes and R. Bauman, 42–50. Publications of the American Folklore Society. Austin: University of Texas Press.

Irvine, Judith. 1992. "Ideologies of Honorific Language." *Pragmatics* 2 (3): 251–62.

———. 1996. "Shadow Conversations: The Indeterminacy of Participant Roles." In *Natural Histories of Discourse,* edited by M. Silverstein and G. Urban, 131–59. Chicago: University of Chicago Press.

———. 2005. "Commentary: Tears and Knots in the Interdiscursive Fabric." *Journal of Linguistic Anthropology* 15 (1): 72–80.

———. 2008. "Subjected Words: African Linguistics and the Colonial Encounter." *Language and Communication* 28:323–43.

Irvine, Judith, and Susan Gal. 2000. "Language Ideology and Linguistic Differentiation." In *Regimes of Language: Ideologies, Politics, Identities,* edited by P. Kroskrity, 35–83. Santa Fe, NM: School of American Research Press.

Jackson, John L. 2005. *Real Black: Adventures in Racial Sincerity.* Chicago: University of Chicago Press.

Jakobson, Roman. 1970. "Shifters, Verbal Categories, and the Russian Verb." In *Selected Writings,* 130–47. The Hague: Mouton.

James Figarola, Joel. 1974. *Cuba, 1900–1928: La república dividida contra sí misma.* Havana: Editorial Arte y Literatura.

———. 1999a. *La muerte en Cuba.* Havana: Ediciones Unión.

———. 1999b. *Los sistemas mágico-religiosos cubanos: Principios rectores.* Caracas: UNESCO.

———. 2001. "Para un nuevo acercamiento a la nganga." *Del Caribe* 35:22–31.

———. 2006a. *Cuba la gran nganga (algunas prácticas de la brujería).* Santiago de Cuba: Ediciones Caserón.

———. 2006b. *La brujería cubana: El palo monte.* Santiago de Cuba: Editorial Oriente.

Jameson, Robert Francis. 1821. *Letters from the Havana during the Year 1820.* London: John Miller.

John, Suki. 2002. "The Técnica Cubana." In *Caribbean Dance from Abakuá to Zouk*, edited by S. Sloat, 73–80. Gainesville: University Press of Florida.

Johnson, E. Patrick. 2003. *Appropriating Blackness: Performance and the Politics of Authenticity.* Durham, NC: Duke University Press.

Johnson, Paul Christopher. 2007. *Diaspora Conversions: Black Carib Religion and the Recovery of Africa.* Berkeley: University of California Press.

———. 2011. "An Atlantic Genealogy of 'Spirit Possession.'" *Comparative Studies in Society and History.* 53 (2): 393–425.

Johnstone, Barbara. 2008. *Discourse Analysis.* Oxford: Blackwell.

Jones, Rhett. 1997. "Why Blacks Are Committed to Blackness." In *Cultural Portrayals of African Americans: Creating an Ethnic/Racial Identity*, edited by J. F. Hutchinson, 49–74. Westport, CT: Bergin and Garvey.

Keane, Webb. 1997a. "Religious Language." *Annual Review of Anthropology* 26:47–71.

———. 1997b. *Signs of Recognition: Powers and Hazards of Representation in an Indonesian Society.* Berkeley: University of California Press.

Keyes, Charles. 1976. "Toward a New Formulation of the Concept of Ethnic Group." *Ethnicity* 3 (3): 202–13.

Khan, Aisha. 2004. *Callaloo Nation: Metaphors of Race and Religious Identity among South Asians in Trinidad.* Durham, NC: Duke University Press.

Kiple, Kenneth F. 1976. *Blacks in Colonial Cuba, 1774–1899.* Gainesville: University Press of Florida.

Klein, Herbert S. 1999. *The Atlantic Slave Trade.* Cambridge: Cambridge University Press.

Knight, Franklin W. 1996. *Race, Ethnicity, and Class: Forging the Plural Society in Latin America and the Caribbean.* Waco, TX: Baylor University.

Knight, Franklin W., and Teresita Martínez-Vergne, eds. 2005. *Contemporary Caribbean Cultures and Societies in a Global Context.* Chapel Hill: University of North Carolina Press.

Kripke, Saul A. 1972. "Naming and Necessity" and "Addenda to 'Naming and Necessity." In *Semantics of Natural Language*, edited by D. Davidson and G. Harman, 253–355 and 763–69, respectively. 2nd ed. Dordrecht, Holland: D. Reidel.

Kutsinski, Vera M. 1993. *Sugar's Secrets: Race and the Erotics of Cuban Nationalism.* Charlottesville: University Press of Virginia.

Lambek, Michael. 1998. "The Sakalava Poiesis of History: Realizing the Past through Spirit Possession in Madagascar." *American Ethnologist* 25 (2): 106–27.

Lane, Jill. 2005. *Blackface Cuba, 1840–1895.* Philadelphia: University of Pennsylvania Press.

Larduet Luaces, Abelardo. 2001. "Reynerio Pérez en el panorama de las creencias de origen bantú en Santiago de Cuba." *Del Caribe* 34:114–15.

Law, Robin. 1997. "Ethnicity and the Slave Trade: 'Lucumi' and 'Nago' as Ethnonyms in West Africa." *History in Africa* 24:205–19.

Leal, Rine. 1975. *Teatro bufo siglo XIX*. 2 vols. Havana: Editorial Arte y Literatura.

———. 1982. *La selva oscura: De los bufos a la neocolonia (Historia del teatro cubano de 1868 a 1902)*. Havana: Editorial Arte y Literatura.

Lee, Benjamin. 1997. *Talking Heads*. Durham, NC: Duke University Press.

Lefebvre, Henri. 1991. *The Production of Space*. Translated by D. Nicholson-Smith. Oxford: Blackwell.

Lemon, Alaina. 2000. *Between Two Fires: Gypsy Performance and Romani Memory from Pushkin to Socialism*. Durham, NC: Duke University Press.

———. 2009. "Sympathy for the Weary State? Cold War Chronotypes and Moscow Others." *Comparative Studies in Society and History* 51 (4): 832–64.

Lévi-Strauss, Claude. 1987. "Chapter 3." In *Introduction to the Work of Marcel Mauss*. Edited by C. Lévi -Strauss, 46–67. New York: Routledge.

Lhamon, W. T. 1998. *Raising Cain: Blackface Performance from Jim Crow to Hip Hop*. Cambridge, MA: Harvard University Press.

Lindsay, Arturo, ed. 1996. *Santería Aesthetics in Contemporary Latin American Art*. Washington, DC: Smithsonian Institution Press.

Lipski, John M. 2005. *A History of Afro-Hispanic Language*. Cambridge: Cambridge University Press.

Loomis, John A. 1999. *Revolution of Forms: Cuba's Forgotten Art Schools*. New York: Princeton Architectural Press.

Lott, Eric. 1993. *Love and Theft: Blackface Minstrelsy and the American Working Class*. New York: Oxford University Press.

Lovejoy, Paul E. 2003. "Ethnic Designations of the Slave Trade and the Reconstruction of the History of Trans-Atlantic Slavery." In *Trans-Atlantic Dimension of Ethnicity in the African Diaspora*, edited by P. E. Lovejoy and D. V. Trotman, 9–42. London: Continuum.

Lucy, John A. 1992. *Language Diversity and Thought*. Cambridge: Cambridge University Press.

———, ed. 1993. *Reflexive Language: Reported Speech and Metapragmatics*. Cambridge: Cambridge University Press.

———. 1997. "Linguistic Relativity." *Annual Review of Anthropology* 26:291–312.

———. 2004. "Language, Culture, and Mind in Comparative Perspective." In *Language, Culture, and Mind*, edited by M. Achard and S. Kemmer, 1–21. Stanford, CA: Center for the Study of Language and Information Publications.

Mahar, William J. 1999. *Behind the Burnt Cork Mask: Early Blackface Minstrelsy and Antebellum American Popular Culture*. Urbana: University of Illinois Press.

Mannheim, Bruce. 1986. "Popular Song and Popular Grammar: Poetry and Metalanguage." *Word* 37:45–75.

Mannheim, Bruce, and Dennis Tedlock. 1995. "Introduction." In *The Dialogic Emergence of Culture*, edited by D. Tedlock and B. Mannheim, 1–32. Urbana: University of Illinois Press.

Manzano, Juan Francisco. (1840) 1981. *The Life and Poems of a Cuban Slave*. Translated by R. R. Madden. Edited by E. J. Mullen. Hamden, CT: Archon Books.

Martí, José. 1976. *Obra completa*. Vol. 2. Havana: Editorial Pueblo y Educación.

Martinez-Alier, Verena. 1989. *Marriage, Class, and Colour in Nineteenth-Century Cuba*. Ann Arbor: University of Michigan Press.

McAlister, Elizabeth A. 2002. *Rara! Vodou, Power, and Performance in Haiti and Its Diaspora*. Berkeley: University of California Press.

McWhorter, John H. 2000. *The Missing Spanish Creoles: Recovering the Birth of Plantation Contact Languages.* Berkeley: University of California Press.

Meek, Barbra A. 2006. "And the Injun Goes 'How!' Representations of American Indian English in White Public Space." *Language in Society* 35 (1): 93–128.

Merleau-Ponty, M. (1962) 1989. *Phenomenology of Perception.* Translated by C. Smith. London: Routledge.

Miller, Ivor. 2005. "Cuban Abakuá Chants: Examining New Linguistic and Historical Evidence for the African Diaspora." *African Studies Review* 48 (1): 23–58.

Millet, José, Rafael Brea, and Manuel Ruiz Vila. 1997. *Barrio, comparsa y carnaval santiaguero.* Santiago de Cuba: Ediciones Casa del Caribe; Santo Domingo: Ediciones Casa Dominicana de Identidad Caribeña.

Mintz, Sidney, and Richard Price. (1976) 1992. *The Birth of African-American Culture: An Anthropological Perspective.* Boston: Beacon Press.

Mirón, Louis F., and Jonathan Xavier Inda. 2000. "Race as a Kind of Speech Act." *Cultural Studies: A Research Journal* 5:85–107.

Montejo Arrechea, Carmen Victoria. 1993. *Sociedades de instruccion y recreo de pardos y morenos que existieron en Cuba colonial: Periodo 1878–1898.* Veracruz: Gobierno del Estado de Veracruz.

Montes Huidobro, Matías. 1987. *Teoría y práctica del catedratismo en "Los negros catedráticos" de Francisco Fernández.* Havana: Editorial Persona.

Moore, Carlos. 1988. *Castro, the Blacks, and Africa.* Los Angeles: Center for Afro-American Studies, University of California.

Moore, Robin. 1997. *Nationalizing Blackness: Afrocubanismo and Artistic Revolution in Havana, 1920–1940.* Pittsburgh: University of Pittsburgh Press.

———. 2006. "Black Music in a Raceless Society: Afrocuban Folklore and Socialism." *Cuban Studies* 37:1–32.

Morrison, Karen Y. 2000. "Civilization and Citizenship through the Eyes of Afro-Cuban Intellectuals during the First Constitutional Era, 1902–1940." *Cuban Studies* 30:76–99.

Mousouris, Melinda. 2002. "The Dance World of Ramiro Guerra: Solemnity, Voluptuousness, Humor, and Chance." In *Caribbean Dance from Abakuá to Zouk*, edited by S. Sloat, 56–72. Gainesville: University Press of Florida.

Mudimbe, V. Y. 1988. *The Invention of Africa.* Bloomington: Indiana University Press.

———. 1994. *The Idea of Africa.* Bloomington: Indiana University Press.

Murakami, Haruki. 2007. *Blind Willow, Sleeping Woman: Twenty-four Stories.* Translated by P. Gabriel and J. Rubin. New York: Vintage International.

Murray, David. 2007. *Matter, Magic, and Spirit: Representing Indian and African American Belief.* Philadelphia: University of Pennsylvania Press.

Murray, David R. 1971. "Statistics of the Slave Trade to Cuba, 1790–1867." *Journal of Latin American Studies* 3 (2): 131–49.

Myers, Kristen. 2005. *Racetalk.* New York: Rowman & Littlefield.

Nathan, Hans. 1962. *Dan Emmett and the Rise of Early Negro Minstrelsy.* Norman: University of Oklahoma Press.

Navarro, Desiderio. 2002. "In medias res publicas: On Intellectuals and Social Criticism in the Cuban Public Sphere." *boundary 2* 29 (3): 187–203.

Noreña, Carlos. 1881. "Los negros curros." In *Tipos y costumbres de la isla de Cuba: Colección de artículos por los mejores autores de este género.* Edited by A. Bachiller y Morales, 127–33. Havana: Miguel de Villa.

Ocasio, Rafael. 2012. *Afro-Cuban Costumbrismo: From Plantation to the Slums.* Gainesville: University Press of Florida.

Ochoa, Todd Ramón. 2010. *Society of the Dead: Quita Manaquita and Palo Praise in Cuba.* Berkeley: University of California Press.

Ochs, Elinor. 1992. "Indexing Gender." In *Rethinking Context: Language as an Interactive Phenomenon,* edited by A. Duranti and C. Goodwin, 335–58. Cambridge: Cambridge University Press.

Ortiz, Fernando. (1906) 1973. *Los negros brujos.* Miami: Ediciones Universal.

———. 1986. *Los negros curros.* Havana: Editorial de Ciencias Sociales.

Ortiz López, Luis A. 1998. *Huellas etnosociolinguísticas bozales y afrocubanas.* Frankfurt: Vervuet Verlag.

Pagliai, Valentina. 2011. "Unmarked Racializing Discourse, Facework, and Identity in Talk about Immigrants in Italy." *Journal of Linguistic Anthropology* 21 (S1): E94–E112.

Palmié, Stephan. 1993. "Ethnogenetic Processes and Cultural Transfer in Afro-American Slave Populations." In *Slavery in the Americas,* edited by W. Binder, 337–63. Wurzburg: Konigshausen and Neuman.

———. 2002. *Wizards and Scientists: Explorations in Afro-Cuban Modernity and Tradition.* Durham, NC: Duke University Press.

———. 2007a. "Ecué's Atlantic: An Essay in Methodology." *Journal of Religion in Africa* 37 (2): 275–316.

———. 2007b. "Genomics, Divination, 'Racecraft.'" *American Ethnologist* 34 (2): 205–22.

———. 2007c. "Introduction: Out of Africa?" *Journal of Religion in Africa* 37 (2): 159–73.

———. 2011. "Historical Knowledge and Its Conditions of Impossibility; or, Why Spirits and Historians Don't Get Along." Paper presented at the annual meeting of the American Anthropological Association, New Orleans, November 18.

Pedroso, Regino. 2005. "Santiago de Cuba, la ciudad de las montañas." In *Santiago de Cuba siglo XX: Cronistas y viajeros miran la ciudad,* edited by R. Duharte Jiménez and E. Recio Lobaina, 114–42. Santiago de Cuba: Editorial Oriente.

Peel, J. D. Y. 1989. "The Cultural Work of Yoruba Ethnogenesis." In *History and Ethnicity,* edited by E. Tonkin and et al., 198–215. London: Routledge.

Peña Montero, Armando. 2012. "Treinta años de una mirada: Conversación con Luis Joaquín Rodríguez Arias, El maestro." *Caserón* 7:42–44.

Pérez, Louis A., Jr. 1999. *On Becoming Cuban: Identity, Nationality, and Culture.* Chapel Hill: University of North Carolina Press.

Pérez, Nancy, Clara Domínguez, Rosa Rodríguez, Orlando Silva, and Danubia Terry. 1982. *El cabildo carabalí Isuama.* Santiago de Cuba: Editorial Oriente.

Pérez Rodríguez, Nancy. 1988. *El carnaval santiaguero.* 2 vols. Santiago de Cuba: Editorial Oriente.

Pérez Sarduy, Pedro, and Jean Stubbs, eds. 1993. *AfroCuba: An Anthology of Cuban Writing on Race, Politics, and Culture.* Melbourne: Ocean Press.

———, eds. 2000. *Afro-Cuban Voices: On Race and Identity in Contemporary Cuba.* Gainesville: University Press of Florida.

Pertierra, Anna Cristina. 2011. *Cuba: The Struggle for Consumption.* Coconut Creek, FL: Caribbean Studies Press.

Philalethes, Demoticus. 1856. *Yankee Travels through the Island of Cuba.* New York: D. Appleton & Co.

Portuondo Zuñiga, Olga. 2000. *Cabildos negros santiagueros. Del Caribe* 32:78–85.

Price, Richard. 1983. *First-Time: The Historical Vision of an African-American People.* Baltimore, MD: Johns Hopkins University Press.

———. 2006. *The Convict and the Colonel: A Story of Colonialism and Resistance in the Caribbean.* Durham, NC: Duke University Press.

Putnam, Hilary. 1977. "Meaning and Reference." In *Naming, Necessity, and Natural Kinds*, edited by S. P. Schwartz, 119-132. Ithaca: Cornell University Press.

Rafael, Vicente L. 2009. "*Conjuración*/Conspiracy in the Philippine Revolution of 1896." In *Words in Motion: Toward a Global Lexicon*, 219–39. Durham, NC: Duke University Press.

Rahier, Jean Muteba. 2003. "Introduction: *Mestizaje, Mulataje, Mestiçagem* in Latin American Ideologies of National Identities." *Journal of Latin American Anthropology* 8 (1): 40–51.

Ramírez Calzadilla, Jorge. 1995. "Religión y cultura: Las investigaciones socioreligiosas. *Temas* 1(March):57–68.

Ramírez Moreira, Luisa María. 2003. *La pintura ingenua: Reino de este mundo.* Santiago de Cuba: Ediciones Catedral.

———. 2009. Essay for art exposition "La Metáfora" by Suitberto Goire Castilla. Santiago de Cuba: Galería Oriente.

———. 2012. "Suitberto Goire Castilla y la gráfica que perdura." *Caserón* 7:3–7.

Rampton, Ben. 1995. *Crossing: Language and Ethnicity among Adolescents.* London: Longman.

Ramsey, Kate. 1997. "Vodou, Nationalism, and Performance: The Staging of Folklore in Mid-Twentieth-Century Haiti." In *Meaning in Motion: New Cultural Studies of Dance*, edited by J. C. Desmond, 345–78. Durham, NC: Duke University Press.

———. 2011. *The Spirits and the Law: Vodou and Power in Haiti.* Chicago: University of Chicago Press.

Ravsberg, Fernando. 2012. "En fotos: Junto a una de las comparsas más populares de La Habana." BBC Mundo. http://www.bbc.co.uk/mundo/video_fotos/2012/08/120806_galeria_carnaval_cuba_mz.shtml.

Remedi, Gustavo. 2004. *Carnival Theater: Uruguay's Popular Performers and National Culture.* Minneapolis: University of Minnesota Press.

Rodney, Walter. 1982. *How Europe Underdeveloped Africa.* Washington, DC: Howard University Press.

Rodríguez-Mangual, Edna M. 2004. *Lydia Cabrera and the Construction of an Afro-Cuban Cultural Identity.* Chapel Hill: University of North Carolina Press.

Román, Reinaldo. 2007. *Governing Spirits: Religion, Miracles, and Spectacles in Cuba and Puerto Rico, 1898–1956.* Chapel Hill: University of North Carolina Press.

Ronkin, Maggie, and Helen E. Karn. 1999. "Mock Ebonics: Linguistic Racism in Parodies of Ebonics on the Internet." *Journal of Sociolinguistics* 3 (3): 360–80.

Rotenberg, Robert. 2001. "Metropolitanism and the Transformation of Urban Space in Nineteenth-Century Colonial Metropoles." *American Anthropologist* 103 (1): 7–15.

Roth-Gordon, Jennifer. 2011. "Discipline and Disorder in the Whiteness of Mock Spanish." *Journal of Linguistic Anthropology* 21 (2): 211–29.

Routon, Kenneth. 2005. "Unimaginable Homelands? 'Africa' and the Abakuá Historical Imagination." *Journal of Latin American Anthropology* 10 (2): 370–400.

———. 2008. "Conjuring the Past: Slavery and the Historical Imagination in Cuba." *American Ethnologist* 35 (4): 632–49.

———. 2010. *Hidden Powers of State in the Cuban Imagination.* Gainesville: University Press of Florida.

Ruiz Hernández, J. Vitelio. 1977. *Estudio sincrónico del habla de Santiago de Cuba.* Santiago de Cuba: Editorial Oriente.

Rushing, Fannie Theresa. 1992. "Cabildos de Nación, Sociedades de la Raza de Color: Afrocuban Participation in Slave Emancipation and Cuba Independence, 1865–1895." PhD diss., University of Chicago.

Samuels, David. 2004. "Language, Meaning, Modernity, and Doowop." *Semiotica* 149:297–323.

Saussure, Ferdinand. 1996. *Course in General Linguistics.* Translated by R. Harris. Chicago: Open Court.

Sawyer, Mark Q. 2006. *Racial Politics in Post-Revolutionary Cuba.* Cambridge: Cambridge University Press.

Schiffrin, Deborah. 1994. *Approaches to Discourse.* Oxford: Blackwell.

Schmidt, Jalane. 2011. "Las calles ordenadas contra 'la brujeria' afro-cubana: Los festivales para la virgen de los años 1930 en Santiago de Cuba." *Del Caribe* 54:41–48.

Schwegler, Armin. 1998. "El palenquero." In *América negra: Panorámica actual de los estudios linguísticos sobre variedades hispanas, portugueses, y criollas,* edited by M. Perl and A. Schwegler, 220–91. Madrid: Iberoamericana.

———. 2006. "Bozal Spanish: Captivating New Evidence from a Contemporary Source (Afro-Cuban 'Palo Monte')." In *Studies in Contact Linguistics: Essays in Honor of Glenn G. Gilbert,* edited by J. Fuller and L. L. Thornburg, 71–100. New York: Peter Lang.

Schwegler, Armin, and Constanza Rojas-Primus. 2010. "La lengua ritual del Palo Monte (Cuba): Estudio comparativo (Holguín/Cienfuegos)." *Revista Internacional de Lingüística Iberoamericana* 8 (15): 187–246.

Scott, David. 1991. "That Event, This Memory: Notes on the Anthropology of African Diasporas in the New World." *Diaspora* 1 (3): 261–83.

Scott, Rebecca J. 1985. *Slave Emancipation in Cuba: The Transition to Free Labor, 1860–1899.* Princeton, NJ: Princeton University Press.

Searle, John. 1969. *Speech Acts: An Essay in the Philosophy of Language.* Cambridge: Cambridge University Press.

Serviat, Pedro. 1986. *El problema negro en Cuba y su solución definitiva.* Havana: Editorial Política.

Shankar, Shalini. 2008. *Desi Land: Teen Culture, Class, and Success in Silicon Valley.* Durham, NC: Duke University Press.

Shaw, Rosalind. 2002. *Memories of the Slave Trade : Ritual and the Historical Imagination in Sierra Leone.* Chicago: University of Chicago Press.

Sheriff, Robin E. 1999. "The Theft of Carnaval: National Spectacle and Racial Politics in Rio de Janeiro." *Cultural Anthropology* 14 (1): 3–28.

———. 2001. *Dreaming Equality: Color, Race, and Racism in Urban Brazil.* New Brunswick, NJ: Rutgers University Press.

Silverstein, Michael. 1976. "Shifters, Linguistic Categories, and Cultural Description." In *Meaning in Anthropology,* edited by K. Basso and H. Selby, 11–55. Albuquerque: University of New Mexico Press.

———. 1979. "Language Structure and Linguistic Ideology." In *Papers from the Parasession on Linguistic Units and Levels,* edited by P. Clyne and et al., 193–247. Chicago: Chicago Linguistic Society.

———. 1992. "The Indeterminacy of Contextualization: When Is Enough Enough?" In *The Contextualization of Language*, edited by P. Auer and A. DiLuzio, 55–76. Amsterdam: John Benjamins.

———. 1993. "Metapragmatic Discourse and Metapragmatic Function." In *Reflexive Language: Reported Speech and Metapragmatics*, edited by J. A. Lucy, 33–58. Cambridge: Cambridge University Press.

———. 2001. "The Limits of Awareness." In *Linguistic Anthropology: A Reader*, edited by A. Duranti, 382–401. Oxford: Blackwell.

———. 2003. "Indexical Order and the Dialectics of Sociolinguistic Life." *Language and Communication* 23 (3–4): 193–229.

———. 2005. "Axes of Evals: Token versus Type Interdiscursivity." *Journal of Linguistic Anthropology* 15 (1): 6–22.

Silverstein, Michael, and Greg Urban. 1996. "The Natural History of Discourse." In *Natural Histories of Discourse*, edited by M. Silverstein and G. Urban, 1–20. Chicago: University of Chicago Press.

Skidmore, Monique. 2003. "Darker Than Midnight: Fear, Vulnerability, and Terror in Making Urban Burma (Myanmar)." *American Ethnologist* 30 (1): 5–21.

Smitherman, Genevra. 2000. *Black Talk: Words and Phrases from the Hood to the Amen Corner.* Boston: Houghton Mifflin.

Stevenson, Robert. 1968. "The Afro-American Musical Legacy to 1800." *Musical Quarterly* 54 (4): 475–502.

———. 1994. "Ethnological Impulses in the Baroque Villancico." *Inter-American Music Review* 14 (1): 67–106.

Stolcke, Verena. 1995. "Talking Culture: New Boundaries, New Rhetorics of Exclusion in Europe." *Current Anthropology* 36 (1): 1–24.

Stoller, Paul. 1995. *Embodying Colonial Memories: Spirit Possession, Power, and the Hauka in West Africa.* New York: Routledge.

Sutton, David. 2004. "Ritual Continuity and Change: Greek Reflections." *History and Anthropology* 15 (2): 91–105.

Taylor, Charles, and Amy Guttman. 1994. *Multiculturalism: Examining the Politics of Recognition.* Princeton, NJ: Princeton University Press.

Taylor, Diane. 2003. *The Archive and the Repertoire: Performing Cultural Memory in the Americas.* Durham, NC: Duke University Press.

Testa, Silvina. 2004. *Como una memoria que dura: Cabildos, sociedades y religiones afrocubanas de Sagua La Grande.* Havana: Centro Cultural Pablo de la Torriente Brau.

Thomas, Susan. 2009. *Cuban Zarzuela: Performing Race and Gender on Havana's Lyric Stage.* Urbana: University of Illinois Press.

Tomlinson, Matt. 2004. "Perpetual Lament: Kava-Drinking, Christianity, and Sensations of Historical Decline in Fiji." *Journal of the Royal Anthropological Institute* 10 (3): 653–73.

Trouillot, Michel-Rolph. 1995. *Silencing the Past: Power and the Production of History.* Boston: Beacon Press.

Turner, Bryan S. 1997. "The Body in Western Society: Social Theory and Its Perspectives." In *Religion and the Body*, edited by S. Coakley, 15–41. Cambridge Studies in Religious Traditions. Cambridge: Cambridge University Press.

Turner, Victor. 1967. *The Forest of Symbols: Aspects of Ndembu Ritual.* Ithaca, NY: Cornell University Press.

———. 1974. *Dramas, Fields, and Metaphors: Symbolic Action in Human Society*. Ithaca, NY: Cornell University Press.

Twine, France Winddance. 1998. *Racism in a Racial Democracy: The Maintenance of White Supremacy in Brazil.* New Brunswick, NJ: Rutgers University Press.

Urban, Greg. 1986. "Ceremonial Dialogues in South America." *American Anthropologist* 88 (2): 371–86.

———. 1989. "The 'I' of Discourse." In *Semiotics, Self, and Society*, edited by B. Lee and G. Urban, 27–51. Berlin: Mouton de Gruyter.

———. 1991. *A Discourse-Centered Approach to Culture.* Austin: University of Texas Press.

———. 1996. *Metaphysical Community*. Austin: University of Texas Press.

———. 2001. *Metaculture: How Culture Moves through the World.* Minneapolis: University of Minnesota Press.

Urciuoli, Bonnie. 1996. *Exposing Prejudice: Puerto Rican Experiences of Language, Race, and Class.* Boulder, CO: Westview Press.

———. 2008. "Skills and Selves in the New Workplace." *American Ethnologist* 35 (2): 211–28.

———. 2009. "Talking/Not Talking about Race: The Enregisterment of *Culture* in Higher Education Discourses." *Journal of Linguistic Anthropology* 19 (1): 21–39.

———. 2011. "Discussion Essay: Semiotic Properties of Racializing Discourses." *Journal of Linguistic Anthropology* 21 (S1): E113–E122.

Valdés Bernal, Sergio. 1987. *Las lenguas de African subsaharana y el español de Cuba.* Havana: Editorial Academía de Ciencias de Cuba.

———. 1996–97. "El legado carabalí en el español de Cuba." *Anuario de Lingüística Hispánica* 12–13:449–56.

Vaughan, Umi, and Carlos Aldama. 2012. *Carlos Aldama's Life in Batá.* Bloomington: Indiana University Press.

Viddal, Grete. 2012. "Vodú Chic: Haitian Religion and the Folkloric Imaginary in Socialist Cuba." *New West Indian Guide* 86 (3–4): 205–36.

Vincent, Amanda. 2006. "Bata Conversations: Guardianship and Entitlement Narratives about the Bata in Nigeria and Cuba." PhD diss., University of London.

Volosinov, V. N. 1973. *Marxism and the Philosophy of Language.* Translated by L. Matejka and I. R. Titunik. Cambridge, MA: Harvard University Press.

Weinreb, Amelia Rosenberg. 2009. *Cuba in the Shadow of Change: Daily Life in the Twilight of the Revolution.* Gainesville: University Press of Florida.

Wertsch, James V. 1998. *Mind as Action.* New York: Oxford University Press.

West-Durán, Alan. 2004. "Rap's Diasporic Dialogues: Cuba's Redefinition of Blackness." *Journal of Popular Music Studies* 16 (1): 4–39.

Whitten, Norman E. Jr. 2003. "Symbolic Inversion, the Topology of *el Mestizaje*, and the Spaces of *las Razas* in Ecuador." *Journal of Latin American Anthropology* 8 (1): 52–85.

Whorf, Benjamin Lee. (1956) 1997. *Language, Thought, and Reality: Selected Writings of Benjamin Lee Whorf.* Cambridge, MA: MIT Press.

Wilce, James M. 2009. *Crying Shame: Metaculture, Modernity, and the Exaggerated Death of Lament.* Chichester: Wiley-Blackwell.

Williams, Brackette F. 1989. "A Class Act: Anthropology and the Race to Nation across Ethnic Terrain." *Annual Review of Anthropology* 18:401–45.

Williams, Lorna. 1995. "The Emergence of an Afro-Cuban Aesthetic." *Afro-Hispanic Review* 14 (1): 48–57.

Wilson, Kenneth G. (1993) 2001. *The Columbia Guide to Standard American English.* Vol. 2009. New York: Columbia University Press.

Wirtz, Kristina. 2004. "Santería in Cuban National Consciousness: A Religious Case of the *Doble Moral.*" *Journal of Latin American Anthropology* 9 (2): 409–38.

———. 2005. "'Where Obscurity Is a Virtue': The Mystique of Unintelligibility in Santería Ritual." *Language and Communication* 25 (4): 351–75.

———. 2007a. "Divining the Past: The Linguistic Reconstruction of 'African' Roots in Diasporic Ritual Registers and Songs." *Journal of Religion in Africa* 37:242–74.

———. 2007b. "Enregistered Memory and Afro-Cuban Historicity in Santería's Ritual Speech." *Language and Communication* 27:245–57.

———. 2007c. "How Diasporic Religious Communities Remember: Learning to Speak the 'Tongue of the Oricha' in Cuban Santería." *American Ethnologist* 34 (1): 108–26.

———. 2007d. "Making Sense of Unintelligible Messages in Divine Communication." *Text and Talk* 27 (4): 435–62.

———. 2007e. *Ritual, Discourse, and Community in Cuban Santería: Speaking a Sacred World.* Gainesville: University Press of Florida.

———. 2009. "Hazardous Waste: The Semiotics of Ritual Hygiene in Cuban Popular Religion." *Journal of the Royal Anthropological Institute* 15:476–501.

———. 2013. "Spirit Materialities in Cuban Folk Religion: Realms of Imaginative Possibility." In *The Social Life of Spirits,* edited by R. Blanes and D. Espírito Santo. Chicago: University of Chicago Press.

———. 2014. "Spiritual Agency, Materiality, and Knowing in Cuba." In *Spirited Things: The Work of "Possession" in Black Atlantic Religions,* edited by P. C. Johnson. Chicago: University of Chicago Press.

Wortham, Stanton. 2001. *Narratives in Action: A Strategy for Research and Analysis.* New York: Teachers College Press.

Wright, Winthrop. 1990. *Cafe con Leche: Race, Class, and National Image in Venezuela.* Austin: University of Texas.

Wurdemann, John George F. 1844. *Notes on Cuba.* Boston: James Munroe and Company.

Yarnow, Dvora. 2003. *Constructing "Race" and "Ethnicity" in America: Category-making in Public Policy and Administration.* Armonk, NY: M. E. Sharpe.

Yelvington, Kevin A. 2001. "The Anthropology of Afro-Latin America and the Caribbean: Diasporic Dimensions." *Annual Review of Anthropology* 30:227–60.

———, ed. 2006. *Afro-Atlantic Dialogues: Anthropology in the Diaspora.* Santa Fe, NM: SAR Press.

Yurchak, Alexei. 2005. *Everything Was Forever, Until It Was No More: The Last Soviet Generation.* Princeton, NJ: Princeton University Press.

Zerubavel, Eviatar. 2003. *Time Maps: Collective Memory and the Social Shape of the Past.* Chicago: University of Chicago Press.

Index

The letters *f*, *m*, or *t* following a page number indicate respectively a figure, map, or table on that page. A boldface page number contains the subject entry's definition.